# Global Environmental Change and Agriculture

NEW HORIZONS IN ENVIRONMENTAL ECONOMICS

**General Editors:** Wallace E. Oates, *Professor of Economics, University of Maryland, USA* and Henk Folmer, *Professor of Economics, Wageningen Agricultural University, The Netherlands and Professor of Environmental Economics, Tilburg University, The Netherlands*

This important series is designed to make a significant contribution to the development of the principles and practices of environmental economics. It includes both theoretical and empirical work. International in scope, it addresses issues of current and future concern in both East and West and in developed and developing countries.

The main purpose of the series is to create a forum for the publication of high quality work and to show how economic analysis can make a contribution to understanding and resolving the environmental problems confronting the world in the twenty-first century.

Recent titles in the series include:

Biodiversity, Conservation and Sustainable Development
Principles and Practices with Asian Examples
*Clem Tisdell*

Green Taxes
Economic Theory and Empirical Evidence from Scandinavia
*Edited by Runar Brännlund and Ing-Marie Gren*

Global Environmental Change and Agriculture
Assessing the Impacts
*Edited by George Frisvold and Betsey Kuhn*

The Political Economy of Environmental Policy
A Public Choice Approach to Market Instruments
*Bouwe R. Dijkstra*

The Economic Valuation of Landscape Change
Theory and Policies for Land Use and Conservation
*José Manuel L. Santos*

Sustaining Development
Environmental Resources in Developing Countries
*Daniel W. Bromley*

Valuing Recreation and the Environment
Revealed Preference Methods in Theory and Practice
*Edited by Joseph A. Herriges and Catherine L. Kling*

Designing Effective Environmental Regimes
The Key Conditions
*Jørgen Wettestad*

Environmental Networks
A Framework for Economic Decision-Making and Policy Analysis
*Kanwalroop Kathy Dhanda, Anna Nagurney and Padma Ramanujam*

The International Yearbook of Environmental and Resource Economics
1999/2000
*Edited by Henk Folmer and Tom Tietenberg*

# Global Environmental Change and Agriculture

## Assessing the Impacts

*Edited by*

George Frisvold
*Department of Agricultural and Resource Economics,*
*University of Arizona*

Betsey Kuhn
*Economic Research Service,*
*US Department of Agriculture*

NEW HORIZONS IN ENVIRONMENTAL ECONOMICS

**Edward Elgar**
Cheltenham, UK • Northampton, MA, USA

Published by
Edward Elgar Publishing Limited
Glensanda House
Montpellier Parade
Cheltenham
Glos GL50 1UA
UK

Edward Elgar Publishing, Inc.
6 Market Street
Northampton
Massachusetts 01060
USA

A catalogue record for this book
is available from the British Library

**Library of Congress Cataloguing in Publication Data**

Global environmental change and agriculture: assessing the impacts /
    edited by George Frisvold, Betsey Kuhn.
       (New horizons in environmental economics)
     Includes bibliographical references.
      1. Global environmental change. 2. Climatic changes—
Environmental aspects. 3. Agriculture—Environmental aspects.
4. Environmental auditing. I. Frisvold, George B. II. Kuhn,
Betsey. III. Series.
GE149.G55 1998
338.1'4—dc21                                   97–32759
                                              CIP

ISBN 1 85898 631 1

Printed and bound in Great Britain by
Biddles Ltd, Guildford and King's Lynn

# Contents

# List of Figures

# List of Tables

# Contributors

Irma Adelman, *Professor in the Graduate School, Department of Agricultural and Resource Economics, University of California at Berkeley*

Roy Darwin, *Economist, Resource Economics Division, Economic Research Service*

Alain de Janvry, *Professor, Department of Agricultural and Resource Economics, University of California at Berkeley*

Kelly Eakin, *Vice President, L.R. Christensen Associates*

George Frisvold, *Associate Extension Specialist, Department of Agricultural and Resource Economics, University of Arizona*

Elise Hardy Golan, *Economist, Food and Rural Economics Division, Economic Research Service*

James Hrubovcak, *Economist, Resource Economics Division, Economic Research Service*

Harry M. Kaiser, *Associate Professor, Department of Agricultural, Resource and Managerial Economics, Cornell University*

Mary Knudson, *Research Associate, Department of Agricultural Economics, Purdue University*

Betsey Kuhn, *Director, Food and Rural Economics Division, Economic Research Service*

Michael LeBlanc, *Deputy Director, Food and Rural Economics Division, Economic Research Service*

Jan Lewandrowski, *Economist, Resource Economics Division, Economic Research Service*

Rinku Murgai, *Economist, Development Economics Research Group, The World Bank*

Ian W.H. Parry, *Economist, Resources for the Future*

Anton Raneses, *Senior Analyst, American Petroleum Institute*

Vernon W. Ruttan, *Regents' Professor, Department of Applied Economics, University of Minnesota*

Elisabeth Sadoulet, *Associate Professor, Department of Agricultural and Resource Economics, University of California at Berkeley*

David Schimmelpfennig, *Economist, Resource Economics Division, Economic Research Service*

Marinos Tsigas, *Economist, Food and Rural Economics Division, Economic Research Service*

Stephen Vogel, *Economist, Food and Rural Economics Division, Economic Research Service*

Paul Winters, *Rockefeller Post-Doctoral Fellow, International Potato Center*

Gary Yohe, *Professor and Chair, Department of Economics, Wesleyan University*

# Acknowledgements

The collection of works presented in this volume is the result of several cooperative research projects that brought together economists from the Economic Research Service of the U.S. Department of Agriculture and leading scholars in agricultural, development and environmental economics. Earlier incarnations of this book's chapters were first presented at a conference co-sponsored by the Economic Research Service and the Farm Foundation.

We would like to thank a number of people who helped make this book possible. We thank John Miranowski for the initial support of the research projects and conference and for sound advice at early stages of this endeavor. We thank Walter Armbruster, Roberta Atkinson, Denice Bess, John Dunmore, Cynthia Ray and Bob Robinson for their help in organizing the conference. Other conference participants, Pierre Crosson, Shantayanan Devarajan, Jae Edmonds, Bruce Gardner, John Horowitz, Erik Lichtenberg, Ramon Lopez, Peter Oram, Raymond Prince, John Reilly and Henry Shands, provided valuable comments on early drafts of these chapters. Margot Anderson, William Anderson, Dennis Cory and Susan Offutt provided continued and patient support of this project in its latter stages. Nancy Bannister, Helen Ferris and Letricia Womack provided excellent word processing and graphics support. Finally, we would especially like to thank Ken O'Neill and Shoshana Mayden for serving as technical editors of this volume.

# 1 Introduction

## George Frisvold and Betsey Kuhn

## 1 ENVIRONMENT, AGRICULTURE AND ECONOMICS

The concept of externalities has long been recognized in neoclassical economics (Marshall, 1910; Pigou, 1932). Discussion of the scarcity of land and other natural resources as a constraint on overall development dates back even further, to the classical economists. While environmental externalities and management of renewable and non-renewable resources have been extensively studied by economists, these were largely partial equilibrium studies of a single sector or single environmental problem (Mishan, 1965; Fisher and Peterson, 1976; Peterson and Fisher, 1977).

It has only been in the last third of this century that economists have made persistent attempts to formally include environmental impacts as a fundamental aspect of all economic activity. As Ayers and Kneese (1969) pointed out in their seminal article, externalities 'are not freakish anomalies in the processes of production and consumption but an inherent and normal part of them'. Early work by Ayers and Kneese (1969) and by Leontief (1970) to include the environment in general equilibrium and input–output analyses was soon followed by a host of modeling efforts attempting to formally include environmental processes and impacts in regional and national models of the economy.[1]

As one takes a more general equilibrium approach, certain critical relationships between the economy and environment become more evident. First, it is often through the agricultural sectors that the environment is linked most strongly to the overall economy. Agriculture, more so than other sectors, is highly sensitive to changes in the environment. Climate change, air pollution, water scarcity and loss of plant genetic diversity are examples of environmental stresses that particularly affect agriculture. At the same time, agriculture and forestry sectors are the major users of land and water resources. As a result, changes in agricultural policies, production and international trade have important environmental ramifications.

Second, evaluating environmental problems requires not just a regional or national perspective, but also an international one. Ecological boundaries such as air-sheds or watersheds seldom match jurisdictional boundaries. Many environmental problems, such as depletion of ocean fisheries, stratospheric ozone depletion, growing greenhouse gas emissions and acid rain, are international in scope. How economies adapt to environmental change depends on their trade patterns and policies. Changing trade patterns, in turn, influence land, water and chemical input use.

Third, there is a vital need for greater understanding of the relationships between agriculture, the environment, poverty alleviation and overall economic growth in developing countries. Agriculture is still a leading sector in developing economies, accounting for significant shares of employment, gross domestic product (GDP) and foreign exchange. Rural populations, especially the rural poor, depend on access to land and natural resources for their livelihoods and are particularly vulnerable to disruptions in agricultural markets and to environmental degradation. Although the role of agricultural growth in overall economic development has long been studied, interactions between development and environmental economists are relatively recent (Hanemann, 1988; Dasgupta and Mäler, 1990).

Fourth, an important research challenge is to make better use of information on environmental relationships in economic modeling. This includes the problem of choosing the appropriate level of detail and aggregation. Relationships between economic activity and the environment are often location-specific.[2] To accurately assess the environmental impacts of economic activity or the economic impacts of environmental policies, one needs to account for these spatial differences. At the same time, one would like to be able to aggregate activities up to economically meaningful units for policy and planning purposes. There is a trade-off between capturing details of complex, often dynamic biophysical processes and maintaining tractability and transparency of analyses.

Formal modeling efforts have followed two paths. The top-down approach incorporates greater detail about particular environmental changes or processes of interest (such as climate change) into the structure of pre-existing sectoral or aggregate economic models. The bottom-up approach begins with detailed specification of biophysical processes and attempts to trace out sectoral economic impacts of changes in environmental quality or policy. Here, less attention may be paid to multi-market linkages across sectors. Either approach requires a great deal of creativity in linking economic and environmental data often collected at different levels of aggregation and for different purposes. Methods, data and modeling assumptions also need to be transparent enough for practitioners of quantitative assessment to understand and test the robustness of results.

Fifth, as one moves from partial to general equilibrium analysis, one must confront a number of second-best problems (Mishan, 1965; Ayers and Kneese, 1969). The ultimate welfare effects of changes in environmental quality or policies will be sensitive to distortions created by pre-existing trade, tax or agricultural income support policies.

## 2    AIMS AND SCOPE OF THE BOOK

This volume examines global environmental constraints on sustained agricultural growth. The chapters emphasize empirical applications to illustrate how to rigorously assess critical linkages between environmental quality, agricultural development and overall economic performance. A wide range of environmental problems are addressed in computable general equilibrium models (CGEs), social accounting matrix (SAM) analysis, national income accounting, risk measurement and models of public finance. While a major focus of the volume is climate change, chapters also address loss of genetic diversity, water pollution, groundwater depletion and soil erosion.

We feel that a major contribution of this volume is its emphasis on applied quantitative analysis. Much has been written about the conceptual problems of accounting for the environment more fully in assessments of agricultural and economic performance. Chapters here move beyond discussion of conceptual issues to take important steps at quantifying environmental and economic relationships. To inform public policy about agriculture, the economy and environmental change, one really needs to quantify the impacts and the trade-offs of policy choices.

A second contribution is that this volume brings the tools and the perspective of development economics to the assessment of environmental problems. The use of CGEs and SAMs are examples of the tools. In terms of perspective, the volume focuses on environmental impacts on households, income distribution, the role of agriculture in overall economic development, vulnerability and the role of institutions (in particular, research institutions and intellectual property rights).

It is our hope that this volume furthers the cross-fertilization of agricultural, environmental and development economics and that it is a useful guide to master's and doctoral students in these fields. For this reason, the methods and data used in the illustrative applications are presented in the necessary clarity and richness of detail to be a useful guide to practitioners of quantitative modeling and analysis. We also hope that the volume will prove useful to planners and policy analysts in international environmental, development and agricultural organizations that are confronting practical problems of environmental and economic assessment.

## 3    AN OVERVIEW OF THE BOOK

This book is organized in three major parts. Part One (Chapters 2 and 3) examines a number of environmental, technological and economic challenges that will confront international agricultural and environmental research systems in the next century. Some of these include global climate change, loss of crop genetic diversity, limits to future expansion of cultivated acreage, limits to sustained yield growth through conventional plant-breeding methods and the persistence of infectious diseases in developing countries. The chapters explicitly consider what institutional changes are needed to enable research systems to meet these challenges. Part Two (Chapters 4 through 6) presents three applications of environmental accounting and indexing to illustrate how environmental quality can be included formally in national income accounts, SAM analyses and probabilistic indicators of sustainability. Part Three (Chapters 7 through 10) examines several questions about global climate change. How and why might climate change affect Asia, Africa and Latin America differently? How will climate change affect different social classes within developing countries? What are the implications of climate change for future land and water resource use? How might carbon taxes interact with pre-existing taxes in an economy? What are promising directions for future research on the economic impacts of climate change on agriculture?

In Chapter 2, Vernon Ruttan provides a broad historical overview of environmental concerns over the latter half of the 20th century and looks forward to resource, institutional, technological and health constraints to sustainable agricultural development in the 21st century. Ruttan emphasizes the role of agricultural, environmental and health sciences in overcoming these constraints with special reference to the needs of developing countries.

Many agricultural, environmental and health problems are closely linked. Agricultural production affects the quantity and safety of drinking water. Global environmental problems such as climate change or ozone depletion can affect agricultural productivity and ultimately nutrition. AIDS and other diseases affect labor availability and productivity in developing countries. Because of these linkages, Ruttan argues that strategies for sustainable agricultural development must be carried out along a broad interdisciplinary front. In Chapter 2, he offers his vision of the types of institutional infrastructure that will be needed to supply future knowledge and technology in the areas of agriculture, resource management and public health. He concludes by discussing how global agricultural, health and environmental research systems can work more effectively with each other.

In Chapter 3, Mary Knudson takes stock of the state of plant genetic diversity in gene banks, in the wild and in farmers' fields and focuses on problems faced by national and international gene banks in managing genetic resources. Knudson points out that, without the preservation of existing plant species, it will become increasingly difficult to continue to create improved crop varieties. Even if gene banks currently have collections representing 90 percent of the determined genetic diversity of major crops in the world, this potential will be wasted if existing collections are not well maintained or catalogued. She concentrates on the incentives for private sector utilization of genetic resources, paying particular attention to the role of intellectual property rights (IPRs). The chapter discusses how IPRs have affected diversity and how IPR systems might be structured to better promote diversity in the future.

In Chapter 4, Elise Golan, Irma Adelman and Stephen Vogel incorporate the impacts of environmental externalities in a SAM. As an illustrative application, the authors develop an environmentally adjusted SAM for California to examine the impacts of groundwater pollution from cotton cultivation. The SAM illustrates how one can quantify the impacts of externalities on the level and distribution of income, production and welfare. Their framework also quantifies the impacts of currently generated externalities on both the current and future economy. Formally accounting for externalities is an important step toward correctly measuring value-added in each sector of an economy as well as measuring the impacts of pollution on household income and overall income distribution. Further, an environmentally corrected SAM can be used to derive more accurate net national product (NNP) measures.

In Chapter 5, Jim Hrubovcak, Michael LeBlanc and Kelly Eakin adjust measures of agricultural and national income in the U.S. economy to reflect depletion of agricultural natural capital (land and water) and the impact of agricultural environmental externalities on producers and consumers in other sectors. The authors cast the environment as a set of natural capital assets providing flows of goods and services to the economy. The authors adjust agricultural and national income to account for soil productivity loss from erosion, changes in water quality and depletion of groundwater stocks. Because of agriculture's small share of total U.S. GDP, accounting for these factors would lead to only minor adjustments in NNP. Adjustments to net farm income are more significant, however. Their estimated adjustments would require net agricultural income to be revised downward by 6 percent ($4 billion).

A weakness of many studies of the effects of climate change is their focus on mean changes in climate variables, such as temperature and precipitation, mean responses to climate change, such as crop yields, or both. There are many cases where one would be interested in the probability of crossing some threshold where climate change impacts are highly non-linear (e.g. crop failures, residential flooding) or irreversible (species extinction).

In Chapter 6, David Schimmelpfennig and Gary Yohe discuss methods for measuring the effects of climate change on ecological or agronomic vulnerability. They develop indexes of vulnerability and sustainability that characterize the probability of crossing one or multiple thresholds. The threshold they consider, for illustrative purposes, is a 10-percent reduction in yields of six major cereal crops. The authors argue that their indexes could be used to help farmers evaluate the need for new technologies by indicating the vulnerability of their current cropping systems to extreme yield loss absent any adaptations. On a broader scale, the indexes identify the scope for crop migration. For example, vulnerability may be reduced if corn production migrates to areas currently specializing in spring wheat. Regional research and extension systems could facilitate adaptation to climate change by anticipating the viability of crops not currently growing in their particular areas. This indexing method could also be applied to estimating the vulnerability of ecosystems, individual species or mariculture to climate change.

In Chapter 7, Harry Kaiser assesses economic studies of the impacts of climate change on agriculture, draws general lessons from these studies, and offers recommendations about which areas of climate change research should be given a high priority in the future. Kaiser makes six general observations about predicted impacts of climate change. First, it will have negative distributional consequences as developing countries fair worse than developed countries. Second, impacts in developed countries may be small relative to their national incomes. Third, economic effects of climate change will be very different than physical yield effects. In general, economic welfare does not change as much as expected yields. Fourth, although climate change is often modeled as occurring instantaneously on a current economy, it will occur gradually over time, with most of the effects felt in future economies. Fifth, agricultural producers and institutions will make adaptations as climate changes. Sixth, estimates of the agronomic and economic effects of climate change depend crucially on assumptions about the magnitude of the $CO_2$ fertilization effect. Although there is evidence that plant productivity increases under higher concentrations of ambient $CO_2$, there is still a great deal of uncertainty about the potential magnitude of this effect.

In response to these observations, Kaiser identifies eight research priorities. First, develop a universal base scenario for both climate and other socio-economic changes to facilitate comparisons between different studies. Second, improve understanding of the $CO_2$ fertilization effect. Third, improve the accuracy and consistency of climate change models.[3] Fourth, assess the effects of climate change on water supply and demand. Fifth, consider impacts of greenhouse gas accumulation of levels higher than the assumed $CO_2$ equivalent doubling used in most studies. Sixth, conduct more dynamic, rather than comparative static, analyses. Seventh, study the potential for institutional adaptations such as more efficient water pricing or changes in farm programs to increase planting flexibility. Finally, link more aggregated macro-models with farm-level micro-models to study climate change impacts in a comprehensive way.

In Chapter 8, Paul Winters, Rinku Murgai, Alain de Janvry, Elisabeth Sadoulet and George Frisvold examine the impacts of climate change on low income, net food-importing developing economies. These economies are likely to be most vulnerable to global environmental and market changes. To examine the economy-wide impacts of climate change, the authors construct three archetype multi-sector, multi-class CGE models representing groups of countries within Asia, Africa and Latin America in the year 2050. Model simulations illustrate the different impacts of climate change on different regions within the developing world. Further, they show how impacts differ across social classes within regions. While national incomes fall in all regions under the climate change scenarios considered, the negative impacts are largest in Africa, where GDP losses range from 6 to 10 percent.

The different regional impacts depend on the relationship between each regional economy and the international market, substitution possibilities within the economy, the relative importance of agriculture and the composition of production in the agricultural sector. Economies that are more able to substitute imported food for domestic foods will be less affected by climate change. Economies with a greater supply responsiveness, with a smaller agricultural sector and with a crop mix less vulnerable to climate change will suffer less than highly agrarian, closed economies. The most important channel of impacts will be via lower food crop yields because food crops make up the bulk of agricultural production in developing countries and because food accounts for a significant share of consumption, particularly among poorer households. The effects of climate change on income distribution are generally regressive, with the disparity impacts increasing as global warming becomes more severe.

In Chapter 9, Roy Darwin, Marinos Tsigas, Jan Lewandrowski and Anton Raneses employ an eight-region CGE model of the world economy to examine the impacts of climate change on land use, agricultural production and other economic activities. The Future Agricultural Resources Model (FARM) combines a geographic information system (GIS) with the CGE. The GIS describes regional land areas in terms of endowments of different classes of land, differentiated by length of growing season. The GIS also describes regional water resources that depend both on temperature and precipitation as well as measures of storage capacity. Endowments of different classes of land and available water (in part) determine regional production structures for forestry, crop and livestock production. These sectors also compete with other sectors in the economy for land and water resources. Production possibilities in each region depend directly on land class and water endowments. Climate change scenarios are imposed on the model by altering regional land class and water endowments. A strength of the approach used in Chapter 9 is the way it links land and water resources to climate conditions and economic activity on a global scale.

The FARM model results suggest that climate change will not dramatically alter global food production or prices, but that there may be significant changes in global land use patterns. Globally, climate change reduces average productivity on existing land, but induces the area under cultivation to expand. Global crop and livestock acreage increases significantly while land in forestry declines. The authors also report results of sensitivity analysis, emphasizing the role of land use change as a mode of adaptation to climate change.

Many of these simulation results raise intriguing questions for future research. For example, the simulation results suggest that cropland in Canada could increase significantly as production moves to higher latitudes. Is this possible given soil and other environmental characteristics of the region? If so, what are the implications for ecosystems and indigenous populations? The simulation results also suggest that land area with climate suitable to support tropical moist forests will contract as a result of climate change. Tropical deforestation would be further increased as forests are converted to crop and pasture acreage. What are the implications of such deforestation for loss of biological diversity? To what extent will $CO_2$ emissions increase from deforestation, inducing even further changes in climate? The authors find that water supplies are likely to increase for the world as a whole but that shortages could occur in some regions, notably Japan. What are the implications of climate change for future conflicts over water resources or for public investment in reservoirs or irrigation infrastructure?

In Chapter 10, Ian Parry examines greenhouse gas abatement policies, focusing on carbon taxes and the use of emissions quotas. Parry explicitly considers interactions between these abatement policies with tax-created distortions in other markets, chiefly the labor market. He discusses revenue-neutral carbon tax experiments where increased revenues from carbon taxes are offset by reductions in labor taxes. These tax shift experiments have three effects. The first is the welfare gain from environmental benefits. The second is a *revenue-recycling effect* where welfare increases as the reduced labor tax raises employment. The third is a *tax interaction effect*, which is the welfare *loss* from the reduction in labor supply induced indirectly by the emissions tax.

Parry argues, based on his own research and that of others, that the tax interaction effect will generally outweigh the revenue-recycling effect. This has important implications for the 'double dividend' hypothesis. In its strongest form this hypothesis holds that, because of revenue recycling, carbon taxes could be justified on tax efficiency gains alone and that environmental improvements could be achieved at little cost. Parry finds the possibility of such a double dividend illusory.

The results of Chapter 10 yield two important policy conclusions. First, the second-best optimal emissions tax is likely *lower* than a first-best Pigouvian emissions tax. In other words, accounting for other taxes in the economy implies that emissions taxes should be lower. Second, because of the revenue-recycling effect, one can make a strong efficiency case for preferring a revenue-raising instrument such as an emissions tax or auctioned emissions quota over a non-revenue-raising instrument such as a non-auctioned emissions quota to reduce carbon emissions.

## NOTES

1. See Forsund (1985) and James (1985) for discussion of these early modeling efforts.
2. This is particularly true for agriculture where, for example, soil characteristics such as erodibility or the potential for leaching of chemicals can vary widely from region to region.
3. For example, general circulation models used to project climate often make widely different predictions of future rainfall. These differences grow larger as the region assessed becomes smaller.

# REFERENCES

Ayers, R. and Kneese, A. (1969), 'Production, Consumption and Externalities', *American Economic Review,* **59,** pp. 282–297.

Dasgupta, P. and Mäler, K.-G. (1991), 'The Environment and Emerging Development Issues', in Fischer, S., de Tray, D. and Shekhar, S. (eds), *Proceedings of the World Bank Annual Conference on Development Economics, 1990,* pp. 101–131.

Fisher, A. and Peterson, F. (1976), 'The Environment in Economics', *Journal of Economic Literature,* **14,** pp. 1–33.

Forsund, F. (1985), 'Input–Output Models, National Economic Models, and the Environment', in Kneese, A. and Sweeney, J. (eds) *Handbook of Natural Resource and Energy Economics: Volume One,* Amsterdam: Elsevier Science Publishers, pp. 32–41.

Hanemann, W.M. (1988), 'Economics and the Preservation of Biodiversity', in Wilson, E.O. (ed.) *Biodiversity,* Washington: National Academy Press, pp. 193–199.

James, D. (1985), 'Environmental Economics, Industrial Process Models, and Regional-Residuals Management Models', in Kneese, A. and Sweeney, J. (eds) *Handbook of Natural Resource and Energy Economics: Volume One,* Amsterdam: Elsevier Science Publishers, pp. 271–324.

Leontief, W. (1970), 'Environmental Repercussions and the Economic Structure: An Input–Output Approach', *Review of Economics and Statistics,* **52,** pp. 262–271.

Marshall, A. (1910), *Principles of Economics,* London: Macmillan.

Mishan, E.J. (1965), 'Reflections on Recent Developments in the Concept of External Effects', *Canadian Journal of Economics and Political Science,* **31,** pp. 1–34.

Peterson, F. and Fisher, A. (1977), 'The Exploitation of Extractive Resources: A Survey', *Economic Journal,* **87,** pp. 681–721.

Pigou, A.C. (1932), *The Economics of Welfare,* London: Macmillan.

PART I


Global Environmental Change:
Implications for Agricultural Research Systems

# 2 Research Systems for Sustainable Agricultural Development

## Vernon W. Ruttan

## 1 INTRODUCTION

In this chapter I summarize the conclusions from a series of consultations and a Bellagio conference involving leading agricultural, environmental and health scientists, conducted with support from the Rockefeller Foundation, to explore the constraints on sustainable growth in agricultural production (Ruttan, 1989, 1992, 1993, 1994). I explore a number of agricultural, resource, environmental and health concerns that will condition the capacity of the agricultural sector to respond to the demands that population and income growth will place on the sector – particularly in the developing countries of Africa, Asia and Latin America. Before doing so, however, I would like to place these concerns about the implications of natural resource availability and environmental change within a broader historical context.

## 2 CONCERNS ABOUT RESOURCES AND THE ENVIRONMENT

We are now in the midst of the third wave of social concern since World War II about the implications of natural resource availability and environmental change for the sustainability of improvements in human well-being.

The first wave of concern in the late 1940s and early 1950s focused primarily on the quantitative relations between resource availability and economic growth, including the adequacy of land, water, energy and other natural resources to sustain growth. The reports of the U.S. President's Water Resources Policy Commission (1950) and the U.S. President's Materials Policy Commission (1952) were the landmarks of the early post-war resource assessment studies generated by this wave of concern. The primary response to this first wave of concern was technical change. In retrospect it appears that a stretch of high prices has not yet failed to induce the new knowledge and new technologies needed to locate new deposits, promote substitution and enhance productivity. If the Materials Policy Commission were writing today, it would have to conclude that there has been abundant evidence of the nonevident becoming evident; the expensive cheap; and the inaccessible accessible (Barnett and Morse, 1963; Ausubel and Sladovich, 1989).

The second wave of concern occurred in the late 1960s and early 1970s. The earlier concern with the potential 'limits to growth' imposed by natural resource scarcity was supplemented by concern about the capacity of the environment to assimilate the multiple forms of pollution generated by growth. The landmarks in this second wave of concern include *Silent Spring* (Carson, 1962) and *The Limits to Growth* (Meadows et al., 1972). An intense conflict was emerging between the two major sources of demand for environmental services. One was the rising demand for environmental assimilations of residuals derived from growth in commodity production and consumption – asbestos in our insulation, pesticides in our food, smog in the air and radioactive wastes in the biosphere. The second was the rapid growth in consumer demand for environmental amenities – for direct consumption of environmental services – arising out of rapid growth in per capita income and high income elasticity of demand for such environmental services as access to natural environments and freedom from pollution and congestion (Ruttan, 1971). The response to these concerns, still incomplete, was the design of local institutions designed to require individual firms and other organizations to bear the costs arising from the externalities generated by commodity production.

Since the mid-1980s these two earlier concerns have been supplemented by a third. These newer concerns center around the implications for environmental quality, food production and human health of a series of environmental changes that are occurring on an international scale. These include issues such as global warming, ozone depletion and acid rain, among others (Committee on Global Change, 1990; Committee on Science, Engineering and Public Policy, 1991). The institutional innovations needed to respond to these transnational changes will be more difficult to design. They will, like the sources of change, need to be transnational or international. Experience with attempts to design incentive-compatible international regimes, such as the Law of the Sea Convention, or even the somewhat more successful Montreal Protocol on reduction of CFC emissions, suggests that the difficulty of resolving free-rider and equity issues imposes a severe constraint on how rapidly effective international regimes can be put in place to resolve these new environmental concerns.

With each new wave of concern, the issues that dominated the earlier wave were recycled. The result is that while the intensity of earlier concerns has receded, in part because of induced technical and institutional changes, the concerns about the relationships between resource and environmental change and sustainable growth in agricultural production have broadened (Graham-Tomasi, 1991). During the 1980s, for example, concerns about the effects of more intensive agricultural production on (a) resource degradation through erosion, salinization and depletion of groundwater and (b) the quality of surface and groundwater through runoff and leaching of plant nutrients and pesticides intensified. Terms that had initially been introduced by the populist critics of agricultural research – such as alternative, low input, regenerative and sustainable agriculture – began to enter the vocabulary of those responsible for agricultural research resource allocation.

# 3   THE AGRICULTURAL TRANSFORMATION

We are in the closing years of the 20th century completing one of the most remarkable transitions in the history of agriculture. Prior to this century almost all the increase in food production was obtained by bringing new land into production. There were only a few exceptions to this generalization in limited areas of East Asia, the Middle East and Western Europe (Hayami and Ruttan, 1985).

By the first decade of the next century, almost all of the increases in world food production must come from higher yields – from increased output per hectare. In most of the world the transition from a resource-based to a science-based system of agriculture is occurring within a single century. Most of the countries of the developing world have been caught up in the transition only since mid-century. Among developing countries, those in East, Southeast and South Asia have proceeded further in this transition than most countries in Latin America and Africa.

Recent historical trends in production and consumption of the major food grains could easily be taken as evidence that one should not be excessively concerned about the capacity of the world's farmers to meet future food demands. World wheat prices, corrected for inflation, have declined since the middle of the last century. Rice prices have declined since the middle of this century (Edwards, 1988; Pingali, 1988). These trends suggest that productivity growth has been able to more than compensate for the rapid growth in demand, particularly during the decades since World War II.

As we look toward the future, however, the sources of productivity growth are not as apparent as they were a quarter century ago. The demands that the developing economies will place on their agricultural producers from population growth and growth in per capita consumption arising out of higher income will be exceedingly high. Population growth rates are expected to decline substantially in most countries during the first quarter of the next century. But the absolute increases in population size will be large and increases in per capita incomes will add substantially to food demand. The effect of growth in per capita income will be more rapid growth in demand for animal proteins and for maize and other feed crops. During the next several decades, growth in food and feed demand rising from growth in population and income will run upwards of 4 percent per year in many countries. Many countries will experience more than a doubling of food demand before the end of the second decade of the next century (Parikh, 1993).

## 4  BIOLOGICAL AND TECHNICAL CONSTRAINTS ON CROP AND ANIMAL PRODUCTION

It seems apparent that the gains in agricultural production required over the next quarter century will be achieved with much greater difficulty than in the immediate past. Difficulty is currently being experienced in raising yield ceilings for the cereal crops that have experienced rapid yield gains in the recent past. The incremental response to increases in fertilizer use has declined. Expansion of irrigated area has become more costly. Maintenance research, the research required to prevent yields from declining, is rising as a share of research effort (Plucknett and Smith, 1986). The institutional capacity to respond to these concerns is limited, even in the countries with the most effective national research and extension systems. Indeed, there was considerable difficulty in many countries during the 1980s in maintaining the agricultural research capacity that had been established during the 1960s and 1970s (Pardey et al., 1991).

It is possible that within another decade, advances in basic knowledge will create new opportunities for advancing agricultural technology that will reverse the urgency of some of the above concerns. Institutionalization of private sector agricultural research capacity in some developing countries is beginning to complement public sector capacity (Pray and Echeverria, 1989). Advances in molecular biology and genetic engineering are occurring rapidly. But the date when these promising advances will be translated into productive technology seems to be receding.

The following five general conclusions are from the first consultation on *Biological and Technical Constraints on Crop and Animal Productivity* (Ruttan, 1989).

First, advances in conventional technology will remain the primary source of growth in crop and animal production over the next quarter century. Almost all increases in agricultural production over the next several decades must continue to come from further intensification of agricultural production on land that is presently devoted to crop and livestock production. Until well into the second decade of the next century, the necessary gains in crop and animal productivity will be generated by improvements from conventional plant and animal breeding and from more intensive and efficient use of technical inputs including chemical fertilizers, pest control chemicals and more effective animal nutrition.

The productivity gains from conventional sources are likely to come in smaller increments than in the past. If they are to be realized, higher plant populations per unit area, new tillage practices, improved pest and disease control, more precise application of plant nutrients, and advances in soil and water management will be required. Gains from these sources will be crop, animal and location specific. They will require closer articulation between the suppliers and users of new knowledge and new technology. These sources of yield gains will be extremely knowledge and information intensive. If they are to be realized, research and technology transfer efforts in the areas of information and management technology must become increasingly important sources of growth in crop and animal productivity.

Second, advances in conventional technology will be inadequate to sustain the demands that will be placed on agriculture as we move into the second decade of the next century and beyond. Advances in crop yields have come about primarily by increasing plant populations per hectare and by increasing the ratio of grain to straw for individual plants. Advances in animal feed efficiency have come largely by decreasing the proportion of feed consumed that is devoted to animal maintenance and increasing the proportion used to produce usable animal products. There are severe physiological constraints to continued improvement along these conventional paths. These constraints are most severe in those areas that have already achieved the highest levels of productivity – as in Western Europe, North America and parts of East Asia. The impact of these constraints can be measured in terms of declining incremental response to energy inputs – both in the form of a reduction in the incremental yield increases from higher levels of fertilizer application, and a reduction in the incremental savings in labor inputs from the use of larger and more powerful mechanical equipment. If the incremental returns to agricultural research should also decline, it will impose a higher priority on efficiency in the organization of research and on the allocation of research resources.

Third, a reorientation of the way we organize agricultural research will be necessary in order to realize the opportunities for technical change being opened up by advances in microbiology and biochemistry. Advances in basic science, particularly in molecular biology and biochemistry, continue to open up new possibilities for supplementing traditional sources of plant and animal productivity growth. A wide range of possibilities was discussed at the consultation – ranging from the transfer of growth hormones into fish to conversion of lignocellulose into edible plant and animal products. The realization of these possibilities will require a reorganization of agricultural research systems. An increasing share of the new knowledge generated by research will reach producers in the form of proprietary products or services. This means that incentives must be created to draw substantially more private sector resources into agricultural research. Within the public sector, research organization will have to increasingly move from a 'little science' to a 'big science' mode of organization. Examples include the Rockefeller Foundation-sponsored collaborative research program on the biotechnology of rice and the University of Minnesota program on the biotechnology of maize. In the absence of more focused research efforts, it seems likely that the promised gains in agricultural productivity from biotechnology will continue to recede.

Fourth, efforts to institutionalize agricultural research capacity in developing countries must be intensified. Crop and animal productivity levels in most developing countries remain well below the levels that are potentially feasible. Access to the conventional sources of productivity growth – from advances in plant breeding, agronomy, and soil and water management – will require the institutionalization of substantial agricultural research capacity for each crop or animal species of economic significance in each agro-climatic region. In a large number of developing countries this capacity is just beginning to be put in place. A number of countries that experienced substantial growth in capacity during the 1960s and 1970s experienced an erosion of capacity in the 1980s. Even a relatively small country, producing a limited range of commodities under a limited range of agro-climatic conditions, will require a cadre of agricultural scientists in the 250–300 range. Countries that do not acquire adequate agricultural research capacity will not be able to meet the demands that they will place on their farmers as a result of growth in population and income.

There are substantial possibilities for developing sustainable agricultural production systems in a number of fragile resource areas. Research underway in the tropical rain forest areas of Latin America and in the semi-arid tropics of Africa and Asia suggests the possibility of developing sustainable agricultural systems with substantially enhanced productivity – even in unfavorable environments. It is unlikely, and perhaps undesirable, that all of these areas become important components of the global food supply system. But enhanced productivity is important to those who reside in these areas – now and in the future. It is important that the research investment in the areas of soil and water management and in farming systems be intensified in these areas.

Fifth, there is a need for the establishment of substantial basic biological research and training capacity in the tropical developing countries. There are a series of basic biological research agendas that are important for applied research and technology development for agriculture in the tropics that receive, and are likely to continue to receive, inadequate attention in the temperate region developed countries. There is also a need for closer articulation between training in applied science and technology and training in basic biology. When such institutes are established they will need to be more closely linked with existing academic centers of research and training than the series of agricultural research institutes established by the Rockefeller and Ford Foundations and the Consultative Group on International Agricultural Research (CGIAR).

# 5 RESOURCE AND ENVIRONMENTAL CONSTRAINTS ON SUSTAINABLE GROWTH

As we look even further into the next century, there is a growing concern about the impact of a series of resource and environmental constraints that may seriously impinge on the capacity to sustain growth in agricultural production. The second consultation focused on issues of resource and environmental constraints on agricultural production.

One set of concerns explored during the consultation focused on the impact of production practices in those areas that have made the most progress in moving toward highly intensive systems of agriculture production. These include loss of soil resources due to erosion, waterlogging and salinization, groundwater contamination from plant nutrients and pesticides, and growing resistance of insects, weeds and pathogens to present methods of control. If agriculture is forced to continue to expand into more fragile environments, such problems as soil erosion and desertification can be expected to become more severe. Additional deforestation will intensify problems of soil loss, degrade water quality and contribute to the forcing of climate change.

A second set of concerns stems from the impact of industrialization on global climate and other environmental changes (Reilly and Bucklin, 1989; Parry, 1990). There can no longer be much doubt that the accumulation of carbon dioxide ($CO_2$) and other greenhouse gases – principally methane ($CH_4$), nitrous oxide ($N_2O$), and chlorofluorocarbons (CFCs) – has set in motion a process that will result in a rise in global average surface temperatures over the next 30–60 years. There continues to be great uncertainty about the climate changes that can be expected to occur at any particular date or location in the future. It is almost certain, however, that the climate changes will be accompanied by rises in the sea level and that these rises will impinge particularly heavily on the islands of Southeast Asia and the great river deltas of the region. Dryer and more erratic climate regimes can be expected in interior South Asia and North America. As a partial offset some analysts have suggested that higher $CO_2$ levels may have a positive effect on yield.

The bulk of the carbon dioxide emissions come from fossil fuel consumption. Carbon dioxide accounts for roughly half of radiative forcing. Biomass burning, cultivated soils, natural soils and fertilizers account for close to half of nitrous oxide emissions. Most of the known sources of methane are a product of agricultural activities – principally enteric fermentation in ruminant animals, release of methane from rice production and other cultivated wetlands and biomass burning. Estimates of nitrous oxide and methane sources have a very fragile empirical base. Some estimates suggest that agriculture and related land use and land use transformation could account for upwards of 25 percent of radiative forcing (Reilly and Bucklin, 1989). Other estimates, that take into account the different lifetimes and chemical transformations of the several greenhouse gases, attribute a significantly smaller share of climate change forcing to agricultural sources (Nordhaus, 1990).

The alternative policy approaches to the threat of global warming can be characterized as *preventionist* or *adaptionist*. A preventionist approach could involve four policy options: (a) reduction in fossil fuel use or capture of carbon dioxide emissions at the point of fossil fuel combustion, (b) reduction in the intensity of agricultural production, (c) reduction of biomass burning and (d) expansion of biomass production. Of these, only energy efficiency and conservation are likely to make any significant contribution over the next generation. Moreover, the pace of capital replacement will limit the speed with which either will occur. Any hope of significant reversal of agricultural intensification, reduction in biomass burning or increase in biomass absorption is unlikely to be realized within the next several decades. The institutional infrastructure or institutional resources that would be required do not exist and will not be in place rapidly enough. We will not be able to rely on a technological fix to the global warming problem. The fixes, whether driven by preventionist or adaptionist strategies, must be both technological and institutional.

This forces me, although reluctantly, into adopting an *adaptionist* approach in attempting to assess the implications of global climate change for future agricultural research agendas. Thus, in this context, an adaptionist strategy implies moving as rapidly as possible to design and put in place the institutions needed to remove the constraints that intensification of agricultural production is currently imposing on sustainable increases in agricultural production. I am referring, for example, to (a) commodity policies – such as those of the United States, the EU countries and Japan – that encourage excessive use of chemical inputs as substitutes for land; and (b) to resource policies, such as those that inhibit the rational conservation, allocation and use of surface and groundwater. If we are successful in designing the policies and institutions needed to deal with existing resource constraints and management, it will place us in a better position to respond to the more uncertain changes that will emerge as a result of future global climate change. In this section I discuss some of the research implications that emerged from the second consultation.

A serious effort to develop alternative land use, farming systems and food systems scenarios for the 21st century should be initiated. A clearer picture of the demands that are likely to be placed on agriculture over the next century, and of the ways in which agricultural systems might be able to meet such demands, has yet to be produced. World population could rise from the present 5 billion level to the 10–20 billion range. The demands that will be placed on agriculture will also depend on the rate of growth of income – particularly in the poor countries where consumers spend a relatively large share of income growth on subsistence – food, clothing and housing. The resources and technology needed to increase agricultural production by a multiple of three- to six-fold will depend on both the constraints on resource availability that are likely to emerge and the rate of advance in knowledge. Advances in knowledge can permit the substitution of more abundance for increasingly scarce resources and reduce the resource constraints on commodity production. Past studies of potential climate change effects on agriculture have given insufficient attention to adaptive change in non-climate parameters. But application of advances in biological and chemical technology, which substitute knowledge for land, and advances in mechanical and engineering technology, which substitute knowledge for labor, have in the past been driven by increasingly favorable access to energy resources – by declining prices of energy. There will be a strong incentive, by the early decades of the next century, to improve energy efficiency in agricultural production and utilization. Particular attention should be given to alternative and competing uses of land. Land use transformation, from forest to agriculture, is presently contributing to radiative forcing through release of $CO_2$ and methane into the atmosphere. Conversion of low intensity agricultural systems to forest has been proposed as a method of absorbing $CO_2$. There will also be increasing demands on land use for watershed protection and biomass energy production.

The capacity to monitor the agricultural sources and impacts of environmental change should be strengthened. It is a matter of serious concern that only in the last decade and a half has it been possible to estimate the magnitude and productivity effects of soil loss, even in the United States. Even rudimentary data on productivity effects of soil loss are almost completely unavailable in most developing countries. The same point holds, with even greater force, for groundwater pollution, salinization, species loss and other environmental problems. It is time to design the elements of a comprehensive agriculturally related resource monitoring system and to establish priorities for implementation. Data on the effects of environmental change on the health of individuals and communities are even less adequate. The monitoring should include a major focus on the effects of environmental change on human populations. There continues to be a lack of firm knowledge about the contribution of agricultural practices to the methane and nitrous oxide sources of greenhouse forcing. Much closer collaboration between production-oriented agricultural scientists, eco-logically trained biological scientists and the physical scientists that have been traditionally concerned with global climate change is essential.

The design of technologies and institutions to achieve more efficient manage-ment of surface and groundwater resources will become increasingly important. During the next century water resources will become an increasingly serious constraint on agricultural production. Agricultural production is a major source of decline in the quality of both groundwater and surface water. Limited access to clean and uncontaminated water supply is a major source of disease and poor health in many parts of the developing world and in the formerly centrally planned economies. Global climate change can be expected to have a major differential impact on water availability, water demand, erosion, salinization and flooding. Development and introduction of technologies and management systems that enhance water use efficiency represent high priorities both because of short- and intermediate-run constraints on water availability and the longer-run possibility of seasonal and geographical shifts in water availability. The identification, breeding and introduction of water efficient crops for dryland and saline environments is potentially an important aspect of achieving greater water use efficiency.

Research on environmentally compatible farming systems should be intensified. In agriculture, as in the energy field, there are a number of technical and institutional innovations that could have both economic and environmental benefits. Among the technical possibilities is the design of new 'third' or 'fourth' generation chemical, biorational and biological pest management technologies. Another is the design of land use technologies and institutions that will contribute to reduction of erosion, salinization and groundwater pollution.

Immediate efforts should be made to reform agricultural commodity and income support policies. In both developed and developing countries producers' decisions on land management, farming systems and use of technical inputs (such as fertilizers and pesticides) are influenced by government interventions such as price supports and subsidies, programs to promote or limit production, and tax incentive and penalties. It is increasingly important that such interventions be designed to take into account the environmental consequences of decisions by landowners and producers induced by the interventions.

A food-system perspective should become an organizing principle for improvements in the performance of existing systems and for the design of new systems. The agricultural science community should be prepared, by the second quarter of the next century, to contribute to the design of alternative food systems. Many of these alternatives will include the use of plants other than the grain crops that now account for a major share of world feed and food production. Some of these alternatives will involve radical changes in food sources. Rogoff and Rawlins (1987) have described one such system based on lignocellulose – both for animal feed and human consumption.

A large-scale program of research on the design of institutions capable of implementing incentive-compatible resource management policies and programs should be initiated. By incentive-compatible institutions, I mean institutions capable of achieving compatibility between individual, organizational and social objectives in resource management. A major source of the global warming and environmental pollution problem is the direct result of the operation of institutions which induce behavior by individuals and public agencies that are not compatible with societal development, some might say survival, goals. In the absence of more efficient incentive-compatible institutional design, the transaction costs involved in *ad hoc* approaches are likely to be enormous.

# 6  HEALTH CONSTRAINTS ON AGRICULTURAL DEVELOPMENT

The third consultation focused on health constraints on agricultural development. One might very well ask why this topic was included in a series of consultations on agricultural research. Since the mid-1960s a number of commonly used health indicators, such as life expectancy and infant mortality, have experienced substantial improvement for almost all developing countries. Concerns about nutritional deficiency as a source of poor health have receded in a large number of developing countries in the last several decades (BOSTID/IOM, 1987; Commission on Health Research for Development, 1990).

Yet there are a number of other indicators that suggest that health constraints could become increasingly important by the early decades of the next century. Daily calorie intake per capita has been declining for as much as two decades in a number of African countries. While dramatic progress has been made in the control and reduction of losses due to infectious disease and in the control of diarrheal disease, little progress has been made in the control of several important parasitic diseases. The sustainability of advances in malaria and tuberculosis control is in doubt. The impact of environmental change on health is a source of increasing concern. The emergence of AIDS, combined with the other health threats, could represent a major threat to economic viability in developing countries.

If one visualizes a number of these health threats emerging simultaneously in a number of countries it is not too difficult to construct a scenario in which there are large numbers of sick people in many villages and cities around the world. The numbers could become large enough to be a serious constraint on food production capacity. It was this set of concerns that guided the dialogue in the third consultation.

**Issues and Priorities for the 21st Century**

Evidence on the question raised at the beginning of the consultation – does health represent a serious constraint on agricultural development? – is at best ambiguous. Scattered data from countries such as India, Indonesia and the Ivory Coast indicate loss of days worked due to sickness in the 5–15 percent range. In the former Soviet Union (FSU) and Poland, substantial numbers of days of work are lost due to respiratory disease associated with atmospheric pollution.

There have been major 'plagues' in the past that resulted in mortality levels sufficient to seriously impinge on food supply. In the 15th century, following the Spanish conquest, the Amerindian population in the basin of Mexico declined by something like 90 percent. Most of the decline was due to a series of epidemics: smallpox, measles, typhus and plague. Famine, associated with the high dependency to working adult ratio, probably accounted for 10–15 percent of the population loss.

The population loss from most historical plagues in Europe and Asia was concentrated in the younger and oldest age groups rather than among the adult population of working age. Many adults had survived earlier attacks and had acquired some degree of immunity. The incidence of death from the European and Asian diseases introduced into the Americas was spread more evenly across the age distribution because everyone was equally susceptible. The AIDS plague is unique in that it is killing people who would be at their most productive age. The result will be a rise in the dependency ratio – the ratio of the old and young relative to workers in the more productive age groups. There are important questions that have not yet been sorted out in the relationships between AIDS and other diseases. One apparent consequence of AIDS in East Africa is a rise in tuberculosis. The World Health Organization has an active program of cooperation with African and other high incidence AIDS countries in estimating HIV infection and AIDS incidences. A further step should be to model the direct and interaction effects of the simultaneous incidence of HIV infection and tropical parasitic and viral diseases on morbidity and on mortality.

**Specific Issues**

I list below some of the more specific research implications that emerged from the consultation on health and agriculture.

First, the capacity to design systems of health delivery that are capable of reducing the incidence of illness continues to elude health policy and planning agencies in both developed and developing countries. The systems that are in place in most countries can be more accurately described as sickness recovery systems rather than health systems. They are health care rather than health maintenance systems. A major deficiency is the lack of a system for providing families and individuals with the knowledge needed to achieve better health with less reliance on the health care system. The point was made several times during the consultation that many countries have been able to design reasonably effective agricultural extension or technology transfer systems to provide farm people with the knowledge about resources and technology needed to achieve higher levels of productivity. But, with few exceptions, we have yet to design an effective system to provide families and individuals with the knowledge in the area of human biology, nutrition and health practice that will enable them to lead more healthy lives.

Second, the residuals produced as a by-product of industrial and agricultural production have become an increasingly important source of illness in a number of countries and regions. The most serious impacts are occurring in the formerly centrally planned economies of Eastern Europe, the FSU and China. Levels of atmospheric, water and soil pollution have resulted in higher mortality rates and reductions in life expectancy. The effects are evident in the form of congenital malformation, pulmonary malfunction and excessive heavy metals in soils and in crops grown on contaminated soils. In some cases the benefits from use of pesticides shift from positive to negative when costs to health are considered (Pingali and Roger, 1995). Many of the health effects of agricultural and industrial intensification are due to inadequate investment in the technology needed to control or manage contaminants. Rapid industrial growth in poor countries, in which investment resources are severely limited, will continue to be accompanied by underinvestment in the technology needed to limit the release of contaminants. The situation that exists in Eastern Europe presents a vision of the future for many newly industrializing countries unless better technology can be made available and more effective management of environmental spillover effects can be implemented.

Third, lack of location-specific or site-specific research capacity represents a major constraint on the capacity of health systems in most developing countries. It is no longer possible to maintain the position that health-related research results can simply be transferred from developed country research laboratories or pharmaceutical companies to practices in developing countries. Local capacity is needed for the identification and analysis of the sources of health problems. Local capacity is also needed for the analysis, design and testing of health delivery systems. The international donor community has been much slower in supporting the development of health research systems than agricultural research systems in the tropics. For example, there is now in place a network of more than a dozen international agricultural research centers (IARCs), sponsored by the Consultative Group on International Agricultural Research, that plays an important role in backstopping national agricultural research efforts.

The only comparable international supported center in the field of health is the Diarrheal Research Center in Bangladesh. Furthermore the capacity to conduct research on tropical infectious and parasitic diseases that was supported by the former colonial countries – the United Kingdom, France, the Netherlands and Belgium – has been allowed to atrophy.

Fourth, high birth rates are both a consequence and a cause of poor health. The demographic transition from high to low birth rates has in the past usually followed a rise in child survival rates. This suggests that improvements in health, particularly of mothers and children, are a prerequisite for decline in population growth rates. But high population growth rates, particularly in areas of high population density, are often associated with dietary deficiencies that contribute to poor health and high infant mortality rates.

The issue of how to achieve high levels of health and low birth rates at low cost in poor societies remains unresolved. Several very low-income countries have achieved relatively high levels of health – as measured by low infant mortality rates and high life expectancy rates – but often a high cost relative to per capita income. Other societies that have achieved relatively high incomes continue to exhibit relatively high infant mortality rates and only moderately high life expectancy levels.

Fifth, more effective bridges must be built, both in research and in practice, between the agricultural and health communities. At present these two 'tribes', along with veterinary medicine and public health, occupy separate and often mutually hostile 'island empires'. But solutions to the problem of sustainable growth in agricultural production and improvement in the health of rural people and the consumers of agricultural commodities requires that each of these communities establish bridgeheads in the other's territory. Multi-purpose water resource development projects have contributed to the spread of onchocerciasis. Successful efforts to control the black fly have reopened productive lands to cultivation. The introduction of improved cultivars and fertilization practices has helped make the productivity growth sustainable. But examples of effective collaboration either in research or in project development are difficult to come by.

# 7   BRIDGING THE ISLAND EMPIRES

The battle to achieve sustainable growth in agricultural production must be fought out along a broad multidisciplinary front (Bell et al., 1994). Poverty undermines health and degrades the environment. Environmental problems such as soil erosion, water logging and salinity, and fertilizer and pesticide residues link the agricultural agenda with issues such as malaria and schistosomiasis control, sanitation, and water and food quality on the health agenda. Environmental changes underway at the global level, such as acid rain, ozone depletion and climate change, will require changes in food production and health practices at the producer and community level. Effective bridges must be built between the 'island empires' of agricultural, environmental and health sciences. Much more effective organizational and institutional linkages must be built between the suppliers of knowledge and technology and the users. Institutions must be designed to place the users in a stronger role relative to the suppliers. In this section, I present the vision of the institutional infrastructure that will be needed to supply the knowledge and technology in the areas of agricultural production, resource management and health that began to take shape in the several consultations at the Bellagio conference.

**Agricultural Research**

This vision is strongly influenced by the experience of attempts, beginning in the late 1950s, to establish a global agricultural research system (Baum, 1986; Ruttan, 1986). For the architects of the post-World War II set of global institutions, meeting world food needs and the reduction of poverty in rural areas were essential elements in their vision of a world community that could ensure all people of freedom from hunger.

In the immediate post-war years much of the burden fell on the United Nations Food and Agriculture Organization (UN/FAO). But John Boyd Orr, the first Director General of the FAO, burdened with the memory of the agricultural surpluses of the 1930s, was highly critical of the view that knowledge and technology represented a serious constraint on agricultural production capacity: 'No research was needed to find out that half the people in the world lacked sufficient food for health, or that with modern engineering and agricultural science the world food supply could easily be increased to meet human needs' (Boyd Orr, 1966, p. 160). In the first two post-war decades, assistance for agricultural development in the poor countries was conducted largely in a technology transfer and community development mode. By the late 1950s, it was becoming apparent, however, that the gains in production from simple technology transfer had largely played themselves out.

The inadequacy of policies based on the technology transfer or extension model led, in the early 1960s, to a reexamination of the assumption about the availability of a body of agricultural technology that could be readily diffused from high agricultural productivity to low productivity countries or regions. The result was the emergence of a new perspective, that agricultural technology, particularly yield-enhancing biological technology, is highly 'location specific.' Evidence was also accumulated that only limited productivity gains could be achieved by the reallocation or more efficient use of the resources available to peasant producers in poor countries.

In the early post-war development literature peasant producers had been viewed as obstacles to agricultural development. They were viewed as bound by custom and tradition and resistant to change. In an iconoclastic work published in 1964, Theodore W. Schultz advanced a 'poor but efficient' view of peasant producers. They were viewed as making effective use of the resources available to them. But they lived in societies in which productivity-enhancing 'high pay-off' inputs were not available to them. Drawing on the experience of the Rockefeller Foundation program in Mexico and case studies by anthropologists and agricultural economists, Schultz identified three 'high pay-off' investments needed to enhance the productivity of peasant producers. These were (a) the capacity of the agricultural research system to generate locally relevant knowledge and technology, (b) the capacity of the industrial sector to develop, produce and market new inputs which embodied the knowledge and technology generated by research, and (c) the schooling of rural people to enable them to make effective use of the new knowledge and technology.

These insights, from experience and analysis, shaped the response to the food crises of the 1960s and 1970s. The immediate response was the transfer of large resources, including food aid, to the food deficit countries. The longer-term response was the mobilization of resources to develop a system of international agricultural research institutes and to strengthen national agricultural research systems.

By the early 1990s the system had expanded from an initial 4 to 18 centers. The initial centers focused their research on the major food crops grown in developing countries – rice, wheat, maize, potatoes and cassava. These were joined in the 1970s by centers focusing on livestock production, animal disease and genetic resources, on arid and semi-arid areas, food policy and the capacity of the national research system. As the new seed-fertilizer technology generated at the CGIAR centers, particularly for rice and wheat, began to become available, some donors assumed that the CGIAR centers could bypass the more difficult and often frustrating efforts to strengthen national agricultural research systems. But experience in the 1960s and the 1970s confirmed the judgement of those who had participated in the organization of the international centers. Strong national research centers were essential if the prototype technology that might be developed at the international centers was to be broadly transferred, adopted and made available to producers.

During 1990–92, five new centers were added to the CGIAR system. In 1990 the International Irrigation Management Institute (IIMI), the International Center for Research on Agro-Forestry (ICRAF) and the International Network for the Improvements of Banana and Plantain (INIBAP) were brought into the CGIAR system. In 1992 the International Center for Living Aquatic Research Management (ICLARM) was added to the system. This expansion was not accompanied by an expansion of the resources available to the system. Support to the system since the early 1990s has actually declined in real terms, producing a 'quiet crisis in the system'.

The crisis has not only been financial. A number of the CGIAR centers are experiencing the difficulties associated with organizational maturity. There is a natural 'life cycle' sequence in the history of research organizations and research programs (Ruttan, 1982, p. 132). When they are initially organized they tend to attract vigorous and creative individuals. As these individuals interact across disciplines and problem areas the organization often experiences a period of great productivity. As the research organization matures, however, there is often a tendency for the research program to settle into 'filling in the gaps' in knowledge and technology rather than achieving creative solutions to scientific and technical problems. Since the early 1980s, a number of the managers of several of the CGIAR institutes have been forced to struggle, during a period of budget stringency, with the problem of how to revitalize a mature research organization.

The location-specific nature of biological technology meant that the prototype technologies developed at the international centers could become available to producers in the wide range of agro-climatic regions and social and economic environments in which the commodities were being produced only if the capacity to modify, adapt and reinvent the technology was available. It became clear that the challenge of constructing a global agricultural research system capable of sustaining growth in agricultural production required the development of research capacity for each commodity of economic significance in each agro-climatic region. One response by the CGIAR donor community was the establishment of a new center, the International Service for National Agricultural Research (ISNAR) to provide analytical and technical assistance to national agricultural research systems in strengthening their organization and management. Another response was, particularly during the 1970s, substantially expanded support for national agricultural research systems.

Efforts to strengthen national research institutes have been only partially successful. The 1970s witnessed a remarkable expansion of agricultural research capacity in a number of developing countries. The national research systems in India, Brazil, Malaysia and a number of other developing countries began to achieve world class status in their capacity to make advances in knowledge and technology available to their farmers. A number of other countries, such as the Philippines, Colombia and Thailand, achieved substantial capacity to conduct research on their major agricultural commodities. During the 1990s, the buffeting of a global recession and debt crisis had the effect of weakening commitment by a number of aid agencies and national governments to the strengthening of agricultural research. In Africa, many national agriculture research systems that received generous external support even during the 1980s have failed to become productive sources of knowledge and technology.

The role of technical support for farmer decision making and the capacity to supply producers with the technical inputs in which the new technology is embodied has been a continuing area of controversy. In general the developing countries have been relatively extension intensive. The ratio of extension workers to agricultural product has been much higher in developing countries than developed countries (Judd et al., 1987). Weak linkages between research and extension and between extension and farmers have represented a serious constraint on the diffusion of new technology (Tendler, 1993). During the late 1970s and early 1980s the World Bank devoted very substantial resources to the support of an intensive 'training and visit' (T & V) system of delivering information about practices and technology to farmers. The system involved a highly regimented schedule in which the field-level worker is involved one day each week in intensive training about the information that he or she must convey to farmers (Benor and Harrison, 1977). In retrospect it appears the system erred in placing the extension worker rather than the farmer, or the farm family, at the center of the technology adoption process.

A second constraint on the effectiveness of the transfer of agricultural practices and technology to producers is the weakness of the private sector as a source of both the supply and delivery of knowledge and technology (Evenson et al., 1987; Pray, 1987). The emergence of more liberal economic policies since the early 1980s in a number of developing countries is, however, leading to rather rapid growth of private sector suppliers of agricultural technology and to increased research by the suppliers.

The global agricultural support system is still incomplete. Inadequacies in both research and extension systems continue to deprive farm families of the support that they need to meet even current food consumption and income needs. Yet the vision of the agricultural support system that will be needed to sustain growth in agricultural production is reasonably clear. During the past several decades, implementation of the vision has been less than adequate in some developed countries and in all but a few developing countries. With the end of the cold war, it may now be possible to extend the vision to farm families in many of the formerly centrally planned economies. One important step will be to place farm families and the farm enterprise in those societies at the center of the agricultural production process. Another important step will be to link the agricultural research systems in the formerly centrally planned economies with the emerging global agricultural research system.

## Health Research

Godfrey Gunatilleke (1993) has outlined a vision of the gains in health status that can be achieved by even a poor society that devotes significant resources in support of an effective national health policy. Sri Lanka has achieved health indicators – a life expectancy of around 70 years and infant mortality below 20 per 1,000 live births – comparable to the levels achieved by many societies that are much more affluent. But a vision of the global health research system needed to sustain national health policy has emerged more slowly than the vision of a global agricultural system. Only within the last decade has the health research community begun to articulate the form that such a system might take.

For most of the last century, since the time of Koch and Pasteur, health research has been thought of principally as laboratory-based biomedical research, seeking 'silver bullets' against specific infections or diseases – new vaccines, new drugs and new surgical techniques. This focus, plus the remarkable improvements in health in recent decades, led to the misperception that all the new knowledge and new technology needed to protect families and communities around the world from debilitation and illness could be generated in the universities, research institutes and pharmaceutical company laboratories of the industrialized countries.

This limited conception was clearly strong but has been changing rapidly. Three gains in perception are especially important. The first is the recognition that health technologies, to be useful, must be applied in particular social settings. Achieving health improvements requires not only technology but also policies, organizations and processes adapted to the varied economic, social, cultural and historical circumstances among and within countries. Even vaccines, the simplest of technologies, cannot be applied in Lagos by the same means as they are in Liverpool.

An effective health research system, capable of conducting the essential national health research, needs epidemiologists, economists, management specialists and other social and policy analysts in addition to biomedical scientists (Lucas, 1993). Such skills are scarce in industrialized countries. They are grossly deficient in developing countries. But they are essential to identify the precise nature of health problems in different national and local settings, and to design, test and apply appropriate solutions.

A second gain in perception is the recognition that the principal actors in achieving improvements in health are individuals and families, especially mothers. Preventing illnesses and promoting health depend first and most of all on 'maternal technology' – the ability to use basic knowledge about nutrition, cleanliness, home remedies and when and how to call on health professionals (Mata, 1988).

An effective health research system, therefore, must be organized not simply to serve physicians but to support the flow of health knowledge and technology to families and communities. It must also provide for the reverse flow of information from families and communities to researchers about the actual nature of health problems and how they are changing. Such a conception of linking researchers directly to primary actors is customary in agriculture, where research results have long been aimed at farmers as decision makers. But it is a recent conception in health even in industrialized countries.

A third gain in perception is the recognition that the world's health research efforts are overwhelmingly concentrated in industrialized countries, seeking technologies to address the diseases of the more affluent societies. Only about 5 percent of global health research financing is directed to the major diseases and health problems of the less developed countries, where more than 90 percent of the world's burden of preventable deaths occur (Commission on Health Research for Development, 1990). An effective global health research system must address this huge imbalance and provide for a large increase in the resources devoted to the health problems of the developing countries.

Combining these three perceptions with the traditional power of biomedical research, one can begin to perceive, dimly, the shape of a global health research system and how to move toward it. Such a system, in health just as in agriculture, will need to be based solidly on national research systems, capable of supporting decision makers as they identify and confront health problems. A national health research system requires, first of all, skills to measure the patterns and determinants of disease, disability and death, and to monitor changes in health status over time. It also requires skills to design, test and evaluate means for applying improved health technologies in local environments, and for making research results available to those who need to use them, from national policy makers to local families. Every nation needs the capacity to conduct such country-specific research to guide its health activities, and the establishment of such capacity should clearly be given top priority (Lucas, 1993).

Beyond the capacity for essential country-specific research, health scientists in every country will wish to join, as and when they can, in the international effort to advance the world's frontiers of knowledge on the social and biological pathologies of ill-health and disability, and on new technologies to overcome them. In poor countries, the conditions for world class science are difficult to establish. Nevertheless, a significant number of developing countries, Thailand, India, Egypt, Mexico and Brazil, to name just a few, are beginning to have the capacity to make significant contributions to world knowledge in the health field.

Thus, national health research systems need to begin with the capacity to guide national health activities, and to go on, as conditions permit, to participate in global frontier research. In most developing countries, there are only rudimentary health research capabilities at present. It is urgent for developing countries, and for the international health assistance community, to commit themselves to building steadily stronger national health research systems. Such systems will need to start small, and to focus initially on the most pressing health problems. But they should be designed with a view to dynamic change over time as financial and personnel resources grow, and as health problems change with the demographic and epidemiological transitions through which the developing countries will pass over the coming decades.

Thinking about how to achieve an effective global health research system thus begins with the development of strong national systems. But national systems must not be thought of as separate, freestanding entities. On the contrary, it is essential that they be linked together by strong international ties, and draw from the common, growing pool of worldwide health knowledge, with each country adapting advances in health science to its own specific circumstances.

Moreover, it would be a mistake to think of a global system as centered in the industrialized countries, with all scientific advances pioneered there and rippling outward to the developing world. We have already seen major health improvements developed in the Third World, as ambulatory therapy for tuberculosis was pioneered in Madras, and oral re-hydration therapy for diarrhea in Dhaka. As the amount and quality of developing country research steadily rise, a global research system will increasingly be multi-centric, one in which the flows of ideas and new knowledge move in all directions along networks of information and collaboration encompassing scientists from many countries, rich and poor alike.

Thus the guidelines for moving toward a global health research system include: (1) the development, as rapidly as feasible, of strong national systems, especially in developing countries where they are currently very weak, and (2) the rapid evolution of international collaborative mechanisms and arrangements. Two aspects of this overall vision received special attention and illumination.

The first is the necessity for building direct relationships between the national health research system and action for health at the community and family level.

Kaseje (1993) has described the elements of a community-based health system in Kenya that he helped design and implement that relies directly on the actions of individual families and communities. The model views the mother as the key health provider. It builds on the strong motivation to carry out her tasks resulting from concern about the current and future well-being of her children and family.

The resources needed to enable families to provide effective health services to their members are very similar to those identified three decades ago by Schultz to enable peasant producers to become effective suppliers of agricultural commodities. The 'high pay-off' health inputs include: (a) the capacities of the health research community to produce the new knowledge and the materials that are appropriate to the resource and cultural endowments of rural communities; (b) the capacity of national, regional and local institutions to make the knowledge and the materials available to families; and (c) formal schooling and informal education of families, particularly mothers, to make effective use of available health information.

There are strong differences of opinion within the international health community as to whether a system of international health research centers, analogous to the CGIAR centers, would be appropriate or effective. On the one hand internationally organized efforts have the advantage of achieving a critical mass of scientists concentrating on and physically located close to high-priority problems. Internationally organized research efforts can focus on specific problems in a multidisciplinary way and demonstrate economies of scale in their operations, making them attractive to external funding. On the other hand, international center salaries are high and their activities, if not carefully targeted, can supersede rather than complement national efforts (Commission on Health Research for Development, 1990, p. 58).

Constraints on foreign assistance funds suggest that it would be unrealistic to expect that resources could be mobilized at present to support a system of international health research centers in the tropics. It seems more likely that most international collaboration in the health field will be through international networks linking scientists in national institutions (both in industrialized and developing countries) in goal-oriented research programs aimed at specific health problems. A successful example of such collaboration is the Special Programme for Research and Training in Tropical Diseases (TDR), co-sponsored by the UN Development Programme, the World Bank and WHO. Started in 1976, TDR focuses on six specific diseases (including malaria, schistosomiasis and leprosy), and in addition to supporting research, invests approximately 25 percent of its annual budget of $30–35 million in strengthening research capacity in developing countries.

While international networks of national centers can work effectively in supporting research on particular diseases, there is one extremely important function they cannot perform. The field of health research conspicuously lacks an overview mechanism. In agriculture, the CGIAR (as distinct from the set of centers it sponsors) has built highly valuable methods for surveying the world-wide agricultural research scene in relation to the needs for research results, reviewing ongoing research activities (both those of the international centers and of other institutions), and proposing changes in current research priorities and institutional arrangements including, where necessary, the development of new research facilities.

There is no analogous, effective, independent organization in the health field for assessing progress in research, especially on developing-country health problems, identifying neglected areas and promoting necessary action. The result is clear. At present, of the three leading infectious disease causes of death in the world (acute respiratory infections, diarrheal diseases and tuberculosis), only diarrhea is addressed by a major, sustained research effort. That is why the Commission on Health Research for Development came to the conclusion that 'a health analogue of the CGIAR assessment and promotion structure could be of great value and should be established' (Commission on Health Research for Development, 1990, p. 59). This objective is clearly an urgent one.

**Environmental Research**

If the global research system for agriculture now faces the challenges of maturity and the system for health confronts those of adolescence, then the global environmental research system still requires early post-natal care.

To be sure, research for environmental conservation has a long and productive history in many parts of the world. Since World War II, this research has been given impetus and direction by at least three waves of concern over the implications of natural resource availability and environmental change for the sustainability of improvements in human well-being. Early work focused on the adequacy and protection of the material base for agricultural and industrial production. By the mid-1970s, increasing attention was also being given to the impact of residuals generated by that production on air and water quality and human health. Today, rapidly growing awareness of global change in the earth system has provided yet another dimension to our environmental concerns.

Most environmental research to date has been performed in universities, initially with support from major philanthropic organizations such as the Ford Foundation. Prodded by the Stockholm Conference on the Global Environment in 1972, national governments have become increasingly involved as supporters, producers and users of environmental research. Over the last decade, there has also been an explosion in the number and variety of non-governmental organizations active on the world's environmental scene, some of them producing research of the highest caliber and relevance (Livernash, 1992). International programs for environmental research have also expanded dramatically since their 'modern' birth in the International Geophysical Year of 1957. Nonetheless, most important international institutions for environmental research are barely 25 years old – for example ICSU's SCOPE, UNESCO's MAB, IIASA and, of course, UNEP (Caldwell, 1990). Today's major research programs on global change – the World Climate Research Program (WCRP), the International Geosphere Biosphere Program (IGBP) and the Human Dimensions of Global Environmental Change Program (HDGEC) – are younger still (Jaeger and Ferguson, 1991; Miller and Jacobson, 1992; Perry, 1991).

This impressive and expanding array of activities nonetheless falls far short of the global system of environmental research needed to provide the knowledge base for sustainable development. Still lacking is a coherent institutional structure that can link the world's environmental researchers both upward to the international level of policy negotiations and downward to the community level consumers, producers, health workers and extension agents on whose actions sustainable development must ultimately depend. In the wake of the Rio 'Earth Summit', however, several initiatives are under discussion that could supply important components of such a system and move it substantially closer to reality.

The most ambitious of these is START (System for Analysis, Research and Training) proposed in 1991 by the IGBP in collaboration with the WCRP and HDGEC. START is planned as 'a global system of regional research networks to stimulate research, modeling, and training activities related to global environmental change in both the natural and social sciences' (IGBP, 1992, p. 5). Its regional focus is based on the realization that global change wears local faces. The origins, the impacts and the options for managing global environmental change will be different in different parts of the world, and must be understood within their local environmental and social contexts. The initial START planning document divided the world into 13 'scientifically coherent' regions (Eddy et al., 1991). Within each region, the research network is planned to consist of one or more research centers plus an unspecified number of regional research sites (e.g. university departments and field stations). The networks aim to provide scientists throughout the world with the knowledge and infrastructure necessary for them to participate fully in ongoing research on global environmental change.

In addition to the comprehensive plans of START, a number of more focused regional initiatives are also being pursued around the world. In Asia, the Smithsonian-sponsored program on Sustainable Management of Tropical Evergreen Forests has linked leading centers throughout Asia in a unique network for research, training and data collection (Ashton, 1991; Lepkowski, 1992). In the Americas, the Inter-American Institute for Global Change Research (IAI) has been established as a 'regional network of research entities . . . [that] seeks to achieve the best possible international coordination of scientific and economic research on the extent, causes and consequences of global change in the Americas' (IGBP, 1991; Declaration of Montevideo, 1992). Close integration with the START initiative has been emphasized throughout the planning of the IAI. In Central and Eastern Europe a number of environmental research, development and training institutions have been formed to address the special problems of this region. One notable example with support from a number of Western countries is the Regional Environmental Center in Budapest. Since its inception in 1989, the Center has helped 'to set up environmental surveys, grassroots and non-governmental organizations, new environmental legislation and remediation campaigns' (*Nature*, 1992). Its major activity has been building a database on environmental conditions in the region, coupled with a computer network to disseminate these data to smaller offices for use by local researchers.

At the global level, increasing attention is being given to the need for a permanent international research institution that could tackle environmental problems that transcend individual regions and link national centers for environmental research into a truly global system. This function is currently performed on a largely *ad hoc* basis, for example through studies of ICSU's Scientific Committee on Problems of the Environment, or the Intergovernmental Panel on Climate Change. But the time may well be ripe for complementing such *ad hoc* efforts with a more permanent home or homes. How these and other initiatives will relate to one another or to existing national research centers is not yet clear. Most of the parties involved seem aware of the need for addressing such relations. Early indications are that their potential complementarities could dominate the inevitable competition for people, programs and funds.

Against this optimistic assessment, however, it must be noted that in the dialogue leading to recent environmental research initiatives, there appears to have been little consideration of appropriate linkages with agricultural and health research systems. This is a serious omission for two reasons. First, it virtually guarantees that many of the lessons painfully learned in the course of building today's relatively mature network of agricultural and health research systems will be lost on the fledgling environmental effort. Second, it perpetuates the 'island empire' problems I referred to at the outset of this chapter. There are several related lessons from the development of today's agricultural and health research systems that should be incorporated in new environmental efforts. As noted above, all of these reflect a growing appreciation of the central role of family and community level decisions in shaping sustainable development.

One reason is that means must be designed to assure that research priorities reflect the environmental problems confronting individual families, farmers and resource users in the field. The small 'charmed circle' of puzzles that excite lab scientists or program administrators should not be allowed to dominate the agenda. The World Bank's report on *Development and the Environment* is surely correct in its conclusion that 'the current environmental debate has paid too little attention to the problems of clean water, urban air pollution, indoor air pollution, and severe land degradation'. Each year these problems kill millions of people, undermine the health of hundreds of millions more, and significantly reduce productivity of people who can least afford it (World Bank, 1992, p. 4; see also Norberg-Bohm et al., 1992).

A second reason is that the temptation to search for universal 'silver bullets' that will solve specific environmental problems whenever and wherever they occur must be resisted. Most causes, impacts and solutions will be intimately associated with particular social circumstances and landscapes. Effective research systems will therefore require significant site-specific components and must avoid focusing activity in a few elite laboratories of the high income countries. The need for elite laboratories will remain, in part because of needs for special research and data processing equipment, and in part because of the need to bring top scientists from many disciplines together for particular aspects of the necessary research. But specific measures must be implemented to assure that such regional centers do not bleed talent, funds and equipment from the essential national and local nodes of the research network. A recognition of the need for simultaneous and complementary strengthening of the local, national and regional dimensions of the emerging global environmental research system seems well embodied in the plans for START (Eddy et al., 1991). But a practical vision of what constitutes 'essential' national environmental research, how this research is to be funded and how it is to be linked to international efforts, has yet to emerge.

A third reason is that a technology transfer strategy for research and development will be no more successful in dealing with environmental problems than it has been for sustaining improvements in agricultural productivity or human health. This applies not only to conventional North–South transfers, but also to the current spate of enthusiasm for grafting the clean energy systems of advanced OECD nations onto the formerly socialist economies of Europe. Less obviously, but perhaps even more importantly, experience in the agriculture and health sectors warns against the wholesale transfer of institutions as a means of enhancing environmental conservation. This is especially the case in the area of common pool resources where an uncritical tendency to transfer solutions based on full private property rights or centralized regulation to small scale, low income situations has had disastrous consequences. Appropriate alternatives often exist, more finely attuned to local social and environmental conditions (Ostrom, 1990). In general, the need is not to transfer environmental technologies and institutions from 'advanced' to 'developing' regions, but rather to promote more widespread sharing of knowledge, know-how and experience around the world. In particular, in environment as in agriculture and health, the need is to enhance the voice and power of users relative to suppliers of needed research and development.

Finally, an effective global environmental research system must be much more broadly inclusive than is presently the case. The need to better incorporate knowledge users in the system has been stressed in this chapter. The environmental research and development potential of the formerly centrally planned economies must be tapped. The private sector must be encouraged as both a supplier and deliverer of the knowledge needed for environmentally sustainable development. Perhaps no single factor has so inhibited the development of effective global research systems for agriculture and health as the failure to promote incentives and reward structures that can induce constructive private sector involvement. In the environmental field, there is a vast potential for private sector engagement in topics as diverse as energy efficiency and biotechnology. But a number of issues involving intellectual property rights, liabilities and government–industry relations will have to be resolved before the potential can be fully tapped for the benefit of sustainable development (Schmidheiny, 1992).

An effective global environmental research system will have many of the features of effective agricultural and health research systems. The behavior of consumers of environmental services and the producers of the residuals – households, farms and factories – that erode environmental amenities will have to be recognized as central to the process of environmental change. The resources that will be needed to place households, farms and factories in a position to respond constructively will depend on: (a) the capacity of the environmental research system to provide the knowledge, including the essential national environmental research, needed by household, farm and factory decision makers; (b) the capacity of national, regional and community institutions to provide the knowledge, technology and incentives to those who make decisions about resource use; and (c) the depth of understanding possessed by household, farm and factory decision makers about the consequences of their own actions and the actions of the economic and political institutions in which they participate.

## 8   PERSPECTIVE

We have argued that the 'island empires' of the agricultural, health and environmental sciences can learn from one another as they strive to build global research systems that can support sustainable development. Whether they can, or even should, move beyond passive learning to active cooperation remains to be seen.

There seems little merit in any grand organizational scheme that would attempt to pull the already diverse networks of research in the respective empires under a single roof. And the most dynamic of the existing empires – that dealing with environmental research – simply does not have enough experience in the tough business of actually running a global network to seem credible as a leader of any major bridging movement.

What does seem both feasible and desirable, however, is to begin some modest effort at active bridge building. At a minimum, the principals of the three empires might agree to meet regularly – perhaps in the spirit of the G-7 Summits – in order that they and their senior staff members could get to know one another and exchange information on current activities. An exploration of possible collaboration in global monitoring and other data gathering activities might be a good early agenda item for such meetings. The new UN Commission on Sustainable Development, established at the 1992 'Earth Summit', would be one logical organization to convene meetings. An International Environmental Organization modeled along the lines of the General Agreement on Tariffs and Trade has been suggested (Esty, 1993).

At a deeper level, it is essential to realize that the global agricultural, health and environmental research systems outlined in this chapter have important common elements. The global systems can be effective only as the underlying sciences – particularly the biological and the social sciences – advance. Advances in the biological sciences and the social sciences are necessary to enlarge the world's understanding of the natural and social phenomena in global change. They are also needed in order to expand the capacity to apply advances in knowledge to the national and human dimensions of development in the poor countries where most of the world's people live.

The need to enlarge scientific capacity in the poorer countries of the world should not be viewed as a burden on either the developed or developing countries. Rather it is an opportunity to multiply the intellectual talent necessary to advance knowledge relevant to the achievement of sustainable development. Completion of the development of global research systems in agriculture, health and environment is a necessary component of a global effort to establish and mobilize the intellectual capacity and energy that will be needed to sustain development.

# REFERENCES

Ashton, P. (1991), *Sustainable Management of Tropical Evergreen Forests: A Program Proposal,* Cambridge, MA: Harvard Institute for International Development, Harvard University, mimeo.

Ausubel, J. and Sladovich, H.E. (eds) (1989), *Technology and the Environment,* Washington, DC: National Academy Press.

Barnett, H.J. and Morse, C. (1963), *Scarcity and Growth: The Economics of Natural Resource Availability,* Baltimore: Johns Hopkins University Press.

Baum, W. (1986), *Partners Against Hunger: The Consultative Group On International Agricultural Research,* Washington, DC: World Bank.

Bell, D., Clark, W. and Ruttan, V. (1994), 'Global Research Systems for Sustainable Development: Agriculture, Health, and Environment', in Ruttan, V. (ed.), *Agriculture, Environment and Health: Sustainable Development in the 21ˢᵗ Century,* Minneapolis: University of Minnesota Press, pp. 358–380.

Benor, D. and Harrison, J.Q. (1977), *Agricultural Extension: The Training and Visit System,* Washington, DC: World Bank.

Board on Science and Technology for International Development (BOSTID) and Institute of Medicine (IOM) (1987), *The U.S. Capacity to Address Tropical Infectious Disease Problems,* Washington, DC: National Academy Press.

Boyd Orr, J. (1966), *As I Recall,* London: MacGib and Kee.

Caldwell, L. (1990), *International Environmental Policy: Emergence and Dimensions,* 2nd edn, Durham, NC: Duke University Press.

Carson, R. (1962), *Silent Spring,* Boston: Houghton Mifflin.

Commission on Health Research for Development (1990), *Health Research: Essential Link to Equity in Development,* London: Oxford University Press.

Committee on Global Change of the Commission on Geoscience, Environment and Resources (1990), *Research Strategies for the U.S. Global Change Research Program,* Washington, DC: National Academy Press.

Committee on Science, Engineering and Public Policy (1991), *Policy Implications of Greenhouse Warming,* Washington, DC: National Academy Press.

Cummings, R.W. (1989), *Modernizing Asia and the Near East: Agricultural Research in the 1990s,* Washington, DC: U.S. Agency for International Development, Bureau for Science and Technology, mimeo.

Declaration of Montevideo (1992), *Declaration of Montevideo on an Inter-American Institute for Global Change Research.* Montevideo.

Eddy, J.A., Malone, T.F., McCarthy, J.J. and Rosswall, T. (1991), *Global Change Systems for Analysis, Research and Training (START),* International Geosphere-Biosphere Program, International Council of Scientific Unions, Report no. 15, Boulder, CO: University Center for Academic Research, Office of Interdisciplinary Earth Sciences.

Edwards, C. (1988), 'Real Prices Received by Farmers Keep Falling', *Choices,* Fourth Quarter, pp. 22–23.

Esty, D.C. (1993), 'GATTing the Greens: Not Just Greening the GATT', *Foreign Affairs,* **72,** pp. 32–36.

Evenson, R.E., Evenson, D.D. and Putnam, J.D. (1987), 'Private Sector Agricultural Inventions in Developing Countries', in Ruttan, V.W. and Pray, C.E (eds), *Policy for Agricultural Research,* Boulder, CO: Westview Press, pp. 469–511.

Graham-Tomasi, T. (1991), 'Sustainability: Concepts and Implications for Agricultural Research Policy', in Pardey, P.G., Roseboom, J. and Anderson, J.R. (eds), *Agricultural Research Policy: International Quantitative Perspectives,* Cambridge: Cambridge University Press, pp. 81–102.

Gunatilleke, G. (1994), 'Health Policy for Rural Areas: Sri Lanka', in Ruttan, V.W. (ed.), *Agriculture, Environment and Health: Sustainable Development in the 21st Century,* Minneapolis: University of Minnesota Press, pp. 209–235.

Hayami, Y. and Ruttan, V.W. (1985), *Agricultural Development: An International Perspective,* 2nd edn, Baltimore: The Johns Hopkins University Press.

International Geosphere-Biosphere Program (IGBP) (1991), 'The Inter-American Institute for Global Change Research', *Global Change Newsletter,* **8,** pp. 4–5.

International Geosphere-Biosphere Program (IGBP) (1992), 'A Quick Start for START: Guidelines for Regional Research Network Centers', *Global Change Newsletter,* **9,** pp. 5–7.

Jaeger, J. and Ferguson, H.L. (eds) (1991), *Climate Change: Science, Impacts and Policy, Proceedings of the Second World Climate Conference,* Cambridge: Cambridge University Press.

Judd, M.A., Boyce, J.K. and Evenson, R.E. (1987), 'Investing in Agricultural Research and Extension', in Ruttan, V. and Pray, C.E. (eds), *Policy for Agricultural Research,* Boulder, CO: Westview Press, pp. 2–38.

Kaseje, D.C.O. (1994), 'Health Systems for Rural Areas: Kenya', in Ruttan, V.W. (ed.), *Agriculture, Environment and Health: Sustainable Development in the 21st Century,* Minneapolis: University of Minnesota Press, pp. 236–256.

Lepkowski, W. (1992), 'U.S.–Japan Global Partnership Action Plan Revived', *Chemical Engineering News,* **70,** pp. 16–18.

Livernash, R. (1992), 'The Growing Influence of NGOs in the Developing World', *Environment,* **34,** pp. 12–20, 41–43.

Lucas, A.O. (1994), 'The Institutional Infrastructure for Health Research in Developing Countries', in Ruttan, V.W. (ed.), *Agriculture, Environment and Health: Sustainable*

*Development in the 21ˢᵗ Century*, Minneapolis: University of Minnesota Press, pp.187–208.

Mata, L. (1988), 'A Public Health Approach to the "Food–Malnutrition–Economic Recession" Complex', in Bell, D.E. and Reich, M.R. (eds), *Health, Nutrition, and Economic Crises: Approaches to Policy in the Third World*, Dover: Auburn House, pp. 265–275.

Meadows, D.H. and Meadows, D.L., with J. Randers and W.W. Behrens III (1972), *The Limits to Growth*, New York: University Books.

Miller, R.B. and Hackobson, H.K. (1992), *Research on the Human Components of Global Change: Next Steps*, Human Dimensions of Global Environmental Change Program, International Social Science Council, Discussion Paper 1, Paris: International Social Science Council.

*Nature* (1992), 'West's Gift Becomes a Model', *Nature*, **355**, p. 672.

Norberg-Bohm, V., Clark, W.C., Baskshi, B., Berkenkamp, J.A., Bishko, S.A., Koehler, M.D., Marrs, J.A., Nielsen, C.P. and Sagar, A. (1992), *International Comparisons of Environmental Hazards*, John F. Kennedy School of Government, Harvard University, CSIA Discussion Paper 92–09, Cambridge, MA.: Harvard University.

Nordhaus, W.D. (1990), 'To Slow or Not to Slow: The Economics of the Greenhouse Effect', New Haven: Department of Economics, Yale University.

Ostrom, E. (1990), *Governing the Commons: The Evolution of Institutions for Collective Action*, Cambridge: Cambridge University Press.

Pardey, P., Roseboom, J. and Anderson, J. (1991), 'Regional Perspectives on National Agricultural Research', in Pardey, P., Roseboom, J. and Anderson, J. (eds), *Agricultural Research Policy: International Quantitative Perspectives*, Cambridge: Cambridge University Press.

Parikh, K. (1993), 'Agriculture and Food System Scenarios for the 21ˢᵗ Century', in Ruttan, V.W. (ed.), *Agriculture, Environment and Health: Sustainable Development in the 21ˢᵗ Century*, Minneapolis: University of Minnesota Press, pp. 26–47.

Parry, M. (1990), *Climate Change and World Agriculture*, London: Earthscan Publications.

Perry, J.S. (1991), 'Global Change: From Rhetoric to Reality', *Reviews of Geophysics*, supplement, **29**, pp. 39–45.

Pingali, P. (1988), *Intensification and Diversification of Asian Rice Farming Systems*, Los Banos, Laguna, Philippines: International Rice Research Institute, Agricultural Economics Paper RR–41.

Pingali, P.L. and Roger, P.A. (eds) (1995), *Impact of Pesticides on Farmer Health and the Rice Environment*, Natural Resource Management and Policy Series, Boston and London: Dordrecht.

Plucknett, D.H. and Smith, N.J.H. (1986), 'Sustaining Agricultural Yields', *BioScience*, **36**, pp. 40–45.

Pray, C.E. and Echeverria, R. (1990), *Determinants and Scope of Private Sector Research in Developing Countries*, International Service for National Agricultural Research (ISNAR), Staff Notes 90–82. The Hague: ISNAR.

President's Materials Policy Commission (1952), *Resources for Freedom*, Washington, DC: U.S. Government Printing Office.

President's Water Resources Policy Commission (1950), *A Water Policy for the American People, Volume One*, Washington, DC: U.S. Government Printing Office.

Reilly, J. and Bucklin, R. (1989), *Climate Change and Agriculture*, World Agriculture Situation and Outlook Report, WAS-55, Washington, DC: Agricultural Research Service, U.S. Department of Agriculture, pp. 43–46.

Rogoff, M.H. and Rawlins, S.L. (1987), 'Food Security: A Technological Alternative', *BioScience*, **37**, pp. 800–807.

Ruttan, V.W. (1971), 'Technology and the Environment', *American Journal of Agricultural Economics,* **53**, pp. 707–717.

Ruttan, V.W. (ed.) (1989), *Biological and Technical Constraints on Crop and Animal Productivity: Report on a Dialogue,* St. Paul, MN: University of Minnesota Department of Agricultural and Applied Economics.

Ruttan, V.W. (ed.) (1990), *Health Constraints on Agricultural Development,* St. Paul, MN: University of Minnesota Department of Agricultural and Applied Economics, Staff Paper P90-74.

Ruttan, V.W. (ed.) (1992), *Sustainable Agriculture and the Environment: Perspectives on Growth and Constraints,* Boulder, CO: Westview Press.

Ruttan, V.W. (1986), 'Toward a Global Agricultural Research System: A Personal View', *Research Policy,* **15**, pp. 307–327.

Schmidheiny, S. (1992), *Changing Course: A Global Business Perspective on Development and the Environment,* Cambridge: MIT Press.

World Bank (1992), *Development and Environment: World Development Report 1992,* Oxford: Oxford University Press.

# 3 Agricultural Diversity: Do We Have the Resources to Meet Future Needs?

## Mary Knudson

## 1 INTRODUCTION

It is no longer necessary to justify the importance of biological diversity in discussions of agricultural productivity. Experts as well as the public have come to realize that the maintenance of agricultural productivity requires a healthy diversity of cultivated varieties. Examples such as the collapse of the Mayan civilization, the tragedy of the Irish potato famines and the southern corn leaf blight of 1970 in the United States are easily and commonly invoked as examples of the threat posed to agricultural productivity from an over-reliance on monotypes. While these examples may provide the most dramatic evidence of the importance of maintaining genetic diversity in agriculture, they are the tip of the agricultural iceberg. Without the preservation of existing species, it will become increasingly difficult to create new and improved plant varieties. The most careful avoidance of monotypic agriculture will be unable to meet future agricultural needs, if not accompanied by the development of more productive plant varieties.

To create improved varieties and to have these improved varieties planted in the field, several conditions must be met. First, plant breeders must have access to a wide selection of existing genetic material. In the first section of this chapter, I assess the degree of genetic diversity in current collections of national and global germplasm banks (hereafter, called gene banks). In this section, I also address the issue of access to these collections. Even if a gene bank holds 90 percent of the determined diversity in the world, this potential will be wasted if existing collections are not well maintained or efficiently cataloged. Policies to help these banks run more efficiently will be identified.

But accessible and relatively complete collections of genetic material are only two necessary conditions for enhancing future agricultural productivity. In addition, private plant breeders and public institutions must make effective use of the resources provided by gene banks. While there will be discussion of the role of the public sector in these matters, this chapter will primarily concentrate on the incentives of the private sector to utilize the resources of the gene banks. The motivation for this focus comes from the charge, often made, that market incentives by themselves will be an insufficient mechanism for the enhancement of genetic diversity, even in the presence of well-stocked and accessible gene banks. If this charge is true, then public policy will have to be directed towards supplementing the actions of free markets. If false, then policy can be more directly targeted towards the enhancement of gene banks.

Gene banks and plant breeders are only the first two steps in a process that ultimately ends with the farmer. While the quality of gene banks and their use determines what varieties farmers may choose from, the choice of variety is ultimately up to the farmer. Enhanced varietal options will be useless without the adoption of these varieties by farmers. A brief discussion of the use of varieties and what characteristics farmers select will shed light on the role diversity plays and what role it should play in these choices.

In terms of policy, this chapter will show that both the gene banks and the use of germplasm by plant breeders could be changed to increase diversity. In particular, the impact of intellectual property rights (IPRs) will be discussed. This should help determine how IPRs affect diversity and how IPRs should be used in the future to promote diversity. Policies stemming from several international agreements on the conservation, maintenance and use of plant germplasm will also be discussed. While differences in ownership values are debated during international negotiations, policies have evolved to resolve these differences so that a strong global policy on conserving, maintaining and using global plant genetic resources may be implemented. Policy prescriptions that could ameliorate the problems of gene banks, the use of germplasm by plant breeders, and the use of property rights by various countries are many – some simple to implement and some not so simple. However, if these policies are implemented, then the future level of diversity within our germplasm collections should be of the caliber necessary to meet agricultural demands over the coming 50 years.

## 2 DIVERSITY DEFINED

Before proceeding into the discussion, a brief note should be made about terms. Biodiversity is a catchword used to cover a set of very different biological characteristics. As typically used, biological diversity is usually meant to cover three types of diversity: genetic diversity, species diversity and ecosystem diversity. *Genetic diversity* refers to the genetic variance between individual plants, animals and microorganisms. For example, a state with the Turkey and Togo varieties of wheat exhibits a greater degree of genetic diversity than a state where only the Turkey variety is grown. *Species diversity*, by contrast, refers to the numbers of different living organisms within a particular area. An area inhabited solely by owls, field mice and the Turkey variety of wheat would thus exhibit a (relatively) greater degree of species diversity, although a minimal level of genetic diversity. *Ecosystem diversity* refers to variance of habitats, biotic communities and ecological processes (McNeely et al., 1990; U.S. Congress, OTA, 1987). If our owl/mouse/Turkey variety area also had a small lake filled with trout, then ecosystem diversity of the area would be increased.

Failure to make a distinction between these types of diversity is a potential source of conflict and misunderstanding. A policy to aid *genetic* diversity by, for example, subsidizing the use of new crop varieties, may decrease *species* variety if the new crops are planted on land that was previously an uncultivated meadow. Following the usual conventions in discussions of crop agriculture, I shall limit my discussion to genetic diversity.

# 3 THREATS TO PLANT GENETIC DIVERSITY

Genetic diversity in crop agriculture is threatened in three ways, all related to the growing of high yielding varieties (HYVs).[1] These are *genetic vulnerability*, *genetic erosion*, and *genetic wipeout* (Wilkes, 1989). While analytically distinct, the first two are often found together, and can often lead to the third.

*Genetic vulnerability* refers to the inability of a plant or crop variety to fight against adverse conditions such as disease or environmental problems (Wilkes, 1989). The National Research Council (NRC, 1993) uses the term: 'to indicate the condition that results when a crop is uniformly susceptible to a pest, pathogen, or environmental hazard as a result of its genetic constitution, thereby creating a potential for disaster' (NRC, 1993, p. 48). The more genetically uniform a crop is (i.e. the lower the genetic diversity), and the more widely this crop is grown, the less likely the entire crop can survive well against unexpected threats. Genetic vulnerability increases as environmental conditions become more favorable to the pest or pathogen or if the pest or pathogen is highly dispersible (NRC, 1993).

The dangers of genetic vulnerability were brought home to U.S. agriculture by the 1970 southern corn leaf blight. By the 1960s, most of the maize grown in the United States was a single cross hybrid,[2] produced using a cytoplasmic–genetic system.[3] The cytoplasmic part of this system all stemmed from one source in Texas. This high degree of genetic uniformity made the corn crop vulnerable to widespread losses from pests or diseases. The cytoplasm was susceptible to southern corn leaf blight (Plucknett et al., 1987) and an outbreak of this blight in the 1970s destroyed 15 percent of the entire U.S. corn crop (Wilkes, 1989).

This disaster alerted American agriculture to the potential problems with the genetic base of crops grown in the United States. In responding to this threat, the National Academy of Sciences (NAS) appointed a special Committee on Genetic Vulnerability in 1970 to determine the United States' level of genetic vulnerability. The results of that study indicated that the genetic vulnerability of corn was hardly unique. Six cotton varieties made up 68 percent of the land planted to cotton; six soybean varieties made up 56 percent of total soybean acreage; six wheat varieties made up 41 percent of total wheat planted; and six inbred lines of maize were used as parents of hybrids which occupied 71 percent of all hybrid maize land (Duvick, 1984).

The U.S. research system demonstrated how well it could react to such a crisis. The year following the corn blight outbreak, farmers were able to plant new hybrids that did not contain the T cytoplasm. This rapid response was achieved through the use of different production technology, international winter nurseries (in Hawaii, Florida, the Caribbean, and Central and South America), and germplasm from throughout the world (United States, Argentina, Hungary and Yugoslavia) (Plucknett et al., 1987).

Concern over genetic vulnerability remains great today. Again, in 1992, the NAS convened to assess it (NRC, 1993). This concern is felt not only in the United States. Because of the widespread use of HYVs with similar genetic backgrounds across the globe, genetic vulnerability for many crops has increased (NRC, 1993; Goodman and Castillo-Gonzalez, 1991).

The second threat to genetic diversity is *genetic erosion*. Genetic erosion is defined as the loss of landraces and wild relatives.[4] Clearly genetic erosion and genetic vulnerability are distinct – an increasing reliance on monocultures need not inevitably mean the loss of wild varieties, for example. But often they are linked, as can be seen from a discussion of the mechanisms of genetic erosion.

Genetic erosion can occur in many ways. First, as farmers come to uniformly adopt new varieties such as HYVs, landraces can disappear (McNeely et al., 1990). Second, as farmers devote more land to commercial agriculture, wild relatives can be displaced. Third, as urban populations press out, wild varieties and landraces can also be displaced. For example, urban development in Mexico and Guatemala threatened the home of teosinte, a wild relative of maize. The Aswan dam in Egypt and overgrazing in West Asia and North Africa threatened wild relatives of many crops (Plucknett et al., 1987). Thus, ironically, increasing the amount of land devoted to agriculture as well as decreasing the amount of land devoted to agriculture can lead to genetic erosion. This genetic erosion can lead to greater reliance on a limited set of varieties – and with it, genetic vulnerability.

The third threat to genetic diversity is the most thorough, *genetic wipeout*. Genetic wipeout is the complete elimination of a genetic resource. Many believe the earth is currently undergoing an extinction episode for plants and animals occurring at a faster rate and on a broader scale than ever before

(McNeely et al., 1990; Wilson, 1988). In agriculture, landraces are becoming extinct because new varieties are replacing them before they are being collected. Even when collected, the landraces may be lost because of inadequate maintenance of germplasm collections.

The US Department of Agriculture (USDA) melon program provides a good example of the danger of genetic wipeout. When a virus threatened the melon crop, researchers were able to come up with resistance genes offering protection against the virus. However, instead of preserving the seeds of the susceptible melon, the seeds were instead destroyed. Predictably, a new disease threatened the new melons, a disease to which the old melons were immune. However, because the old variety was lost, breeders had to search for and collect a new set of melon seeds to breed resistance into commercial varieties (Wilkes, 1989). This effort could have been avoided had genetic wipeout of the old seeds been avoided. (Simply storing seeds is not sufficient to avoid genetic wipeout. The same results can occur if seeds within collections are not rejuvenated often enough.)

The above discussion shows how important it is to be alert to genetic erosion, vulnerability and wipeout in agriculture. While one may wish that these problems would go away by themselves, future trends such as population growth, global warming and environmental degradation promise to only exacerbate our current predicament (McNeely et al., 1990; Plucknett et al., 1987). Because our diversity in the wild is decreasing, and because little evolution or adaptation occurs once a plant is held in a collection, future diversity rests on the makeup of germplasm collections. If this diversity decreases, it affects the future base of our crop production system (McNeely et al., 1990). The question becomes, 'do we have the genetic resources to respond to new environmental problems?' To answer this question, we must look at gene banks, the primary resource for preserving plant genetic diversity.

## 4   GENE BANKS FOR *EX SITU* PRESERVATION

One of the most successful methods for the preservation of germplasm has been the gene bank. A gene bank is a form of *ex situ* preservation of plants.[5] Plants are preserved in an environment outside of their normal habitat, usually as a seed or a cutting (U.S. Congress, OTA, 1987). Table 3.1 presents a listing of the different storage technologies utilized for different plants.

Gene banks fall into one of two types. The first type is referred to as an active (or medium-term) collection. In active collections, plants are made available for use in ongoing breeding programs. For seeds, these collections are stored at 5 degrees Celsius. Seeds in this state have a life expectancy of 5 to more than 20 years depending on many factors. For other plants, such as

*Global Environmental Change and Agriculture*

woody, clonally propagated plants, the plants are maintained in greenhouses, orchards and *in vitro* plant cultures, which entails a shorter life expectancy.

*Table 3.1   Storage technologies for germplasm of different plants*

| Plant group | Storage form | Field collections | *In vitro* culture | Cool temperature | Liquid nitrogen | Collection |
|---|---|---|---|---|---|---|
| Cereals/grain legumes | S | | X | R | B, A | |
| Forage legumes/ grasses | S | | X | R | B, A | |
| | P | X | X, R | X | A | |
| Vegetables | S | | X | R | B,A | |
| | P | X | R | R | R | A |
| Forest trees | S | | X | R | B, A | |
| | P | X | R | R | | B, A |
| Roots and tubers | S | | X | | B, A | |
| | P | X | X, R | R | R | A |
| Temperate fruit and nuts | S | | X | R | B, A | |
| | P | X | X, R | R | R | A |
| Tropical fruit and nuts | S | | X | R | A | |
| | P | X | R | R | R | A |
| Ornamentals | S | | X | R | A | |
| | P | X | X, R | | | A |
| Oilseeds | S | | X | R | B, A | |
| | P | X | R | R | | A |
| New crops | S | | X | R | B, A | |
| | P | X | X, R | | | A |

*Notes:*
S = seed; P = plant; X = currently in use; R = under research and development.
B = base collection available; A = active collection available.

*Source:*
Adapted from U.S. Congress OTA, *Technologies to Maintain Biological Diversity*, OTA-F-330, Washington, DC: U.S. Government Printing Office, March, 1987, Table 7-6.

The second type of gene bank is the base collection. These are duplicates of the active collection and serve as a backup. Plants in this collection are stored at −10 to −20 degrees Celsius, with a life expectancy of 20 to 50 years or more. Some base collections have experimented with cryogenic storage in liquid nitrogen, a newer storage technology. Cryogenic preservation works on all plants, including those plants not stored as seed, thus avoiding the shorter life expectancies of greenhouse-preserved plants. Cryogenic preservation also promises to extend the life expectancy of stored plants to over 100 years (Towill and Roos, 1989). Outside of cryogenics, biotechnology may also be able to contribute to storage technologies in the future. For example, plant materials can be distributed as meristem cultures and stored as individual genes in the form of isolated DNA (Day, 1995).[6]

### The International Gene Bank System

The primary international organizations that deal with the conservation of plant genetic resources are (adapted from Hawtin, 1994, pp. 3–5):

1. the Food and Agriculture Organization (FAO), which with the Commission on Plant Genetic Resources oversees policy on the status of ownership of global germplasm resources. The FAO is also overseeing an International Network of *Ex Situ* Base Collections that maintains germplasm under agreed storage standards;
2. the Consultative Group on International Agricultural Research (CGIAR), an association of 17 International Agricultural Research Centers (IARCs) and about 40 governmental and private donors, conserves and uses plant germplasm; collections made in a particular country will be carried out in partnership with the country concerned;
3. other UN agencies such as the UN Environment Programme (UNEP), which oversees the implementation of the Convention on Biological Diversity;
4. international non-governmental organizations, such as the World Wide Fund for Nature, the World Resources Institute and the Rural Advancement Foundation International.[7]

Of these organizations, the CGIAR is the principal player with the largest *ex situ* collections in the world and, therefore, will be the focus of this section. (See Table 3.2 for more details on the CGIAR centers[8]). The World Bank, FAO and UN Development Programme (UNDP) cosponsor the CGIAR system; the World Bank hosts a secretariat. A Technical Advisory Committee with a secretariat at FAO in Rome advises the CGIAR system on important research policy decisions and oversees reviews of the IARCs. Of the 17 IARCs, 13 are directly involved with the conservation and use of genetic resources (Hawtin, 1994; Ruttan, 1982).

The use of germplasm sets the CGIAR's strategy apart from other international organizations that are involved with the conservation of germplasm. The IARCs have over '500,000 accessions, and distribute annually about 110,000 samples to more than 120 countries around the world' (Hawtin, 1994, p. 5). (See Table 3.3 for a listing of the five largest national plant germplasm systems and major international research centers.)

*Table 3.2    CGIAR centers*

CIAT – Centro Internacional de Agricultura Tropical. Cali, Colombia. Founded in 1967. Focuses on germplasm development (global mandate for beans, cassava and forages, and a regional mandate for rice); and on resource management research in Latin America and the Caribbean (with research efforts in land use, hillsides, forest margins and savannas).

CIFOR – Center for International Forestry Research. Bogor, Indonesia. Founded in 1992. Focuses on conserving and improving productivity of tropical forest systems.

CIMMYT – Centro Internacional de Mejoramiento de Maiz y Trigo. Mexico City, Mexico. Founded in 1966. Focuses on crop improvement. Research covers maize, wheat, barley and triticale.

CIP – Centro Internacional de la Papa. Lima, Peru. Founded in 1970. Focuses on potato and sweet potato improvement.

ICARDA – International Center for Agricultural Research in the Dry Areas. Aleppo, Syria. Founded in 1975. Focuses on improving farming systems for North Africa and West Asia. Research covers wheat, barley, chickpea, lentils, pasture legumes and small ruminants.

ICLARM – International Center for Living Aquatic Resources Management. Metro Manila, Philippines. Founded in 1977. Focuses on improving production and management of aquatic resources in developing countries.

ICRAF – International Center for Research in Agroforestry. Nairobi, Kenya. Founded in 1977. Focuses on mitigating tropical deforestation, land depletion and rural poverty through improved agroforestry systems.

ICRISAT – International Crops Research Institute for the Semi-Arid Tropics. Patancheru, India. Founded in 1972. Focuses on crop improvement and cropping systems. Research covers sorghum, millet, chickpea, pigeonpea and groundnut.

IFPRI – International Food Policy Research Institute. Washington, DC. Founded in 1975. Focuses on identifying and analyzing policies for meeting food needs of the developing countries, particularly the poorer groups within these countries. Research covers ways to achieve sustainable food production and land use, improve food consumption and income levels of the poor, enhance the links between agriculture and other sectors of the economy, and improve trade and macroeconomic conditions.

IIMI – International Irrigation Management Institute. Colombo, Sri Lanka. Founded in 1984. Focuses on improving and sustaining the performance of irrigation systems through better management.

IITA – International Institute of Tropical Agriculture. Ibadan, Nigeria. Founded in 1967. Focuses on crop improvement and land management in humid and sub-humid tropics; farming systems. Research covers maize, cassava, cowpea, plantain, soybean, rice and yam.

ILRI – International Livestock Research Institute. Nairobi, Kenya. Founded in 1995 with the consolidation of two CGIAR livestock centers. Focuses on tropical crop–livestock systems, collaboration with national research systems, and ruminant genetics, health and feed resources.

IPGRI – International Plant Genetic Resources Institute. Rome, Italy. Established in 1993 as the successor to the FAO's International Board on Plant Genetic Resources. IPGRI's mandate is to advance the conservation and use of plant genetic resources.

IRRI – International Rice Research Institute. Manila, Philippines. Founded in 1960. Focuses on global rice improvement in major rice environments; irrigated, rain-fed lowland, upland, deepwater and tidal wetland.

ISNAR – International Service for National Agricultural Research. The Hague, Netherlands. Founded in 1979. Focuses on strengthening national agricultural research systems through improvement in their policy planning, organization and management.

WARDA – West Africa Rice Development Association. Bouaké, Cote d'Ivoire. Founded in 1970. Focuses on improving rice varieties and production methods among smallholder farm families in the upland/inland swamp continuum, the Sahel and mangrove swamp environments.

*Source:*

Adapted from G. Hawtin, 'The contribution of the CGIAR and other international organizations to the conservation of plant genetic resources', in D. Witmeyer and M.S. Strauss (eds), *Building Global Cooperation*, Washington, DC: American Association for the Advancement of Science, 1994.

*Table 3.3    Estimates of germplasm holdings in the five largest national plant germplasm systems and major international centers*

| Country/center | Crops | Total |
|---|---|---|
| United States | All crops | 450,000[a] |
| China | All crops | 400,000 |
| Former Soviet Union | All crops | 325,000 |
| IRRI[b] | Rice | 86,000 |
| ICRISAT[b] | Sorghum, millet, chickpeas, peanut, pigeonpea | 86,000 |
| ICARDA[b] | Cereals, legumes, forages | 77,000 |
| India | All crops | 76,000 |
| CIMMYT[b] | Wheat, maize | 75,000 |
| CIAT[b] | Common bean, cassava forages | 66,000 |
| Japan | All crops | 60,000 |
| IITA[b] | Cowpea, rice, root crops | 40,000 |
| AVRDC[c] | Alliums (onion, garlic, shallot), Chinese cabbage, common cabbage, eggplant, mungbean, pepper, soybean, tomato, other vegetables of regional importance | 38,500 |
| CIP[b] | Potato, sweet potato | 12,000 |

*Notes:*
a = 1994 number provided by H. Shands, personal communication. The rest of the numbers are found in the NRC source listed below.
b = acronyms are listed in Table 3.2.
c = AVRDC stands for Asian Vegetable Research and Development Center.

*Source:*
Adapted all with the exception of the U.S. estimate from Table 2 in the Executive Summary, in the National Research Council, *Managing Global Genetic Resources: Agricultural Crop Issues and Policies,* National Academy Press, 1993. The U.S. estimate is from H. Shands, personal communication, 1994.

The International Plant Genetic Resources Institute (IPGRI, formerly the International Board on Plant Genetic Resources or IBPGR) was established for the sole purpose of conserving, maintaining and using plant germplasm (Hawtin, 1994). Although IPGRI does not have any germplasm collection itself, it is the central coordinator for the international gene bank system, setting up priorities, helping governments establish national gene banks and research institutions, and aiding other IARCs in locating and preserving genetic material.

IBPGR was initially set up to assess and implement active germplasm programs for rice, wheat, maize, sorghum and millets and Phaseolus beans. Within its first decade of operation, however IBPGR found that the loss of genetic diversity was proceeding at a rate much faster than previously thought. In response, germplasm programs were established for an additional 42 second priority and 37 third priority crops, and some more for crops of lesser priority (Williams, 1984).

Under the auspices of the IBPGR, from 1970 to 1990, the number of gene bank institutions throughout the world grew from 5 to over 50. By 1990, 96 countries had genetic resources programs and 21 more carried out related activities (Williams, 1984). IBPGR had several agreements for active collections, which are often used in ongoing breeding programs.[9] The IBPGR also had agreements with 38 institutions to hold designated base collections of seed crops (Holden, 1984).

While working with all countries, IPGRI has a mandate to aid in development. It therefore provides funds mostly to developing countries and to research that will aid developing countries. For example, IPGRI uses its field staff to work with scientists and governments in developing countries to assist in developing national genetic resource programs (Williams, 1984, 1989). It has different field and research programs to fit the needs of the various countries, and puts interdisciplinary teams together to work on a problem and/or crop.

Balancing scientists' needs for access to genetic materials with the desire of developing nations to preserve their genetic heritage is difficult. To reach a balance, most of the gene banks operating within the CGIAR system observe the following guidelines first set by the IBPGR:

1. germplasm shall be available to all bona fide scientists and researchers, regardless of political or institutional affiliation;
2. collections made in a particular country will be carried out in partnership with the country concerned;
3. half of all samples collected will be left in the country of origin, and all germplasm collections will be duplicated elsewhere[10] (McNeely et al., 1990, p. 65).

These guidelines are consistent with the CGIAR's 1989 policy of not claiming ownership of plant germplasm and of seeing the CGIAR system as a trustee of germplasm for the world community and particularly for developing countries (Hawtin, 1994).

Two factors account for the success of this international system of germplasm exchange. First, with its long-running contacts to established breeding programs (most importantly the CGIAR), the IPGRI is in a unique position to link those interested in obtaining germplasm with the correct gene bank. Since the system is not directly tied to one government, information flows even more easily than would otherwise be the case. Second, the breeding institutions help share the costs of germplasm preservation, either by holding duplicates in their home institution or by providing funds to preserve germplasm of crops they consider important. This cost-sharing scheme helps keep the system's costs down, and thus contributes to its success, although the costs of all gene banks are expected to rise in the near future as seeds in many active programs will soon need to be rejuvenated (Wilkes, 1989).

**Global Germplasm Collections**

How effective are current global gene bank efforts? Table 3.4 shows recent estimates of the number of gene bank accessions of major crops worldwide. Within each crop, there are different categories of genetic resources. Typically, they can be broken up into five: current or recent cultivars, obsolete cultivars, landraces, wild and weedy species, and special genetic stocks (such as elite and current breeder lines) (Keystone Dialogue, 1988). Tables 3.4 and 3.5 group all the accessions, with wild accessions and landraces referred to separately.

*Table 3.4    Conservation status of major crops*

| Crop | Number of accessions | | | Cultivars (%) | | |
|---|---|---|---|---|---|---|
| | In gene banks | Distinct accessions | In the wild | Not collected | Collected landraces | Collected wild species |
| Wheat | 410,000 | 125,000 | 10,000 | 10 | 95 | 60 |
| Grain, oil legumes | 260,000 | 132,000 | 10,000+ | 30–50 | NA | NA |
| Rice | 250,000 | 120,000 | 5,000 | 10 | 75 | 10 |
| Sorghum | 95,000 | 30,000 | 9,500 | 20 | 80 | 10 |
| Maize | 100,000 | 50,000 | 15,000 | 5 | 95 | 15 |
| Soybean | 100,000 | 30,000 | 7,500 | 30 | 60 | 30 |
| Common potato | 42,000 | 30,000 | 15,000 | 10–20 | 95 | 40 |
| Yams | 8,200 | 3,000 | 60 | High | 40 | 5 |
| Sweet potato | 8,000 | 5,000 | 550 | >50 | 50 | 1 |

*Source:*
The first five columns are from National Research Council, *Managing Global Genetic Resources: Agricultural Crop Issues and Policies,* National Academy Press, 1993, Table 1, Executive Summary. The last two columns are from Table 6.1 in D.L. Plucknett, N.J.H. Smith, J.T. Williams and N.M. Anishetty, *Gene Banks and the World's Food,* Princeton: Princeton University Press, 1987.

Tables 3.4 and 3.5 show that there are large numbers of accessions, with greater numbers for the more economically important crops. There are over 2.5 million crop accessions, with accessions of 1.2 million in cereals, 369,000 in legumes and grasses, 137,000 in vegetables and 74,000 in root crops (Plucknett et al., 1987). The large number of legumes and grass accessions reflects their importance as feed for livestock worldwide. Perhaps the most important point from Table 3.5 is the distinct sample column. The numbers are much lower than the numbers of accessions, indicating the high level of overlap between gene bank accessions. For example, over two-thirds of the wheat accessions represent overlap. Part of this overlap is due to policies, such as those of IPGRI, that require collections to be duplicated as insurance against loss from natural disasters, human error or political upheaval. However, this duplication is expensive and, at times, unnecessary (Plucknett et al., 1987).

It is clear that gene banks have succeeded admirably in accumulating a high proportion of existing landraces. For example, over 80 percent of the landraces

Table 3.5   Estimated number of gene bank accessions worldwide

| Crop | Number of | | | Coverage percentages | |
|------|-----------|---|---|---------------------|---|
|  | Accessions | Distinct samples | Collections of 200+ accessions | Landraces | Wild species |
| **Grains:** | | | | | |
| Wheat | 410,000 | 125,000 | 37 | 95 | 60 |
| Barley | 280,000 | 55,000 | 51 | 85 | 20 |
| Rice | 215,000 | 90,000 | 29 | 75 | 10 |
| Maize | 100,000 | 50,000 | 34 | 95 | 15 |
| Sorghum | 95,000 | 30,000 | 28 | 80 | 10 |
| Oats | 37,000 | 15,000 | 22 | 90 | 50 |
| Pearl millet | 31,500 | 15,500 | 10 | 80 | 10 |
| Finger millet | 9,000 | 3,000 | 8 | 60 | 10 |
| Other millets | 16,500 | 5,000 | 8 | 45 | 2 |
| Rye | 18,000 | 8,000 | 17 | 80 | 30 |
| **Pulses:** | | | | | |
| *Phaseolus* | 105,500 | 40,000 | 22 | 50 | 10 |
| Soybean | 100,000 | 18,000 | 28 | 60 | 30 |
| Groundnut | 34,000 | 11,000 | 7 | 70 | 50 |
| Chickpea | 25,000 | 13,500 | 15 | 80 | 10 |
| Pigeonpea | 22,000 | 11,000 | 10 | 85 | 10 |
| Pea | 20,500 | 6,500 | 11 | 70 | 10 |
| Cowpea | 20,000 | 12,500 | 12 | 75 | 1 |
| Mungbean | 16,000 | 7,500 | 10 | 60 | 5 |
| Lentil | 13,500 | 5,500 | 11 | 70 | 10 |
| Faba bean | 10,000 | 5,000 | 10 | 75 | 15 |
| Lupin | 3,500 | 2,000 | 8 | 50 | 5 |
| **Root crops:** | | | | | |
| Potato | 42,000 | 30,000 | 28 | 95 | 40 |
| Cassava | 14,000 | 6,000 | 14 | 35 | 5 |
| Yams | 10,000 | 5,000 | 12 | 40 | 5 |
| Sweet potato | 8,000 | 5,000 | 27 | 50 | 1 |
| **Vegetables:** | | | | | |
| Tomato | 32,000 | 10,000 | 28 | 90 | 70 |
| Cucurbits | 30,000 | 15,000 | 23 | 50 | 30 |
| Cruciferae | 30,000 | 15,000 | 32 | 60 | 25 |
| *Capsicum* | 23,000 | 10,000 | 20 | 80 | 40 |
| *Allium* | 10,500 | 5,000 | 14 | 70 | 20 |
| Amaranths | 5,000 | 3,000 | 8 | 95 | 10 |
| Okra | 3,600 | 2,000 | 4 | 60 | 10 |
| Eggplant | 3,500 | 2,000 | 10 | 50 | 30 |
| **Forages:** | | | | | |
| Legumes | 130,000 | n.a. | 47 | n.a. | n.a. |
| Grasses | 85,000 | n.a. | 44 | n.a. | n.a. |

*Note*:
n.a. = data not available.

*Source:*
Adapted from D.L. Plucknett, N.J.H. Smith, J.T. Williams and N.M. Anishetty, *Gene Banks and the World's Food,* Princeton: Princeton University Press, 1987, Table 6.1.

of wheat, maize, sorghum, chickpeas (pulse), pigeonpeas (pulse) and potatoes have been accumulated. This is also true for barley, oats, pearl millet, rye and tomatoes (Table 3.5). More troubling is cassava, a major crop which nonetheless has a coverage rate of only 35 percent (Table 3.5). Overall, however, these coverage rates are quite high, and indicate the priority given to collecting landraces by the international genetic resource community.

The coverage rates for wild species, by contrast, are quite low, sometimes alarmingly so. Only 10 percent of the wild rice species and 15 percent of the wild maize species have been collected (Table 3.5). Such lack of coverage makes these and other wild species more susceptible to genetic wipeout.

Across categories, only root crops obviously lag as a group. This is due to the difficulties involved in storing roots, arising from their greater bulk, shorter longevities and tendency to germinate in storage. Vegetable germplasm can be collected much more easily than root crops, and can be stored more easily in the form of seeds. Nonetheless, vegetable collection lagged behind root collection until 1980, when the IBPGR and other national and regional programs began a more strenuous collection of vegetables. The size of accessions doubled within five years. To date, most of the significant diversity of landraces has been collected. The collection of wild species of vegetables is also good, better than that of cereals and grain legumes, in part due to the effort of IPGRI.

### Problems of the Global Gene Bank System

Despite the relatively successful performance of the international gene bank system in collecting plant species, there are problems. One major problem alluded to earlier is the lack of progress in collecting many of the wild species. As HYVs are increasingly utilized, the problem of collecting these wild species will only become more difficult, if not impossible (due to genetic wipeout).

Another major problem is the continued maintenance of high-quality personnel at the gene banks. Many gene banks have been successful because of the leadership, management skill and broad scientific background of their curators. Gene bank systems may find these curators hard to replace. There are no formal programs for training curators (Ph.D. or equivalent), technicians, scientists (M.S., Ph.D. or equivalent) or personnel for gene banks (Keystone Dialogue, 1988). In addition, the pool of potential plant breeders is diminishing as young scientists seek to study microbiology over plant breeding and as the traditional plant breeding slots in universities are being allocated to microbiology (Kloppenburg, 1988). Furthermore, the scientific and technical competency of germplasm workers has not kept up with advances in preservation technology, biosystematics, cell biology and biotechnology (Chang et al., 1989; Keystone Dialogue, 1988). Hence, in the future, a lack of well-trained curators and staff at gene banks could compromise the viability of germplasm collections.

A number of measures could be taken to maintain high-quality personnel. All gene banks should adopt a policy of selecting a successor to a retiring curator early enough so that they can be trained slowly with the existing curator. Formal training programs such as IRRI's training program on rice conservation (Chang et al., 1989) could be expanded. Other ways to improve training are: provision of better informal teaching aids such as video tapes, courses offered on biotechnology methods, quarantine requirements, database design and management, and undergraduate curricula that include genetic resources (Keystone Dialogue, 1988).

A second major problem involves redundancy among collections. For example, from a survey of germplasm conservators and users of barley germplasm, of its 250,000 accessions, only 50,000 are unique (NRC, 1993). Duplication can (and does) occur when gene banks obtain two samples of the same plant known by two different names (Chang et al., 1989). Estimates of redundancy in collections range from 10 percent to as high as 60 percent (Plucknett et al., 1987; Chang et al., 1989; Holden, 1984). While some redundancy is necessary as a security measure, this insurance is purchased at the cost of not having financial resources for other valued uses. It also creates an inflated perception of the collected diversity within the germplasm system.

A way to reduce excessive redundancy would be to first determine whether enough diversity has been collected and then work on the genetic evaluation of the accessions. The following is a hierarchical method that could be used to determine the level of duplicates among collections: accession name, pedigree history, geographic origin and seed source; comparison of seed and plant morphology and electrophoreses and restriction fragment length polymorphism (Chang et al., 1989). IPGRI has already instituted a registration and monitoring process, and this has helped with some of these problems. Curators could also agree on the genotypes or populations to concentrate on, which could reduce duplication (Holden, 1984). Nevertheless, more attention needs to be paid to whether significant diversity has been captured in the collections. This may be costly to achieve and some centers may not have the means to do it (Plucknett et al., 1987).

A third problem facing gene banks is the problem of maintaining genetic integrity (the genetic structure of a population of plants) (Keystone Dialogue, 1988; NRC, 1993). This is more of a problem for plants that sexually propagate. Clonal plants are more easily maintained since they reproduce asexually and, therefore, identically, although somatic (nonsexual) mutations may still occur. Appropriate propagation and rejuvenation programs must be designed carefully for each crop (Chang et al., 1989). More research needs to be done on recalcitrant seeds and on *in vitro* methods (McNeely et al., 1990; Williams, 1989). Furthermore, guidelines need to be established to determine the most effective size of a gene bank and its collection.

Another major problem involves the gathering of information, particularly with passport, characterization and evaluation data (Day, 1995; NRC, 1993). Few centers have adequate passport data on the source of the species, and those are not often verified (Plucknett et al., 1987). Characterization data describe phenotypic traits that are highly heritable and largely unaffected by the environment. Evaluation data comprise more variable qualities such as yield and disease resistance and are highly valuable to breeders selecting germplasm for a breeding program (Day, 1995; NRC, 1993). Sixty-five percent of all accessions have no basic data; 80 percent have no data on useful characteristics (i.e. mode of propagation); and 95 percent lack evaluation data (i.e. germinability tests (McNeely et al., 1990)). Clearly, a central file for the global accessions for each crop needs to be made, and records need to be computerized and standardized (Chang et al., 1989; Keystone Dialogue, 1988). Fortunately, a system-wide database is under development (Shands, 1994b). With such a system, the accessions would less likely be duplicated and would be more accessible to other scientists, promoting efficient collaboration between gene banks and other scientific programs (Williams, 1989).

There are also problems with information on the genetics of landraces and of wild species (NRC, 1993). The information on landraces is either fragmentary or non-existent (NRC, 1993). So little is known about some wild species that they are often categorized in the wrong genus. For example, in the early 1970s, the wild species of the world sorghum collections were improperly categorized. With incorrect information, one can easily lose the species (Harlan, 1984; Williams, 1989).

One solution to decrease the information collection and regeneration workload would be for the banks to identify a core subset of accessions that represent the diversity of the crop. Efforts then could be placed on gathering information such as passport, characterization and evaluation data on this set of accessions. This would also aid in regeneration of the material (NRC, 1993).

A final problem for international gene banks is funding. More funding would help alleviate many of these problems. However, this in itself is a problem. Over the next five years, a conservative estimate of money put towards plant gene resources is $55 million (Plucknett et al., 1987, p. 143). Many agree that this is too little towards a system that is so important to global crop production and to global welfare. The CGIAR system has recently faced decreased funding, which is compounded by inflation. As a result, four of the IARCs will be merged and the number of scientists and national employees has decreased (Powledge, 1993/94). Agricultural research centers in developing countries are hurting even more. Special financial attention needs to be given to gene banks in Eastern Europe where problems range from inadequate electricity, repairs, maintenance, refrigeration equipment, education and training, technical journals and computers (Powledge, 1993/94).

## The U.S. Gene Bank System

The U.S. national germplasm system is considered by many to be the best in the world (Goodman and Castillo-Gonzales, 1991). The United States has had a policy on germplasm since the 19th century, when a formal system for plant exploration and development of new crop species was set up within USDA. In 1946, out of concern for lost germplasm due to inadequate maintenance facilities, the USDA enacted the Agricultural Marketing Act, authorizing 'regional centers to maintain and develop germplasm' (U.S. Congress, OTA, 1987 p. 233). The National Plant Germplasm System (NPGS) helps carry out this mission. The NPGS is a network of cooperating institutions, agencies and research units of the federal, state and private sectors. It ensures adequate genetic diversity for improving crop productivity and reducing genetic vulnerability by collecting, maintaining, evaluating and making available seed and clonal germplasm of crops and potential crops (Shands et al., 1989). A more recent goal of the NPGS system is to regenerate seed in the active and base collections and to determine the level of duplications, aided by the Germplasm Resources Information Network (GRIN) database.

The NPGS has three functional elements: operations, advising and administration. NPGS operations cover the collection and preservation of plant germplasm as well as the release of seed and information. The Agricultural Research Service (ARS) of the USDA funds and staffs these operations, but state universities also provide significant financial and personnel support (Shands et al., 1989). Working collections are primarily held in four Regional Plant Introduction Stations (RPISs) at Griffin, Georgia, Ames, Iowa, Geneva, New York and Pullman, Washington. Special genetic stock collections (including nine Clonal Repositories, the USDA Small Grains Collection, Soybean Collection, Cotton Collection, Potato Collection and the World Rice Collection) are also held at several other places in the United States (Chang et al.,1989; U.S. Congress, OTA 1987). In 1994, accessions in the NPGS seed working collections numbered 450,000 (Shands, 1994b; see Shands et al., 1989 for more details on these working collections).

Duplications of working and commodity collections are held as a base collection at the National Seed Storage Laboratory (NSSL) at Fort Collins, Colorado. Instituted in 1958, the NSSL's mission is for long-term preservation of plant germplasm with 85 percent viability. NSSL seed is used when seed from other collections reaches a significant low point in viability (Shands et al., 1989).

Crops that cannot be stored as seed are housed at the National Clonal Germplasm Repositories (NCGR). These include many fruit and nut species. Currently, the working and base collections of these plants are not separated due to the high cost of maintaining clonal plants (Chang et al., 1989), although advances in technology may change this. Accessions at NCGR and in quarantine at Beltsville, Maryland number 24,720 (Shands et al., 1989).

The National Germplasm Resources Laboratory at Beltsville, Maryland supports the repositories of the NPGS. More specifically, the Plant Exchange Office deals with plant explorations and links the United States with other countries in the movement of plant germplasm. The National Plant Germplasm Quarantine Center ensures that germplasm entering the United States is free of economically important diseases or insects. The GRIN database gathers information about plant germplasm collections and makes information available via an Internet gopher (Shands et al., 1989; U.S. Congress, OTA, 1987).

Advisory elements advise and counsel the NPGS. These include 'the National Plant Genetic Resources Advisory Council (NPGAC) and more than 40 Crop Advisory Committees (CAC)' (Shands et al., 1989). The most influential of these is the NPGAC, which advises the Secretary of Agriculture and the Director of the National Genetic Resources Program about 'the assembly, description, maintenance, and effective utilization of living resources', including crops, wild species and landraces (Shands et al., 1989 p. 109). Nine members come from non-federal public and private sectors, are appointed by the Secretary and can serve up to two consecutive terms.

The CACs are national technical working groups of specialists on a particular crop (Shand et al., 1989; Chang et al., 1989), drawn from the federal, state and private sectors. These specialists offer analysis and data and advise gene banks on the status of that crop's germplasm, including issues of genetic vulnerability and gaps in present collections (Chang et al., 1989).

Federal and state governments offer administrative support through the funding and personnel support. The federal government offers support via ARS ranging from collecting germplasm to the release of new varieties. Federal funding of NPGS was at $20.9 million in financial year 1994 (Shands, 1994a). State Agricultural Experiment Stations (SAES) contribute an estimated $15–20 million towards NPGS. (This figure would be higher if research on basic genetics and on the early stages of plant breeding were included.) The USDA's Cooperative State Research, Education and Extension Service has acted as a liaison between the Federal Government and SAES on state research with a national scope.

## Problems with the U.S. Gene Bank System

Criticisms of the U.S. gene bank system touch on all the elements that make up a good gene bank system, that is, infrastructure, managerial expertise, a strong scientific community, well-trained personnel and adequate financing (Goodman and Castillo-Gonzalez, 1991). Of these, infrastructural difficulties are most pressing.

Critics argue that the NSSL has not maintained seed viability. A 1981 General Accounting Office report found that only half the seeds from active

NPGS collections were sent to the NSSL. Furthermore, 63 percent of the active collections were inadequately stored, resulting in decreased seed viability (U.S. Congress, OTA, 1987).

A particular infrastructural problem is lack of storage space. In the late 1980s, the NSSL was almost filled to capacity (Goodman and Castillo-Gonzalez, 1991; U.S. Congress, OTA, 1987). More funds were needed to expand and update facilities. To alleviate the NSSL space problem, some regional programs stored their own base collections, thus using up scarce resources better used elsewhere (U.S. Congress, OTA, 1987). The NSSL has added a major new addition that has quadrupled its previous capacity (Shands, 1994b).

In addition, the four RPISs of the NPGS system have been criticized for their accession evaluations. Even though these stations evaluate important agricultural traits necessary to catalog accessions, their evaluations are often not extensive enough to meet users' needs, making these accessions inaccessible. The problem may well be one of having the resources necessary to hire well-trained scientists to conduct the tests. If it were not possible to increase funds in this area, another way to accomplish the goal would be to allow breeders who require specific traits for an ongoing research program to test and evaluate accessions held in the RPISs. An additional benefit of this approach is that the tests would be done in the environment of the breeder's choice – helping to characterize phenotypic expression under the desired environment (U.S. Congress, OTA, 1987).[11]

The infrastructure and funding of CACs have also been criticized. CACs members are volunteers, paying for their own room, board and travel to CAC meetings. Naturally, the frequency of CAC meetings varies more than would be the case if the federal government subsidized committee meetings. While the USDA has felt that its current CAC funding support is adequate, the OTA found otherwise (U.S. Congress, OTA, 1987). As policy comes to be more influenced by CAC input, the level of support of this important institution will have to be carefully monitored. Furthermore, some from industry believe the role of industry has been under-represented (Duvick, 1991).

Finally, documentation and characterization data are often missing for accessions, making them less useful to plant breeders. However, the U.S. germplasm system distributes more seed worldwide than any other institution (Goodman and Castillo-Gonzalez, 1991).

This rather imposing list of difficulties should not gainsay the advances made in germplasm collection within the United States. At the same time, the increasing need for genetic diversity requires that steps be taken to improve the system. Clearly, this has already been recognized. ARS has tried to centralize program responsibilities into one office. This could improve coordination between collections, improve the GRIN database and provide more clarity on funding priorities (U.S. Congress, OTA, 1987). However, there needs to be greater funding for the infrastructure and the NPGS – more personnel and scientists need to be hired, more training of personnel and scientists needs to be done, and more joint programs for conducting research and rejuvenating seeds must be done and coordinated well.

# 5   USE OF GERMPLASM

The germplasm stored in gene banks can potentially contribute a number of characteristics to new varieties, such as resistance to disease and tolerance to drought, which can maintain or even increase yields. But even in the best of worlds, there will be a significant delay between the enhancement of germplasm and the release of new varieties. It generally can take 8 to 15 years to develop a new variety (Knudson, 1988; Plucknett et al., 1987). In some cases, it can take even longer. To understand genetic diversity, then, we must focus our attention on the step from germplasm to release of a commercial variety. Furthermore, even the release of a new commercial variety will have no effect on genetic diversity unless the farmer utilizes that new commercial variety. This section will therefore treat the issue of farmer adoption of seed varieties as well.

**The Use of Parental Pools**

In 1981, Donald Duvick, the senior vice president of research at Pioneer Hi-Bred International, Inc., conducted a survey of leaders of 125 plant-breeding firms covering five major crops (cotton, soybean, wheat, hybrid sorghum and hybrid maize). The survey attempted to determine the genetic diversity of the parental pools used by breeders as well as the varieties and hybrids that farmers grew.[12] The response rate of the survey was 81 percent (101 replies) (Duvick, 1984). This is an exceptionally important and informative survey, and must take a rather large place in any discussion of genetic diversity. Duvick's survey attempted to provide four measures of genetic diversity in U.S. agriculture. These were *cultivar concentration, diversity in time, genetic reserves* and *diversity in breeding pools.*

*Cultivar concentration* was defined as the proportion of total cropland devoted to the six most popular varieties. The higher the cultivar concentration, the lower the genetic diversity of the crop. Over the 1970s, cultivar concentration for cotton decreased from 68 percent to 38 percent. Similar reductions were found for maize (measured as inbreds used as one parent in a hybrid). Soybean cultivar concentration decreased from 56 percent to 42 percent, and wheat concentration decreased from 41 percent in 1970 to 38 percent in 1979. No information was available for sorghum. A study by Smith (1988), however, shows that an increase in numbers of varieties does not necessarily show an increase in genetic diversity. The varieties may have a common ancestry (NRC, 1993).

*Diversity in time* measures the market life of a variety. All of the leading varieties of 1970 for all five crops had been replaced by 1980, primarily because the new varieties were superior in at least one important trait. Hence, over the course of years, new varieties took over the fields, increasing diversity in time. The estimated average life spans of varieties for major crops were seven years for maize, eight years for cotton and sorghum, and nine years for soybeans and wheat. All breeders stated that they thought this life span would shorten in the future due to the expected release of superior varieties in the future and increased private sector activity.

Diversity in time could also increase because of monocultural production, where genetic resistance to pests breaks down more rapidly due to the lack of natural biological barriers to a pest (Reid, 1992). There are three ways these barriers can be broken down: changes in the pathogen or in its effect, a pathogen moves to a new biome or changes in agronomic practices (NRC, 1993). In such cases, new varieties have to be introduced that are pest resistant. Wheat is a good example of how genetic diversity over time can work. Wheat is very susceptible to rust. The product life-cycle of wheat varieties has always been short, in part to generate some diversity over time in hopes of fighting rust epidemics. More recently, progress has been made on the resistance genes such that there is longer-term resistance to the pathogen. There has been no outbreak of a rust epidemic since the 1950s in the United States due to these different measures (NRC, 1993).

*Genetic reserves* refer to populations of lines developed during a breeding program. Different types of reserves exist, based on where the cultivar falls in the breeding development process. The *first-line* reserves are cultivars just out of advanced yield trials and currently planted on the farm. They are usually not grown over large areas, but the number per crop may be high (averaging around 30 per crop for cotton, soybeans and wheat; and 134 and 454 for sorghum and maize hybrids). *Second-line* reserves are those cultivars in advanced yield trials. They number in the thousands, many of which are found not to be superior to current cultivars and are put into storage. Varieties in preliminary yield trial stages are in *third-line* reserve, and also number in the thousands.

The parental pools, from which these reserve lines are drawn, offer an even more genetically diverse selection. As a breeding strategy evolves, less and less plants are available. At the end of the process, just a few plants are released as a variety. But they are selected out of a large and diverse group. If the need arises, a breeder can go back into the reserve lines and select a particular plant and release it. Simply looking at the number of released varieties is insufficient for determining the true genetic diversity in U.S. breeding programs. In fact, Duvick argues that from 500 inbred lines, 124,750 genetically different maize hybrids can be created. These hybrids would be diverse with respect to disease and pest resistance, environmental tolerance and yield potential. However, Duvick found there are 2,800 inbred maize lines available in the United States, making a case that there is more than enough diversity within the parental pools of plant breeders. The results for other crops are similar.

Respondents from all five major crops stated that they had increased the diversity of their breeding pools, particularly through the use of landraces. The proportion of respondents replying that the breeding base in their programs was 'broader' than in 1970 was 77 percent for maize, 78 percent for soybeans, 85 percent for wheat, 87 percent for cotton and 100 percent for sorghum (Duvick, 1984). Breeders for all five crops stated that they found their elite adapted lines were some of the most important sources of useful pest resistance and stress tolerance (see Tables 3.6 and 3.7).[13] Elite lines have been shown to increase productivity via yields, resistance to pests and diseases, and tolerance to environmental stress on top of more efficiently using nutrients. Consistent increases in genetic yield potential through elite material have been found in sorghum, soybean, cotton and wheat (Smith and Duvick, 1989). Duvick claims

*Table 3.6    Major sources of needed pest resistance (percentage of respondents using each source)*

| Crop | Elite adapted | Elite unadapted | Landraces | Related species |
|------|---------------|-----------------|-----------|-----------------|
| Cotton | 41 | 65 | 35 | 35 |
| Soybean | 79 | 70 | 33 | 24 |
| Wheat | 95 | 95 | 50 | 50 |
| Sorghum | 63 | 75 | 38 | 38 |
| Maize | 83 | 61 | 39 | 17 |
| All crops | 76 | 72 | 39 | 17 |

*Source:*
Table 18 in D.N. Duvick, 'Genetic Diversity in Major Farm Crops on the Farm and in Reserve', *Economic Botany*, **38**, 1984, pp. 161–178.

*Table 3.7    Major sources of stress tolerance (percentage of respondents using each source)*

| Crop | Elite adapted | Elite unadapted | Landraces | Related species |
|------|---------------|-----------------|-----------|-----------------|
| Cotton | 65 | 29 | 0 | 0 |
| Soybean | 88 | 27 | 9 | 0 |
| Wheat | 100 | 35 | 20 | 5 |
| Sorghum | 75 | 50 | 13 | 0 |
| Maize | 83 | 26 | 13 | 0 |
| All crops | 84 | 31 | 8 | 1 |

*Source:*
Table 21 in D.N. Duvick, 'Genetic Diversity in Major Farm Crops on the Farm and in Reserve', *Economic Botany*, **38**, 1984, pp.161–178.

this result speaks to the adequacy of diversity within germplasm collections and that, contrary to criticisms, elite material has not been narrowed by the search for increased yield. Some examples of this 'hidden diversity' in elite lines that could be traced back to exotic material are resistance to a new viral form of corn lethal necrosis and resistance to a new disease, maize chlorotic-dwarf virus.

If breeders cannot find the appropriate genetic diversity within their own pool, they usually will look first to other sources of improved germplasm. These can be found in national, regional and international screening nurseries and through performance trials of USDA, IARCs and some land grant university experiment stations. Unfortunately, fewer than half of the respondents stated that they were happy with the U.S. germplasm collections and services (13 percent were very dissatisfied). Reasons varied, but the most important were the small size of collections, the loss of items due to improper reproduction and storage, and lack of documentation on collection as to agronomically-relevant traits such as descriptor information and passport data (Duvick, 1984, p. 171; NRC, 1993). As a result, breeders would have to screen many accessions 'more or less blindly'. Breeders are also reluctant to use landraces and wild species because they do not want to bring in unfavorable genes and a chance of breaking favorable linkages found in the current parental pool plants. This is truer of breeders of the cereals who have long-standing breeding programs (NRC, 1993). Those breeders who depend heavily on gene banks work on crops with 'little or no history of improvement', that is, pulses (beans or lentils), some root crops, vegetables and some industrial crops (NRC, 1993, p. 62).

Overall, then, this survey provides evidence that (at least as of 1981) diversity was increasing on farms (decreased concentration and increasing through time) and within breeding programs. In fact, as Duvick notes, 'very few breeding program directors said without qualification, "Yes, genetic vulnerability is a serious problem in my crop"' (Duvick, 1984, p. 171). Brown reiterates this claim, 'the need to continually improve cultivars in order to retain farmers' business has led to increased genetic diversity' (Brown, 1988, p. 225). Of the major crops, wheat breeders showed the most concern, partly because wheat has been very vulnerable to epidemics of leaf and stem rust over the past 75 years. In addition, public breeders were more concerned about genetic vulnerability than private breeders. This may be a result of the fact that many public breeders have to work with the basic breeding stock, and thus would be more sensitive to potential problems in genetic diversity.

Although the Duvick survey found that breeders relied on elite lines, no one feels that the parental pool and selection should remain only on elite lines. According to the NRC report, 'plant breeders ... , generally agree that the need for genetic diversity within the economically important plant species has never been greater' (NRC, 1993, p. 173). New sources of diversity are needed to meet future problems and many private breeders are including more exotic and wild germplasm. Wild germplasm is usually used for sources of disease and pest resistance (Table 3.7) (Harlan, 1984).[14] But they also have been found to increase yields, as they have for oats (Frankel and Brown, 1984). However, wild species can bring problems into a breeding strategy, such as negative traits that are difficult to eliminate.[15] More research is needed not only in collecting and documenting wild species and landraces, but also in how to incorporate useful traits into otherwise superior germplasm.

**Farmer Use of Germplasm**

Farmers have taken advantage of new varieties developed from these breeding pools. The life span of a variety is expected to continue to drop in the United States. The typical life span of a variety in a developed country is four to ten years (Plucknett et al., 1987). Varieties are typically replaced where they are no longer resistant to a particular disease or pest, when different environmental or consumer pressures emerge, or when better material becomes available.

The payoff from these new varieties can be easily quantified. In the United States, rice, barley, soybeans, wheat, cotton and sugarcane yields doubled; tomato yields tripled; and maize, sorghum and potato yields quadrupled, between 1930 and 1980 (Reid, 1992). Rates of yield increase for wheat, maize, sorghum and soybeans range between 1 and 3 percent per year (Duvick, 1986). Maize production, for example, has increased at a rate of 3 percent per year for the past 50 years, a trend that is expected to continue (Duvick, 1984). Similar productivity gains can be found for the United Kingdom, where yields for wheat increased at a 3 percent annual rate from 1949 to 1984 (NRC, 1993). Increased use of inputs also contributed to this rate of increase, most impor- tantly the addition of synthetic nitrogen fertilizer. In the 1940s, nitrogen fertilizer became relatively cheaper and offered farmers a means to increase production in the face of limiting factors such as land. Wheat, for example, was put under many government acreage programs, cutting the amount of wheat acreage in half from 1949 to 1970 (Knudson, 1988). Given these rates of yield gain, one can expect that these crops will yield 15 percent more by the year 2000 than they did in 1985 (Duvick, 1986).

Plant breeding and genetic resources have contributed much to these pro- duction increases. Half (or nearly half) of the increases in U.S. yields can be credited towards plant breeding (Reid, 1992). For example, one study showed that maize yields increased from 1930 to the 1980s due to better weed control (13 percent of the yield increase), synthetic nitrogen fertilizer (19 percent), the transition to hybrids (16 percent) and other general breeding improvements (46 percent) (Duvick, 1986). Breeding efforts thus make up the lion's share of yield increases and sustained yield increase will be heavily dependent on future breeding improvements. Breeding improvements are themselves heavily dependent on the maintenance of genetic diversity in gene banks.

None of this speaks to genetic vulnerability. For farmers to adopt a new variety it usually has to show superior performance. Farmers are not concerned about such issues as genetic vulnerability unless it affects their own production system, such as an epidemic of the level of the southern corn leaf blight (NRC, 1993). Hence, much is left up to plant breeders and research institutions to see that adequate genetic diversity is present in commercial agriculture. There should be some concern here. The 1994 NRC report, along with some other studies, suggests that there is some regional and global genetic vulnerability (Goodman and Castillo-Gonzalez, 1991).

In looking at wheat, maize and rice within the United States and throughout the world, only in wheat does there appear to be some increase in genetic diversity. In the United States, the number of wheat varieties has grown from 263 in 1969 to 429 in 1984. The land devoted to the ten leading varieties has decreased since 1969. In a survey of 17 wheat breeders, Cox et al. (1986) found that the reliance on landraces and other species has increased. In fact, 14 breeders were using crosses with other species, and this accounted for 2 to 4 percent of their crosses, advanced lines and releases (NRC, 1993). Unfortunately, in developing countries, the trend is the opposite for wheat. They are devoting more land to a few HYVs, making a case for increased genetic vulnerability (NRC, 1993). As for maize, while Duvick (1984) claims that genetic vulnerability is decreased, Smith (1988) claims otherwise.

In the United States, maize's genetic diversity, based on isozyme data for 138 commercial hybrids used in 1986 and compared with one in 1981, was about the same for the Corn Belt. The time frame is very short, however, especially considering the length of time it takes to produce a hybrid. However, there is little evidence that more exotic germplasm is being introduced into breeding programs. For one thing, sensitivity to day-length delays this introduction. Still Duvick's (1984) survey claims good genetic diversity has been found in the improved parental pools.

In the developing world, from 1961–65 to 1983–85, maize production increased 84 percent, with an annual growth rate of 4 percent. Improved genotypes, either through hybrids or open-pollinated varieties, were grown on half of the maize area in developing countries. In the other half, adoption of new hybrids or varieties was low. This could result for several reasons including an inadequate seed distribution system particularly in remote areas, farmer preference for landraces and unique niches (NRC, 1993). There is a reliance on a just a few hybrids or improved varieties in these developing countries.

In the United States and Japan, rice is genetically vulnerable. The genetic background is very narrow. Plus, in many developing countries where adoption of HYVs is high, there is a reliance on just a few rice cultivars. Cytoplasmic uniformity, found with the southern corn leaf blight in maize, is also a concern in hybrid rice.

The picture of global genetic vulnerability is not promising. Not only does global genetic vulnerability exist, but also raises questions as to the world's ability to face future epidemics. Due to the lack of research infrastructure, many developing countries cannot easily introduce more diversity or resistant genes. In the case of an epidemic, this could be disastrous for a country. Furthermore, many of these countries may not be able to 'reintroduce' previously grown landraces. Landraces have been lost due to such factors as the adoption of HYVs and the loss of agricultural land.

Although it is the farmer who decides what to grow, their short-run, private incentives will not necessarily match society's long-run incentives to maintain genetic diversity. Plant breeders, governments and international agencies such as the IARCs all have a role to play to ensure that our agricultural systems are genetically diverse and sustainable.

## Economic Benefits of Germplasm Use

How can we assess the economic benefits of the system of gene banks, breeding programs and farmer adoption? While it is difficult to measure the costs and benefits in monetary terms, it appears that the benefits of gene banks are high (Plucknett et al., 1987). Germplasm has increased United States agricultural production by about $1 billion annually (U.S. Congress, OTA, 1987). Other profits from germplasm stem from their yield, quality and nutritive contributions as well as decreasing the cost of sustaining yields. For example, genetic resistance to fungi and bacteria is very profitable as it replaces expensive chemical applications for resistance that offer only temporary control (Plucknett et al., 1987).

An example of benefits comes from the case of maize streak virus in West Africa. This disease was a threat there and could have caused production to drop to zero. However, due to crossing two maize accessions with resistance to the pathogen, resistant lines and hybrids were available in ten years. The value of having the entire maize production system saved is not small (Goodman and Castillo-Gonzalez, 1991).

Given these benefits, it is disconcerting to note that genetic diversity appears to merit the same underinvestment as occurs in many other agricultural research projects. While specific rates of return for gene banks as a whole do not exist, many studies on the contribution of agricultural research to productivity put rates of return of R&D investments between 10 and 15 percent above inflation (Ruttan, 1982), and gene banks would appear to be no different. Further research is required to understand why this underinvestment continues to occur.

# 6   POLICIES AFFECTING GERMPLASM COLLECTION

Public policies have a large impact on the status of global genetic resources. In this section, I analyze both international and U.S. policies, attempting to understand how these policies have affected genetic diversity in agriculture, particularly in regards to global genetic resource exchange. There is concern that an increase in intellectual property rights (IPRs) will restrict global genetic resources exchange. These IPRs further bring up the question of who owns what genetic resources. The section takes us from the establishment of global IPRs of plant germplasm with the International Union for the Protection of New Plant Varieties to the most recent UN Convention on Biological Diversity

## Intellectual Property Rights: International Policy

The first major IPR agreement that affected major crops on an international scale was the 1961 International Convention for the Protection of New Varieties of Plants. Responding to ongoing trends in Breeder's Rights within European nations, parties to the convention signed a treaty establishing the International Union for the Protection of New Plant Varieties, known by the acronym UPOV. The provisions of the treaty are very general, establishing a minimum standard for the level and form of protection, and giving each signatory country the ability to easily make more extensive provisions. Two exemptions are permitted within UPOV: a farmer's exemption, allowing farmers to reuse their seed for planting, and a research exemption, allowing scientists to use protected material within this breeding program (Barton and Siebeck, 1991). Each country must define what makes a variety eligible for protection, that is, uniformity, superiority, and so forth. In return, the country is given some proprietary rights over the use of the variety. Member countries are allowed reciprocal rights and protected varieties can be used in other scientists' breeding programs (Perrin et al., 1983). Twenty countries (including the United States and the more recent additions of Australia, Canada, Hungary, Japan and Poland) are currently members of UPOV (Barton and Siebeck, 1991).

The UPOV has changed since its inception, responding to issues raised over ownership of genetic resources. Both the farmer and research exemptions were revised in March of 1991 (Anon., 1993/94; Reid, 1992). UPOV now prohibits the production of propagating material, including sexual and asexual reproduction, without the permission of the breeder. Before the revision, production of propagating material was allowed if it was not for commercial use. Within this revision, 'an exemption authorized, but does not require, member countries to allow farmers to save seed for planting on their own holdings' (Anon., 1993/94, p. 58). In the United States, this exemption has been challenged in the Supreme Court case of *Winterboer v. Asgrow Seed Co.* (Anon., 1993/94). The

Winterboers were accused of selling an unreasonably large amount of their seed to neighboring farmers. Historically, such resale of seed has been allowed, as long as less than 50 percent of income comes from seed sales. The decision in the Supreme Court could alter the way seed is exchanged between farmers or reduce incentives to develop new varieties depending on who wins.[16]

The research exemption in UPOV has also been modified. Countries are allowed to impose a royalty fee on researchers whose products are 'essentially derived' from a previously protected variety (NRC, 1993; Reid, 1992).

> Essentially derived varieties [are defined] as new varieties which are predominantly derived from an initial variety with only one or a few clearly distinguishing characteristics. Essentially derived varieties may be protected, but only with the permission of the owner of the initial variety. (Anon., 1993/94, p. 58)

Other changes to UPOV are: the protection of all plant genera and first generation hybrids, even if they are not grown in that country; the extension of Breeder's Rights to harvested materials, which 'prevents importation of harvested material through unauthorized use of a protected material from a country where protection is not granted' (Anon., 1993/94, p. 58); and the extension of protection time from 18 to 20 years and from 18 to 25 years for non-woody and woody plants, respectively (Anon., 1993/94).

The significance of UPOV is that it offers plant breeders greater global IPRs with the intent of providing incentives to breeders to develop more and better varieties. In other cases of intellectual property protection, there seems to be some tolerance by the holder of the IPR when a developing country uses it without compensation to the holder. The developing country uses the product or technology at such a relatively low level that there is not a significant market impact. But the developing country benefits from using it, helping it to become more developed and, hence, a bigger potential market. Once the country becomes more developed and a bigger user of the protected technology or product, then the holder of the IPR expects to be compensated (Evenson, 1990). A similar situation could be seen with IPRs and crop varieties (Plucknett et al., 1987).

Another international IPR policy comes from the Uruguay Round of the General Agreement on Tariffs and Trade, which was negotiated from 1986 to 1993 with some 108 countries. This agreement established minimum standards for IPRs, which would include Breeder's Rights. In exchange for accepting IPRs, developing countries would be given access to developed country markets for products such as agricultural products and textiles (Barton and Siebeck, 1991). Those countries not honoring these IPRs could have trade sanctions imposed against them (Frisvold and Condon, 1998).

The granting of IPRs for plant varieties does raise some concerns. One concern with the UPOV lies in fear of a decreased exchange of plant genetic resources among certain countries (Chang et al., 1989; Shands, 1994a). There is a trend for public institutions, which traditionally have treated their research products as public goods, to act more like a private institution. United States universities are seeking IPRs and restricting access to their research – either for financing research or as a means to ensure that others do not misappropriate their ideas or materials or to prevent future legal conflicts over patent infringements (Barton and Siebeck, 1991; NRC, 1993). Public institutions in Europe have become privatized, such as the Plant Genetics Institute in England (Shands 1994a). Publicly developed inbred lines of maize are not freely accessible in other countries (Goodman and Castillo-Gonzalez, 1991). Restriction to germplasm need not only come from IPRs, however. Countries can restrict the importation and exportation of germplasm. For example, pepper from India, oil palm from Malaysia, coffee from Ethiopia and tea from Sri Lanka are prohibited from being exported in the form of breeding material (NRC, 1993). The result of such trends could be decreased germplasm availability and decreased genetic diversity.

Like most controversial policies there are many sides to the issue. If there were no means of legal protection, institutions could use trade secrecy, making seed less available. Hybrid corn is an example where parental inbred lines are a trade secret and only the hybrid is sold (NRC, 1993).

Another concern deals with the growth of developing countries' seed industry. Consider a developing country that relies heavily on foreign countries for their seed. One may envision a scenario where the developing country will continually be left behind. The foreign firm will gain market strength, making it more difficult for a domestic research system, that may be inadequate to begin with, to conduct research and develop new varieties that can compete with the foreign firm. If a national goal is to develop a strong national research program, then the government must set policy so appropriate technology can be transferred between the foreign firm and the public sector. One method could be to grant a research exemption to the universities in that country so they could use this seed in their breeding programs. The stronger the developing country's research program is, the less of a concern it becomes that IPRs are granted (Shands, 1994a).

A developing country will need a good strategy to benefit from international IPRs. Even if they establish plant breeder's rights, it doesn't mean it will help them. In Argentina and Chile, plant breeder's rights were ineffective without an established seed certification program and the ability to enforce their legislation (Reid, 1992). A good strategy not only includes trained scientists, good personnel and good facilities, but it also includes consistent funding over the long-term. As many developing countries do not have those resources, assistance will have to come from developed countries.

## Intellectual Property Rights: U.S. Policy

Since 1970, the United States has instituted two major changes in IPR policy, the Plant Variety Protection Act (PVPA) and utility patents (UPs) that are consistent with UPOV. The PVPA, instituted in 1970 and amended in 1981, gives patent-like protection over several crops to plant breeders for a period of 18 years. While the main aim of the PVPA was to induce private plant breeders to invest more in varietal development, studies have shown that public as well as private programs have been affected by its passage. Since 1970, the private sector has increased R&D investments in plant breeding, particularly in soybeans and wheat (Butler and Marion, 1985; NRC, 1993; Perrin et al., 1983). A more recent study by Knudson and Pray (1991) showed that the PVPA might have influenced the direction of public research in soybeans, wheat, hybrid corn, hybrid sorghum and cotton. Public research increased rapidly after the PVPA was passed.

While these figures suggest that the PVPA has been a powerful tool for enhancing research, two exemptions may limit its potential. Protected varieties can be used in research programs and farmers can plant, sell or trade their seed as long as their primary occupation is growing crops. These exemptions could have large market ramifications, and cause some firms to drop their research programs. Knudson and Hansen (1990) found that this second exemption could result in a market loss of $39 million and $62 million in 1986–87 and 1987–88 for the Corn Belt, Plains and Pacific Northwest wheat market. Given the under-investment in maintaining gene banks, such losses in funds may well have serious impacts in terms of genetic diversity.

The PVPA was amended in 1994, making U.S. law conform with inter-national standards set by the UPOV. Farmers are no longer permitted to sell seed without a license from the owner of the variety. They may, however, save seed for replanting (Fuglie et al., 1996).

The importance of these exemptions diminished with the 1985 *ex parte Hibberd* case. This decision extended the 1980 *Diamond v. Chakrabarty* ruling to include plants, seeds, tissue cultures, hybrid plants and hybrid seeds. As a result, a plant breeder could attain a UP for 17 years. UPs are significant in that they do not contain a farmer or research exemption clause and can cover multiple varieties or individual components of a variety. Both public and private research institutions have used UPs and show every indication of increasing their use of them. A survey of SAESs showed that the number of experimental stations that plan to use UPs will almost double from 19 to 37. UPs for wheat, corn and soybean varieties will account for most of this increase (Brooks, 1989).

Even disregarding the issue of exemptions, there are several arguments against the PVPA and other intellectual rights for crops. The most important involves the 'crowding out' of the public sector from plant breeding. As property rights enable firms to attain profits, they will compete with the public sector, eventually diminishing the role played by the latter. This affects genetic diversity in three ways. The first recognizes the strategic interaction of firms. Once property rights are established, the fear of losing a market advantage may also lead to a decreased exchange. But the consequence of decreased exchange is that germplasm will not be available for use in developing many new varieties. Second, property rights might mean that plants which are genetically diverse but not obviously profitable will tend to be under-collected, leading to problems in meeting unexpected needs for germplasm.

Finally, as breeding becomes more oriented towards market forces, there is the potential for the diversion of plant breeding efforts towards the development of genetically trivial traits (Kloppenburg, 1988; Stallman, 1990). The economic rationale for the development of trivial traits lies in the low time investment of such efforts, its independence from the need to maintain a diverse set of germplasm (and thus costly germplasm programs), and the potential gain in market share. These actions may affect the public sector as well, as plant breeding institutes become more interested in developing more varieties (although trivial) in hopes of gaining more market recognition.

Supporters of IPRs such as the former director of research for Pioneer Hi-Bred, Dr Donald Duvick, argue that IPRs increase genetic diversity. By maintaining breeding pools and marketing an increasingly wide range of crop varieties, seed companies promote genetic diversity. There is some evidence to support the view that genetic diversity in agriculture has not been negatively affected by public policies. Cox et al. (1986) found that genetic diversity has increased for hard red winter wheat and soft red winter wheat.[17] The number of hard red winter wheat varieties increased, as did the genetic diversity of those varieties. Prior to the passage of the PVPA, increases in soft red winter wheat were accompanied by a decrease in genetic diversity. After passage, however, an increase in varieties was accompanied by an increase in genetic diversity, pointing perhaps to the diversity-enhancing effect of property rights. Pray and Knudson (1994) confirm these observations. They present a regression analysis of data on hard red winter wheat in the three principal wheat states from the early 1960s to 1988. Their results indicate that the PVPA has not affected the genetic diversity of hard red winter wheat in the United States. In fact, the PVPA had a positive (although statistically insignificant) impact. Public agricultural research appropriations, however, had a positive and significant impact on wheat genetic diversity, although there was some evidence of a diminishing marginal return.

A 1990 survey of 84 plant-breeding firms also reveals important information about firm reaction to these policies (Pray et al., 1993). The PVPA seemed to have had a positive impact on the exchange of information, but the respondents were split evenly on whether the PVPA had a positive or negative impact on the exchange of germplasm itself. In contrast, UPs were seen as having a negative impact on germplasm exchange, and respondents saw UPs as having little impact on information exchange.

As for profits, firms responded that the PVPA had a positive impact on profits, bringing along with it an increase in research expenditures. UPs had less of an impact, although given the long development times required for a new variety, it is probably too soon to expect to see profits from UPs. One could look at R&D expenditures to see if firms have changed their practices based on the expectation of increased profits, but firms reported little effect on R&D investments from UPs. This result does not, however, appear to be supported by preliminary regression analysis, which in fact indicates that UPs do stimulate R&D in plant breeding and biotechnology firms (Pray et al., 1993).

These studies suggest that IPRs have led to an increase of both profits and R&D and, most importantly for this study, have done so without diminishing the genetic diversity of agriculture. These results support the conclusion of Plucknett et al. (1987) that 'no evidence has emerged that protection of private plant variety rights impedes the conservation, exchange, and utilization of crop germplasm' (Plucknett et al., 1987, p. 39).

### Genetic Resources as a Heritage of Humankind

The granting of IPRs is not the only ownership issue regarding plant genetic resources. A more basic question is, who owns the plant genetic materials of the world, including the elite lines, varieties, and hybrids developed by research institutions? Since 1983, many international conventions and treaties have addressed this question. The debate includes the ability to grant IPRs, but is expanded to include holding the world's plant genetic resources as a trust for future generations. Two big issues come out of these conventions: what will happen to genetic resource exchange and what will happen to the future of our genetic diversity?

The International Undertaking on Plant Genetic Resources was passed in 1983 at the biennial conference of the Food and Agricultural Organization (FAO). The Undertaking stated that all plant genetic resources, ranging from wild relatives to varieties which took many years for plant breeders to develop, were to be considered 'a common heritage of mankind' and therefore should be a public good to all and freely exchanged (Keystone Dialogue, 1988; Kloppenburg and Kleinman, 1987, p. 29). The Undertaking also called for placing and organizing global base collections under the auspices of the FAO (Swaminathan, 1988). The FAO Commission on Plant Genetic Resources was instituted to see that the Undertaking was fulfilled. 'Its objective was to ensure that plant genetic resources of economic and social value, particularly for agriculture, will be explored, preserved, evaluated and made available for plant breeding and scientific purposes' (Keystone Dialogue, 1988, p. 26). While this

Undertaking was enthusiastically supported by many developing countries, many industrialized nations and a number of developing countries did not support it. As a result the provisions of the Undertaking were not officially binding (Frisvold and Condon, 1998). (As of 1988, 114 countries either became members of the Undertaking or have followed it (Keystone Dialogue, 1988).) Knowing the arguments made by both sides will be a useful way to get a handle on the conflicts that continue to emerge as international policy tries to deal with this complex issue. To many, the conflict over the ownership and access to genetic resources is one of the biggest obstacles to a clear, effective global strategy governing our genetic resources (Reid, 1992).

The main justification for the Undertaking is based on the global trends in use and exchange of germplasm. Many of the industrialized countries have crops that originated outside their borders. For example, over 98 percent of United States agricultural crops are non-native (McNeely et al., 1990, p. 57). These countries have received and continue to receive free germplasm from informal global channels or through formal channels such as the CGIAR system. They use this germplasm to develop superior varieties, varieties which are then sold back to the donor country, despite the fact that the donor country contributed significantly to the variety's genetic makeup. This exchange pattern raises a number of questions. How should donor countries be compensated for varieties that could not be developed without their germplasm resources? If donor countries do not charge developed countries for their initial contribution, why should they be charged for the final variety? Finally, even if donor countries do not import the developed variety with their germplasm in it, should they not be compensated in some way for the value added to the variety from their donated germplasm? These questions become more pressing when one recognizes that developing countries have contributed 95.7 percent of the genetic resources found in global crop production – the developed world only contributed a few crops (Kloppenburg and Kleinman, 1987). There is a growing belief that these resources are assets that can benefit the economies of developing countries (Reid, 1992).

Against these arguments are raised a number of points. First, there is an established interdependence of countries for food crops. Both the Northern and Southern hemispheres are dependent on each other. Most regions of the world (outside of the Indo-Chinese, Hindustanean and West Central Asiatic areas) receive more than 50 percent of their genetic resources from outside areas (Kloppenburg and Kleinman, 1987; Reid, 1992). For example, much of the wild germplasm flow has been North–North or South–South (Table 3.8). Second, many countries, particularly the developed ones, have established national and international IPRs on their varieties. Enforcing the Undertaking would thus lead to a major disruption in the structure of international IPRs. Third, the flow of germplasm of advanced material is probably in the North–South direction (NRC, 1993). Finally, the market for raw genes is an inefficient and underdeveloped one. Germplasm only becomes valuable after research and development (although this is also true of landraces), and the use of this germplasm does not deprive a country of that resource (Brown, 1988).

*Table 3.8   Flows of wild germplasm*

| Crops improved with wild germplasm | Source of germplasm | | | |
|---|---|---|---|---|
| | Number of crops | Industrialized countries | Developing countries | Both |
| Crops grown largely (>70%) in industrialized countries | 10[a] | 6 | 1 | 3 |
| Crops grown largely (>70%) in developing countries | 8[b] | 0 | 8 | 0 |
| Crops grown in both developing and in industrialized countries | 6[c] | 0 | 1 | 5 |

*Notes:*

a:   crops are: barley, oats, potato, sunflower, carrot, grapes, apple, pear, strawberry, sugar beet.
b:   crops are: rice, cassava, sweet potato, oil palm, sesame, sugarcane, rubber, cacao.
c:   crops are: wheat, maize, tomato, peas, tobacco, cotton.

*Source:*

W.V. Reid, *Genetic Resources and Sustainable Agriculture: Creating Incentives for Local Innovation and Adaptation,* Nairobi: Acts Press, African Centre for Technology Studies, 1992.

In 1987, The Keystone Center in Colorado established a series of sessions that tackled questions surrounding plant genetic resources. In Session I they discussed *ex situ* conservation of plant genetic resources. This session tried to resolve differences over genetic resource and IPRs and tried to develop a strategy and recommendations for the 'availability, use, exchange and protection of plant germplasm' (Keystone Dialogue, 1988, p. 2).[18] The people who attended the Dialogue were significant players in the international germplasm exchange system. The Keystone Dialogue recommendations have been used in subsequent international agreements such as revisions of the Undertaking and the UN Convention on Biological Diversity.

Three key elements for resolving these property rights differences came out of the Keystone Dialogue. First was the concept that genetic resources were a common heritage 'held in trust by present generations for future generations' (Keystone Dialogue, 1988, p. 13).

Second, plant breeders' rights were recognized, noting the 'decision of whether an individual country would employ any form of intellectual property protection, or none, is solely a national prerogative' (Keystone Dialogue, 1988, p. 15). This represented a divergence from the FAO Undertaking. However, the

Dialogue recommended that a farmer exemption clause should apply for all forms of IPR protection so that farmers would maintain the right to re-grow their seed from their harvested seed.

Third, the concept of Farmers' Rights was developed. Farmers' Rights recognizes that farmers everywhere have developed landraces and that localities and regions throughout the world develop and maintain minor crops (Keystone Dialogue, 1988). The concept of Farmers' Rights eventually was adopted by the Undertaking. Starting from a discussion in June 1986 at the First session of the FAO's Commission on Plant Genetic Resources, and at the Second session of the FAO's Commission on Plant Genetic Resources in 1989, (and in line with the Keystone Dialogue), the Undertaking had an Agreed Interpretation where Farmers' Rights were defined 'as a right to international funding in return for the germplasm developed by farmers over the centuries' (Barton and Siebeck, 1991, p. 12).

The concept of Farmers' Rights is fundamentally different from plant breeders' rights, however. In the latter case, plant breeders can obtain intellectual property protection supported by the force of law to obtain compensation for improving plant varieties. In contrast, the concept of Farmers' Rights represents a non-compulsory moral obligation to developing countries for past contributions to crop genetic improvements (Frisvold and Condon, 1998). Although the FAO established an international fund to implement Farmers' Rights, contributions were to be made by countries on a voluntary basis. Contributions to this fund have remained insignificant.

The Keystone Dialogue also recommended that global plant genetic resource conservation efforts, such as the *ex situ* base collections, be organized on a global basis, with the FAO, the IARCs, non-governmental organizations, the International Union for the Conservation of Nature and Natural Resources, and IPGRI forming an advisory committee. The committee would oversee, assess, review and monitor global plant genetic conservation strategies (Keystone Dialogue, 1988).

Another recent international agreement affecting plant genetic resources is the United Nations Convention on Biological Diversity (CBD). The CBD was opened for signature at the UN Conference on Environment and Development in Rio de Janeiro in 1992. Its objectives are:

> the conservation of biological diversity, the sustainable use of its components and the fair and equitable sharing of the benefits arising out of the utilization of genetic resources, including by appropriate access to genetic resources and by appropriate transfer of relevant technologies, taking into account all rights over those resources and to technologies, and by appropriate funding. (UNEP, 1992)

The CBD designates the Global Environmental Facility (GEF) of the World Bank, the UNDP and the UNEP as the interim institutional mechanism to finance implementation of the Convention.

Language in the CBD over plant genetic resources was drafted with pharmaceutical development more than seed variety development in mind. However, the CBD has important implications for agricultural genetic resources, while subsequent meetings to implement the CBD have focused increasingly on agricultural biodiversity (Frisvold and Condon, 1998). The CBD upholds nations' sovereign rights over their genetic resources. It also formalizes the right of nations to use property rights over genetic resources to gain a greater share of the benefits from technologies that use those resources.

Appropriate burden sharing was mentioned, with those developed countries that benefit the most from genetic resources sharing the greatest burden. Furthermore, the CBD states that governments are required to develop national plans and programs; access to genetic resources is encouraged on mutually agreed terms; and the equitable sharing of the benefits arising from exploiting plant genetic resources is promoted (Hawtin, 1994, p. 2).

The CBD also states that any benefit-sharing agreements between contracting parties must honor IPRs. President Clinton signed the CBD on June 4, 1993 (NRC, 1993). In the Clinton Letter of Submittal to the United States Senate:

> The Administration will therefore strongly resist any actions taken by the Parties to the convention that will lead to inadequate levels of protection of intellectual property rights, and will continue to pursue a vigorous policy with respect to the adequate and effective protection of intellectual property rights in negotiations on bilateral and multilateral trade agreements. (Powledge, 1993/94, p. 46)

The U.S. Senate has yet to ratify the CBD, however.

Also at the UNCED Earth Summit in Rio, 172 nations (including the United States) adopted Agenda 21. Agenda 21 was meant to be a global plan of action to address both global environmental problems and sustainable development issues in developing countries. A number of key elements from Agenda 21 (particularly its Preamble and Chapter 14) pertain to plant genetic resources. The plan: (a) calls for countries to strengthen programs and institutions concerned with plant genetic resources, (b) calls for establishment of *ex situ* base collections, (c) foresees strengthened North–South links in genetic resource conservation and use, (d) recognizes the need for future research, and (e) stresses the importance of information and data exchange (Hawtin, 1994).

Both the CBD and Agenda 21 recognized the strong role that national programs play in the conservation of plant genetic resources. These programs range from the management of gene banks, to the training of plant breeders and other scientists involved with plant genetic resources, to non-governmental organizations and private firms, to the farmer concerned about the diversity present in his field. However, even a wealthier developed country may have problems in meeting these goals. For the developing country, it will be even more difficult. For a global plant genetic resource conservation program to work, a global financial plan must be in place. Developing countries will depend strongly on others for financial assistance over the long term to meet these goals.

The CBD and Agenda 21 face familiar problems if they are to be implemented successfully. Adequate funding needs to be provided. A unified international plant genetic resource conservation system needs to be established. Information on accessions needs to be not only standardized, but also computerized and available to all. International, regional, national and local programs should work together to determine the conservation and use of a location's genetic materials. *Ex situ* and *in situ* conservation methods should be used (Shands, 1994a).

While these international agreements have taken a number of steps toward addressing controversies over genetic resource ownership, there remain concerns over how new IPR regimes might affect the exchange of germplasm. Will there be less exchange of germplasm? Will public institutions have more restrictions to access to their genetic resources? Will genetic diversity decrease, hence increasing genetic vulnerability? Some evidence suggests that IPRs will not decrease genetic diversity, but it is a situation to be watched carefully and on a micro level. Agricultural research structures vary for all countries; each will differ in their response to changing IPRs.

In 1989 the CGIAR established a policy stating that the Centers are trustees for the world's germplasm and indicating that they see their materials as available to all. This answers some of the concerns regarding how public institutions will behave with regard to IPRs.

In keeping with the international conventions in trying to establish a unified global plant genetic resource system, the CGIAR has just signed an agreement with the FAO where the gene banks are placed under the auspices of the FAO while the IARCs are the trustees. This would make the CGIAR system a part of the International Network of *Ex Situ* Base Collections, a part of the FAO (Powledge, 1993/94). Furthermore, in 1993, the CGIAR established an eight-member 'stripe committee' to 'study how the CGIAR discharges its responsibilities for plant genetic resources conservation' (Powledge, 1993/94 p. 6). The term 'stripe' refers to the fact that the committee assessed only one facet (or stripe) of the CGIAR's multiple functions. The committee's goal was to make recommendations regarding how CGIAR should change to assist in international biodiversity policy, such as implementation of the CBD and how to educate the rest of the international community about the strong role the CGIAR has played in international germplasm conservation. [19]

## Some Solutions

Because of the recent work of the NRC on managing global genetic resources and because of the breadth and depth of this work, some of its recommendations that pertain to the North–South conflict and to IPRs are presented here. With respect to the North–South conflict, the NRC agrees with the previous treaties' plant breeders' rights, Farmers' Rights and recognition of national sovereignty. However, within this there can be conflict. NRC's solutions are:

(1) negotiate a treaty that defines a compromise position on the intellectual property and free flow of crop germplasm, (2) create an international payment mechanism, more likely a system linked to the value of seed sales, whose proceeds would support genetic diversity conservation programs, and (3) focus attention on strengthening plant breeding and building biotechnology research capacity in the developing world rather than on legal arrangements. This would restore reciprocity between the industries of the developed and developing countries. (Day, 1995, p. 5)

With respect to IPRs, the NRC looks to respect IPRs while not restricting germplasm flow. It is concerned about adequate availability of protected material placed in depositories, maintaining a research exemption clause and whether technology-importing countries will honor process patents. With respect to public institutions, the NRC recommends that they not restrict the availability of their material, particularly to developing countries, out of fear of legal conflict with other research institutions. They should employ the use of royalty-free licenses (Day, 1995). The CGIAR system has a policy where they will not apply for IPR protection of germplasm held in trust and are looking at ways this policy could be applied to recipients of their accessions (Hawtin, 1994).

Funding remains a problem. The NRC projects that only 30 to 40 base collection germplasm banks are needed to maintain our genetic resources. While developed countries can support their own programs, developing countries will need outside assistance. About $240 million annually will be needed for programs, evaluation of accessions and documentation. To help keep this in perspective, 1993 global commercial seed sales were an estimated $30 billion (Day, 1995).

Finally, the NRC recommends that to maintain biodiversity, a fund must be created that supports the basic principles of the International Undertaking on Plant Genetic Resources of the FAO. The FAO, IPGRI and other CGIAR centers must work together along with national systems. The CGIAR now has 'no formal legal basis for action among governments' (NRC, 1993 p. 26). But they are leaders in conserving plant resources. Perhaps they should set up some alliance with the FAO in that they consult the FAO over important policy issues (NRC, 1993).

# 7   THE FUTURE OF AGRICULTURAL BIODIVERSITY

This survey of current trends in agricultural biodiversity shows that the future may be rosier than pessimistic projections of crises might predict. International institutions are doing an excellent job of acquiring landraces of the major global crops. Domestically, policy innovations such as the PVPA appear to have enhanced both profits and productivity without diminishing genetic diversity.

But it would be incorrect to paint too promising a picture. Overall, the international research community has not attained the same level of coverage of wild species for the major crops. With habitat conversion and other trends crowding out these species, future acquisition may either be prohibitively expensive or simply impossible, as these species are wiped out. If we cannot reverse population growth, global warming and the other trends jeopardizing wild plant species, at least we could mitigate some of the damage by collecting genetic resources before they vanish forever. This would be an especially good project now that international collections are close to completing their acquisition of landraces.

The acquisition of species is only one (albeit a highly visible) means of meeting the need for genetic diversity. Yet a plant that is acquired and dies through poor preservation techniques or is lost in a bewildering and archaic database is just as much a source of lost genetic variation as the loss of that plant through monocultural cropping patterns. We have seen that much needs to be done, both in the physical treatments of the gene banks and in their informational systems, to enhance existing supplies. It bears repeating that what happens to a plant once it enters the gene bank is just as important to preserving future genetic diversity as what happens to it in the field. Policies should be undertaken to ensure that gene banks run more efficiently. Individual gene banks need to ensure that they have the continual leadership to ensure good management. Governments and international groups must make sure that the information of all gene banks is centrally documented using similar standards.

A third area of concern is the use of these accessions by plant breeders. Global genetic vulnerability may be a potential problem. More diversity needs to be built into the parental pools from which breeders draw to develop varieties or hybrids.

A fourth area of concern is the degree of conflict between donor and recipient countries over the structure of property rights governing genetic material. Given the evidence that the assignment of property rights does not diminish genetic diversity, nations may be more willing than previously to entertain some stronger forms of international IPRs in agriculture. Such property rights could well provide (through increased profits) the funds required to enhance the acquisition, maintenance and cataloging of plant species. Such efforts will enable the United States and other nations to maintain and perhaps increase existing agricultural productivity, gains that will be crucially dependent upon advances in plant breeding and ultimately upon the quality and variety of germplasm available to plant breeders.

At the same time, there must be some assurance by IPR holders that the exchange of germplasm flow will not decrease. Either research exemptions could be maintained or special free licenses could be given to research institutions.

A final area of concern is funding. Without an adequate long-term financial strategy at the national or international level, the concerns mentioned above will be difficult to tackle. Governments, firms, non-governmental organizations and international organizations need to understand the value of biodiversity to global agricultural production. Without this understanding, underinvestment in plant genetic diversity will continue.

In conclusion, the first steps to ensuring adequate genetic diversity for the future have been taken. Good collections have been set up and are functioning well. International agreements have been made with regard to future strategy of conserving, maintaining and using plant genetic resources. The next several steps now must be taken to make sure that these genetic resources are accessible to future generations. If these steps are taken, then genetic diversity in gene banks, parental pools and in the field should enable us to meet the demands of the next century.

## NOTES

1.  HYVs are usually thought of as a product of the Green Revolution. HYVs are found in wheat, rice, maize, sorghum, beans, groundnuts, cassava and potatoes. Their success is due in large part to the simultaneous use of technologies; chemical inputs, irrigation, new tillage practices and improved management technologies.
2.  A hybrid is the first generation of a cross between two genetically dissimilar parents.
3.  A cytoplasmic–genetic system refers to a system that requires genes from both the nucleus and the cytoplasm of a cell in order to be expressed.
4.  Landraces are cultivated crop species that have evolved from a wild species and from which a farmer has done some selection for several years (Poehlman, 1979). Landraces are usually found in farmers' fields in developing countries. Wild relatives or wild species refer to plants that may or may not be cultivated but are found in the wild and are related to plants grown for crop production.
5.  Other forms exist, such as *in situ* preservation, which is the preservation of plants in their natural habitat such as on-farm conservation. While *in situ* preservation is being used somewhat on a global basis, and may increase in the future, *ex situ* preservation is still the major form of germplasm maintenance for crop plants today. As a result, this chapter will concentrate on *ex situ* preservation. For a more detailed discussion of these and other forms of germplasm preservation, see McNeely et al., (1990)
6.  Biotechnology can also be used to manage, characterize and use germplasm, but currently it is expensive and time consuming and needs much expertise to do so (Day, 1995). Therefore, it is a technology that will not be used much yet, particularly in developing countries.
7.  See Hawtin (1994) and Keystone Dialogue (1988) for a more detailed listing of other UN agencies and non-governmental organizations.
8.  With a decrease in funding the CGIAR will merge four of the IARCs (Powledge, 1993/4).
9.  The current numbers of ongoing collections of major crops are as follows: Wheat has 31; barley 28; rice 25; maize 21; sorghum 15; millets 12; soybean 13; common bean 23; lima bean 2; groundnut 14; cowpea 7; chickpea 7; pigeon pea 2; lentil 2; faba bean 4; mung bean 6; pea 10;

potato 11; sweet potato 5; and cassava 3. See Williams (1984, 1989) for more details on these listings.

10. This last guideline is a precaution to guard against natural disasters and political upheavals.

11. Phenotypic expression is the physical appearance of a plant as opposed to the genetic constitution of a plant (genotype) (Poehlman, 1979).

12. Parental pools are the plant population, which are used as parents in breeding programs.

13. Stress tolerance refers to tolerance to excessive heat, drought, low soil fertility, cool temperatures or rapid fluctuation from one environmental extreme to another.

14. There are several examples of what a wild species has provided. Potato has received resistance to bacterial wilt, scab, virus leafroll, virus X, virus Y, hopperburn and nematodes. Tomato, a high valued crop in the United States, has received resistance to Verticilium and Fusarium wilts, bacterial canker, bacterial wilt, grey leaf spot, leaf wound, Septoria leaf spot, curly top virus, mosaic virus, three kinds of spotted wilt virus, Phytophthora fruit rot and root knot nematode. Tomato's commercial success seems dependent on its wild species' contributions (Harlan, 1984).

15. A breeding strategy for backcrossing is often used to eliminate the negative traits so that only the good ones exist. Backcrossing is crossing the progeny with one of its parents or with a genetically equivalent organism (Poehlman, 1979, p. 463). Sometimes, however, the negative traits have been found to be tightly linked with the desirable traits, making it impossible to use this wild species as a source for this particular trait.

16. The Supreme Court has subsequently ruled in favor of Asgrow Seed Company, limiting the scope of the farmer's exemption (Editor's note).

17. In the United States, there are five market classes of wheat. They include hard red winter, hard red spring, soft red winter, white and durum. They are grown in different parts of the country, and vary somewhat in the amount and type of protein they have.

18. The Dialogue discussed both *ex situ* and *in situ* conservation strategies. For *ex situ* germplasm collections, they looked at the (1) scientific and technical aspects of germplasm conservation, (2) equity and ownership issues, such as those found in the North–South debate, and (3) organization of an international germplasm system. However, for the purposes of this chapter, we discuss only how property rights are affected.

19. Many associates of the CGIAR system were surprised at the UNCED at how unaware the rest of the world was of their work. The committee will also address whether more coherence amongst international organizations is needed; strategies to finance future conservation; what species should be included; whether non-food crops should become CGIAR responsibility; how to incorporate eco-regional responsibilities; and how to make use of advances in molecular biology.

# REFERENCES

Anon. (1993/94), 'New PVPA amendments proposed by Senator Bob Kerrey would bring United States into compliance with UPOV', *Diversity,* **9–10** (double issue), p. 46.

Barton, J.H. and Siebeck, W.E. (1991), 'Intellectual property issues for the International Agricultural Research Center. What are the options?', Report prepared for the Consultative Group for International Agricultural Research (CGIAR) Secretariat, Washington, DC.

Brooks, H.J (1989), 'Questionnaire on maintenance of free exchange of plant germplasm', Unpublished memo, Agricultural Research Service, November 17.

Brown, W.L. (1988), 'Plant genetic resources: a view from the seed industry', in Kloppenburg, J. (ed.), *Seeds and Sovereignty: The Use and Control of Plant Genetic Resources*, Durham, NC: Duke University Press, pp. 218–230.

Butler, L.J. and Marion, B.W. (1985), 'The impacts of patent protection on the U.S. seed industry', College of Agriculture and Life Sciences, University of Wisconsin: North Central Regional Research Publication No. 304.

Chang, T.T., Dietz, S.M. and Westwood, M.N. (1989), 'Management and use of plant germplasm collections', in Knutson, L. and Stoner, A.K. (eds), *Biotic Diversity and Germplasm Preservation, Global Imperatives,* Dordrecht: Kluwer Academic Publishers, pp. 127–160.

Cox, T.S., Murphy, J.P. and Rodgers, D.M. (1986), 'Changes in genetic diversity in the Red Winter Wheat regions of the United States', *Proceedings of the National Academy of Science,* **83**, pp. 5583–5586.

Day, P.R. (1995), 'Opening Statement for the NRC report', *Managing Global Genetic Resources: Agricultural Crop Issues and Policies,* January 31.

Duvick, D.N. (1984), 'Genetic diversity in major farm crops on the farm and in reserve', *Economic Botany,* **38**, pp. 161–178.

Duvick, D.N. (1986), 'Plant breeding: past achievements and expectations for the future', *Economic Botany,* **40**, pp. 289–297.

Duvick, D.N. (1991), 'Industry and its role in plant diversity', *Forum for Applied Research and Public Policy,* **6**, pp. 90–94.

Evenson, R.E. (1990), 'Intellectual property rights, R&D, inventions, technology purchase, and piracy in economic development: an international comparative study', in Evenson, R.E. and Ranis, G. (eds), *Science and Technology: Lessons for Development Policy,* Westview Special Studies in Science and Technology, Boulder, CO: Westview Press in cooperation with the Economic Growth Center, Yale University, pp. 325–355.

Frankel, O.H. and Brown, A.H.D. (1984), 'Plant genetic resources today: a critical appraisal', in Williams, J.T. and Holden, J.H.W. (eds), *Crop Genetic Resources: Conservation and Evaluation,* London: George Allen and Unwin.

Frisvold, G. and Condon, P. (1998), 'The Convention of Biological Diversity and Agriculture: implications and unresolved debates', *World Development,* **26**, pp. 551–570.

Fuglie, K., Ballenger, N., Day, K., Klotz, C., Ollinger, M., Reilly, J., Vaasavada, U. and Yee, J. (1996), *Agricultural Research and Development. Public and Private Investments Under Alternative Markets and Institutions,* Natural Resources and Environment Division, Economic Research Service, U.S. Department of Agriculture, Agricultural Economic Report Number 735.

Gale, J.S. and Lawrence, M.J. (1984), 'The decay of variability', in Williams, J.T. and Holden, J.H.W. (eds), *Crop Genetic Resources: Conservation and Evaluation,* London: George Allen and Unwin, pp. 77–101.

Goodman, M.M. and Castillo-Gonzalez, F. (1991), 'Plant genetics: politics and realities', *Forum for Applied Research and Public Policy,* **6**, pp. 74–78.

Harlan, J.R. (1984), 'Evaluation of wild relatives of crop plants', in Williams, J.T. and Holden, J.H.W. (eds), *Crop Genetic Resources: Conservation and Evaluation,* London: George Allen and Unwin, pp. 212–222.

Hawtin, G. (1994), 'The contribution of the CGIAR and other international organizations to the conservation of plant genetic resources', in Witmeyer, D. and Strauss, M.S. (eds), *Building Global Cooperation,* Washington, DC: American Association for the Advancement of Science, pp. 1–13.

Holden, J.H.W. (1984), 'The second ten years', in Williams, J.T. and Holden, J.H.W. (eds), *Crop Genetic Resources: Conservation and Evaluation*, London: George Allen and Unwin, pp. 275–285.

Keystone Dialogue (1988), 'Final report of The Keystone International Dialogue on Plant Genetic Resources. Session I: *ex situ* conservation of plant genetic resources', Aug. 15–18, Keystone, Colorado, The Keystone Center.

Kloppenburg, J.R. (1988), *First the Seed: The Political Economy of Plant Biotechnology*, New York: Cambridge University Press.

Kloppenburg, J.R. and Kleinman, D.L. (1987), 'Seeds and sovereignty', *Diversity*, **10**, pp. 29–33.

Knudson, M. (1988), 'The research and development of competing biological innovations: the case of semi- and hybrid wheats', unpublished Ph.D. dissertation, University of Minnesota.

Knudson, M. and Hansen, L.T. (1990), 'Examination of winter wheat yield response to seed source', *Journal of Production Agriculture*, **3**, pp. 551–557.

Knudson, M.K. and Pray, C.E. (1991), 'Plant variety protection, private funding, and public sector research priorities', *American Journal of Agricultural Economics*, **73**, pp. 882–886.

McNeely, J.A., Miller, K.R., Reid, W.V., Mittermeier, R.A. and Werner, T.B. (1990), *Conserving the World's Biological Diversity*, International Union for Conservational Nature and Natural Resources, Gland, Switzerland; World Research Institute, Conservation International, World Wildlife Fund, WWF–U.S. and the World Bank, Washington, DC.

National Research Council (NRC) (1993), *Managing Global Genetic Resources: Agricultural Crop Issues and Policies*, Washington, DC: National Academy Press.

Perrin, R.K., Kunnings, K.A. and Ihnen, L.A. (1983), 'Some effects of the U.S. Plant Variety Protection Act of 1970', Department of Economics and Business, North Carolina State University: Economics Research Report No. 46, August 1983.

Plucknett, D.L., Smith, N.J.H., Williams, J.T. and Anishetty, N.M. (1987), *Gene Banks and the World's Food*, Princeton: Princeton University Press.

Poehlman, J.M. (1979), *Breeding Field Crops*, 2nd edition, Westport: AVI Publishing Company, Inc.

Powledge, F. (1993/94), 'Genetic resources issues dominate CGIAR agenda, more challenges and less money for beleaguered group', *Diversity*, **9–10** (double issue), p. 46.

Pray, C., Knudson, M. and Masse, L. (1993), 'Impact of changing intellectual property rights on U.S. plant breeding R&D', unpublished paper.

Pray, C.E. and Knudson, M.K. (1994), 'Impact of intellectual property rights on genetic diversity: the case of wheat', *Contemporary Economic Policy*, **12**, pp. 102–112.

Reid, W.V. (1992), *Genetic Resources and Sustainable Agriculture: Creating Incentives for Local Innovation and Adaptation*, Nairobi: Acts Press, African Centre for Technology Studies.

Ruttan, V.W. (1982), *Agricultural Research Policy*, Minneapolis: University of Minnesota Press.

Shands, H.L. (1994a), 'Some potential impacts of the United Nations Environment Program's Convention on Biological Diversity on the international system of exchanges of food crop germplasm', in Witmeyer, D. and Strauss, M.S. (eds), *Building Global*

*Cooperation*, Washington, DC: American Association for the Advancement of Science, pp. 27–38.

Shands, H.L. (1994b), personal communication.

Shands, H.L., Fitzgerald, P.J. and Eberhart, S.A. (1989), 'Program for plant germplasm preservation in the United States: the U.S. National Plant Germplasm System', in Knutson, L. and Stoner, A.K. (eds), *Biotic Diversity and Germplasm Preservation, Global Imperatives,* Dordrecht: Kluwer Academic Publishers, pp. 97–115.

Smith, J. (1988), 'Diversity of United States hybrid maize germplasm: isozymic and chromatographic evidence', *Crop Science,* **28**, pp. 63–69.

Smith, J.S.C. and Duvick, D.N. (1989), 'Germplasm collections and the private plant breeder', in Brown, A.H.D., Frankel, O.H., Marshall, D.R. and Williams, J.T. (eds), *The Use of Plant Genetic Resources,* Cambridge: Cambridge University Press, pp. 17–32.

Stallman, J.I. (1990), 'Plants, patents and public research priorities', *Choices,* **5**, pp. 8–11.

Swaminathan, M.S. (1988), 'Seeds and property rights: a view from the CGIAR system', in Kloppenburg, J. (ed.), *Seeds and Sovereignty: The Use and Control of Plant Genetic Resources*, Durham, NC: Duke University Press, pp. 231–253.

Towill, L.E. and Roos, E.E. (1989), 'Techniques for preserving of plant germplasm', in Knutson, L. and Stoner, A.K. (eds), *Biotic Diversity and Germplasm Preservation, Global Imperatives,* Dordrecht: Kluwer Academic Publishers, pp. 380–403.

United Nations Environment Programme (1992), Convention on Biological Diversity, June 5, 1992.

U.S. Congress, Office of Technology Assessment (1987), *Technologies to Maintain Biological Diversity*, OTA-F-330, Washington, DC: U.S. Government Printing Office, March.

Wilkes, G. (1989), 'Germplasm preservation: objectives and needs', in Knutson, L. and Stoner, A.K. (eds), *Biotic Diversity and Germplasm Preservation, Global Imperatives,* Dordrecht: Kluwer Academic Publishers, pp. 13–41.

Williams, J.T. (1984) , 'A decade of crop genetic resources research', in Williams, J.T. and Holden, J.H.W. (eds), *Crop Genetic Resources: Conservation and Evaluation*, London: George Allen and Unwin, pp. 1–17.

Williams, J.T. (1989), 'Plant germplasm preservation: a global perspective', in Knutson, L. and Stoner, A.K. (eds), *Biotic Diversity and Germplasm Preservation, Global Imperatives,* Dordrecht: Kluwer Academic Publishers, pp. 81–96.

Wilson, E.O. (1988), 'The current state of biological diversity', in Wilson, E.O. (ed.), *Biodiversity,* Washington, DC: National Academy Press, pp. 3–18.

PART II

Environmental Accounting and Indexing

# 4 Environmental Distortions and Welfare Consequences in a Social Accounting Matrix Framework

**Elise Hardy Golan, Irma Adelman and
Stephen Vogel**

## 1 PRECIS

The economic activities of agents give rise to environmental externalities. These externalities vary in extent by type of activity, by specific impact of environmental damage, and by severity and coverage. The externalities introduce distortions in the economy that result in a change in the distribution of welfare. The objective of this chapter is to provide a framework for explicitly examining the impact that environmental externalities have on the level and distribution of income, production and, ultimately, welfare. The analysis will consider the distributional impact of environmental distortions on economic activity and welfare within the current economy and between the current and the future economy.

In the analysis presented here, we propose to evaluate the impact that environmental externalities have on welfare using changes in the levels of consumer and producer surpluses, which accrue to different activities and agents in both the current and future economies. By associating these surpluses with externality costs in a social accounting matrix (SAM), the method proposed here provides an operational framework for quantifying the magnitude of these environmental distortions and tracing the distribution of the resultant rents among all the sectors and institutional actors in the current economy. The analysis of externality distortions in the current economy is strengthened by estimation of the impact of the currently generated externalities on the future economy. Three types of future damage categories are identified and an estimation approach is developed for each category. The estimation techniques include the construction of a future externality SAM, the construction of a multiplier matrix model and direct allocation of welfare changes. In the final step of the analysis, the 'externality SAM' and the present-value results of the future damage estimates are subtracted from the original SAM to arrive at an environmentally corrected representation of the flows generated by the activities of the economy.

Making environmental distortions explicit is an important step in deriving a correct evaluation of the true value-added in each sector and in making clear the impact of pollution on the per capita income of households, and hence on income distribution. In this way, the environmentally corrected SAM and SAM multiplier results can be used to derive an environmentally corrected Net National Product (NNP) measure. This environmentally correct NNP measure is an improvement over standard measures in that it accounts for current distortions in value-added due to environmental externalities and accounts for environmental damage that is 'debited' to future generations.

The environmentally corrected NNP measure derived with the environmental SAM and multiplier results takes into account both intergenerational and current distortions in production, consumption and welfare that arise from environmental externalities. However, the environmental prices used in the analysis are not derived from an optimal growth path and do not represent optimal prices. Instead, these prices reflect estimates of surplus changes that occur because of the damage sustained by current and projected victims of the externality. The damage and surplus change estimates, and hence the environmental prices, are agent and sector specific. The environmentally corrected NNP number is not more or less sustainable than unadjusted NNP.

The analysis recognizes the constraints inherent in empirical valuation techniques and differentiates between environmental valuation methods that utilize actual market-based techniques and those that utilize non-market techniques.

The methodology proposed here is analogous to that used to quantify the rents arising from quantitative restrictions in international trade (Buchanan and Tullock, 1965; Bhagwati and Srinivasan, 1981; Krueger, 1983). However, in this research, we are more concerned than these authors with making explicit how the rents are distributed among firms, consumers and the government, and among wages, profits, consumption and savings. There are also elements of our approach in the Little–Mirrlees (1974) project evaluation methodology. Our analysis is more general-equilibrium than the actual (though not conceptual) Little–Mirrlees project analysis methodology, and entails the quantification of the distributive consequences arising from the use of market prices instead of environmental prices.

In section 2, economic accounting for environmental externalities is discussed. Section 3 discusses environmental externalities and welfare distortions. In section 4 the changes in consumer and producer welfare that arise from environmental distortions are examined. In section 5, environmental accounting within the context of a SAM is discussed and a brief literature review is given.

In section 6, a schematic externality SAM is used to trace through the distributional effects of environmental distortions. Section 7 presents the calculations for an environmentally corrected NNP. In section 8, the methodology developed in sections 5–7 is applied to the construction of an agriculturally oriented SAM for California which is used to examine the welfare impacts of groundwater contamination generated by the California cotton sector. The conclusion is presented in section 9.

# 2  ENVIRONMENTAL DISTORTIONS AND THE ACCOUNTING SYSTEM

Throughout the 1970s and 1980s, environmentalists sparked public awareness of the interconnectedness of the economy and the environment, or vice versa. Growing awareness in the developed countries concerning pollution, resource degradation and irreversible depletion of natural resources was matched by a concern in developing countries that economic programs that encouraged rapid, unsustainable exploitation of natural resources were at best shortsighted and at worst destructive. In both developed and developing countries, there is continuing recognition that natural resources and environmental amenities are important determinants of the growth, stability and welfare of a socio-economic system.

Efforts to quantify concerns about the economy's impact on the environment, and to illustrate different policy scenarios, have been hindered by the standard System of National Accounts (SNA). In the framework detailed in the 1968 SNA, there is only a limited accounting of the contribution of the environment to the economy, and an even more limited accounting of the impact of the economy on the environment. The 1990 SNA and its Satellite System for Integrated Environmental and Economic Accounting (SEEA) attempt to redress many of the shortcomings of the earlier SNA. However, in spite of the progress made in revising the standard system of accounts, the debate concerning economic accounting and the environment continues.

At the very heart of the debate on environmental accounting is the concern that the benefits and costs of environmental exploitation are unfairly distributed, whether between industry and consumers, between rich and poor, or between today and tomorrow. Although the focus of this concern has been on intergenerational equity in the enjoyment of the earth's natural resources, it has been accompanied by renewed concern that the management and exploitation of natural resources often result in an inequity in the current distribution of the costs and benefits of resource use. At the extreme, environmental exploitation and environmental externalities can lead to the impoverishment of certain sectors of an economy while other sectors prosper.

Much of the concern about the distribution of natural resource and environmental use arises from the observation that incomplete prices (and incomplete property rights) can lead to environmental externalities in which all of the costs and benefits of resource use do not accrue to a single agent. Examples of environmental externalities are abundant. They range from the classic negative example of the smoke from a factory blackening the drying clothes of a neighboring laundry to the classic positive example of the benefits to an apple orchard from the cross-pollinating services provided free of charge by a neighboring apiary. Other examples include a factory that dumps waste into a stream that is used for fishing and swimming, and a hillside lumber operation that results in soil erosion which reduces the profitability of farms located at the base of the hill. The examples can be inter-regional or global, as in the case of ivory embargoes and the livelihoods of elephant hunters and their families, or in the case of chlorofluorocarbons and the destruction of the earth's ozone layer. The examples can also be intergenerational, as in the case of economic production today that results in irreparable damage to the environment.

Even more importantly, environmental externalities and incorrect valuation of the costs and benefits of natural resource use can lead to a misallocation of research and development funds, government subsidies and defensive expenditures. This misallocation can trigger structural change in the economy that further encourages inappropriate resource use.

Though we restrict our discussion to the distribution of the costs and benefits associated with environmental externalities, the distinction between externalities and exclusivity, particularly when considering intergenerational distortions, becomes blurred. An externality produced by the current economy could have such devastating effects on the environment that future economies could not use or enjoy certain aspects of the environment. Through the externality, the current economy precludes use by future generations of a non-degraded environment. The current economy essentially assumes exclusive use-rights over certain aspects of the environment through the production of the externality.

## 3    ENVIRONMENTAL EXTERNALITIES AND WELFARE DISTORTIONS

The concept of an 'externality' was introduced by Marshall (1920) and has been widely applied in the environmental economics literature. In general, there are two conditions necessary for an externality to exist (the definition presented here is from Baumol and Oates (1988)). First, an externality exists whenever some individual's (say A's) utility or production function includes real variables whose values are chosen by others without particular attention to the effects on A's welfare. Second, the decision maker, whose activity affects the utility levels of others or enters the production functions of others, does not receive (pay) compensation equal in value to the resulting benefits (or costs).

As a result of an externality of the sort described above, a wedge is introduced between the marginal private product (or cost) and the marginal social product (or cost). The fact that the producer does not include social marginal cost in his profit calculus results in over-production of the good, over-production of pollution, and a larger producer surplus than would be achieved if the producer had paid all the costs of production including pollution costs.

Analysis of environmental externalities from the point of view of the deviation between private and social costs and benefits situates the discussion within the framework of the theoretical welfare analysis of Pigou (1920). The Pigouvian approach to externalities involves calculating the dollar-compensation that must be paid in order to compensate for the reallocation of welfare that results from the deviation between social and private costs and benefits. The change in welfare that results from the externality is measured by the change in consumer or producer surplus, where consumer surplus is defined as the area under the ordinary (Marshallian) demand curve and above the price line, and producer surplus is defined as the area above the supply curve and below the price line. Consumer and producer surplus are money measures of welfare changes.

The use of consumer and producer surplus to measure consumer and producer benefits was proposed by Dupuit and further developed by Marshall. Producer surplus and its sister measurement 'quasi rent' have been generally recognized as accurate money measures of changes in producer welfare, but consumer surplus has been deemed to be an unsatisfactory measure of consumer well-being (see Just et al. (1982) for a detailed analysis of consumer surplus and welfare measures).

A basic criticism of consumer surplus arises from the fact that this measure is based on the Marshallian demand curve, which holds income rather than utility constant as one moves along the curve. This fact poses a number of problems when assessing the welfare change arising from price or quantity changes. It has been demonstrated that the conditions under which consumer surplus actually measures a true, unique 'surplus of utility' are restrictive. These conditions specify that (a) the marginal utility of income must be constant with respect to price and/or income change, and (b) income elasticities must be the same for all goods for which prices change and zero if income changes. Strict satisfaction of these conditions poses unrealistic restrictions on preference schedules and, as a result, consumer surplus measures have been discredited on theoretical grounds. Welfare economists prefer other measures, namely Hicksian willingness-to-pay measures, which hold utility rather than income constant.

Unfortunately, economists are, more often than not, unable to generate willingness-to-pay measures, or the expenditure curves which can serve as the basis for their construction. As a result, welfare economists have developed guidelines to express the margin of error that should be expected in using consumer surplus rather than 'true' willingness-to-pay measures, as expressed by compensating and equivalent variation. Willig (1976) found that consumer surplus can be used for approximating compensating and equivalent variation in single-price-change cases where the change in consumer surplus is a very small fraction of total income. In this case, using consumer surplus as an estimate for compensating or equivalent variation typically entails less than a 5 percent error.

The study presented here adheres to the conditions for using consumer surplus 'without apology'. In the examples we consider, it is reasonable to assume that for most consumers, the magnitude of the changes in consumer surplus in relation to income will be quite small. In addition, each price change is examined individually.

# 4   SURPLUS MEASURES OF ENVIRONMENTAL EXTERNALITIES

The manner in which environmental externalities translate into positive or negative incremental changes in consumer or producer surplus is examined next. A change in surplus can arise from unregulated externalities as well as from economic policy designed to control externalities. Surplus measures of distortions in unregulated and regulated economies are both examined below.

**Environmental Distortions in Unregulated Economies**

In principle, the prices generated by economies that do not take account of environmental externalities can lead to four types of rents. First, are the rents enjoyed by the externality-causing industry and its clients. Second, are the negative rents suffered by industries that are negatively affected by the externality. Third, are the rents accruing to industries that supply goods or services providing some defense against the externality. Fourth, are the rents suffered by households and individuals that are affected directly by the negative externality. Each of these four types of externalities is examined.

The first type of rent involves the externality-generating industry. For the pollution-originating sector, not taking account of the negative externalities which they generate or of the environmental services which they enjoy free of charge (or at less than full price) is equivalent to a producer subsidy; their subsidized supply curve is to the right of the 'environmentally correct' supply curve and they are the beneficiaries of producer rents. As a result, these producers generate more employment, and the purchasers of their products, both other producers and final-demand users, benefit from lower market prices, which give rise to a positive incremental purchaser surplus. In addition, increased production on the part of the polluting firm leads to increased demand for inputs (derived demand), thus increasing the producer surplus of those industries which supply these inputs.

Second are the negative rents suffered by industries that are perversely affected by the externality. Producers on whom environmental damage is inflicted are, in effect, taxed. Their supply curve is to the left of the supply curve that would obtain in the absence of externalities and they employ fewer workers; the users of their products pay too high a price and incur negative purchaser surplus. Those industries supplying inputs to the pollution-damaged producers also experience a fall in demand for their goods and a corresponding decrease in their producer surplus.

In addition to the upward shift in their marginal cost curves, certain industries affected by the externality could experience a direct fall in demand. Household valuation of polluted goods and services versus unpolluted goods and services could result in a direct downward shift in demand. For example, demand for recreation areas or attractions that are degraded by an externality will go down, as will demand for housing in polluted areas.

The third type of rent is a result of an increase in demand for goods and services that provide defense against the externality. Industries that provide these goods and services experience an upward shift in demand, resulting in an increase in producer surplus.

With the fourth type of (negative) rents, those agents directly affected by negative externalities from the pollution-generating sector (e.g. households living near an air-polluting factory) are also, in essence, taxed. They incur negative consumer rents from the pollution which must be subtracted from the positive consumer rents they get as purchasers of the polluter's output. For consumers, the negative rents induced by pollution arise from a decline in health and life expectancy, and from a decrease in the general quality of life. As a result of the pollution, households might spend more on defensive goods and services. This could result in a redistribution of expenditure and savings.

## Distortions Through Environmental Regulation

The manner in which environmental regulations compensate or correct for the distortions introduced into the system by environmental externalities can itself introduce a whole set of distortions into the system. For example, in the case of regulation through quantity controls, such as product bans or restrictions, firms directly affected by the regulation have a kinked supply curve. To the extent that the regulation is effective, both suppliers and demanders are rationed. In this case, the producers that are directly affected experience a change in producer surplus (that may be either positive or negative) and the purchasers of their products experience a negative incremental purchaser surplus. This negative effect extends to industries that supply the controlled firm and to depressed employment levels in all negatively impacted industries. By contrast, the firms and agents that purchase commodities that were negatively affected by the environmental effect experience a positive producer or purchaser surplus due to the regulation. This is also true of firms that supply these industries.

In the case of environmental regulation through input restrictions, such as pesticide bans, the producer cost curve and hence the supply curve shifts up to the left, at least in the short run, in reaction to higher-priced inputs which must be used instead of the banned or restricted input. The extent and duration of the shift depend on the existence or development of non-polluting substitute inputs or of technologies which reduce the use of polluting inputs.

Again, the producers that are directly affected experience a negative incremental producer surplus and the purchasers of their products experience a negative incremental purchaser surplus. Firms that supply these industries will also be affected. In contrast, the firms and agents that purchase commodities that are negatively affected by the environmental effect experience a positive producer or purchaser surplus due to the regulation. Firms that supply these industries will be positively affected. The level of employment will be redistributed from industries that are negatively impacted by the restrictions to those that are positively impacted.

Another type of 'correctional distortion', though it does not involve regulation, can be added to the list above. These distortions arise through defensive expenditures, or clean-up costs undertaken by the government to compensate for environmental distortions that have remained unchecked. Expenditures on the part of the government that are not accompanied by a taxation scheme that taxes environmental users in proportion to the environmental damage they inflict will continue to 'subsidize' the polluting industries.

The shift in government expenditure toward environmental defensive goods and services generates surplus and new employment in industries producing these goods and services. If government expenditure is curtailed in other areas in order to compensate for the increase in defensive expenditure, then surplus and employment in these areas could decrease.

## 5   ENVIRONMENTAL DISTORTIONS AND THE SAM

The distribution of the costs and benefits of an externality can have an important impact on an economy's distribution of welfare. As illustrated above, distributional impacts occur between agents that are directly affected by the externality and those that are only indirectly affected; between workers in pollution-generating industries and workers in pollution-suffering industries; and between purchasers of environmentally subsidized products and purchasers of products which are more expensive or of lesser quality because of the externalities. A partial equilibrium evaluation of the incidence of these externalities will not suffice since the net impact of the environmental distortions is often unpredictable and hard to evaluate without an economy-wide quantitative framework. Every change in externality or pollution control has an impact on all other prices and quantities. One must capture the direct and indirect percolation of rents throughout the system to understand the real extent to which particular activities or enterprises benefit or suffer from the externality and the extent to which different consumers or types of consumption benefit from the externality. For this reason, a general equilibrium framework such as a SAM is essential for understanding the extent of the impact of environmental distortions on the economy.

The SAM was developed by Sir Richard Stone, and has been used to model a wide array of economies for policy analysis and economic planning. (See Pyatt and Round (1977) and Pyatt and Roe (1977) for bibliographies and examples.) The SAM is a form of double entry accounting in which the accounting entities in national income and product accounts and in input–output production accounts are presented as debit (expenditures) and credit (receipts) in balance sheets of institutions and activities. Activities may include agricultural and non-agricultural production (or any disaggregation of the two). Institutions include households, firms, government and the rest of the world. Entries in the SAM include intermediate input demands between production sectors, income (value-added) paid by production sectors to different types of labor or capital, the distribution of wages across different household groups, and the distribution of household-group expenditures across savings, consumption of domestically produced goods, and services and imports. A government account collects income from activities and households and allocates it to government consumption, investment, transfers to production activities and households, savings and payments to foreigners (for imports and debt service and repayment).

The total product of each activity in the SAM must be earmarked for some use, inside or outside the economy (intermediate demand, consumption, investment, government demand or exports). Total gross receipts of each activity must be allocated to some entity inside or outside the economy (purchases of inputs from other activities, payment to labor and capital, imports, taxes and savings).

By convention, columns of the SAM represent expenditures while rows indicate receipts. The salient characteristic of SAMs, derived from double entry accounting, is that the sum of receipts (row sums) and the sum of expenditures (column sums) must be equal for each and every account in the system. The SAM accounting framework thus identifies the source and destination of every dollar circulating in the economy. Another salient feature of the SAM is that the SAM categories to which incomes and expenditures are assigned are the same on the revenue and expenditure sides, so that the SAM is a square matrix.

The great strengths of the SAM are its comprehensiveness and its flexibility in portraying diverse institutional settings and economic structures and in providing a framework for addressing different policy issues. The SAM is superior

to the National Accounts Framework in that it includes a portrayal of interactions within a particular account (e.g. production, enterprises or households).
Each of the accounts in the National Accounts is expanded from a scalar into a
matrix. The SAM is also superior to the input–output framework in that it en-
dogenizes incomes and consumption and thereby permits accurate appraisal of
the full effects of specific changes.

In the economic/accounting literature, the interest in a SAM accounting
framework was motivated by a number of issues, two of which will be touched
on here. First, a SAM, unlike the National Income Accounts (NIAs), provides a
flexible framework for data organization that is compatible with alternative
analytical uses; the SAM framework is capable of integrating an accounting
framework and modeling applications (Hanson and Robinson (1991) give a
good examination of the role of SAMs in linking data and modeling requirements.) The SAM framework and general equilibrium models, which are built
upon it, are of particular interest when a partial equilibrium approach is not
sufficient.

The second motivating factor behind the introduction of the SAM framework
was the refocusing of interest by economists from macro to micro issues. Sir
Richard Stone (1961) describes this motivation in the following way:

> The term social accounting, as opposed to national accounting, is used to denote the
> activity of designing and constructing a system of accounts which will embrace all
> the ramifications of an economy, as far as these are measurable ... The transition
> from national accounts to social accounts involves ... the replacement of a simple
> structure by a more elaborate one. (p. 110)

In the economic literature, the shift from NIAs to SAMs, and the desire to
examine all of the 'ramifications' in an economy, involved the resurgence of
interest in issues involving micro or structural analysis such as the extent and
incidence of poverty, income distribution and industrial structural change. A
SAM provides a vehicle for this research in that it reconciles micro accounts
with macro accounts to provide a framework to examine not just the interplay
of micro elements in the economy, but also the impact of micro shocks on
structural change, income distribution, and so on.

In the environmental accounting literature, the reasons for the use of the
SAM framework have tended to mirror the reasons for its inception, though
most of the current work involving SAMs and the environment has tended to
focus on the role of the SAM in providing a link between environmental
accounting and general equilibrium modeling. Bojo et al. (1990), Dasgupta and
Mäler (1991), Mäler (1991) and Weale (1992) use the SAM framework to examine the general equilibrium consequences of different environmental
accounting approaches. Bojo et al. use the SAM framework to illustrate the
types of modifications which should be made to the accounting system to better
reflect defensive expenditures, damage to individuals from environmental deg-

radation, and the depreciation of natural stocks. Mäler develops a Net Welfare Measure, and then uses the SAM framework to illustrate how environmental resources should be included in national accounting systems, and how the conventional NNP measure should be adjusted to reflect sustainable income. Weale develops an environmental SAM for Indonesia (where the SAM is taken from Khan and Thorbecke (1988) and the environmental linkages are taken from Repetto et al. (1989)) to examine accounting techniques used to measure the depletion of natural resources and the cost of repairing environmental damage. Through the development of the environmental Indonesian SAM, Weale also describes the role that the SAM framework can play in linking environmental national accounts to an environmental/economic model. The system of statistics he presents with his SAM is consistent with the structure of the SNA, and can be consolidated to the tables in the SEEA described by Bartelmus et al. (1991). The framework he develops in his SAM is also consistent with the modeling needs of environmental economists. In Weale's SAM he identifies three types of environmental/economic linkages: land degradation, deforestation and depletion of oil reserves, and he is able to derive a set of environmental multipliers for these three resource issues. Weale is able to demonstrate that the modeling of environmental effects is possible with only a slight adjustment of a 'typical' SAM.

Resosudarmo and Thorbecke (1995) develop a SAM of Indonesia that incorporates the linkages between economic production, air pollution and health costs. Their analysis utilizes the strengths of the SAM in differentiating between socio-economic groups, and they examine the impact of environmental management on household incomes for different socio-economic classes. Unfortunately the linkage between the economy, air pollution and income is not complete in that morbidity is not linked back to employment and income.

In the work of Bergman (1991), the SAM framework (in this instance, a computable general equilibrium model) is used to examine the general equilibrium effects of emission control programs of $SO_x$, $NO_x$ and $CO_2$ on input and output prices and the allocation of resources in the Swedish economy. Bergman (1991) develops a computable general equilibrium (CGE) model that includes markets for both emission permits and technologies for emission control, and examines the general equilibrium effects of emission reduction policies. His objective is to highlight the necessity of using general equilibrium analysis as opposed to partial equilibrium analysis, as is standard practice, to examine emission controls for major pollutants. His findings suggest that

> ... under certain conditions environmental policy measures have general equilibrium effects. Unless these general equilibrium effects are taken into account, policy analyses might give a distorted picture of a set of proposed environmental policies. The reported results also suggest that the implementation of reasonably large computable general equilibrium models is a feasible undertaking, and that models of this type can be useful as a device for ex ante policy evaluation. (Bergman, 1991, p. 60)

Aside from the work by Resosudarmo and Thorbecke (1995), the use of the SAM for environmental accounting and modeling has not extended to distributional or structural change issues. And yet, the very nature of environmental externalities, and the corresponding distortions that they create in the economy, calls for an examination of the welfare-distribution impacts. Through the creation of an environmental externality SAM, we will attempt to provide a framework for examining the welfare distribution consequences of environmental externalities.

## 6   THE EXTERNALITY SAM

Each environmental externality gives rise to a set of interconnected flows that can be portrayed in an 'externality SAM'. The measured flows in market economies capture only the rectangles circumscribed by the observed market prices and the observed quantities sold. But, in the presence of environmental externalities, the observed prices and quantities are very poor indications of the real values and costs of the commodities exchanged in the market. The externality SAM indicates the changes in the values of the flows arising from specific environmental externalities.

Production forms the core of economic activities and generates direct environmental consequences that trickle through from one sector to another, through the purchase of intermediate inputs. Production also generates value-added, which is distributed to economic institutions as income. As a result, households, enterprises, government and the rest of the world all experience externalities from the environmental effects generated by production. In addition, institutions themselves generate direct environmental effects, which impact on each other as well as on production (e.g. air pollution from cars may reduce agricultural yields). Institutions also purchase the net output of production. These purchases are another path through which externalities from production are transmitted. They also offer a mechanism through which changes in consumption patterns can affect the structure of output and, hence, the degree of pollution.

The purpose of the externality SAM is to provide a relief map of the distribution of environmental distortions in the economy. The externality SAM separates those flows in the economy which are generated by environmental externalities from other flows in the economy, and in this way provides a sharp evaluation of those who benefit from the environmental distortion and those who are made worse off because of the distortion. The externality SAM provides a mapping of the negative or positive increments to producer or consumer welfare in the economy. The externality SAMs also indicate the taxes and lump sum transfers that must be added to the market price-based SAM economy to induce the same behavior and income for all institutions and sectors as would have obtained in the absence of the externality under the existing non-market regulations.

The general equilibrium nature of the SAM provides a more accurate picture of who benefits and who loses from pollution (once higher round interactions are evaluated) than a partial equilibrium approach. As a result, the SAM framework enables one to trace through the ultimate incidence of any particular type of economic intervention to reduce pollution. It can therefore also be used to anticipate where the strongest political resistance to environmental legislation or environmental taxes is going to come from and where the strongest support for such measures can be mobilized.

The methods used to derive the externality SAMs are analogous to those discussed in Adelman et al. (1991). We illustrate these procedures by reference to rents and externalities arising from water pollution in agriculture. The derivation of externality SAMs due to air pollution and land degradation and for other sectors of the economy is conceptually similar. The actual estimation of the environmental distortions is done in two steps. First, we estimate the price equivalents of the environmental distortions in each sector of the economy. Second, we use information contained in a SAM plus information on elasticities to evaluate the direct and indirect rents received by each activity and agent and to distribute these rents to factors, enterprises, households and government; and between current consumption, investment and the public deficit.

## Ecological Prices in an Accounting Matrix

The estimation of ecological or environmental prices is an important and controversial element in green accounting. The ultimate meshing of environmental and economic accounting depends on generating the cost of the externality or of the 'corrected' versus the 'uncorrected' price of the environmental good or service.

Much of the literature on environmental pricing and economic accounting is concerned with computing environmental prices that are associated with an optimal growth path. By contrast, the corrected prices computed here do not represent optimal prices, in the sense that they are not derived from an economy on an optimal growth path. The prices computed here do not represent sustainable prices any more than do market-generated prices. Rather, these prices are an economic valuation of environmental services in cases where these services are not traded in the market.

The economic literature on environmental valuation is growing at a great pace and a methodology for estimating the value of non-marketed environmental services is quickly being established (see Navrud (1994) for a comprehensive review). Resource and environmental economists have conducted studies to estimate the value of a wide range of environmental services; from the value of fishable, swimable and boatable water, to the value of clean air in residential areas; from the value of biodiversity, to the value of the western spotted owl; and from the value to residents of Nebraska of clean water in Alaska, to the value today of a forest tomorrow. The array of methodologies that economists use to derive money value amounts includes the contingent valuation, travel cost, hedonic pricing and cost-of-illness methods. For the construction of the externality SAM, we rely on the fairly extensive research that has been conducted in California on environmental valuation. To convey the extent of work done in this area, one bibliography on the effects of air pollution and acid rain on agriculture (Barse et al., 1985) includes 21 entries concerning the economic effects on crop producers and consumers.

The manner in which the cost of the externality is estimated has important philosophical and methodological implications for incorporating environmental externalities into an accounting system. Costs that are calculated from market transactions (such as the tabulation of defensive expenditures, travel cost method, cost-of-illness method and the hedonic price method) are fundamentally different from those calculated using non-market valuation techniques (such as the contingent valuation method and any method where preferences are not translated into actual money transactions). Costs that are calculated from actual market transactions are firmly linked to the rest of the economy and can have reverberations on the rest of the system. The SAM, or any accounting system, registers these costs in the current account as changes in the allocation of expenditure and production. Damage estimates of this sort could also be forwarded for payment by future economies.

By contrast, though non-market money measures of the value of environmental amenities might accurately translate environmentally derived welfare into money terms for comparison with other money measures, these non-market estimates impact differently on the rest of the economy because, though incurred, they are not paid. Estimates that rely on non-market measures of externality costs provide an indication of welfare loss that is not translated into economic activity. The benefits of the externality resonate throughout the economic accounts, but the effects of these unpaid costs are not measurably linked to the economy. Nevertheless, these estimates mirror a decline in welfare. In the analysis presented here, we have chosen to allocate damages of this sort to the future economy, and discussion of their incorporation into the economic accounts follows the development of the current account schematic SAM.

### The Current Account Water Externality SAM

In this section, we locate the rents that arise from water pollution on a schematic externality SAM. Conceptually, each entry in the schematic SAM reflects the changes in producer and purchaser surpluses for each sector or agent that generates water pollution or uses water (Table 4.1).

We begin unraveling the effects of environmental distortions on the economy by calculating the cost of the environmental externality. The cost of the environmental externality is used to derive the change in consumer and producer surplus that accrues to the victims of the externality. This calculation is pivotal, in that the change in the victims' producer and consumer surplus serves to determine the benefit of the externality that accrues to the polluting industry. The change in producer and consumer surplus that accrues to the downstream industries and consumers represents the amount of the subsidy that is paid to the polluting industry. This subsidy to the polluting firm has an impact throughout the economy in that it redirects production and consumption. In this analysis, 'environmental prices' are derived by calculating the pre-subsidy equilibrium prices.

The first step in calculating the externality SAM is to identify the defensive or other compensatory expenditure flows in the original SAM, that is, the amount that is paid by the victims of the externality to those industries or services that provide some defense or alternative against the externality. For each sector and each industry, it is then necessary to establish the change in producer and consumer surplus for the sufferers of the externality. The next step is to determine the negative change in consumer and producer surplus that results from the externality but is not registered in the current accounts (i.e. changes measured by non-market methods). The total negative change in surplus represents the benefit to the polluting industry; it is the subsidy that is enjoyed by the polluting industry.

Table 4.1 illustrates the types of flows that are generated by the externality. In the discussion that follows, the change in flows that arise from the externality is examined for each block of the schematic SAM.

### Block A

The first effect registered in Block A is that the polluting industry enjoys lower input prices due to the 'environmental subsidy'. The environmental subsidy shifts the producer's marginal cost curve, resulting in a new equilibrium price and quantity (where the exact change in price, quantity and revenue depends on the elasticities of supply and demand). In Block A, this increase in production is allocated according to share coefficients to those activities that produce an input for the polluting industry.

The second effect registered in Block A is that intermediate demand enjoys lower cost inputs from the freely polluting industry. The environmental subsidy leads to a reduced selling price for the output of the subsidized industry and this is passed on to both intermediate and final demand. As a result, the marginal cost curve of industries that use cotton as an input shifts downward generating a new equilibrium price, quantity and revenue. Block A allocates the change in revenue among inputs according to the share coefficients.

*Table 4.1   The schematic externality SAM*

| | Activities<br>Agriculture, other industries | Value-Added<br>Labor, capital, depreciation |
|---|---|---|
| **Activities**<br><br>Agriculture<br><br>Other<br>industries | *Block A*<br>Polluting industry and its suppliers increase production as a result of the externality.<br><br>Suppliers of environmental defense expand supply to match increased demand.<br><br>Industries injured by the externality decrease production.<br><br>Intermediate demand enjoys (suffers) lower (higher) priced inputs.<br><br>Decrease in productivity due to pollution. | |
| **Value-Added**<br><br>Labor<br><br>Capital<br><br>Depreciation | *Block B*<br>Change in value-added divided between wages and profits.<br><br>Change in depreciation. | |
| **Institutions**<br>Enterprises<br><br>Households | | *Block D*<br>Changes in returns to capital and returns to labor allocated to households and enterprises. |
| **Exogenous flows**<br><br>Government<br><br>Gross investment<br><br>Rest of world | *Block C*<br>Change in value-added tax revenue and tariff revenue due to externality-induced redistribution of production.<br><br>Change in imported input demand. | *Block E*<br>Change in employer's portion of social security tax revenue due to net change in household income.<br><br>Change in unincorporated profit-tax revenue.<br><br>Change in savings for unincorporated businesses.<br><br>Change in foreign investment in unincorporated businesses. |
| **Row total** | | |

| *Institutions* | *Exogenous Flows* | Column |
|---|---|---|
| Enterprises, households | Government investment | total |

*Block F*

Increase in expenditure on goods and services that experience a decrease in price due to the externality.

Increase in expenditure on environmental defensive goods and services.

Decrease in expenditure on goods and services that experience a rise in price due to the externality.

*Block I*

Change in government expenditure in response to change in relative prices induced by the externality. Increase in government defensive expenditures.

Change in investment due to externality-induced changes in productivity and capital use.

Change in type and quantity of exports in response to relative price changes induced by the externality.

*Block G*

Changes in corporate earnings as a result of the externality distributed to households.

*Block H*

Change in income tax revenue.

Change in incorporated business profit-tax revenue.

Change in foreign investment in incorporated businesses.

Industries that supply goods or services that defend against the externality also enjoy a positive change in surplus. As a result of the externality these industries experience an increase in demand. Block A records the increase in the production of environmentally defensive goods and services as well as the increase in demand (and production) for inputs to environmentally defensive industries.

Block A also records the negative impacts of the externality on the production of 'downstream' industries. Due to the externality, these industries experience an upward shift in their marginal cost curves and a reduction in production. This upward shift in marginal cost arises because of the increase in defensive expenditures. The resultant decrease in production entails a decrease in other inputs. Both the increase in defensive inputs and the decrease in other inputs are registered in Block A.

For producers, the change in water rent directly due to environmental damage is also registered in Block A. The quantity element of this rent consists of the change in productivity due to pollution, if any, applied to the base quantities of resources used; the price equivalent is valued at the non-polluted price.

## Block B

The rents in the activity rows cascade down through the SAM to the value-added accounts. The change in value-added that is induced by the externality is divided between the wage bill and profits. Since the rents recorded in the activity rows imply changes in the 'true' intermediate costs, they affect value-added and its components. To allocate the change in value-added between wages and profits requires a theory of how the labor market operates in each sector. In sectors in which labor has substantial market power, one would assume that workers can protect the purchasing power of their real wages. In these sectors, one must add to the wage rates of each labor skill the increased cost of the re-priced direct and indirect water component of their consumption bundle. In sectors with an elastic supply of labor at a fixed money wage, and a largely non-unionized or weak labor force, such as agriculture, no adjustment to the wage rate is made, though there is an increase in the wage bill due to increased levels of hiring. The change in the wage bill due to water pollution includes both the effect of purchaser surplus and the effect of productivity change. The overall change in rent flows to labor in each sector is the difference between the wage bill with and without water pollution.

The changes in rents that accrue to capital as profits and investment funds are the residual account. The residual must be calculated from the new value-added minus the change in the wage bill, the change in the price of inventories and the change in depreciation. The change in value-added is the change in the rent from intermediates and is the column sum of the rent entries in the activity rows for each sector. The inventory rent is calculated by multiplying the inventory vector of final demand by $(I-A)^{-1}$ inverse, where $A$ is the input–output table of the water externality SAM.

Block B also records the change in capital equipment use and depreciation. The change in depreciation reflects two effects of the externality: first, those industries which use water as an input in the production process incur increased depreciation due to lower-quality water inputs; and second, those industries which enjoy increased (decreased) production due to the externality also incur increased (decreased) depreciation, this time because of higher (lower) use rates for capital.

## Block C

The entries in Block C that accrue to government are the change in taxes. The entries in the activity columns of this row include the change in value-added taxes, computed on the change in value-added that arises as a result of the externality and the change in tariff revenue computed on the change in imported inputs that arises as a result of the externality.

Block C also records the impact of the externality on the importation of inputs from the rest of the world. Imports will experience an increase in demand from those industries that benefit from the externality (the polluting industry, inputs to the polluting industry and pollution-defense industries), and a decrease in demand from those industries that are harmed by the externality (downstream industries and their input industries). The size of the change will depend on the shift in demand due to the externality, and on the elasticities of supply and demand for each imported input.

## Block D

In Block D, we examine institutions as the final repositories of rent. Enterprises absorb the change in returns to capital for incorporated businesses, while households absorb both the change in returns to labor and the change in returns to capital for unincorporated businesses. Block D registers the increase in the return to capital and labor enjoyed by subsidized enterprises, and the decrease in the return to capital and labor suffered by the activities which are harmed by the externality. The change in the return to capital considered here is already net of any change in depreciation or change in the price of inventories.

## Block E

In the government row, Block E records the change in social security tax due to the net change in household income as a result of the externality. It also records the change in profit-tax revenue from unincorporated businesses that results from the externality. In the capital account row, Block E records the change in savings net of depreciation on the part of unincorporated businesses. In the rest of world accounts, Block E records the change in foreign investment in unincorporated businesses. The SAM holds investment proportionate to income.

## Block F

Moving across the activity row, Block F records both the change in surplus due to the fact that final demand enjoys lower cost goods from the pollution industry, and the change in surplus due to the fact that final demand faces higher cost goods from those industries that are negatively affected by the externality. Block F also registers the increased expenditure by households for goods and services that provide some defense against the externality. This increase is matched by a decrease in other consumption goods that is also registered in Block F.

Block F also records the direct health and quality of life changes experienced by households as a result of the externality. Total damages of this sort consist of the price equivalent of the change in utility of the decrease in the quality of water multiplied by the consumption of water in the base, plus the value of change in health and life expectancy due to lower water quality, plus the value of the decrease in quality of life due to water pollution. The health component can be estimated from the increase in health expenditures due to water pollution; the life expectancy component can be evaluated from the present value of the earnings stream due to shorter working life, if any, induced by water pollution. The quality of life component can only be estimated using a non-market valuation method. These values are reflected in a decrease in final demand proportionate to the change in welfare generated by the externality and the income elasticity of each good in the consumption basket.

## Block G

In Block G the change in corporate earnings resulting from the externality is allocated among households (distributed earnings) down the enterprise column.

## Block H

In Block H, the change in corporate earnings resulting from the externality is allocated between the capital account (investment/savings) and the government (business profit tax). For computational purposes, it can be assumed that the marginal rate of investment is the same as the average rate. These changes are recorded in the enterprise column. The rest of the world accounts in the enterprise column record the change in foreign investment in incorporated businesses that results from the externality. In the household column, Block H records the change in income tax paid by households due to changes in the wage bill and distributed earnings. The household column in Block H also records the change in savings by households that results from the externality.

## Block I

The first entries in Block I are the changes in government expenditure that result from externality-induced changes in relative prices. Government expenditure also changes to include an increase in environmentally defensive expenditures as a result of the externality.

The second entries in Block I allocate the change in gross investment among the activity rows, where the change in gross investment is a result of changes in productivity and capital use that result from the externality.

The third entries in Block H record the fact that, just like agents in the domestic accounts, rest of the world purchasers benefit from the externality when purchasing goods or services from the polluting industry, and the reverse when purchasing goods or services from industries that are harmed by the externality.

### Future Damages

The current account externality SAM records both the cost and benefits of environmental externalities in those cases where the damages are realized in the current economy. However, in many instances, the costs of an environmental externality are not borne by the current economy, but are passed on to a future generation. In these cases, the future generation does not enjoy the benefits of the externality but pays the residual damages. Not only do future generations pay a price for current externalities, but also there is often a cumulative or time element involved with environmental degradation so that the future consequences of environmental mismanagement could be more severe than those manifested in the current economy. For example, the siltation of waterways that poses only a minor inconvenience today could lead to a decrease in the fish population and habitat that could severely restrict commercial and recreational fishing activities in the future. Or, the beauty of a natural lake could be destroyed to such an extent that future generations can no longer enjoy it. Or, the health consequences of contaminated groundwater might only become evident after years of water consumption.

Not only does the future economy inherit the cost of environmental externalities, but it also inherits the direction of growth that was established in the previous economy. In the presence of environmental externalities, particularly 'unpaid' externalities, the direction of growth is established on the basis of incomplete environmental prices that provide faulty signals for the direction of growth and development.

The impact of externalities on the future economy could be estimated in a number of ways depending on the type of damage. The type of damages we will consider are environmental defensive expenditures or other damages that trigger a redistribution of economic activity; damages that entail a decline in productivity due to a degraded resource base; and damages that reflect a direct fall in welfare due to the externality. The analyses that we describe for examining the impact of these damages on the future economy can also be used for examining the impact of these damages on the current economy.

Damages that involve defensive expenditure or any damage that results in a direct reallocation of production and consumption in the future economy could be estimated through the construction of a future SAM. In the same way that the current externality SAM traces the distributional changes that arise in the current economy, the future SAM traces the distributional changes in the future economy that result from externalities generated and enjoyed in the current economy. The costs of the externality trickle through the future economy in the same way that they trickle through the current economy except that in the future economy they are not offset by the positive change in welfare that was generated by the current externality. In the future economy, no industries receive an externality 'subsidy', which means that the first set of positive entries in Block A of the schematic SAM do not take place in the future economy (unless the future economy generates its own set of externalities, in which case a whole new set of damages and benefits must be calculated).

In order to trace the impact on the future economy of damages that result from a decrease in productivity due to a degraded resource base, a multiplier matrix is generated from the original SAM. Damages of the sort generated by decreases in productivity are an 'exogenous shock' to the future economy, and though they could be incorporated in a future externality SAM, the SAM multiplier framework is a more expeditious framework for estimating the general equilibrium impacts that this type of damage will have on the future economy.

The multiplier matrix illustrates the relationship between exogenous injections and endogenous income and production levels, and through the construction of the multiplier matrix, it is possible to trace the impact of exogenous change on every endogenous account in the future economy. The construction of the SAM model is easily understood by considering the decomposition of a SAM presented in Table 4.2.

*Table 4.2   Decomposition of a SAM*

|  | Endogenous accounts | Row totals | Exogenous accounts | Row totals | Row totals |
|---|---|---|---|---|---|
|  | *Endogenous 1* |  | *Exogenous 1* |  |  |
| Endogenous accounts | $Y_{11}$ $Y_{12}$ $Y_{13}$<br>$Y_{21}$ $Y_{22}$ $Y_{23}$<br>$Y_{31}$ $Y_{32}$ $Y_{33}$ | $N = BY'$ | $X_{14}$ $X_{15}$<br>$X_{24}$ $X_{25}$<br>$X_{34}$ $X_{35}$ | $X$ | $N + X = Y'$ |
|  | *Endogenous 2* |  | *Exogenous 2* |  |  |
| Exogenous accounts | $Y_{41}$ $Y_{42}$ $Y_{43}$<br>$Y_{51}$ $Y_{52}$ $Y_{53}$ |  | $X_{44}$ $X_{45}$<br>$X_{54}$ $X_{55}$ |  |  |
| Column totals | $X$ |  |  |  |  |

Define $Y$ as the vector of column totals of endogenous accounts (i.e. the column totals of block *Exogenous 1* plus block *Exogenous 2*). Define $N$ as the vector of row totals of block *Endogenous 1* and $X$ as the vector of row totals of block *Exogenous 2*. A basic feature of any SAM is that the row and column sums must balance. This means that:

$$Y' = N + X$$

Noting that $N$ equals $BY$, where $B$ is the matrix of share coefficients for block *Endogenous 1*, this equation can be rewritten as:

$$Y' = BY' + X$$

Solving for $Y$,

$$Y' = (I - B)^{-1} X$$

where $(I-B)^{-1}$ is the SAM multiplier, $M$. Element $M_{ij}$ in $M$ represents the effect on sector (account) $i$ of an increase in exogenous demand for sector (account) $j$. With the multiplier matrix, an exogenous change is traced through to calculate the general equilibrium impact on the incidence and distribution of economic activity.

The third type of damage involves direct changes in welfare that are not translated into economic activity. This type of damage indicates the direct decline in well-being that results from the externality. Damages of this sort include the decrease in enjoyment of natural sites due to pollution (both use and non-use values). The benefits of the externality resonate throughout the economic accounts, but the effects of these unpaid costs are not measurably linked to the economy. Nevertheless, these estimates mirror a decline in welfare, which we reflect with a drop in real future income.

### From Externality SAM to Environmentally Adjusted SAM

Examination of the externality SAM and the results of the future damage analyses gives a picture of the distortions that arise as a result of environmental externalities in the distribution of production, consumption, income and welfare in both the current and future economies. To arrive at an environmentally adjusted portrayal of the current economy in which the distortions caused by the environmental externalities are removed, the current externality SAM is added to the actual SAM. To arrive at an environmentally adjusted SAM that includes natural resource depletion and degradation as they impact future activities, the present value of the results of the future damage analyses are added to the current environmentally adjusted SAM. Together, the environmentally adjusted SAM and the present-value future damage estimates, provide a description of the true costs and benefits of the externality to each sector of the economy.

On the basis of the calculations described above, an NNP index number that more accurately reflects current and future welfare can be calculated. This is done in the next section.

# 7   GREEN ACCOUNTING AND THE EXTERNALITY SAM

At its strongest, the quest for a more accurate economic accounting of the environment has been a quest for economic indicators that more truly measure a society's welfare. This approach is taken by Dasgupta and Mäler (1991), who reaffirm both the need and possibility of generating NNP measures which can be used to evaluate well-being.

> What we are after are present and future well-being and methods of determining how well-being is affected by policy. And it is not an accident that the index which, when properly computed, can be used toward this end is net national product. (p. 106)

We are in sympathy with the desire to interpret NNP as a measure of welfare, and the NNP number that we derive is a more accurate reflection of welfare. Nevertheless, we recognize that in the current calculations of the SNA there are many elements of welfare that are not correctly included, thereby reducing the effectiveness of NNP as a measure of welfare. In our NNP calculations we only correct for distortions caused by the specific environmental distortions under investigation.

The outline presented in Table 4.3 provides a guide to the way NNP is presented in the SAM framework (for a detailed discussion of SAMs and NIAs see Hanson and Robinson, 1991). By definition, GNP equals value-added plus indirect taxes. NNP equals GNP minus depreciation.

Through incorporation of the economic effects of environmental externalities in the current account externality SAM and the current environmentally adjusted (CEA) SAM, it is shown that environmental externalities trigger changes to value-added and depreciation throughout the current economy. These changes result in changes in GNP and NNP. Through calculation of the impact of externality damages on the future economy with the methods described above, the impact of environmental damages on future value-added is estimated. By combining the NNP number calculated with the environmentally adjusted SAM with the discounted future damage estimates, an environmentally adjusted NNP that accounts for future and current externality distortions can be derived.

The approach we have outlined for accounting for environmental externalities is substantially different from most approaches outlined in the literature. Our treatment of the major issues in environmental accounting is clarified in the next section.

*Table 4.3   The schematic NNP SAM*

| | *Activities* Agriculture, other industries | *Value-Added* Labor, capital, depreciation | *Institutions* Enterprises, households | *Exogenous Flows* Government, investment, Rest of world |
|---|---|---|---|---|
| *Activities* Agriculture Other Industries | *Block A* | | *Block F* | *Block I* |
| *Value-Added* Labor Capital Depreciation | *Block B* Value-added Depreciation | | | |
| *Institutions* Households Enterprises | | *Block D* Employee compensation Distributed earnings on capital | *Block G* | |
| *Exogenous flows* Government Investment Rest of world | *Block C* Value-added tax | *Block E* | *Block H* | |
| Total | NNP | National income | | |

## Green Accounting Issues

In broad terms, the debates surrounding the generation of environmentally adjusted national statistics can be organized into three concerns:

1.   Economic accounts that do not incorporate the environment are inadequate for planning and present a distorted picture of economic activity.
2.   Environmentally defensive expenditures are treated inconsistently in standard accounts and often overstate economic performance.
3.   Due to neglect of environmental depletion or degradation, GDP (Gross Domestic Product) and NDP (Net Domestic Product) measures calculated from the standard SNA do not represent sustainable income.

Each of these concerns is examined below.

### Distortion of the economic information system

In the 1968 SNA, natural resources and the environment are not included in balance sheets or assessed by environmental quality indicators. Through its failure to adequately register the economic services rendered by the environment and natural resources, the 1968 system does not fulfill its role as an information system. Specifically, neglecting environmental and natural resources distorts the accounts in two ways. First, these accounts overlook the production of some undesirable outputs (e.g. pollution), and second, they overlook or undervalue a number of environmental inputs to production. Through its distorted or incomplete accounting, it is argued that the 1968 SNA or any similar system cannot serve as a database or information system for policy makers, researchers or economic modelers.

Through the development of the CEA SAM and the future damage analyses, we account for environmental externalities such as pollution and provide a valuation for environmental goods or services that are unpriced. The CEA SAM and the future damage analyses provide a thorough mapping of the impacts of environmental distortions on the incidence and distribution of economic activity in both the current and future economies. The CEA SAM and the future damage analyses provide a picture of economic activity that is undistorted by environmental externalities.

### Defensive expenditures

The 1968 SNA offers a poor indication of a society's efforts to defend against environmental degradation. On the one hand, economic growth that results in pollution, the congestion of parks and the irreversible depletion of natural resources is mirrored by a positive change in GNP, while on the other hand, efforts to preserve a healthy environment and a sustainable natural resource base often result in a negative change in GNP. The perversity of this situation is further complicated by the fact that the 1968 SNA treats certain defensive expenditures (measures to reduce or avoid environmental damage) incurred by industry as intermediate expenditures which are netted out of final value-added, while those defensive expenditures undertaken by households and governments are generally treated as final goods, and are therefore included as productive contributions to national output.

There is much debate in the literature as to whether defensive expenditures should be deducted from GDP in order to provide a better estimate of sustainable income and whether estimates of damages to the environment as a result of economic activity should be accounted for. There is also a certain amount of contention concerning just what type of expenditure qualifies as a 'defensive' expenditure.

On one side of the debate is the argument that the purchase of goods or services for protection against environmental degradation improves well-being, and that in this respect, there is nothing different about defensive expenditures from other expenditures. This point is argued by Bojo et al. (1990), who contend that if defensive expenditures are deducted from final demand, the NNP calculation that results will be absurd because increases in welfare could trigger a fall in NNP. The other side of the debate argues that defensive expenditures are not indications of improvements in human well-being, that they are instead indications of environmental degradation. Beckerman (1972) supports this point and argues that defensive expenditures are 'anti-bads' and represent a drop in real income.

In the development of the environmentally adjusted SAM and the future damage analyses, we take a middle ground between the two sides of the argument presented above. We do not deduct environmental defense expenditures from national income, but we do expose the distortions that result in the economy as a result of externalities and defensive expenditures in order to reveal the direction of economic activity that might have obtained in the absence of these distortions. Exposure of environmental distortions allows for identification of the part of economic activity that reflects defensive expenditures.

## Depreciation

The first step on the road to recognizing the inconsistencies in the SNA with regard to depreciation was to establish, or rather reestablish, the notion of the 'environment as capital'. El Serafy (1992) traces the notion of natural capital back to the classical and early neoclassical economists. In particular, he claims that Alfred Marshall viewed the distinction between land and capital in their capacity as factors of production as rather artificial. Stressing the capital quality of land (which El Serafy equates with Nature in this instance), Marshall (1920) is quoted:

> ... all that lies just below the surface has in it a large element of capital, the produce of man's past labour. Those free gifts of nature, which Ricardo classed as the 'inherent' and 'indestructible' properties of the soil, have been largely modified; partly impoverished and partly enriched by the work of many generations of men. (Marshall, 1920, p.147)

The case put by modern environmentalist and environmental economists is that the decision to husband, maintain or deplete natural resources is strictly analogous to the decision to create, maintain or deplete man-made capital. This being the case, the SNA should record environmental and natural resources as alternative forms of capital, and register the depletion or degradation of these resources, part of which represents the depreciation of natural capital.

The issues of natural capital depreciation and the degradation or depletion of natural resources have generated a lot of debate in the environmental accounting literature, but these issues generate even more debate when taken in tandem with the issue of sustainability. The recognition of nature as capital is an integral part in defining sustainable income. The notion of true, or 'sustainable income' can be traced to Sir John Hicks' definition of income. In fact, on the basis of Hicks' definition, Daly (1989) asserts that the term 'sustainable income' is redundant. Hicks' definition of income is as follows:

> The purpose of income calculation in practical affairs is to give people an indication of the amount that they can consume without impoverishing themselves. Following out this idea, it would mean that we ought to define a man's income as the maximum value that he can consume during a week, and still expect to be as well off at the end of the week as he was at the beginning. Thus, when a person saves, he plans to be

better off in the future; when he lives beyond his income, he plans to be worse off. Remembering that the practical purpose of income is to serve as a guide for prudent conduct, I think it is fairly clear that this is what the central meaning must be. (Hicks, 1939, p. 172)

Clearly, it is argued, any definition of income, including GDP or even NDP as defined by the 1968 SNA, which does not allow for the depreciation of all capital or production assets, including environmental and natural resources, does not give a true indication of how much a nation can consume and 'still expect to be as well off at the end of the week'. Such measures of income are not true measures of income in the Hicksian sense of the term. Hence, the current SNA overstates income because it does not account for the consumption or degradation of natural resources.

Of course, differences exist among experts on how to adjust national accounts to reflect sustainability goals, or even whether conventional GDP measures should be adjusted. Many economists insist that both GDP and NDP in the SNA must be corrected according to the Hicksian definition of income (El Serafy, 1989). Others insist that the core accounts of the SNA and the traditional measures of GDP and NDP must remain intact and that sustainability concerns should be addressed through the computation of new measures of 'sustainable social net national product', 'sustainable income' or environmentally adjusted net domestic product ('EDP') and environmentally adjusted net income ('ENI') (Bartelmus, 1989; Daly, 1989; Pearce, 1989; Harrison, 1989a, 1989b; Stahmer, 1992; Lutz, 1992). The UNEP/World Bank approach to this issue was decided at an expert meeting on environmental accounting and the SNA in November 1988. At this meeting it was decided that it is currently impossible to value, in monetary terms, all of the functions provided by the environment and that 'replacing GDP with a more sustainable measure of income is not yet feasible'. In addition, though the Hicksian definition of income was adopted by an SNA expert group meeting in 1989, GDP will continue to be defined in the revised SNA without adjustment for the degradation of natural capital. Allowance for an environmentally adjusted GNP will be made through a system of satellite accounts.

Whether incorporated directly into the core accounts or included in satellite accounts, the mode of accounting for natural capital depreciation or environmental depletion or degradation must be determined, and a number of different approaches have been adopted. In one approach, the value of the amount of the resource that has been used up is simply deducted from national income and any new resource discoveries are credited to national income (Repetto et al., 1989; Pearce et al., 1989). In another approach, capital gains are included (Eisner, 1985, 1988). In the approach proposed by El Serafy (1989), the value of the extracted natural resources is deducted, but in addition, a permanent component is calculated for the revenue generated by the exploitation of an exhaustible resource, and this permanent component is added back to national income. This permanent component is calculated by multiplying an estimate of the opening value of the stock of the resource by the real interest rate.

In developing the environmentally adjusted SAM and the future damage analyses, we have not attempted to calculate sustainable income, growth, development or NNP. The environmental prices used in the analysis are not derived from an optimal growth path and do not represent optimal prices. Though we include future damages in the current accounts, the inclusion of these costs in current economic calculations does not necessarily make them sustainable.

Our hesitancy to embrace a sustainable interpretation of environmentally adjusted NNP stems from discomfort with the notion that there is a basis for defining 'sustainability'. While a lot has been written about sustainable development, the concept is not well defined. The most appropriate definition would appear to be in welfare terms. Sustainable development would consist of a development process which allows for some non-negative rate of long-term increase in per capita welfare accompanied by some non-negative rate of population growth. But this definition begs many important issues: What rates of welfare growth and population growth should be stipulated? Is the distribution of welfare to be taken as given at the initial distribution or can it be changed to achieve increases in welfare? Are institutions for access to labor markets, education, international trade and resources to be assumed as given? Are changes in the composition of consumption possible? Can there be changes in consumer tastes that allow for less resource-intensive growth paths? What changes in technology are to be taken into account? What role is international trade to play in this process? Clearly the definition of sustainable development does not require the maintenance of the stock of each resource *ad infinitum*. Substitution among resources in the production of individual commodities, substitution among commodities in the composition of output, conservation, changes in the distribution of income, defensive expenditures and international trade can all contribute to save particular types of resources at the national level without lowering the rate of growth of welfare.

For all of these reasons, we consider the environmental NNP measure derived with the CEA SAM and the future damage analyses to be a better representation of economic activity and welfare, but not necessarily of sustainable welfare. In the next section we develop an empirical example and apply the SAM framework to the California cotton sector and water externalities.

## 8   CALIFORNIA COTTON WATER EXTERNALITY SAM

California, one of the largest and most diverse agricultural states in the nation, serves as an ideal database with which to examine issues of agricultural pollution. Agriculture in California is a rich and varied industry. California farmers produce more than 250 crops, and for the past 45 consecutive years, California has led the nation in farm production and farm income. On just 3 percent of U.S. farmland, California farmers produce more than half of the country's fruits, vegetables and nuts, and approximately 10 percent of all U.S. agricultural exports are shipped by California farmers.

The 83,000 farms in California comprise 17.1 million acres of pasture and rangeland, and 10.89 million acres of cropland, which includes 8.5 million acres of irrigated land. California farm real estate (land and buildings) is valued at $60 billion. Total net income for California agriculture exceeded $7 billion in 1990, which corresponds to an average of $82,710 per farming operation, or $228 per acre. In 1992 California farmers sold an estimated $18.1 billion of farm products. California's farm population is less than 1 percent of the state's total population, but it is estimated that California agriculture directly or indirectly contributes $63 billion, more than 9 percent of the gross state product.

Agriculture clearly plays an important role in California, and the role of agriculture in creating environmental externalities and welfare distortions in the California economy is certainly worth investigating. For the presentation of the methodology developed here, we have chosen to focus on California cotton cultivation and its contribution to groundwater and surface water degradation. We chose cotton and water externalities as our example because of the richness of the supporting research and because of the relative importance of the cotton crop. California is the second largest cotton producer in the country, and with a value of $930 million (1994), cotton is the fifth most important crop in California. In addition, all cotton fields in California are irrigated.

In the empirical example presented here, the redistribution of welfare in the economy of California due to water contamination (both surface and groundwater) that is caused by the cotton sector is examined. This example calculates the distortions that arise in the allocation of resources, production, consumption, income and ultimately welfare due to the fact that cotton cultivation does not bear the total cost of water degradation and soil erosion. In the first step, an agriculturally oriented SAM for California is developed. Next, the damages attributable to cotton cultivation because of its degradation of groundwater and surface water are estimated, and the costs and benefits of the cotton water externality are allocated among the sectors and agents in the economy. Third, an externality SAM for groundwater contamination due to cotton cultivation is presented. The difference between the externality SAM and the original SAM is then calculated to arrive at an environmentally adjusted SAM. Multipliers are derived for both the original SAM and the environmental SAM in order to highlight the change in the operation of the two economies.

### The California Agriculture SAM

The SAM for California was constructed from output files supplied by IMPLAN (Impact Analysis for Planning). IMPLAN is a modeling system designed for constructing regional accounts and input–output tables. The 1982 version of IMPLAN produces a SAM summarizing macroeconomic flows, that is, a SAM with a set of single commodity and activity accounts in lieu of an input–output table.[1] To build a complete California SAM with a disaggregated set of production activities, the transactions, regional institutional demands and factor income matrices were grafted on to the summary SAM.

The California SAM is disaggregated into 22 production accounts, 5 institutional accounts, 2 factor income accounts, 2 'rest of the world' accounts and a capital account. There are 9 agricultural activities: livestock, cotton, food grains, feed grains, hay and grass seed, fruits, tree nuts, vegetables and miscellaneous crops. There are 13 non-agricultural production activities: forest products, food processing, non-agricultural industries, oil gas and refining, agricultural chemicals, textiles, wood and paper products, non-agricultural chemicals, rail, trucking, air transport, utilities and services. Production activities pay for factor services to the capital and labor accounts. Institutions comprise low, medium, and high income households, as well as government and enterprise accounts. The domestic trade account records flows of exports, imports and income transfers between California and the rest of the United States. The foreign trade account records these flows between California and foreign countries. The California SAM is presented in Table 4.A.1.

## Groundwater Contamination – Damage Estimates

In recent years, concern over the extent of pollution generated by agriculture, particularly groundwater pollution, has grown rapidly. As observed by Crutchfield (1988), several factors have contributed to this development. First, is the increased use of agricultural chemicals; application rates of fertilizers tripled between 1960 and 1985. This increase is combined with a decrease of point pollution sources due to the construction of municipal and industrial treatment plants. Hence, not just the absolute, but also the relative importance of agricultural non-point pollution has grown. In addition, continuing studies by the Environmental Protection Agency (EPA) and U.S. Department of Agriculture (USDA) have highlighted the extent of groundwater contamination.

The damages due to groundwater contamination are primarily sustained by household consumers of groundwater for drinking purposes. In the terminology developed earlier, they are subsidizing cotton (and all agriculture) by the amount of the 'cost' of the externality. Determining the cost of the externality to household groundwater consumers, or conversely the level of the subsidy that is paid to cotton producers, is a crucial element in the construction of the externality SAM.

A first step in estimating the cost of contaminated groundwater is to estimate the extent of potential groundwater contamination from agricultural chemicals. Nielsen and Lee (1987) conducted a comprehensive nationwide survey of water

pollution due to agriculture under the auspices of USDA. In the Nielsen and
Lee study, information about agricultural chemicals is combined with data on
pesticide and fertilizer use by region and by crop, and incorporated into the
DRASTIC model, which rates an area's relative vulnerability to groundwater
contamination based on the area's hydro-geologic characteristics.[2] Combining
the index of vulnerability from the DRASTIC model with information on
population use of groundwater for drinking purposes yields estimates of the
percentage of the population at risk from agricultural groundwater contamination. For California, Nielsen and Lee find that 4,736,915 people with private
wells are at risk from agricultural groundwater contamination and that 4,115
people who use public water systems that depend on groundwater are at risk
from groundwater contamination.

For the purposes of this study, we need to further specify the at-risk population to indicate those at risk from contamination due to cotton cultivation. The
first step of that task is undertaken by Crutchfield et al. (1991) in their survey
of cotton agricultural chemical use and farming practices in 1989. In this study,
Crutchfield et al. use a DRASTIC-type model to derive estimates of groundwater vulnerability due to cotton cultivation. Their results for California are
presented in Tables 4.4 and 4.5.

Combining the estimates of groundwater vulnerability due to cotton with
those on the at-risk population generated by Neilsen and Lee (1987) produces a
rough estimate of the population that is at risk from groundwater contamination
due to cotton cultivation. It is estimated that 44,200 households in California
are at risk from groundwater contamination due to cotton cultivation.

*Table 4.4    Groundwater vulnerability potential: pesticide leaching*

|  | Potential 1 | Potential 2 | Potential 3 | Potential 4 | Unknown |
|---|---|---|---|---|---|
| 1,000 acres | 15 | 36 | 66 | 177 | 756 |
| Percentage | 1 | 3 | 6 | 17 | 72 |

*Note:*
Potential 1 and Potential 4 signify the most vulnerable and least vulnerable classifications respectively. The 'Unknown' category accounts for uses of agricultural chemicals that were not included
in the assessment procedure.

*Source*: Crutchfield et al., (1991).

*Table 4.5    Groundwater vulnerability potential: nitrate leaching*

|  | High vulnerability | Medium vulnerability | Low vulnerability |
|---|---|---|---|
| 1,000 acres | 792 | 257 | 0 |
| Percentage | 75 | 24 | 0 |

*Source*: Crutchfield et al. (1991).

Identification of the population at risk, and the activities that contribute to creating the risk, still leaves the difficult task of assessing exactly what the risk is and, even more difficult, of assessing the cost of the risk. In the absence of this type of information, economists have turned to a number of other techniques to derive estimates of the cost of groundwater contamination. Raucher (1986) takes a damages-avoided approach to analyze the cost and benefits of landfill containment. Nielsen and Lee (1987) propose using the cost of household remedial options (such as filters and other water treatment systems) as an estimate of damages. In order to go beyond use-value estimates, and to evaluate option or existence value, Carson et al. (1991) developed a contingent valuation study to estimate the value of protecting groundwater resources from possible contamination even when they are not needed for drinking water. For our analysis, we will remain within the realm of use-values, more because of data constraints than because of philosophical stance, and will use the estimates of filtration cost generated by Neilsen and Lee (1987).

In order to generate the total and per household costs of cotton chemical contamination of groundwater, we start with an average filtration installation cost estimate of $200 which we depreciate over five years to yield a yearly cost of $40. This amount is added to the yearly maintenance estimate of $200, bringing total yearly filtration cost to $240 per household. Adding an average household's yearly expenditure on water, which is $243, to the costs of filtration yields a yearly household water bill of $483. This means that a household that is at risk from groundwater contamination would need to pay almost double that paid by a risk-free household in order to assure itself of uncontaminated water. The per gallon water price for these households jumps from $1 per 570 gallons to $1.98 per 570 gallons. Assuming a price elasticity of water of $-0.4$ (Schmidt and Plaut, 1993), the change in consumer surplus per year for each at-risk household is estimated at $-$237. The total change in the welfare of all household consumers of groundwater due to the groundwater externality generated by cotton cultivation is $-$10,475,400 (1980 dollars). Expressed in 1982 dollars, the total cost of groundwater damage due to California cotton cultivation is $-$12,267,913.

The total groundwater cost estimate represents the subsidy that California cotton receives from households due to the fact that cotton producers do not assume the full cost of groundwater damages resulting from cotton cultivation. However, in the current account SAM, this externality benefit or subsidy is not 'funded'. The majority of groundwater consumers have not modified their behavior in response to the potential health danger posed by contaminated groundwater. The available data suggest that most groundwater consumers have not installed filters, experienced more sick-days or incurred higher medical bills. Though the cost of the cotton externality does not manifest itself in the current accounts, the quality of the nation's groundwater reserves is being degraded. The current economy is passing the potential cost of groundwater contamination to some future date. In the externality SAM, the benefits of the cotton externality are allocated among the various agents in the current economy, but the costs are allocated to future households.

## Surface Water Contamination and California Cotton – Damage Estimates

Surface water contamination from agriculture arises through soil erosion and pesticide and chemical runoff. Downstream activities such as fishing, recreation, utilities, industries and navigation all suffer damages and increased operating costs due to soil erosion and agricultural chemicals in surface water. In addition, the erosion caused by cultivation can compromise the long-term productive capacity of the land. The on-site and off-site damages caused by soil erosion and runoff from California cotton cultivation are examined below.

### On-site damages
The agricultural productive capacity of the land is weakened by soil erosion from cultivation. As a result of this erosion, soil fertility and crop yields decline. According to Strohbehn and Alt (1987), if present levels of erosion continue for the next 100 years, the decline in crop yields could translate into average annual losses of over $1 billion (this number includes annual fertilizer losses). On the national level, it is estimated that cotton yields would fall by 4.5 percent over the next 100 years. Extrapolating from the national estimates supplied by Strohbehn and Alt (1987), we estimate that the annual yield loss to California cotton due to soil erosion is approximately $549,400 (1982 dollars).

### Off-site damages
For the estimates for the off-site monetary damages imposed by erosion from agricultural land we use those reported in the appendix of Strohbehn (1986) and in Ribaudo (1987). The major source for these estimates is a comprehensive report on off-farm damages from soil erosion compiled by Edwin Clark and his colleagues for the Conservation Foundation (Clark et al., 1985). In this report, Clark extrapolates from available data sources to arrive at estimates of the monetary value of erosion damage to six primary in-stream activities and seven primary off-stream activities. Ribaudo (1987) builds on the best estimates reported by Clark to arrive at a best estimate of annual off-site damage from agricultural soil erosion. His estimate of $3 billion per year (1983 dollars) is almost three times larger than Clark's estimate of $1.3 billion per year (1980 dollars). Adjusting for inflation still leaves a difference of more than 1 billion dollars between the two estimates.

The discrepancy between these two estimates makes clear an observation that both sets of authors freely acknowledge. The nature of the available data, which rely both on extrapolation from small geographic areas to national levels and on extrapolations based on uncertain assumptions about physical relationships and resource valuations, means that researchers can only hope to produce very approximate estimates. In addition, as observed by Clark, some potentially significant impacts of soil erosion, both positive and negative, have been excluded from these estimates meaning that the full costs of agricultural soil erosion could differ substantially. The estimates reported by Ribaudo and by Clark are subject to a wide margin of error. Nevertheless, despite the shortcomings of the damage estimates currently available, these are the best estimates and represent an enormous outlay of time and effort. These damage estimates also represent a significant improvement over the common practice of setting the cost of environmental externalities at zero.

For the analysis here, we use the estimates reported in Strohbehn (1986). Table 4.6 presents the estimates of the total damage from soil erosion by activity as reported by Strohbehn. To arrive at a national estimate of damage due to agricultural erosion, Strohbehn (1986) estimates that erosion damage due to agriculture accounts for approximately half of all erosion damage, or $3.5 billion per year (1983 dollars).

The next step is to determine what percentage of California agricultural damages can be attributed to erosion from cotton cultivation. Cotton cultivation accounts for 3.68 percent of total California cultivation, or 1,105 thousand acres, but not all of this acreage is particularly susceptible to erosion. The first step in estimating the contribution of cotton to erosion damage expense in Cali-

*Table 4.6   National off-site damage from all soil erosion by type of damage (in millions of 1983 dollars)*

| Activity | Erosion damage | |
|---|---|---|
| | Total (in millions) | Percentage |
| Freshwater recreation | 1,889 | 27.0 |
| Marine recreation | 544 | 7.6 |
| Commercial freshwater fishing | 55 | 0.8 |
| Commercial marine fishing | 353 | 4.9 |
| Water storage | 1,097 | 15.1 |
| Navigation | 680 | 9.5 |
| Flooding | 887 | 12.4 |
| Drainage ditches | 214 | 3.4 |
| Irrigation ditches | 107 | 1.5 |
| Irrigated agriculture (salinity) | 28 | 0.4 |
| Municipal water treatment | 121 | 1.7 |
| Municipal and industrial users | 1,086 | 15.0 |
| Steam electric power plants | 54 | 0.7 |
| Total | 7,115 | 100.0 |

*Source:* Strohbehn (1986).

fornia is to examine the physical vulnerability of California cotton acreage to erosion. Crutchfield et al. (1991) use a model developed by Ribaudo (1989) to estimate soil erosion and sediment delivery to surface water for cotton cropland. Of the 14 states surveyed by Crutchfield et al., California had the lowest erosion rates due to cotton cultivation. Table 4.7 presents California cotton soil erosion totals and regional averages.

*Table 4.7    Estimated soil erosion and sediment delivery to surface waters from cotton cropland*

| State/region | Erosion rate (Tons/acre/year) | Total gross erosion (Tons) | Total sediment delivered (Tons) |
|---|---|---|---|
| California | 0.4 | 448 | 205 |
| Delta | 10.1 | 30,030 | 16,793 |
| Southeast | 8.3 | 7,037 | 3,323 |
| Southern Plains | 3.2 | 16,046 | 7,761 |
| West | 0.8 | 1,062 | 483 |

*Source:* Crutchfield et al. (1991).

Because off-site damage is due to both the amount of sediment in the water and the amount of agricultural pollutants, such as pesticides, that find their way into surface water, the information on pure erosion rates must be augmented with information on the potential of chemicals used in cotton cultivation to end up in surface water. Building on a screening procedure for calculating the delivery of pesticides to surface water, Crutchfield et al. (1991) categorize cotton cropland according to its potential for pesticide losses. Potential 1 indicates cropland that is most vulnerable to pesticide losses, while potential 3 indicates cropland that has little or no likelihood of pesticide loss. The California estimates from the Crutchfield et al. report are presented in Table 4.8.

The information presented in Table 4.8 seems to indicate that California cotton cultivation is not a major source of erosion or of surface water pollution. We estimate that less than half (40 percent) of California cotton acreage contributes to surface water erosion damage costs. We estimate that 4.47 percent, or approximately $1.5 million, of California erosion damages due to agriculture are attributable to cotton cultivation. Table 4.9 presents our estimates of damage by activity. Because the California SAM is in 1982 dollars, the dollar amounts in Table 4.9 have been converted from 1983 dollars to 1982 dollars using the Consumer Price Index.

In order to trace the flow of damage expenses in the California SAM, those activities that sustain damage were grouped into categories that correspond to the sectors included in the California SAM. Second, the exact nature of the damage sustained by each sector was examined in order to allocate correctly the increased expenditure in the SAM. For example, the raw data gave estimates on water-treatment costs. We determined that the sector in the SAM that

*Table 4.8   Surface water vulnerability potential for California cotton acreage*

|  | Pesticides attached to sediment | Pesticides dissolved in runoff |
|---|---|---|
| Potential 1 |  |  |
| Cotton acres (thousands) | 183 | 139 |
| Cotton acres (percent) | 17 | 13 |
| Potential 2 |  |  |
| Cotton acres (thousands) | 100 | 140 |
| Cotton acres (percent) | 10 | 13 |
| Potential 3 |  |  |
| Cotton acres (thousands) | 25 | 49 |
| Cotton acres (percent) | 2 | 5 |
| Unknown |  |  |
| Cotton acres (thousands) | 742 | 722 |
| Cotton acres (percent) | 71 | 69 |

*Source*: Crutchfield et al. (1991).

*Table 4.9   Off-site damage from California cotton soil erosion by type of damage ($1982)*

| Activity | Erosion damage | |
|---|---|---|
|  | Total | Percentage |
| Freshwater recreation | 392,400 | 27.0 |
| Marine recreation | 110,500 | 7.6 |
| Commercial freshwater fishing | 11,200 | 0.8 |
| Commercial marine fishing | 71,200 | 4.9 |
| Water storage | 263,500 | 18.1 |
| Navigation | 138,100 | 9.5 |
| Flooding | 180,200 | 12.4 |
| Drainage ditches | 49,400 | 3.4 |
| Irrigation ditches | 21,800 | 1.5 |
| Irrigated agriculture (salinity) | 5,800 | 0.4 |
| Municipal water treatment | 24,700 | 1.7 |
| Municipal and industrial users | 174,400 | 12.0 |
| Steam electric power plants | 10,200 | 0.7 |
| Total | 1,453,400 | 100.0 |

sustains this type of damage is utilities. The raw data described the process involved in water treatment (chemical treatment) as well as the inputs to the process (cleaning agents, materials and labor). We used this information to allocate the damage payments to non-agricultural chemicals, non-agricultural industry and labor. The precise allocation of damage expenses for each sector is described below.

In determining the allocation of expenditure, we often needed to develop rough estimates because data sources were not always explicit about expenditure. In particular, we needed to develop rules of thumb in allocating increased capital expenses. In cases where damage expenditure included increased capital costs, we allocated part of the increase to capital depreciation in order to account for increased wear and tear of existing equipment and the remainder to investment in new equipment. Determining the breakdown between increased depreciation and investment depends on the amount of excess capacity in the sector under investigation. We do not have this information and therefore relied on a best-guess rule; in each case we allocated 25 percent of the increase in capital cost to depreciation and 75 percent to new investment. The type of damage payments by sector are described below.

**Utilities – $298,400**

*Water treatment costs – $24,700*   Agricultural soil erosion deposits sediment and other contaminants in water bodies and reservoirs that supply drinking water. The increase in water-treatment costs corresponds to the costs of removing suspended solids and other contaminants from municipal water supplies. In the SAM, we allocated $2,470 (10 percent) to non-agricultural chemicals for the purchase of cleaning agents; $7,410 (30 percent) to non-agricultural industry for the purchase of other materials; and $14,820 (60 percent) to labor.

*Water storage costs – $263,500*   The increase in water storage costs corresponds to the cost of dredging existing reservoirs or constructing new or extra capacity reservoirs to compensate for the loss in capacity due to soil erosion. In the SAM, $184,450 (70 percent) of the increased cost was allocated to increased capital expense; $26,350 (10 percent) to non-agricultural industry; and $52,700 (20 percent) to labor. Capital expenses were allocated between depreciation $47,430 (25 percent) and investment in new machines $137,020 (75 percent).

*Steam electric power plants – $10,200*   For steam power plants and other water cooling facilities, soil erosion increases the amount of sediment and algae in the water thus decreasing the efficiency of the plant. Removal of algae from condensers requires increased purchase of chemicals for chlorination treatments and increased labor costs. In the SAM, $4,080 (40 percent) was allocated to non-agricultural chemicals and $6,120 (60 percent) to labor.

**Government Services – $246,966**

*Navigation – $138,100*   Damage to navigation consists of the increased dredging costs that must be sustained in order to keep channels and harbors clear of erosion-caused siltation. The Army Corps of Engineers performs approximately half of the dredging activities while state and local authorities perform the other half. In the SAM we allocated these increased costs to labor $96,670 (70 percent) and equipment $41,430 (30 percent). Equipment costs were distributed between depreciation $10,358 (25 percent) and investment $31,072 (75 percent).

*Flooding – $59,466*   This amount represents damages to government property and structures and government clean-up costs incurred as a result of flood sedimentation and increased flood heights due to stream aggradation. This amount is the result of a rough division of the total flood damage amount presented by Strohbehn (1986) between government, households, agriculture and non-agricultural industries. In the SAM, we allocated the flood damages incurred by government services between capital expenses $14,866 (25 percent) and labor $44,600 (75 percent). Capital expenses were distributed between depreciation $3,716 (25 percent) and investment $11,150 (75 percent).

*Drainage ditches – $49,400*   Some soil eroded from agricultural fields is deposited in drainage ditches where it can cause localized flooding. To prevent this, state and local highway departments remove the sediment from drainage ditches. In the SAM we allocated the increase between labor $34,580 (70 percent) and capital $14,820 (30 percent). Capital expenses were distributed between depreciation $3,705 (25 percent) and investment $11,115 (75 percent).

**Agriculture – $51,026**

*Flooding – $23,426*   This damage amount represents the long-term loss of productivity associated with sedimentation due to flooding of relatively fertile agricultural land. This amount is lost *potential* production.

*Irrigation ditches – $21,800*   Soil erosion clogs irrigation canals and substantially increases costs for sediment removal and weed control in irrigation canals. In the SAM we allocated half of the increased cost, or $10,900, to labor and the other half to non-agricultural industry for the purchase of materials.

*Salinization – $5,800*   Salt, which enters irrigation water through irrigation return flows or through erosion of saline soils, can reduce crop yields. These damages are also a measure of potential forgone production.

## Households – $111,612

*Flooding – $54,060*  This amount represents the damages to household property and structures directly due to sedimentation and increased flood heights due to stream aggradation. In the SAM, 20 percent or $10,812 of this amount was allocated to non-agricultural industry for the direct purchase of materials and new structures; and 80 percent or $43,248 was allocated to construction and other services. It should be noted that household labor is not accounted for in most accounting systems.

*Municipal and industrial users – $57,552*  Even after water is treated for suspended sediment and harmful contaminants, dissolved minerals, salts and other materials can still reduce the efficiency and durability of water-using equipment in industries and homes. The amount included here represents the estimated annual costs to households of demineralizing water and repairing or replacing scaled or corroded machinery. In the SAM, we allocated $11,510 (20 percent) to non-agricultural chemicals; $17,266 (30 percent) to non-agricultural industry; and $28,776 (50 percent) to services for repairs and replacements.

## Services – $502,900

*Freshwater recreation – $392,400 and marine recreation – $110,500*  Soil erosion damages water recreation industries through the destruction of fish habitat, siltation of recreation facilities and eutrophication of waterways. The basis for the national estimates of damages sustained by the water recreation sector used by Clark et al. (1985) is a number of site-specific studies conducted by different researchers. The environmental amenities that contribute to the value of a recreation site usually do not have market prices, and efforts to generate money values must depend on techniques such as contingent valuation, hedonic pricing or the travel cost methods. These estimates of damages to recreation depend to a large extent on non-market valuation of fishable, boatable and swimable water. Though it is difficult to determine exactly what percentage of the final estimate measures 'lost enjoyment', we hazard that a large portion, say 60 percent ($301,740) of the estimated damages to recreation depends on non-market valuation of enjoyment while another 20 percent ($100,580) depends on non-market valuations of forgone income. Probably only a very small percentage of the damages corresponds to expenditures that the industry has actually incurred in order to compensate for agricultural soil erosion. For the SAM we allocated $100,580 (20 percent) to services for the construction of improved recreation facilities.

## Non-Agricultural Industry – $242,496

*Municipal and industrial users – $116,848*    Even after water is treated for suspended sediment and harmful contaminants, dissolved minerals, salts and other materials can still reduce the efficient operation and durability of water-using equipment in industries and homes. The amount included here represents the estimated annual costs to industry of demineralizing water and repairing or replacing scaled or corroded machinery. In the SAM we allocated $23,370 (20 percent) to non-agricultural chemicals; $35,054 (30 percent) to non-agricultural industry; $23,370 (20 percent) to labor; and $35,054 (30 percent) to services for professional repairs and replacements.

*Commercial freshwater fishing – $11,200 and commercial marine fishing – $71,200*    The damage assessment method used to estimate the cost to marine fishing from soil erosion is based on a model of biological productivity functions to estimate the impact on productivity of changes in water quality (Bell and Canterbery, 1975). These predictions are then combined with an economic model of supply and demand to determine the economic losses due to productivity changes. Freeman (1982) extrapolated from Bell and Canterbery's (1975) estimates to derive freshwater fishing damages. Strohbehn (1986) uses the relationship between the damages to recreation fishing (freshwater) from agricultural soil erosion as reported by Clark et al. (1985) to determine the percentage of marine and freshwater commercial productivity losses that can be attributed to agricultural soil erosion. The amount of damage attributed to marine and freshwater commercial fishing does not represent costs that these industries actually incurred, but forgone potential output.

*Flooding – $43,248*    This amount represents the damages to industrial property and structures directly attributable to sedimentation and increased flood heights due to stream aggradation. In the SAM, 80 percent or $34,598 of this amount was allocated to services for construction and repair, while 20 percent or $8,650 of the damage amount was allocated to labor.

## The Cotton Water Externality SAM

The first step in creating the cotton water externality SAM is to allocate the benefits of the externality to the cotton industry and to cotton consumers. In this example, cotton enjoys a subsidy of $14,270,713. This subsidy includes both potential unpaid damage amounts and damage amounts that have been paid in the current year. It represents the difference between the private cost and the public (current and future) cost of the externality. Because of this difference, the marginal cost curve of the cotton industry is lower than it should be, the equilibrium price of cotton is lower and the equilibrium quantity greater.

We rely on supporting studies to estimate the change in cotton price and quantity that results from the externality and the shift in cotton's marginal cost curve. Lichtenberg et al. (1988) estimate that a 1 percent increase in the cost of producing cotton in California reduces cotton production by 0.36 percent. Howitt (1991) estimates that a 1 percent increase in production in California would lead to a decrease in farm price of 0.154 percent. Applying these two estimates to the environmental subsidy received by cotton in this example indicates an increase in cotton revenue of approximately $4.5 million. The increase in production results in an increase in input use in cotton production that is allocated down the cotton column according to input shares. The increase input use by cotton cultivation translates into increased demand for inputs. These increases are allocated by shares down all cotton direct and indirect input columns.

Cotton consumers also enjoy a benefit from the externality in the form of lower cotton prices; this fact is mirrored in row 2 of Table 4.A.2, the externality SAM, which records the increase in cotton expenditure across demand. For final demand, an increase in cotton expenditure that was not matched by an increase in income or revenue was set against a decrease in other expenditure to meet budget restrictions.

Industries that supply defensive goods or services to the victims of the externality also realize an increase in demand because of the externality. This increase is allocated by shares among the inputs to the industry, and then again among the inputs to the inputs of the industry.

Industries that are victims of the externality, and must pay to offset the damage caused by the externality, experience an upward shift in their marginal cost curve. This shift translates into a higher equilibrium price and a lower equilibrium quantity than would have obtained without the externality. The relative shifts in price and quantity, and the resulting increase or decrease in revenue, depend on the elasticities of supply and demand for the industries and services in question. In the example examined here, only utilities whose demand is inelastic experience an increase in revenue as a result of the increase in marginal cost. In the externality SAM, the fall in revenue and production for the victimized industries is allocated among the inputs to each industry according to the input coefficients for the industry. The fall in expenditure (or increase in the case of utilities) on the externality-ridden good or service that results from the increase in price is allocated proportionately among the purchasing sectors. It is assumed that households decrease other consumption and savings activities in order to offset the increase in defensive expenditures. This decrease is allocated according to household expenditure coefficients.

To summarize, the steps in creating the externality SAM are delineated below. First, the initial winners and losers from the externality are identified, that is, who generates the externality and who suffers from the externality. In some cases there will be numerous agents that benefit or lose, and an individual agent could simultaneously benefit and lose from an externality.

The second step is to derive the cost of the externality to the losers. Focusing on the cost of the externality to the losers keeps the analysis consistent with analyses involving a compensation principle; the cost of the externality becomes the compensation that winners would have to pay losers in order to justify the continuance of the externality. For this analysis, this externality cost represents the 'subsidy' that is paid by the sufferers of the externality to the generators of the externality.

In the third step, the 'payers' of the subsidy decrease consumption (in the case of households) or production (in the case of activities) in reaction to the subsidy. The distribution of the decrease in consumption depends on the income elasticity of each good and service in the consumption basket. The decrease in production depends on the elasticity of supply and demand for the good in question. The distribution of the decrease in production among the factors and inputs to production depends on the elasticity of demand for these inputs, and on the bargaining position of labor and capital.

In the fourth step, the increase in production in the polluting industry is calculated according to the interaction between the subsidy-augmented supply curve and the demand curve for cotton. The resultant increase in production or in revenue is distributed among the factors and inputs in production according to the elasticities of cotton's demand for these inputs, and to the bargaining position of labor and capital.

The California cotton-water externality SAM is presented in the Appendix. It should be noted that the externality SAM has not been balanced; this step is taken when the environmentally adjusted SAM is calculated.

**Future Damages**

With the cotton water externality, a large portion of the damages caused by the externality is debited to the future economy. Some of these damage amounts reflect losses in productivity and some reflect a direct loss in welfare due to environmental degradation. The impact of damages that measure losses in productivity are analyzed with a multiplier matrix as described below. Analysis of the direct welfare damages follows the multiplier discussion.

In order to trace the impact that unpaid productivity damages incurred in the current economy might have on the future economy, a multiplier matrix is generated from the original California SAM. Productivity damage amounts that are forwarded for payment to the future economy are fed through the SAM multiplier to yield the impact that these damages will have on the future economy. The multiplier matrix illustrates the relationship between exogenous injections and endogenous income and production levels. The multiplier matrix makes it possible to trace the impact of exogenous change on every endogenous account in the future economy.

In the cotton water example, $1,063,346 of the externality damages measure productivity losses that are passed directly to the future economy. This amount represents 7 percent of the total damages caused by the combined water externalities. Of this amount, $29,226 represents the expected decline in agricultural production due to salinization and sedimentation. Commercial fishing is projected to experience a fall in production of $82,400, and recreational fishing and water recreation services are expected to experience a fall in income of $402,320. The cotton industry is projected to sustain a fall in production of $549,400 due to soil erosion. These numbers are fed through a multiplier matrix that is based on the original California SAM. The results indicate the overall damage in productivity that will be sustained by the future economy as a result of externality damages and a degradation of the resource base. The direct impact of the decline in the resource base will be a drop in productivity in the sectors that directly depend on the resource in question. The decrease in productivity triggers changes throughout the economy as indicated by the multiplier. The structure of the multiplier matrix also reflects the pattern of development established with incomplete environmental prices, thereby further indicating misdirected growth.

In addition to the productivity damages sustained by the future economy as a result of the surface water externalities, the future economy also inherits a degraded groundwater resource. As a result of the low-quality groundwater available to future households, it can be argued that future groundwater consumers are less well off than current groundwater consumers. Even if they do not incur higher medical expenses or experience more sick-days as a result of the contaminated water, they nevertheless consume lower-quality water than their current day counterparts. The reduction in welfare due to lower-quality water that was established in section 4.8 is equivalent to $12,267,913. This amount represents 86 percent of the total damages caused by the cotton water externalities. In our analysis, this amount is deducted directly from future household real income to reflect the change in real welfare. This fall in welfare is allocated among the household income groups based on each income group's portion of total household utility expenditures. In the absence of information on water consumption by income group, we used utility expenditures as a proxy for the distribution of water consumption among the income groups. Since households do not actually alter their purchases as a result of this drop in welfare, we do not feed this portion of the future damage through the multiplier analysis.

In order to incorporate future damage amounts into the current accounts, the present values of the results of the multiplier analysis and of the direct drop in welfare are calculated. The discount rate is set at 3 percent, an approximation to the 'natural' rate of growth of California, which is selected to be at a midpoint between the rate of population growth for California (2.2 percent) and the rate of GDP growth for California (3.4 percent). Table 4.10 shows the present value results of the multiplier experiment and the direct fall in welfare.

*Table 4.10    Present value of future damages ($1982)*

| | Reductions due to: | |
| --- | --- | --- |
| | Fall in productivity | Direct fall in welfare |
| Livestock | 16,693 | |
| Cotton | 539,057 | |
| Food grains | 2,938 | |
| Feed grains | 5,335 | |
| Hay and grass | 4,974 | |
| Fruits | 14,008 | |
| Tree nuts | 2,501 | |
| Vegetables | 14,161 | |
| Miscellaneous crops | 1,849 | |
| Forest products | 93,778 | |
| Food processing | 66,937 | |
| Non-agricultural industries | 261,189 | |
| Oil, gas and refining | 120,791 | |
| Agricultural chemicals | 17,471 | |
| Textiles | 15,937 | |
| Wood and paper | 12,098 | |
| Non-agricultural chemicals | 19,131 | |
| Rail | 4,978 | |
| Services | 1,234,998 | |
| Trucking | 19,331 | |
| Air transportation | 23,132 | |
| Utilities | 48,131 | |
| Labor | 730,971 | |
| Capital | 519,988 | |
| Enterprises | 323,698 | |
| Households: | | |
| Low income | 68,387 | 2,382,119 |
| Medium income | 468,542 | 5,955,298 |
| High income | 378,355 | 3,573,178 |
| Government | exogenous | |
| Investment | exogenous | |
| Rest of world domestic | exogenous | |
| Rest of world | exogenous | |

## The Environmentally Adjusted SAM and NNP Calculations

In order to examine the environmental distortions as summarized by the externality SAM in relationship to the complete economy, the externality SAM is subtracted from the original SAM to yield a CEA SAM. The CEA is presented in the Appendix (see Table 4.A.3).[3] The flows of the CEA SAM are adjusted by the value of the flows that are generated by the environmental externality. The CEA SAM illustrates the reduction in cotton cultivation and consumption and in defensive industries that would occur if the externality was assumed by the cotton industry. It also illustrates the increase in production and consumption of goods and services provided by industries that are currently harmed by the externality that would occur if the externality were removed.

In order to expand the analysis of the impact of the externality to include future damages, the present value results of the multiplier analysis and the direct decrease in welfare are presented alongside the current results. In the first three columns of Table 4.11, the sector totals for the original SAM and the CEA SAM are compared. In the last two columns, the results of the future damage estimates are compared with the current account estimates.

As in the original California SAM, the effects in Table 4.11 are in millions of dollars. Because of this, many of the lesser effects simply drop out; this does not indicate zero change in these sectors. In the CEA and in the multiplier experiments, changes due to the environmental externality percolate throughout the economy and every account experiences some change. A blank entry in Table 4.11 indicates a change that rounds to less than $100,000.

*Table 4.11    Matrix totals ($1,000,000)*

| | Original SAM | Current environmental change | Current environmental change (%) | Future damage | Total change (%) |
|---|---|---|---|---|---|
| Livestock | 4644.2 | | | | |
| Cotton | 1126.0 | -4.6 | -0.4 | -0.5 | -0.45 |
| Food grains | 609.3 | -0.3 | -0.05 | | -0.5 |
| Feed grains | 896 | -0.1 | -0.01 | | -0.01 |
| Hay and grass | 651.6 | -0.2 | -0.03 | | -0.03 |
| Fruits | 2748.9 | | | | |
| Tree nuts | 616.4 | 0.1 | 0.02 | | 0.02 |
| Vegetables | 2794.7 | | | | |
| Miscellaneous crops | 379.8 | 0.1 | 0.03 | | 0.03 |
| Forest products | 4794.2 | -0.6 | -0.012 | -0.1 | -0.0146 |
| Food processing | 30360.9 | | | -0.1 | -0.0003 |
| Non-ag. industry | 166854.7 | -0.2 | -0.0001 | -0.3 | -0.0003 |
| Oil, gas and ref. | 33406.4 | -0.1 | -0.0003 | -0.1 | -0.0006 |
| Ag. chemicals | 528.7 | -0.2 | -0.04 | | -0.04 |
| Textiles | 6165.4 | | | | |
| Wood and paper | 6255.4 | -0.1 | -0.002 | | -0.002 |
| Non-ag. chemicals | 7168.2 | -0.1 | -0.002 | | -0.002 |
| Rail | 1858.1 | 0.2 | 0.01 | | 0.01 |
| Services | 343348.8 | -1.2 | -0.0003 | -1.2 | -0.0007 |
| Trucking | 7470.3 | 0.1 | 0.001 | | 0.001 |
| Air transportation | 9202.5 | -0.1 | -0.001 | | -0.001 |
| Utilities | 12538.4 | -0.1 | -0.0008 | | -0.0008 |
| Labor | 229311.2 | -0.5 | -0.0002 | -0.7 | -0.0005 |
| Capital | 120726.1 | -0.4 | -0.0003 | -0.5 | -0.0007 |
| Enterprises | 88838.6 | -0.6 | -0.0007 | -0.3 | -0.001 |
| Households: | | | | | |
| Low income | 41589.4 | | | -2.5 | -0.006 |
| Medium income | 158971.2 | -0.01 | -0.00006 | -6.4 | -0.004 |
| High income | 115955.5 | -0.01 | -0.00008 | -4 | -0.0035 |
| Government | 199767.2 | -0.1 | -0.00005 | na | -0.00005 |
| Investment | 102082.4 | -0.1 | -0.00009 | na | -0.00009 |
| Rest of world domestic | 137539.0 | -0.5 | -0.0004 | na | -0.0004 |
| Rest of world | 40668.8 | | | na | |

Table 4.11 summarizes the incidence of distortions generated by the California cotton industry's water use. The third column of the Table reflects the impact of cotton's water externalities on California's current activities and incomes. In the current period, the effect of the externalities on the economic activity is to overstate 'true' gross economic activity by $8.9 million in the unadjusted SAM.

Non-agricultural output is overstated in the unadjusted SAM by $2.4 million. In the non-agricultural sector, the largest effect is in services, where output is overstated by $1.2 million. This is because both cotton and environmental defensive industries are heavy users of services in their production.

In the non-agricultural sector, only rail and trucking are understated in the unadjusted SAM and hence experience an increase in output with the reduction of the externality. The direction of change for rail and trucking is difficult to explain as cotton is an important client for both of these forms of transportation. Increased rail or trucking use by tree-crops or miscellaneous crops after the externality is not large enough to explain the direction of change. Secondary and third round effects must combine to explain the change.

Another puzzling observation is the small net impact that the externalities have on food processing and textiles. These two industries are the largest users of cotton and one would expect larger benefits from the cotton 'subsidy' to trickle down to input demand. Examination of both the magnitude of the cotton price change that results from the externalities, and of the input coefficients for cotton in textile and food processing, highlights the observation that throughout the SAM, the second and third round effects of the externality are small. In food processing, which is the largest industrial user of cotton, the input coefficient on cotton is .0027. The change in cotton price as a result of the externality is .07 percent. Assuming an elasticity of 1.5 percent for calculating the change in quantity produced due to a change in input price, it is possible to estimate the change in food processing output due to the change in cotton price. In this case, the increase is approximately equivalent to $81,000. Taken alone, a change of this magnitude is negligible in an economy that is described in units of millions of dollars. For this reason many, if not most, of the secondary effects of the externality are negligible.

Due to the overstatement of output in both the agricultural and non-agricultural sectors, the total current account impact of the water externalities generated by cotton on value-added is overstated by about $1 million. As a result, incomes are overstated in the unadjusted SAM, with enterprise income the most overstated.

In the exogenous accounts, economic activity is overstated by $700,000 in the unadjusted SAM. The largest overstatement occurs in the rest of the world domestic, which is the largest consumer of cotton. Investment is overstated by about $100,000 in the unadjusted accounts which is explained both by increased investment in industries bolstered by the externality and also by the fact that some of the defensive expenditures (such as additional water-storage facilities) generate investment.

The fourth column of Table 4.11 reflects the impact of cotton's water externalities on California's future activities and incomes. The numbers represent the results of the multiplier analysis and the direct drop in welfare that occurs because of the externalities. The results presented in column five indicate that when future damages are considered, current economic activity is overstated to an even greater extent than revealed by the calculations in columns three and four. Inclusion of future damages indicates that economic activity, as measured by the unadjusted current SAM, overstates 'true' gross economic activity by an additional $16.7 million. This overstatement is almost twice as large as the overstatement due to the current account adjustments. It is noteworthy that all the externalities generated by cotton affect future generations negatively. While there are current costs and benefits, the major impact of the externalities is to shift the costs of current externality damages to future generations.

The major industries injured by the externality in the future are cotton, non-agricultural industries (commercial fishing) and services (recreational fishing and water recreation). Inclusion of future damages indicates that total productive output is overstated by an additional $2.3 million in the unadjusted SAM.

The overstatement of output in the production sectors due to future damages results in an overstatement in value-added of $1.2 million. As a result, incomes are overstated in the unadjusted SAM, with enterprise income the most overstated. In addition to the impact of value-added on income, incomes are further overstated due to the direct drop in real welfare and real income that results from the externality. Because of this direct drop, future households bear the brunt of currently generated externalities. In absolute terms, middle income households are most affected, with an overstatement of $6.4 million. High income households follow with an overstatement of $4 million, and low income households are least affected in absolute terms, with an overstatement of $2.5 million. In relative terms, the percentage overstatement is the largest for low income households and lowest for high income households.

Calculation of the current environmentally adjusted SAM and of the future damage estimates provides an indication of the changes in the level and distribution of economic activity that arises from the environmental externality. The current environmentally adjusted SAM and the future damage estimates also provide a basis with which to calculate an environmentally adjusted NNP. The overstatement of value-added described by the externality adjustments is reflected in the NNP calculations. In the unadjusted accounting system, NNP is overstated by $2.2 million. Of this amount, adjustment for only current externality distortions results in an overstatement of $1 million. The multiplier analysis adds another $1.2 million to the overstatement of value-added in the unadjusted SAM due to future distortions.[4]

Future damages that result in a direct drop in welfare do not affect NNP calculations. These damages do change real income, and in the cotton water externality example, real income is overstated by $14 million in the unadjusted SAM. This overstatement is larger than the overstatement in NNP by an order of magnitude. In most analyses, NNP and national income would be the same. In our case, they are not the same because there is a change in household welfare that does not flow through value-added because it is not reflected in a change in expenditures. This direct change in household welfare is directly due to the externality. In many ways, this direct change in welfare is like an increase in the price of a 'utility'. Due to this price change, the correspondence between NNP and real income shifts downward despite the fact that the correspondence between NNP and money income remains the same.

In interpreting the results, bear in mind that cotton uses only 3.68 percent of California's agricultural land, and is not one of the heaviest polluters. Nevertheless, the distortions caused by the cotton water externalities affect NNP, real welfare and both the incidence and allocation of economic activity.

# 9  CONCLUSION

With the SAM framework, the information conveyed by the environmentally adjusted NNP measure is expanded to present distributional ramification of the externality. The SAM analysis gives a better accounting of the true costs and benefits of environmental externalities. The general equilibrium nature of the SAM provides a more accurate picture of who benefits and who loses from pollution once higher round interactions are evaluated than a partial equilibrium approach. The SAM framework, combined with the economic valuation of environmental externalities, provides a method for analyzing the distribution and incidence of the costs and benefits of environmental exploitation, whether between industry and consumers, between rich and poor, or between today and tomorrow. Through the creation of the environmentally adjusted SAM and the future damage analyses, it is possible to account for the impact of environmental distortions.

Moving from the unadjusted accounting system to the environmentally adjusted system is equivalent to removing the distortions imposed by the environmental externality. Piercing the veil of incorrect externality prices reveals that society is worse off than it realizes. The level of economic activity portrayed in the unadjusted accounts is higher than would have occurred with the correct environmental prices and this fact is reflected in the environmentally adjusted NNP measure. Current activity that is triggered by the externality is at the expense of both current and future resource users though in the example presented here, the major burden of the cost of the externality is borne by the future economy.

# APPENDIX A    THE SAM TABLES

*Table 4.A.1    The California SAM*

| Sector | Livestock | Cotton | Food grains | Feed grains | Hay and grass | Fruit | Tree nuts |
|---|---|---|---|---|---|---|---|
| Livestock | 555.3 | 10.6 | 11.1 | 32.5 | 14.3 | 5.8 | 1.3 |
| Cotton | 1.3 | 11.3 | 0.1 | 0.1 | 0.1 | 1.6 | 0.4 |
| Food grains | 6.1 | 0.6 | 20.4 | 0.1 | 0.1 | 0.8 | 0.2 |
| Feed grains | 344.6 | — | — | 39.0 | — | — | — |
| Hay and grass | 564.2 | 1.1 | 0.1 | 2.4 | 2.8 | 1.4 | 0.3 |
| Fruits | 2.8 | 2.5 | 0.3 | 0.3 | 0.2 | 3.3 | 0.8 |
| Tree nuts | 0.6 | 0.6 | 0.1 | 0.1 | 0.1 | 0.7 | 0.2 |
| Vegetables | 2.5 | 1.7 | 0.2 | 0.2 | 0.2 | 2.3 | 0.5 |
| Miscellaneous crops | 0.4 | 0.3 | — | 1.5 | 1.2 | 0.4 | 0.1 |
| | | | | | | | |
| Forest products | 189.5 | 171.9 | 20.2 | 20.6 | 16.8 | 308.2 | 60.5 |
| Food processing | 872.9 | 0.4 | 0.3 | 0.6 | 0.5 | 0.8 | 0.1 |
| Services | 68.9 | 23.4 | 17.6 | 26.7 | 21.5 | 169.3 | 17.3 |
| Non-agricultural industry | 66.3 | 52.0 | 62.0 | 77.4 | 63.8 | 205.9 | 45.7 |
| Oil, gas and refining | 3.9 | 27.9 | 16.3 | 30.5 | 24.6 | 51.5 | 8.1 |
| Agricultural chemicals | 1.5 | — | — | 1.0 | 0.9 | 5.6 | 1.4 |
| Textiles | 8.7 | 0.4 | 0.2 | 0.4 | 0.4 | 8.2 | 1.5 |
| Wood and paper | 17.2 | 4.8 | 2.6 | 6.0 | 4.8 | 9.5 | 1.7 |
| Non-agricultural chemicals | 15.4 | 1.6 | 2.9 | 3.6 | 2.9 | 5.2 | 0.6 |
| Railroads | 307.7 | 205.1 | 126.1 | 142.6 | 116.9 | 171.0 | 41.2 |
| Trucking | 64.1 | 5.0 | 4.0 | 8.1 | 6.6 | 13.6 | 1.9 |
| Air transport | 2.1 | 1.1 | 0.1 | 0.2 | 0.2 | 6.3 | 1.1 |
| Utilities | 25.3 | 23.3 | 6.7 | 16.3 | 13.7 | 39.5 | — |
| | | | | | | | |
| Labor | 279.9 | 148.3 | 30.7 | 30.2 | 21.8 | 588.3 | 132.0 |
| Capital | 401.9 | 283.1 | 176.3 | 265.9 | 196.4 | 812.3 | 244.0 |
| | | | | | | | |
| Enterprises | — | — | — | — | — | — | — |
| Low income households | — | — | — | — | — | — | — |
| Medium income households | — | — | — | — | — | — | — |
| High income households | — | — | — | — | — | — | — |
| | | | | | | | |
| Government | 117.7 | 14.8 | 12.7 | 22.6 | 13.6 | 47.9 | 11.1 |
| Capital account | — | — | — | — | — | — | — |
| Domestic imports | 715.2 | 128.2 | 93.1 | 158.6 | 120.7 | 277.5 | 42.6 |
| Rest of world imports | 8.1 | 6.2 | 5.0 | 8.6 | 6.9 | 11.9 | 2.0 |
| | | | | | | | |
| Total | 4644.2 | 1126.0 | 609.3 | 896.0 | 651.6 | 2748.9 | 616.4 |

| Vege-tables | Misc. crops | Forest prod. | Food proc. | Non-ag. industries | Oil, gas, and ref. | Ag. chem. | Tex-tiles | Wood and paper |
|---|---|---|---|---|---|---|---|---|
| 9.5 | 1.3 | 58.2 | 2716.6 | 0.7 | — | — | 5.9 | 3.8 |
| 0.8 | 0.1 | 0.6 | 81.6 | 0.2 | — | — | 12.0 | — |
| 0.4 | — | 0.3 | 211.5 | 0.4 | — | — | — | — |
| — | — | 3.1 | 216.0 | — | — | 1.7 | — | — |
| 0.7 | 0.1 | 10.0 | — | — | — | — | — | — |
| 1.7 | 0.2 | 1.2 | 934.4 | — | — | — | — | 0.1 |
| 0.4 | — | 0.3 | 34.1 | — | — | — | — | — |
| 60.9 | 0.1 | 0.8 | 530.1 | — | — | — | — | — |
| 0.2 | 14.3 | 0.2 | 173.1 | 0.8 | — | — | 0.3 | 2.2 |
| | | | | | | | | |
| 146.2 | 10.8 | 192.6 | 83.2 | 151.1 | 0.5 | 0.1 | 19.9 | 173.3 |
| 0.8 | 0.1 | 21.4 | 3282.5 | 59.0 | 9.0 | 2.3 | 2.0 | 3.3 |
| 52.7 | 8.0 | 186.7 | 3766.4 | 39140.8 | 1293.7 | 48.7 | 186.1 | 424.2 |
| 92.8 | 17.1 | 260.7 | 277.1 | 2739.2 | 9931.8 | 45.5 | 42.7 | 155.6 |
| 40.4 | 8.0 | 116.8 | 3.0 | 14.2 | 4.8 | 17.2 | 0.2 | 1.1 |
| 6.5 | — | 14.9 | 9.3 | 417.4 | 1.9 | 0.5 | 795.1 | 12.2 |
| 7.4 | 0.1 | 4.2 | 184.8 | 2806.7 | 4.4 | 5.2 | 17.1 | 1120.3 |
| 7.8 | 1.5 | 42.0 | 137.7 | 1860.7 | 226.4 | 17.9 | 43.0 | 128.5 |
| 5.0 | 0.8 | 7.7 | 143.3 | 470.1 | 34.8 | 5.1 | 3.7 | 53.9 |
| 229.6 | 52.9 | 586.1 | 1800.3 | 19200.9 | 3078.6 | 45.5 | 399.7 | 321.3 |
| 21.2 | 2.5 | 27.9 | 562.4 | 1735.1 | 89.8 | 17.1 | 30.8 | 66.1 |
| 12.5 | 0.1 | 61.2 | 116.4 | 1274.5 | 81.9 | 4.7 | 28.3 | 27.6 |
| 30.8 | 15.5 | 48.3 | 304.0 | 1604.6 | 627.0 | 17.1 | 38.2 | 103.9 |
| | | | | | | | | |
| 374.5 | 33.3 | 1646.1 | 4308.6 | 57650.8 | 1535.6 | 60.9 | 1631.7 | 1465.6 |
| 1384.1 | 158.2 | 711.4 | 2947.5 | 5209.7 | 4571.9 | 78.8 | 437.0 | 456.4 |
| | | | | | | | | |
| — | — | — | — | — | — | — | — | — |
| — | — | — | — | — | — | — | — | — |
| — | — | — | — | — | — | — | — | — |
| — | — | — | — | — | — | — | — | — |
| | | | | | | | | |
| 37.2 | 5.2 | 110.7 | 947.4 | 2343.2 | 1696.3 | 8.6 | 48.5 | 52.6 |
| — | — | — | — | — | — | — | — | — |
| 259.3 | 47.5 | 651.1 | 5802.5 | 27464.2 | 6999.0 | 139.0 | 2257.0 | 1567.6 |
| 11.0 | 2.1 | 29.6 | 787.0 | 2710.4 | 3219.1 | 12.7 | 166.4 | 115.7 |
| | | | | | | | | |
| 2794.7 | 379.8 | 4794.2 | 30360.9 | 166854.7 | 33406.4 | 528.7 | 6165.4 | 6255.4 |

*Table 4.A.1   (continued)*

| Sector | Non-ag. chemicals | Rail | Services | Truck | Air trans. | Utilities | Labor | Capital |
|---|---|---|---|---|---|---|---|---|
| Livestock | 2.0 | — | 147.2 | — | 0.3 | — | — | — |
| Cotton | — | — | 0.2 | — | — | — | — | — |
| Food grains | — | — | 0.3 | 0.2 | — | — | — | — |
| Feed grains | — | — | 87.0 | — | — | — | — | — |
| Hay and grass | 0.9 | — | 0.4 | — | — | — | — | — |
| Fruits | — | — | 30.5 | — | — | — | — | — |
| Tree nuts | — | — | 0.1 | — | — | — | — | — |
| Vegetables | — | — | 163.1 | — | — | — | — | — |
| Miscellaneous crops | 14.3 | — | 3.5 | — | — | — | — | — |
| | | | | | | | | |
| Forest products | 8.6 | 0.3 | 557.2 | 0.3 | 0.5 | 1.0 | — | — |
| Food processing | 83.0 | 0.3 | 4716.1 | 0.6 | 10.8 | 0.9 | — | — |
| Services | 915.9 | 344.6 | 13973.5 | 131.9 | 320.6 | 675.1 | — | — |
| Non-agricultural industry | 663.9 | 169.9 | 3338.4 | 543.9 | 2231.6 | 1998.9 | — | — |
| Oil, gas and refining | 14.3 | 0.9 | 29.2 | — | — | 0.4 | — | — |
| Agricultural chemicals | 2.5 | 0.4 | 353.4 | 4.6 | 3.8 | 0.8 | — | — |
| Textiles | 29.1 | 0.6 | 591.9 | 4.4 | 3.1 | 17.8 | — | — |
| Wood and paper | 505.0 | 1.2 | 1114.2 | 4.1 | 4.1 | 21.7 | — | — |
| Non-agricultural chemicals | 43.9 | 57.7 | 214.0 | 26.7 | 4.8 | 80.6 | — | — |
| Railroads | 793.7 | 142.5 | 58323.8 | 944.4 | 1791.9 | 498.1 | — | — |
| Trucking | 94.7 | 11.2 | 1198.8 | 999.9 | 82.8 | 39.5 | — | — |
| Air transport | 52.2 | 4.2 | 1708.5 | 15.1 | 651.7 | 18.3 | — | — |
| Utilities | 113.4 | 5.5 | 3468.9 | 18.0 | 28.2 | 1406.6 | — | — |
| | | | | | | | | |
| Labor | 1466.7 | 820.8 | 133637.5 | 3112.7 | 2237.1 | 1519.5 | — | — |
| Capital | 901.6 | 114.0 | 83278.4 | 1138.9 | 339.8 | 2700.5 | — | — |
| | | | | | | | | |
| Enterprises | — | — | — | — | — | — | — | 70209.4 |
| Low income households | — | — | — | — | — | — | 12239.4 | −335.0 |
| Medium income households | — | — | — | — | — | — | 108599.0 | 4767.8 |
| High income households | — | — | — | — | — | — | 77163.1 | 7717.7 |
| | | | | | | | | |
| Government | 120.8 | 63.8 | 20580.3 | 196.8 | 331.8 | 461.9 | 31309.7 | — |
| Capital account | — | — | — | — | — | — | — | 37866.8 |
| Domestic imports | 1205.6 | 110.0 | 14113.4 | 307.5 | 411.1 | 3022.8 | — | 499.6 |
| Rest of world imports | 136.1 | 10.3 | 1719.1 | 20.4 | 748.4 | 73.9 | — | — |
| | | | | | | | | |
| Total | 7168.2 | 1858.1 | 343348.8 | 7470.3 | 9202.5 | 12538.4 | 229311.2 | 120726.1 |

| Enterprises | Households | | | Government | Capital account | Domestic exports | Foreign exports | Total |
|---|---|---|---|---|---|---|---|---|
| | Low | Medium | High | | | | | |
| — | 94.2 | 267.6 | 167.3 | 1.4 | 21.6 | 504.2 | 11.5 | 4644.2 |
| — | 0.1 | 0.6 | 0.5 | 136.6 | 8.3 | 552.5 | 316.8 | 1126.0 |
| — | 0.1 | 0.4 | 0.4 | 41.6 | 11.1 | 5.6 | 308.4 | 609.3 |
| — | 1.6 | 5.7 | 4.8 | — | 2.7 | 0.1 | 189.6 | 896.0 |
| — | 3.2 | 19.8 | 18.8 | 0.1 | — | 14.5 | 10.6 | 651.6 |
| — | 76.4 | 208.0 | 147.9 | 0.2 | — | 1056.8 | 281.3 | 2748.9 |
| — | 3.5 | 12.2 | 10.4 | — | — | 362.3 | 190.8 | 616.4 |
| — | 95.8 | 283.9 | 184.2 | 0.7 | — | 1348.2 | 119.3 | 2794.7 |
| — | 0.1 | 0.5 | 0.4 | 5.0 | — | 156.8 | 4.3 | 379.8 |
| | | | | | | | | |
| — | 43.3 | 175.2 | 193.2 | 14.1 | — | 2157.0 | 78.3 | 4794.3 |
| — | 2152.1 | 6864.1 | 4516.0 | 129.9 | 4.0 | 5954.5 | 1672.6 | 30360.9 |
| — | 963.8 | 4329.2 | 4034.1 | 12363.9 | 29941.2 | 38185.5 | 15223.2 | 166854.7 |
| — | 683.6 | 2834.7 | 1959.2 | 215.4 | 29.3 | 141.1 | 4461.1 | 33406.4 |
| — | 2.9 | 10.0 | 8.5 | 6.4 | 1.8 | 1.3 | 84.4 | 528.7 |
| — | 436.3 | 1692.2 | 1770.7 | 392.2 | 100.3 | 45.7 | 94.3 | 6165.4 |
| — | 99.0 | 365.9 | 295.6 | 20.6 | 8.6 | 221.9 | 426.8 | 6255.4 |
| — | 290.6 | 893.8 | 674.6 | 292.3 | 19.0 | 468.8 | 366.9 | 7168.2 |
| — | 52.5 | 133.5 | 158.9 | 124.0 | 40.9 | 1.5 | 162.7 | 1858.1 |
| — | 20549.8 | 70644.3 | 63019.4 | 30817.8 | 2957.9 | 54771.1 | 11268.4 | 343348.7 |
| — | 198.9 | 506.4 | 438.9 | 763.7 | 106.6 | 147.8 | 225.0 | 7470.3 |
| — | 548.1 | 1393.7 | 1658.8 | 560.9 | 41.8 | 415.2 | 515.6 | 9202.4 |
| — | 590.7 | 1819.9 | 1321.7 | 301.7 | 0.3 | 529.9 | 19.5 | 12538.4 |
| | | | | | | | | |
| — | — | — | — | — | — | 16578.7 | — | 229311.2 |
| — | — | — | — | — | — | 13918.2 | — | 120726.1 |
| | | | | | | | | |
| — | 3365.2 | 3835.6 | 1365.8 | 10062.5 | — | — | — | 88838.6 |
| 8457.2 | — | — | — | 17878.9 | 3348.9 | — | — | 41589.4 |
| 27946.4 | — | — | — | 17658.1 | — | — | — | 158971.3 |
| 27209.5 | — | — | — | 3865.3 | — | — | — | 115955.5 |
| | | | | | | | | |
| 22143.3 | 6284.6 | 31131.3 | 10441.0 | 50711.7 | 20500.0 | — | — | 199767.2 |
| 3082.2 | 71.7 | 12826.2 | 7588.3 | 39537.6 | 1109.7 | — | — | 102082.4 |
| — | 4350.7 | 16187.3 | 13816.7 | 10754.8 | 21399.1 | — | 4637.3 | 137539.0 |
| — | 630.6 | 2529.2 | 2159.2 | 3109.7 | 22429.2 | — | — | 40668.8 |
| | | | | | | | | |
| 88838.6 | 41589.4 | 158971.2 | 115955.5 | 199767.2 | 102082.4 | 137539 | 40668.8 | 1879868.0 |

*Table 4.A.2   The California cotton externality SAM*

|  | Live-stock | Cotton | Food grains | Feed grains | Hay and grass | Fruit | Tree nuts | Vegeta-bles |
|---|---|---|---|---|---|---|---|---|
| Livestock | 277 | 3843 | -12 | -50 | -15 | -6 | -2 | -12 |
| Cotton | 397 | 7547 | 30 | 30 | 30 | 483 | 121 | 244 |
| Food grains | -5 | 217 | -48 | — | — | -1 | — | — |
| Feed grains | -246 | — | — | -111 | — | — | — | — |
| Hay and grass | -381 | 372 | — | -7 | -6 | -5 | — | -1 |
| Fruits | -2 | 905 | — | — | — | -7 | -2 | -6 |
| Tree nuts | -1 | 217 | — | — | — | -1 | — | — |
| Vegetables | -1 | 616 | — | — | — | -5 | -2 | -165 |
| Miscellaneous crops | — | 109 | — | — | 2 | — | — | — |
| Forest products | 95 | 62448 | -23 | -33 | -17 | -387 | -52 | -206 |
| Food processing | 435 | 145 | — | 1 | — | — | — | — |
| Services | 13 | 8492 | 738 | 1039 | 736 | 3223 | 742 | 3506 |
| Non-agricultural industry | 34 | 18891 | -73 | -124 | -61 | -261 | -39 | -131 |
| Oil, gas and refining | 2 | 10136 | -19 | -48 | -23 | -66 | -8 | -55 |
| Agricultural chemicals | 1 | — | — | -1 | -1 | -7 | -2 | -8 |
| Textiles | 4 | 145 | — | — | — | -9 | -2 | -12 |
| Wood and paper | 9 | 1744 | -3 | -10 | -4 | -11 | -1 | -12 |
| Non-agricultural chemicals | 8 | 581 | -3 | -5 | -3 | -8 | -1 | -8 |
| Railroads | 122 | 74463 | -164 | -243 | -122 | -233 | -40 | -348 |
| Trucking | 33 | 1817 | -5 | -14 | -7 | -18 | -1 | -32 |
| Air transport | 1 | 400 | — | — |  | -7 | -2 | -16 |
| Utilities | 319 | 8743 | 72 | 169 | 150 | 426 | — | 326 |
| Labor | 140 | 53876 | 727 | 1042 | 742 | 2747 | 647 | 3068 |
| Capital | 202 | 40326 | -1735 | -2604 | -1714 | -8001 | -1739 | -9157 |
| Enterprises | — | — | — | — | — | — | — | — |
| Low income households | — | — | — | — | — | — | — | — |
| Medium income households | — | — | — | — | — | — | — | — |
| High income households | — | — | — | — | — | — | — | — |
| Government | 66 | 5381 | -13 | -31 | -11 | -53 | -11 | -47 |
| Capital account | — | — | — | — | — | — | — | — |
| Domestic imports | 1444 | 46582 | -87 | -200 | -111 | -339 | -35 | -287 |
| Rest of world imports | 14 | 2249 | -6 | -14 | -7 | -14 | -1 | -15 |

| Misc. crops | Forest products | Food proc. | Non-ag. industry | Oil, gas and ref. | Ag. chemicals | Tex-tiles | Wood and paper | Non-ag. chemicals |
|---|---|---|---|---|---|---|---|---|
| -2 | 727 | -1046 | — | — | — | -3 | -3 | 60 |
| 30 | 191 | 24821 | 61 | — | — | 3648 | — | — |
| — | 4 | -348 | — | — | — | — | — | — |
| — | 35 | -345 | — | — | 28 | — | — | — |
| — | 113 | — | — | — | — | — | — | 26 |
| — | 13 | -1546 | — | — | — | — | — | — |
| — | 4 | -53 | — | — | — | — | — | — |
| — | 9 | -886 | — | — | — | — | — | — |
| -38 | 3 | -267 | -1 | — | — | — | -3 | 414 |
| -16 | 2406 | -31 | -89 | — | 2 | -11 | -116 | 258 |
| — | 268 | -1264 | -40 | -7 | 41 | -1 | -2 | 2496 |
| 422 | 2277 | -2578 | 710 | -1335 | 866 | -162 | -408 | 27268 |
| -26 | 3256 | -107 | -1571 | -7270 | 823 | -24 | -102 | 19964 |
| -12 | 1459 | -1 | -8 | -3 | 312 | — | — | 430 |
| — | 185 | -4 | -180 | -1 | 9 | -451 | -8 | 76 |
| — | 52 | -71 | -1691 | -3 | 94 | -10 | -744 | 874 |
| -3 | 524 | -53 | 22286 | -166 | 325 | -24 | -87 | 15184 |
| -1 | 96 | -56 | -303 | -24 | 92 | -2 | -36 | 1320 |
| -84 | 7260 | -875 | 55180 | -2561 | 818 | -268 | -246 | 23788 |
| -4 | 349 | -217 | -977 | -65 | 310 | -18 | -43 | 2848 |
| — | 765 | -45 | -803 | -60 | 85 | -17 | -19 | 1571 |
| 162 | 1182 | 3502 | 18502 | 7066 | 515 | 437 | 1179 | 4771 |
| 386 | 20559 | -1659 | -2790 | -1123 | 1103 | -926 | -975 | 44106 |
| -1109 | 8886 | -1136 | -79759 | -3347 | 1427 | -249 | -304 | 27111 |
| — | — | — | — | — | — | — | — | — |
| — | — | — | — | — | — | — | — | — |
| — | — | — | — | — | — | — | — | — |
| — | — | — | — | — | — | — | — | — |
| -5 | 1394 | -290 | -1111 | -876 | 158 | -25 | -25 | 3650 |
| — | — | — | — | — | — | — | — | — |
| -56 | 8152 | 303 | -15683 | -5123 | 2518 | -1281 | -1039 | 36271 |
| -4 | 370 | -203 | -1577 | -2357 | 229 | -94 | -76 | 4094 |

Table *4.A.2 (continued)*

| | Rail | Services | Truck | Air transp. | Utilities | Labor | Capital | Enter-prises |
|---|---|---|---|---|---|---|---|---|
| Livestock | — | 35 | — | — | — | — | — | — |
| Cotton | — | 61 | — | — | — | — | — | — |
| Food grains | — | — | — | — | — | — | — | — |
| Feed grains | — | -91 | — | — | — | — | — | — |
| Hay and grass | — | — | — | — | — | — | — | — |
| Fruits | — | -25 | — | — | — | — | — | — |
| Tree nuts | — | — | — | — | — | — | — | — |
| Vegetables | — | -173 | — | — | — | — | — | — |
| Miscellaneous crops | — | -2 | — | — | — | — | — | — |
| Forest products | — | 129 | — | — | -2 | — | — | — |
| Food processing | — | 1060 | — | -5 | -2 | — | — | — |
| Services | -190 | -1009 | -80 | -235 | 24347 | — | — | — |
| Non-agricultural industry | -41 | 746 | -160 | -969 | -29058 | — | — | — |
| Oil, gas and refining | — | 12 | — | — | -1 | — | — | — |
| Agricultural chemicals | — | 83 | -1 | -2 | -2 | — | — | — |
| Textiles | — | 118 | -1 | -2 | -160 | — | — | — |
| Wood and paper | -1 | 684 | -1 | -2 | 6267 | — | — | — |
| Non-agricultural chemicals | -14 | 51 | -9 | -2 | -1103 | — | — | — |
| Railroads | -49 | 106937 | -372 | -958 | -7310 | — | — | — |
| Trucking | -3 | 275 | -294 | -35 | -551 | — | — | — |
| Air transport | -1 | 390 | -5 | -285 | -173 | — | — | — |
| Utilities | 65 | 42207 | 210 | 325 | -3581 | — | — | — |
| Labor | -207 | 29919 | -917 | -971 | 51795 | — | — | — |
| Capital | -28 | -52809 | -336 | -147 | 145427 | — | — | — |
| Enterprises | — | — | — | — | — | — | -9419 | — |
| Low income households | — | — | — | — | — | 3380 | 45 | -1103 |
| Medium income households | — | — | — | — | — | 29995 | -639 | -3643 |
| High income households | — | — | — | — | — | 21311 | -1035 | -3546 |
| Government | -18 | 7320 | -56 | -142 | -6533 | 8648 | — | -2886 |
| Capital account | — | — | — | — | — | — | -5080 | -402 |
| Domestic imports | -28 | 3549 | -90 | -178 | -43652 | — | -67 | — |
| Rest of world imports | -3 | 434 | -7 | -326 | -1070 | — | — | — |

| Households | | | Government | Capital account | Domestic exports | Foreign exports |
|---|---|---|---|---|---|---|
| Low | Medium | High | | | | |
| -100 | -196 | -69 | — | — | -135 | -1 |
| 30 | 183 | 152 | 41388 | 2529 | 168185 | 96465 |
| — | — | — | -117 | -14 | -9 | -409 |
| -3 | -9 | -7 | — | -3 | — | -244 |
| -7 | -28 | -24 | — | — | -22 | -12 |
| -184 | -378 | -255 | — | — | -1623 | -376 |
| -7 | -18 | -14 | — | — | -547 | -250 |
| -223 | -566 | -360 | -1 | — | -2100 | -162 |
| — | -1 | — | -14 | — | -224 | -5 |
| | | | | | | |
| -45 | -107 | -123 | -22 | — | -579 | -4 |
| -2353 | -4466 | -2485 | -205 | — | -1599 | -113 |
| 1467 | 9092 | 8637 | -23195 | -9159 | -21700 | -5583 |
| -741 | -1859 | -1082 | -339 | 1 | -38 | -300 |
| -3 | -2 | — | -10 | — | — | -5 |
| -468 | -1127 | -959 | -619 | -1 | -13 | -6 |
| -102 | -219 | -186 | -32 | — | -59 | -28 |
| 1523 | 4917 | 3764 | 175390 | — | -126 | -24 |
| -52 | -97 | -69 | -195 | — | — | -10 |
| -15681 | -21053 | -12434 | -29420 | -314 | -21197 | -2382 |
| -223 | -319 | -252 | -1203 | — | -40 | -15 |
| -597 | -925 | -895 | -884 | -1 | -112 | -35 |
| 6361 | 20485 | 15054 | 3145 | 4 | 6167 | 233 |
| | | | | | | |
| — | — | — | — | — | -4445 | — |
| — | — | — | — | — | -3739 | — |
| | | | | | | |
| -1464 | -230 | 57 | -15861 | — | — | — |
| — | — | — | -28184 | -20 | — | — |
| — | — | — | -27835 | — | — | — |
| — | — | — | -6094 | — | — | — |
| | | | | | | |
| -3294 | -4220 | -425 | -81673 | -1990 | — | — |
| -84 | -8387 | -4147 | -13446 | -6 | — | — |
| -4568 | -9969 | -7187 | -16895 | -117 | — | -311 |
| -657 | -1580 | -1141 | -4901 | -141 | — | — |

*Table 4.A.3    The current environmentally adjusted SAM*

| Sector | Live-stock | Cotton | Food grains | Feed grains | Hay and grass | Fruit | Tree nuts | Vege-tables |
|---|---|---|---|---|---|---|---|---|
| Livestock | 555.3 | 10.5 | 11.1 | 32.5 | 14.3 | 5.8 | 1.3 | 9.5 |
| Cotton | 1.3 | 11.2 | 0.1 | 0.1 | 0.1 | 1.6 | 0.4 | 0.8 |
| Food grains | 6.1 | 0.6 | 20.4 | 0.1 | 0.1 | 0.8 | 0.2 | 0.4 |
| Feed grains | 344.6 | — | — | 39.0 | — | — | — | — |
| Hay and grass | 564.2 | 1.1 | 0.1 | 2.4 | 2.8 | 1.4 | 0.3 | 0.7 |
| Fruits | 2.8 | 2.5 | 0.3 | 0.3 | 0.2 | 3.3 | 0.8 | 1.7 |
| Tree nuts | 0.6 | 0.6 | 0.1 | 0.1 | 0.1 | 0.7 | 0.2 | 0.4 |
| Vegetables | 2.5 | 1.7 | 0.2 | 0.2 | 0.2 | 2.3 | 0.5 | 60.9 |
| Miscellaneous crops | 0.4 | 0.3 | — | 1.5 | 1.2 | 0.4 | 0.1 | 0.2 |
| Forest products | 189.5 | 171.0 | 20.2 | 20.6 | 16.8 | 308.2 | 60.5 | 146.2 |
| Food processing | 872.9 | 0.4 | 0.3 | 0.6 | 0.5 | 0.8 | 0.1 | 0.8 |
| Services | 68.9 | 23.3 | 17.6 | 26.7 | 21.5 | 169.3 | 17.3 | 52.7 |
| Non-agricultural industry | 66.3 | 51.7 | 62.0 | 77.4 | 63.7 | 205.9 | 45.7 | 92.8 |
| Oil, gas and refining | 3.9 | 27.8 | 16.3 | 30.5 | 24.6 | 51.5 | 8.1 | 40.4 |
| Agricultural chemicals | 1.5 | — | — | 1.0 | 0.9 | 5.6 | 1.4 | 6.5 |
| Textiles | 8.7 | 0.4 | 0.2 | 0.4 | 0.4 | 8.2 | 1.5 | 7.4 |
| Wood and paper | 17.2 | 4.8 | 2.6 | 6.0 | 4.8 | 9.5 | 1.7 | 7.8 |
| Non-agricultural chemicals | 15.4 | 1.6 | 2.9 | 3.6 | 2.9 | 5.2 | 0.6 | 5.0 |
| Railroads | 307.7 | 204.1 | 126.1 | 142.6 | 116.8 | 171.0 | 41.2 | 229.6 |
| Trucking | 64.1 | 5.0 | 4.0 | 8.1 | 6.6 | 13.6 | 1.9 | 21.2 |
| Air transport | 2.1 | 1.1 | 0.1 | 0.2 | 0.2 | 6.3 | 1.1 | 12.5 |
| Utilities | 25.3 | 23.2 | 6.7 | 16.3 | 13.7 | 39.5 | — | 30.8 |
| Labor | 279.9 | 147.6 | 30.7 | 30.2 | 21.8 | 588.3 | 132.0 | 374.5 |
| Capital | 401.9 | 282.5 | 176.3 | 265.8 | 196.2 | 812.3 | 244.0 | 1384.3 |
| Enterprises | — | — | — | — | — | — | — | — |
| Low income households | — | — | — | — | — | — | — | — |
| Medium income households | — | — | — | — | — | — | — | — |
| High income households | — | — | — | — | — | — | — | — |
| Government | 117.7 | 14.7 | 12.7 | 22.6 | 13.6 | 47.9 | 11.1 | 37.2 |
| Capital account | — | — | — | — | — | — | — | — |
| Domestic imports | 715.2 | 127.6 | 93.1 | 158.6 | 120.6 | 277.5 | 42.6 | 259.3 |
| Rest of world imports | 8.1 | 6.2 | 5.0 | 8.6 | 6.9 | 11.9 | 2.0 | 11.0 |
| Total | 4644.2 | 1121.4 | 609.0 | 895.9 | 651.4 | 2748.9 | 616.5 | 2794.7 |

| Misc. crops | Forest prod. | Food proc. | Non-ag. industry | Oil, gas, and ref. | Ag. chemicals | Textiles | Wood and paper | Non-ag. chemicals | Rail |
|---|---|---|---|---|---|---|---|---|---|
| 1.3 | 58.2 | 2716.6 | — | — | — | 5.9 | 3.8 | 2.0 | — |
| 0.1 | 0.6 | 81.5 | — | — | — | 12.0 | — | — | — |
| — | 0.3 | 211.4 | — | — | — | — | — | — | — |
| — | 3.1 | 215.7 | — | — | 1.7 | — | — | — | — |
| 0.1 | 10.0 | — | — | — | — | — | — | 0.9 | — |
| 0.2 | 1.2 | 934.4 | — | — | — | — | — | — | — |
| — | 0.3 | 34.0 | — | — | — | — | — | — | — |
| 0.1 | 0.8 | 530.2 | — | — | — | — | — | — | — |
| 14.3 | 0.2 | 173.1 | — | — | — | 0.3 | 2.2 | 14.3 | — |
| 10.8 | 192.6 | 83.3 | 146.4 | — | 0.1 | 19.9 | 173.3 | 8.6 | 0.3 |
| 0.1 | 21.4 | 3282.6 | 58.3 | 9.2 | 2.3 | 2.0 | 3.3 | 83.0 | 0.3 |
| 8.0 | 186.7 | 3766.6 | 39139.8 | 1293.9 | 48.7 | 186.1 | 424.2 | 915.9 | 344.6 |
| 17.1 | 260.7 | 277.0 | 2741.0 | 9931.6 | 45.5 | 42.7 | 155.6 | 663.9 | 169.9 |
| 8.0 | 116.8 | 3.2 | 17.3 | 4.8 | 17.2 | 0.2 | 1.1 | 14.3 | 0.9 |
| — | 14.9 | 9.5 | 417.7 | 1.8 | 0.5 | 795.1 | 12.2 | 2.5 | 0.4 |
| 0.1 | 4.2 | 185.0 | 2805.8 | 4.6 | 5.2 | 17.1 | 1120.3 | 29.1 | 0.6 |
| 1.5 | 42.0 | 137.6 | 1859.5 | 226.3 | 17.9 | 43.0 | 128.5 | 505.0 | 1.2 |
| 0.8 | 7.7 | 143.2 | 464.8 | 34.9 | 5.1 | 3.7 | 53.9 | 43.9 | 57.7 |
| 52.9 | 586.0 | 1800.0 | 19200.2 | 3078.5 | 45.5 | 399.7 | 321.3 | 793.7 | 142.5 |
| 2.5 | 27.9 | 562.4 | 1735.4 | 89.8 | 17.1 | 30.8 | 66.1 | 94.7 | 11.2 |
| 0.1 | 61.2 | 116.2 | 1272.8 | 81.8 | 4.7 | 28.3 | 27.6 | 52.2 | 4.2 |
| 15.5 | 48.3 | 304.1 | 1603.8 | 627.0 | 17.1 | 38.2 | 103.9 | 113.4 | 5.5 |
| 33.3 | 1645.9 | 4308.6 | 57651.4 | 1535.8 | 60.9 | 1631.7 | 1465.6 | 1466.7 | 820.8 |
| 158.2 | 711.3 | 2947.4 | 5214.2 | 4571.8 | 78.8 | 437.0 | 456.4 | 901.6 | 114.0 |
| — | — | — | — | — | — | — | — | — | — |
| — | — | — | — | — | — | — | — | — | — |
| — | — | — | 7.9 | — | — | — | — | — | — |
| — | — | — | — | — | — | — | — | — | — |
| 5.2 | 110.7 | 947.3 | 2338.9 | 1696.0 | 8.6 | 48.5 | 52.6 | 120.8 | 63.8 |
| — | — | — | — | — | — | — | — | — | — |
| 47.5 | 651.0 | 5802.7 | 27470.8 | 6999.1 | 139.0 | 2257.0 | 1567.6 | 1205.6 | 110.0 |
| 2.1 | 29.6 | 787.4 | 2708.7 | 3219.3 | 12.7 | 166.4 | 115.7 | 136.1 | 10.3 |
| 379.9 | 4793.6 | 30360.9 | 166854.5 | 33406.3 | 528.5 | 6165.4 | 6255.3 | 7168.1 | 1858.3 |

*Table 4.A.3 (continued)*

| Sector | Services | Truck | Air trans. | Utilities | Labor | Capital | Enter-prises |
|---|---|---|---|---|---|---|---|
| Livestock | 145.3 | — | 0.3 | — | — | — | — |
| Cotton | — | — | — | — | — | — | — |
| Food grains | — | 0.2 | — | — | — | — | — |
| Feed grains | 100.7 | — | — | — | — | — | — |
| Hay and grass | — | — | — | — | — | — | — |
| Fruits | 21.3 | — | — | — | 12.0 | — | — |
| Tree nuts | — | — | — | — | 13.2 | — | — |
| Vegetables | 163.7 | — | — | — | — | — | — |
| Miscellaneous crops | 12.6 | — | — | — | — | — | — |
| Forest products | 563.8 | 0.3 | 0.5 | 1.0 | — | — | — |
| Food processing | 4709.6 | 0.6 | 10.8 | 0.9 | — | — | — |
| Services | 13967.8 | 131.9 | 320.6 | 675.1 | — | — | — |
| Non-agricultural industry | 3333.9 | 543.9 | 2231.6 | 1998.9 | — | — | — |
| Oil, gas and refining | 32.9 | — | — | 0.4 | — | — | — |
| Agricultural chemicals | 348.8 | 4.6 | 3.8 | 0.8 | — | — | — |
| Textiles | 586.3 | 4.4 | 3.1 | 17.8 | — | — | — |
| Wood and paper | 1107.2 | 4.1 | 4.1 | 21.7 | — | — | — |
| Non-agricultural chemicals | 203.1 | 26.7 | 4.8 | 80.6 | — | — | — |
| Railroads | 58320.0 | 944.4 | 1791.9 | 498.1 | — | — | — |
| Trucking | 1186.3 | 999.9 | 82.8 | 39.5 | — | — | — |
| Air transport | 1699.2 | 15.1 | 651.7 | 18.3 | — | — | — |
| Utilities | 3461.4 | 18.0 | 28.2 | 1406.6 | — | — | — |
| Labor | 133638.3 | 3112.7 | 2237.1 | 1519.5 | — | — | — |
| Capital | 83272.8 | 1138.9 | 339.8 | 2700.4 | — | — | — |
| Enterprises | — | — | — | — | 21.5 | 70170.2 | — |
| Low income households | — | — | — | — | 12086.8 | — | 8435.8 |
| Medium income households | 29.0 | — | — | — | 108619.3 | 4691.4 | 27950.8 |
| High income households | 30.4 | — | — | — | 77187.5 | 7639.1 | 27213.7 |
| Government | 20569.7 | 196.8 | 331.8 | 461.9 | 31320.8 | — | 22145.4 |
| Capital account | — | — | — | — | 30.3 | 37800.6 | 3088.4 |
| Domestic imports | 14128.0 | 307.5 | 411.1 | 3022.9 | 19.3 | 424.5 | 4.0 |
| Rest of world imports | 1715.6 | 20.4 | 748.4 | 73.9 | — | — | — |
| Total | 343347.6 | 7470.4 | 9202.4 | 12538.3 | 229310.7 | 120725.7 | 88838.0 |

| Households | | | Government | Capital account | Domestic exports | Foreign exports | Total |
|---|---|---|---|---|---|---|---|
| Low | Medium | High | | | | | |
| 94.6 | 270.2 | 166.1 | — | 22.7 | 505.7 | 11.1 | 4644.2 |
| — | — | — | 135.3 | 9.8 | 550.9 | 315.7 | 1121.4 |
| — | — | — | 48.2 | 12.1 | — | 308.2 | 609.0 |
| 1.6 | — | — | — | — | — | 189.5 | 895.9 |
| 3.4 | 19.1 | 20.5 | — | — | 13.9 | 10.4 | 651.4 |
| 75.8 | 206.7 | 147.0 | — | — | 1056.9 | 281.3 | 2748.9 |
| 3.4 | — | 9.2 | — | — | 362.5 | 191.1 | 616.5 |
| 95.4 | 284.7 | 183.7 | — | — | 1348.7 | 118.9 | 2794.7 |
| — | — | — | — | — | 154.7 | 4.0 | 379.9 |
| 43.0 | 174.0 | 192.5 | 16.5 | — | 2155.6 | 78.2 | 4793.6 |
| 2152.3 | 6865.5 | 4516.3 | 134.8 | 5.5 | 5952.9 | 1672.7 | 30360.9 |
| 963.9 | 4328.4 | 4033.6 | 12368.8 | 29942.6 | 38186.4 | 15223.6 | 166854.5 |
| 683.4 | 2835.3 | 1958.6 | 216.2 | 29.9 | 142.9 | 4461.1 | 33406.3 |
| 2.9 | 11.0 | 10.0 | — | — | — | 84.4 | 528.5 |
| 436.0 | 1691.0 | 1769.5 | 397.1 | 101.5 | 46.2 | 94.6 | 6165.4 |
| 98.8 | 365.2 | 295.5 | 25.1 | 10.2 | 222.8 | 427.0 | 6255.3 |
| 290.8 | 896.2 | 673.7 | 295.9 | 21.6 | 469.0 | 367.0 | 7168.1 |
| 52.2 | 134.1 | 161.7 | 133.8 | 45.3 | — | 163.0 | 1858.3 |
| 20549.7 | 70643.9 | 63019.5 | 30819.6 | 2959.7 | 54772.3 | 11269.3 | 343347.6 |
| 199.3 | 507.5 | 438.8 | 771.4 | 109.9 | 147.5 | 224.9 | 7470.4 |
| 547.4 | 1389.0 | 1658.4 | 573.8 | 42.6 | 418.2 | 516.0 | 9202.4 |
| 590.7 | 1820.9 | 1321.0 | 306.1 | — | 534.2 | 19.1 | 12538.3 |
| — | — | — | — | — | 16577.5 | — | 229310.7 |
| — | — | — | — | — | 13919.8 | — | 120725.7 |
| 3365.2 | 3838.3 | 1369.6 | 10073.1 | — | — | — | 88838.0 |
| — | — | — | 17749.5 | 3317.4 | — | — | 41589.4 |
| — | — | — | 17672.8 | — | — | — | 158971.2 |
| — | — | — | 3884.8 | — | — | — | 115955.4 |
| 6285.0 | 31130.1 | 10440.3 | 50714.4 | 20501.2 | — | — | 199767.1 |
| 72.6 | 12834.3 | 7590.9 | 39550.8 | 1114.3 | — | — | 102082.3 |
| 4351.1 | 16191.0 | 13821.3 | 10770.6 | 21405.1 | — | 4637.6 | 137538.5 |
| 630.9 | 2534.6 | 2157.5 | 3108.8 | 22430.8 | — | — | 40668.8 |
| 41589.4 | 158971.2 | 115955.4 | 199767.1 | 102082.3 | 137538.5 | 40668.8 | 1879858.6 |

## NOTES

1.  For the analysis presented here, the 1982 database is used because output from the 1990 IMPLAN database does not permit construction of a macro summary SAM.
2.  The DRASTIC model, developed by the EPA in the 1980s, uses a numerical ranking system that assigns relative weights to various hydrological and geological factors to obtain an index of relative groundwater pollution potential (Aller et al., 1987).
3.  The method used to balance the CEA SAM is the generalized cross-entropy method developed by Golan et al. (1994).
4.  It should be noted that the multiplier analysis does not provide information on the exogenous accounts, including government (indirect taxes) and investment (depreciation). As a result, a full adjustment to NNP cannot be calculated on the basis of these future damages.

## REFERENCES

Adelman, I., Berck, P. and Vujovic, D. (1991), 'Using Social Accounting Matrices to Account for Distortions in Non-market Economies', *Economic Systems Research*, 3, pp. 269–298.

Ahmed, Y., El Serafy, S. and Lutz, E. (eds) (1989), *Environmental Accounting for Sustainable Development*, Washington, DC: World Bank.

Aller, L., Bennett, T., Lehr, J.H., Petty, R. and Hackett, G. (1987), *DRASTIC: A Standardized System for Evaluating Ground Water Pollution Potential Using Hydrogeologic Settings*, U.S. Environmental Protection Agency Report EPA/600/2-87/035, Ada, Oklahoma: Robert S. Kerr Environmental Research Laboratory, U.S. EPA.

Barse, J., Ferguson, W. and Whetzel, V. (1985), *Effects of Air Pollution and Acid Rain on Agriculture: An Annotated Bibliography*, Washington, DC: Natural Resource Economics Division, Economic Research Service, U.S. Department of Agriculture, ERS Staff Report No. AGES850702.

Bartelmus, P. (1989), 'Environmental Accounting and the System of National Accounts', in Ahmed, Y., El Serafy, S. and Lutz, E. (eds), *Environmental Accounting for Sustainable Development*, Washington, DC: World Bank.

Bartelmus, P., Stahmer, C. and van Tongeren, J. (1991), 'Integrated Environmental and Economic Accounting: Framework for a SNA Satellite System', *Review of Income and Wealth*, 37, pp. 111–148.

Baumol, W. and Oates, W. (1988), *The Theory of Environmental Policy* (2nd Edition), New York: Cambridge University Press.

Beckerman, W. (1972), '"Environment", "Needs", and Real Income Comparisons', *The Review of Income and Wealth*, 18, pp. 333–339.

Bell, F. and Canterbery, E.R. (1975), *An Assessment of the Economic Benefits Which Will Accrue to Commercial and Recreational Fisheries from Incremental Improvements in the Quality of Coastal Waters*, Tallahassee: Florida State University.

Bergman, L. (1991), 'General Equilibrium Effects of Environmental Policy: A CGE-Modeling Approach', *Environmental and Resource Economics*, 1, pp. 43–61.

Bhagwati, J.N. and Srinivasan, T.N. (1981), 'The Evaluation of Projects at World Prices Under Trade Distortions: Quantitative Restrictions, Monopoly Power in Trade and Non-traded goods', *International Economic Review*, 22, pp. 385–399.

Bojo, J., Mäler, K.-G. and Unemo, L. (1990), *Environment and Development: An Economic Approach*, London: Kluwer Academic Publishers.

Buchanan, J.M. and Tullock, G. (1965), *The Calculus of Consent*, Ann Arbor, MI: University of Michigan Press.

Carson, R., Hanemann, W.M., Alberini, A., Kanninen, B., Martin, K. and Mitchell, R. (1991), *Valuation of Non-market Aspects of Water Systems*, Technical Report for Project UCLA-W-722 to the Water Resources Center, University of California.

Clark, E.H., Haverkamp, J.A. and Chapman, W. (1985), *Eroding Soils: The Off-Farm Impacts*, Washington, DC: The Conservation Foundation.

Committee of International Development Institutions on the Environment (CIDIE) (1992), *The Present State of Environmental and Resource Accounting and Its Potential Application in Developing Countries*. Presented at the Environmental and Natural Resource Accounting Workshop, UNEP Headquarters, Nairobi, 24–26 February.

Crutchfield, S.R. (1988), 'Agricultural Externalities and Environmental Policy: Re-Emergence of an Old Issue', paper prepared for the Annual Meetings, American Agricultural Economics Association, Knoxville, Tennessee.

Crutchfield, S.R., Ribaudo, M.O., Setia, P., Letson, D. and Hansen, L. (1991), *Cotton Production and Water Quality, An Initial Assessment, Resources and Technology Division*, Economic Research Service, U.S. Department of Agriculture, Staff Report AGES 9105.

Daly, H. (1989), 'Toward a Measure of Sustainable Social Net National Product', in Ahmed, Y., El Serafy, S. and Lutz, E. (eds), *Environmental Accounting for Sustainable Development*, Washington, DC: World Bank.

Dasgupta, P. and Mäler, K.-G. (1991), 'The Environment and Emerging Development Issues', in Fischer, S., de Tray, D. and Shekhar, S. (eds), *Proceedings of the World Bank Annual Conference on Development Economics, 1990*, pp. 101–131.

Eisner, R. (1985), 'The Total Incomes System of Accounts', *Survey of Current Business*, **65**, pp. 24–48.

Eisner, R. (1988), 'Extended Accounts for National Income and Product', *Journal of Economic Literature*, **26**, pp. 1611–1684.

El Serafy, S. (1989), 'The Proper Calculation of Income from Depletable Natural Resources', in Ahmed, Y., El Serafy, S. and Lutz, E. (eds), *Environmental Accounting for Sustainable Development*, Washington, DC: World Bank.

El Serafy, S. (1992), 'The Environment as Capital', in Lutz, E. (ed.), *Toward Improved Accounting for the Environment*, Washington, DC: World Bank.

Freeman, M.A., III (1982), *Air and Water Pollution Control: A Benefit-Cost Assessment*, New York: John Wiley and Sons.

Golan, A., Judge, G. and Robinson, S. (1994), 'Recovering Information from Incomplete or Partial Multi-Sectoral Economic Data', *Review of Economics and Statistics*, **76**, pp. 541–549.

Hanson, K. and Robinson, S. (1991), 'Data, Linkages and Models: US National Income and Product Accounts in the Framework of a Social Accounting Matrix', *Economic Systems Research*, **3**, pp. 215–232.

Harrison, A. (1989a), 'Introducing Natural Capital into the SNA', in Ahmed, Y., El Serafy, S. and Lutz, E. (eds), *Environmental Accounting for Sustainable Development*, Washington, DC: World Bank.

Harrison, A. (1989b), 'Environmental Issues and the SNA', *Review of Income and Wealth*, **35**, pp. 377–389.

Hicks, J. (1939), *Value and Capital*, Oxford: Oxford University Press.

Howitt, R.E. (1991), *Water in California: A Resilient System Under Pressure*, UC/AIC Position Paper No. 91-1, Davis: University of California.

Just, R., Hueth, D. and Schmitz, A. (1982), *Applied Welfare Economics and Public Policy*, Englewood Cliffs, NJ: Prentice-Hall.

Kahn, H.A. and Thorbecke, E. (1988), *Macro Economic Effects and Diffusion of Alternative Technologies within a Social Accounting Matrix Framework: The Case of In-*

*donesia*, London: Gower Publishing Co. (For the World Employment Programme of the International Labour Office.)

Krueger, A.O. (1983), *Alternative Trade Strategies and Employment: Synthesis and Conclusions*, Chicago, IL: University of Chicago Press.

Lichtenberg, E., Zilberman, D. and Ellis, G. (1988), *Economic Spillover Effects of Regulating Water Use in the San Joaquin Valley*, Department of Agricultural and Resource Economics, University of California, Berkeley, unpublished draft.

Little, I.M.D. and Mirrlees, J.A. (1974), *Project Appraisal and Planning for Developing Countries*, London: Heinemann.

Lutz, E. (ed.) (1992), *Toward Improved Accounting for the Environment*, Washington, DC: World Bank.

Mäler, K.-G. (1991), 'National Accounts and Environmental Resources', *Environment and Resource Economics*, **1**, pp. 1–15.

Marshall, A. (Eighth Edition, 1920), *Principles of Economics*, London: Macmillan and Co.

Navrud, S. (1994), *Pricing the European Environment*, Oslo: Scandinavian University Press.

Nielsen, E.G. and Lee, L.K. (1987), *The Magnitude and Costs of Groundwater Contamination from Agricultural Chemicals*, Agricultural Economic Report #576, USDA, ERS.

Pearce, D., Markandya, A. and Barbier, E.B. (1989), *Blueprint for a Green Economy*, London: Earthscan Publications Ltd.

Pigou, A.C. (1920), *The Economics of Welfare*, London: Macmillan.

Pyatt, G. and Roe, A.R. (1977), *Social Accounting for Development Planning with Special Reference to Sri Lanka*, London: Cambridge University Press.

Pyatt, G. and Round, J. (1977), 'Social Accounting Matrices for Development Planning', *Review of Income and Wealth*, **23**, pp. 339–364.

Raucher, R.L. (1986), 'The Benefits and Costs of Policies Related to Groundwater Contamination', *Land Economics*, **62**, pp. 33–45.

Repetto, R., Magrath, W., Wells, M., Beer, C. and Rossini, F. (1989), *Wasting Assets: Natural Resources in the National Income Accounts*, Washington, DC: World Resources Institute.

Resosudarmo, R. and Thorbecke, E. (1995), *The Impact of Environmental Management on Household Incomes for Different Socio-economic Classes: The Case of Air Pollutants in Indonesia*, Department of Agricultural, Resource and Managerial Economics, Cornell University, draft.

Ribaudo, M. (1987), *Agriculture's Impact on Water Quality, Agricultural Resources – Agricultural Land Values and Markets Situation and Outlook Report*, USDA, ERS, AR-6, pp. 30–33.

Ribaudo, M. (1989), *Water Quality Benefits from the Conservation Reserve Program*, AER-606, U.S. Department of Agriculture, Economic Research Service.

Schmidt, R.H. and Plaut, S.E. (1993), 'Water Policy in California and Israel', *Federal Reserve Bank of San Francisco Economic Review*, **3**, pp. 42–55.

Stahmer, C. (1992), 'System for Integrated Environmental and Economic Accounting (SEEA) of the United Nations', Paper presented at a symposium on Environmental Resources in National Accounting, Ein Gedi, Israel, 30 Nov.–4 Dec.

Stohbehn, R.W. (ed.) (1986), *An Economic Analysis of USDA Erosion Control Programs*, AER Report No. 560, USDA, ERS.

Stohbehn, R.W. and Alt, K. (1988), *An Economic Perspective of Soil Conservation Policy, Agricultural Resources – Agricultural Land Values and Markets Situation and Outlook Report*, USDA, ERS, AR-6, pp. 33–39.

Stone, R. (1961), *Input–Output and National Accounts*, Paris: Organization for European Economic Cooperation.

Stone, R. (1977), 'Foreword' in Pyatt, G. and Roe, A.R., *Social Accounting for Development Planning with Special Reference to Sri Lanka*, London: Cambridge University Press.

Weale, M. (1992), *Environmental Statistics and the National Accounts*, Working Paper, Department of Applied Economics and Clare College, Cambridge.

Willig, R.D. (1976), 'Consumer Surplus without Apology', *American Economic Review*, **66**, pp. 589–597.

# 5 Environmental Accounting and Agriculture

## James Hrubovcak, Michael LeBlanc and Kelly Eakin

## 1 INTRODUCTION

National income accounting is one of the most important economic policy-making tools developed in the last 50 years. Detailed information derived from the accounts provides the basis for economic interpretations of changes in the nation's income and wealth. These national income and product accounts (NIPA) through their measures of Gross Domestic Product (GDP) and Net National Product (NNP) often provide the only meaningful indicators of the effects of public policy interventions. Nearly from the inception of national income accounting, however, economists have criticized the NIPA by identifying inconsistencies with the underlying theory and the empirical application of the theory.

Early criticism of the NIPA focused on the treatment of capital, leisure and government expenditures. Recent critiques, with historical roots in the early 1970s, question the use of NNP as a measure of social welfare because it does not account for the value of changes in the stock of natural resources, nor does it include the value of environmental goods and services. Critics question the credibility of the accounts because natural and reproducible capital are treated asymmetrically and the value of non-marketed environmental goods and services is not captured (Prince and Gordon, 1994).[1] NNP, it is argued, is not a useful measure of long-term sustainable growth. The failure to explicitly consider the environment in the accounts misrepresents the current estimate of well-being, distorts the representation of the economy's production and substitution possibilities, and fails to inform policy makers on important issues related to economic growth and the environment.

Several attempts to adjust income measures to account for the environment exist. It is most common for these studies to focus on accounting for natural resource depletion (Repetto, 1992a, 1992b; Smith, 1992; Nestor and Pasurka, 1994; U.S. Department of Commerce, 1994).[2] Theoretical and empirical problems persist, however, particularly when the level of environmental services and damages is estimated. For example, no consistent approach for the treatment of 'defensive expenditures' in response to or in anticipation of environmental injury has emerged from the literature (Ahmad et al., 1989).

Our intent in this chapter is to more accurately measure economic well-being. Improving the measure of current economic activity requires incorporating non-market final goods and bads into the existing accounts. Economic well-being, however, extends beyond current economic activity and must also reflect future production possibilities. We begin by developing a theoretically consistent framework for incorporating natural capital and environmental goods into the existing income accounts. Next, we empirically apply the framework and adjust agricultural income and national income to reflect the depletion of agricultural natural capital (land and water) and the non-market effects of agricultural production on output in other sectors and on consumer utility.

The theoretical framework developed for this study is grounded on the work of Arrow and Kurz (1970), Weitzman (1976), Solow (1986), Hartwick (1990) and Mäler (1991). Weitzman has shown that the current value Hamiltonian in a neoclassical growth model of the aggregate economy can be interpreted as NNP.[3] Solow incorporated exhaustible resources as distinct capital assets into Weitzman's treatment of NNP. Hartwick and Mäler extended Solow's approach to capture renewable resources and environmental capital (pollution abatement). In our analysis, the Hartwick–Solow–Weitzman framework is extended to include three production sectors (agriculture, non-agriculture and household production). This extension allows us to adjust measures of agricultural and national income. Rather than viewing non-market environmental goods as externalities, we follow the prescription of Solow (1992) and cast the environment as a set of natural capital assets providing flows of goods and services to the economy. Economic use of natural capital results in feedback effects. For example, depletion of the stock of natural capital reduces future flows of goods and services from the environment, while degradation from disposal of residuals results in costs imposed on third parties. In addition, firms and households are allowed to make expenditures for pollution abatement and control.

Results from a dynamic optimization model are utilized to adjust NNP and net farm product (NFP) for the use of natural capital assets. In addition, NNP reflects the value of net changes in capital goods (net investment) and the value of net changes in the stock of natural capital. Optimizing the current value Hamiltonian yields scarcity values for all capital stocks including natural capital. The optimization process, therefore, generates relationships for adjusting current NNP to account for the current value of the loss of natural capital stocks from using exhaustible resources and depleting and degrading renewable and environmental resources.

Theoretical results from our model mirror Hartwick's results. That is, GDP includes priced resource input flows and these flows from capital stocks should be offset by deductions from GDP to incorporate the value of changes in natural resource capital stocks to arrive at NNP.[4] Our empirical application suggests only minor changes are necessary when natural resource effects are incorporated into the national income accounts. Adjustments to the national accounts are minor because agricultural production is a small component of U.S. GDP (less than 2 percent) and most extra-agricultural effects are currently captured in GDP. Larger changes are warranted, however, in the adjustment of net agricultural income. Most effects represent income transfers between agriculture and other sectors.

Agricultural income is adjusted to reflect the value of changes in the stocks of 'effective' farmland, water quality and the stock of groundwater. These natural capital stocks may change due to damages associated with agricultural production. Specifically, the effects of soil erosion on agricultural productivity and income, the economic effects of decreased surface-water quality and the depletion of groundwater stocks are presented as examples of the potential scope of accounting adjustments needed in the agricultural sector. We adjust income for changes in the stock of groundwater because in some regions of the United States there has been a sustained withdrawal of groundwater stocks. Our estimated adjustments would require net agricultural income to be revised downward by $4 billion (6 percent). These estimated adjustments to net farm income are consistent with a view of U.S. agriculture where environmental problems exist and where the resource base is depreciating. However, they also suggest that agriculture's contribution to social welfare far exceeds the environmental damages and deterioration of the stock of natural capital resulting from the production of food.

## 2 NATIONAL INCOME ACCOUNTING

The NIPA were developed primarily to monitor the macroeconomic performance of the economy. The most widely used measure of economic activity is GDP. GDP is highly correlated with employment and capacity utilization and therefore central to how business cycles are defined and tracked.

A simple circular flow diagram is a powerful model to illustrate the flow of final goods and services from the business sector to the household sector and the concurrent flow of factor services from households to firms (Figure 5.1). In a monetized economy, goods and services exchange for consumer expenditures while primary factors of production (endowments of capital, labor and land) exchange for wages and salaries, rent, interest and profit. The circular flow model suggests two methods for measuring the monetary value of current GDP: flow of output and flow of income. In a flow-of-output approach, all expenditures on final goods and services are added together. This measure captures the transactions from the 'upper loop' of the circular flow model and includes the value of new capital (gross investment), government purchases of goods and services, and net exports. The flow-of-income alternative yields an equivalent measure of GDP

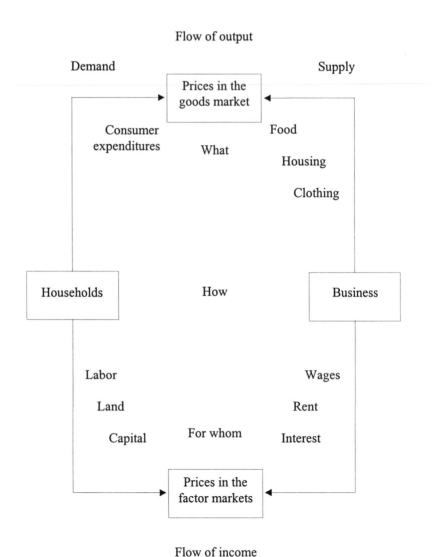

Figure 5.1   Circular flow model

and is computed by summing payments to the primary factors of production. Because GDP is a measure of final goods and services, purchases of intermediate goods must be excluded. The failure to exclude intermediate goods and services from national income results in 'double counting' and an overstatement of the level of economic activity.

Table 5.1 summarizes the NIPA for 1992. The table illustrates the flow-of-income and flow-of-output approaches. Though arrived at in different ways, the calculations of national income and GDP are equal in either case ($6 trillion). The flow-of-income approach includes compensation of employees ($3.6 trillion), proprietors' income ($0.4 trillion), corporate profits ($0.4 trillion), net interest ($0.4 trillion), and rental income (-$8.9 billion). The flow-of-output approach

*Table 5.1   Overview of the existing NIPA accounts, 1992 (billion dollars)*

| Flow of income | | Flow of output | |
|---|---|---|---|
| Compensation of employees | 3,582.0 | Personal consumption expenditures | 4,139.9 |
| Proprietors' income | 414.3 | Gross domestic investment | 796.5 |
| Corporate profits | 407.2 | Government purchases | 1,131.8 |
| Net interest | 442.0 | Net exports | -29.6 |
| Rental income | -8.9 | | |
| *National income* | 4,836.6 | *GDP* | 6,038.6 |
| | | | |
| Business transfer payments | 27.6 | Business transfer payments | -27.6 |
| Individual tax and non-tax liability | 502.8 | Individual tax and non-tax liability | -502.8 |
| Subsidies less government surplus | -2.7 | Subsidies less government surplus | 2.7 |
| Consumption of fixed capital | 657.9 | Consumption of fixed capital | -657.9 |
| Gross national income | 6,022.2 | | |
| Statistical discrepancy | 23.6 | Statistical discrepancy | -23.6 |
| Gross national income | 6,045.8 | | |
| Rest of world net factor income | -7.3 | Rest of world net factor income | 7.3 |
| *GDP* | 6,038.5 | *National income* | 4,836.7 |

*Source*:   U.S. Department of Commerce, Bureau of Economic Analysis, Survey of Current Business (1993).

includes expenditures on final goods and services by households ($4.1 trillion), the government ($1.1 trillion) and gross investment by firms ($0.8 trillion).[5]

Net of taxes, the largest single item differentiating GDP from national income is the consumption of fixed capital or depreciation. For 1992, U.S. GDP exceeded $6 trillion while national income approached $5 trillion. Depreciation of the U.S. capital stock was estimated at $657.9 billion or about 11 percent of GDP. The concept of capital stock depreciation is particularly important when we turn our attention to natural capital and environmental assets.

Table 5.2 summarizes the calculation of farm income for 1992 using a flow-of-income approach. Gross farm income in 1992 was $84.4 billion or about 1.4 percent of U.S. GDP. While wage income (compensation to employees) is by far the largest income category at the national level (74 percent of U.S. national income), proprietors' income (65 percent) and net interest (15 percent) are the largest components of net farm income. Consumption of fixed capital in agriculture is 26 percent of gross farm income, over twice as large as the aggregate national rate.

Income accounts are subject to mis-measurement by either improperly including or excluding items. Including the exchange of intermediate goods and services in the measure of national income is an example of improper inclusion. Similarly, counting transfer payments or non-productive redistributions such as social security payments, welfare payments and agricultural deficiency payments as gross income is inconsistent with the received definition of national income.

*Table 5.2    Summary of farm income, 1982, 1987, 1992 (billion dollars)*

| Flow of income components | 1982 | 1987 | 1992 |
|---|---|---|---|
| Compensation of employees | 10.2 | 9.4 | 11.9 |
| Proprietors' income | 24.6 | 31.3 | 43.7 |
| Corporate profits | 1.1 | 1.1 | 1.0 |
| Net interest income | 18.1 | 12.5 | 10.2 |
| Net farm income | 54.0 | 54.3 | 66.8 |
| Indirect tax and non-tax liability | 3.3 | 3.6 | 4.4 |
| Subsidies less current government surplus | -2.4 | -13.9 | -8.4 |
| Consumption of fixed capital | 22.0 | 22.0 | 21.6 |
| Gross farm product | 76.9 | 66.0 | 84.4 |

*Source*: U.S. Department of Commerce, Bureau of Economic Analysis, Survey of Current Business (various years).

Improper exclusion occurs when the value of a final good or service is not included in the accounts. This occurs when a good or service is traded in informal markets commonly referred to as the 'underground economy'. Often these transactions in the form of 'cash-only' arrangements are undertaken to avoid taxes. 'Non-market' goods and services are also often excluded from the income accounts because they are difficult to measure. Examples include unpaid housework and child-care and environmental goods and services. In some cases, market values have been imputed for 'non-market' goods and the income accounts adjusted accordingly. The value of housing services received from owner-occupied houses is the best example.

The treatment of several elements in the accounts remains controversial and unclear. Leisure, for example, has properties associated with a normal economic good. Yet, whether and how to include the consumption of leisure in the national income accounts is unresolved. Another example is criminal activity. Criminal activity is typically viewed as reducing not enhancing social welfare and therefore not included in GDP. Legal gambling services in Nevada and New Jersey are, however, included. Excluding criminal transactions reflects a moral judgement about the desirability of illegal goods and services as indicators of social well-being. The cost of this moral judgement is to reduce the accounts' usefulness as a measure of economic activity.

Government expenditures on military defense, police and environmental clean-up add to the conventionally measured income accounts. Nordhaus and Tobin (1972) argue, however, that increases in these expenditures reflect the increasing 'disamenities of urban life' that decrease social well-being. Similarly, increases in household 'defensive' expenditures on items like mace and bottled water may signal a decrease in social welfare.

# 3   ENVIRONMENTAL ACCOUNTING

Environmental accounting addresses the improper exclusion of the services provided by environmental goods and the asymmetric treatment of natural capital and reproducible capital within the existing accounts. Including the provision of environmental goods and services greatly increases the complexity of properly adjusting the income accounts. Environmental goods and services rarely have observed market prices or easily measurable market quantities. The absence or incompleteness of these markets can have distorting effects on the goods for which markets exist. Even if environmental goods and services are not included in the accounts, their existence may cause distortions in the relative prices in traditionally measured sectors. If so, the view of measured NNP as the current consumption value of a dynamically optimal resource allocation is flawed.

Income accounting in the United States does not correct for price distortions. In developing countries, however, significant effort is made to correct income accounts for market distortions when the correction may be important for deciding among competing investment projects. The implicit rationale for not adjusting market prices in developed countries is that markets are well developed and distortions, to the extent they exist, are small. However, price distortions with respect to environmental and agricultural goods may be relatively large.

Changes in environmental quality have multiple effects across sectors and consumers. Producers are affected because changes in environmental quality can affect the productivity of other resources. Consumer utility is affected directly through changes in consumption and indirectly through effects in option or existence value. Environmental effects are, therefore, a mixture of private good, public good and quasi-public good effects.

The income accounts can be extended using the flow-of-output approach to value environmental goods and services produced. To avoid double counting, it is important to capture only the value of final environmental goods and services. Accounting for intermediate external effects is needed only to compute sectoral income. If, however, an accurate measure of national income alone is sought, then intermediate external effects can be ignored. In many cases externalities are intermediate goods whose value is imbedded in a bundle of final goods and services. Including intermediate goods in the income accounts is double counting. A similar argument holds for the flow-of-income approach. Economic rents generated by a non-market externality are captured in payments to factors of production.

Accounting for non-market goods requires adjusting GDP for environmental goods and services and transactions from the informal or underground economy. If changes to income consist largely of accounting for environmental effects, then adjusted aggregate income might be termed 'green GDP'. Adjusting GDP requires deriving a shadow price and physical measure for each final non-market good. No information is necessary on intermediate goods.

There is considerable agreement that national accounts, although flawed, are useful measures of economic performance and these accounts can be modified or extended to improve the measure of economic activity. Some economists have argued for developing alternative accounting systems. Satellite accounts, a related but separate set of environmental accounts, may be a preferred alternative to further diluting the quality of the market-based data with imputed transactions. Critics of integrating the accounts argue that, although flawed, the current income accounts reasonably represent the market economy. Satellite environmental accounts would include current market environmental expenditures as well as shadow accounts for non-market environmental goods. A complete system of satellite environmental accounts would allow the analyst to calculate the non-market adjustments and trace productivity effects across sectors.

The United Nations System for Integrated Environmental and Economic Accounting is a set of satellite environmental accounts supplementing the current System of National Accounts.[6] The intent is to develop an environmental accounting framework consistent with the concepts and principles underlying conventional income. Harrison (1989) presents criteria for guaranteeing the satellite accounts are complementary to, rather than a substitute for, the current accounts. A primary requirement is the parallel treatment of 'natural capital' (natural resources) and reproducible capital in the national accounts.

Although there have been other attempts to capture environmental effects in national accounts (Nordhaus and Tobin, 1972), Nestor and Pasurka (1994) is the most ambitious. Nestor and Pasurka disaggregate the U.S. input–output tables into environmental and non-environmental components. Adopting the framework of Schafer and Stahmer (1989), Nestor and Pasurka divide the environmental account into three categories. The 'internal environmental protection sector' captures intermediate goods and services produced and used within the environmental protection industry. The 'external environmental protection sector' captures the purchase of intermediate inputs from outside the sector. Examples include waste disposal, sewage treatment and environmental construction activities. The 'final demand sector' for environmental protection includes fixed capital formation for environmental protection, direct pollution abatement activities by governments and households, and net exports of environmental protection goods.

The Nestor and Pasurka approach is consistent with the proposed system for environmental and economic accounts (United Nations, 1993) and indicates the importance of environmental protection activities in GDP. Through disaggregation, they estimate the 1982 total value-added for environmental protection to be 0.3 percent of GDP. This is less than 20 percent of the $80.6 billion (1.7 percent of real GDP) estimate of real pollution and abatement control expenditures for 1991 (Rutledge and Leonard, 1993). While the Nestor and Pasurka approach provides more information on the contribution of market expenditures on environmental protection, it does not change the overall measure of GDP because it does not include non-market activities.

## 4   NNP AND WELFARE

NNP is the premier indicator of current market-based economic activity. NNP has also been promoted and, more importantly, interpreted as an indicator of social welfare. Samuelson (1961) rejected all current income concepts as meaningful welfare measures and argued instead for a 'wealth-like magnitude' such as the present discounted value of future consumption. Weitzman (1976) bridged the gap between Samuelson's argument for a wealth-based indicator of welfare and current measures of income by demonstrating that NNP captures both current consumption and the present value of future consumption. A current income concept and a wealth-like magnitude, he argues, 'are merely different sides of the same coin'.

Weitzman's results are illustrated in Figure 5.2. The production possibilities frontier, $B'B$, represents the economy's technical ability to transform investment goods into consumption goods. The budget constraint, $C'C$, represents society's willingness to trade off future consumption for current consumption which depends on the rate at which society discounts future consumption. The economy is located at point $A$ on the production possibilities frontier $B'B$. Optimal consumption and net investment are given by $C'$ and $dk^*/dt$. Real NNP is geometrically represented as $OC'$. The only point where measured income is supported by production is at $A$. $OC'$ is a strictly hypothetical consumption level at the present time, because the largest permanent consumption level obtainable is $OB'$. Production and income are equivalent only at $A$, unless the transformation of investment goods into consumption goods does not exhibit diminishing marginal returns. That is, if the production possibilities frontier is linear, $OB'$ is income, where income is interpreted as the maximum consumption possible. The correct measure of 'income' or NNP at the dynamic optimum is indicated by $A$. The level of constant consumption $OC'$ gives the same present value of welfare as the discounted maximum welfare received along the optimal consumption path. Thus, Weitzman calls $OC'$ the stationary equivalent of future consumption.

Weitzman argues that income accounts, properly measured, provide a measure of the welfare of society and give concrete economic form to the concept of sustainability. The current income accounts do not adequately measure welfare or sustainable income because they fail to consider non-market environmental goods and services and the degradation or depletion of non-renewable resources.

If natural capital has a market, but is excluded from the accounts, then the accounts fail to accurately measure true NNP. The only correction needed to adjust the national accounts is to deduct the value of the natural capital consumption (resource depletion). If natural capital does not have a market, however, or the market price is distorted, then adjusting the accounts for natural capital consumption is not as straightforward. Difficulties arise because there is a non-optimal level of resource depletion and the shadow price of resource depletion, an endogenous value, differs from the socially optimal price. Similarly, if natural capital is substitutable for reproducible capital, properly measured NNP also represents the maximum level of sustainable income for society. However, if natural capital cannot substitute for reproducible capital, the link between aggregate NNP and sustainable income is more problematic.

## 5    APPLICATION FRAMEWORK

This analysis treats the environment and natural resources as natural capital assets generating a flow of services. Such a treatment allows for substitution between natural and reproducible capital and is consistent with notions of weak

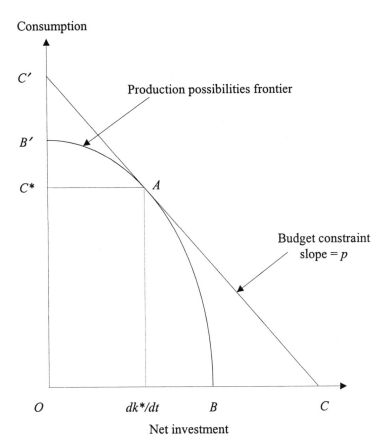

*Figure 5.2   National income*

sustainability. By adjusting national income for changes in environmental quality and natural resource stocks, the national accounts provide a more accurate economic interpretation of changes in a nation's assets. This approach implies information about stocks on their own is not a sufficient statistic for well-being.

The model developed here draws significantly on Hartwick (1990) and Mäler (1991). Our work differs from previous work in that our model includes three production sectors (agriculture, non-agriculture and household production), three roles for land, and equations describing the change in 'effective' productivity of farmland, surface-water quality and the stock of groundwater over time. Land, surface-water quality and the stock of groundwater are treated as natural capital.

Land in its natural state contributes directly to social welfare but is not used in any production sector. Land is used in the agricultural sector and also contributes directly to social welfare by providing rural landscape. We distinguish between the productivity of farmland and its role in providing rural landscape because efforts to increase productivity are not likely to provide added rural landscape. The third use of land is as an input in the production of non-agricultural goods. This land makes no direct contribution to social welfare, but influences welfare by contributing to the production of non-agricultural goods and services.

Water quality directly contributes to social welfare and is also an input into the production of non-agricultural goods. Agricultural production, however, adversely affects water quality as a result of soil erosion and chemical runoff. We adjust income for changes in groundwater stocks because in some regions there has been sustained withdrawal of groundwater over time.

Each of our natural capital assets are regenerative or renewable but may be exhausted from over-use if the rate of use exceeds the natural and managed regenerative rate of the asset. The net rate of regeneration is the rate at which the stock of the asset changes over time.[7] For land, surface-water quality and the stock of groundwater, the net rate of regeneration depends on the intensity of use, the natural rate of regeneration and the effectiveness of management to offset the intensity of use of the asset. Land, for example, is usable until the productivity of soil for producing agricultural goods approaches zero. The loss in soil productivity is offset by the soil's natural capability to regenerate itself. The productivity of soil to produce agricultural goods is also enhanced (managed) by applying labor, intermediate inputs (fertilizer) and capital to improve soil quality.

Surface-water quality is characterized in a similar fashion. Natural regenerative processes offset surface-water quality deterioration. The net rate of regeneration is a function of water quality damage from agricultural production, the natural rate of regeneration and the effectiveness of management to offset degradation. The treatment of groundwater is more problematic because there may be resource degradation associated with the water stock's quantity and quality. Treatment of groundwater in this analysis does not consider changes in groundwater quality.

While agriculture's share of NNP includes a deduction for the consumption of reproducible capital, a similar deduction is not made for other types of capital including farmland or natural resource stocks such as water quality or water quantity. In addition, NNP is not adjusted for externalities associated with agricultural production. For example, agriculture's contribution to NNP is not reduced by off-site damages to water quality associated with soil erosion.

Farm income is adjusted to reflect changes in the effective level of farmland in agriculture over time and the damages associated with soil erosion on surface-water quality. We also correct farm income for the sector's contribution to the overall decline in the stock of groundwater. Because data are limited, the value of scenic preservation of farmland and the value to society of land in its natural state are not addressed. Nor do we correct GDP or NNP for the value of leisure or the production of household output.

The work of Weitzman (1976) and Arrow and Kurz (1970) provides the necessary connection between the current value Hamiltonian and NNP. In their work and our model, net welfare is expressed as the linearized version of the current value Hamiltonian. NNP is reduced to the sum of the social value of an economy's consumption and the social value of the changes in its capital stocks. By capital stocks we mean manufactured or reproducible capital as well as natural capital stocks.

Net welfare measured in terms of final goods and services is:

$$NWM \approx \frac{\partial U}{\partial q}\left[\frac{\partial q}{\partial n_1}n_1 + \frac{\partial q}{\partial k_1}k_1 + \frac{\partial q}{\partial Z_1}Z_1 + \frac{\partial q}{\partial T_1}T_1 + \frac{\partial q}{\partial W_1}W_1\right]$$

$$+\frac{\partial U}{\partial x_2}\left[\frac{\partial x}{\partial n_2}n_2 + \frac{\partial x}{\partial k_2}k_2 + \frac{\partial x}{\partial Y}Y + \frac{\partial x}{\partial L_2}L_2\right]$$

$$-\frac{\partial U}{\partial x_2}[x_3 + x_4 + x_5 + x_6 + I_1 + I_2 + I_3 + I_4 + I_5 + I_6]$$

$$+\frac{\partial U}{\partial Y}Y$$

$$+\sum_{i=1}^{6}\mu_i\dot{k}_i + \rho_3\dot{T}_1 + \rho_4\dot{Y} + \rho_5\dot{W}_1$$

For the interested reader, the theoretical model is developed in detail in Appendix A. The first line of the net welfare equation represents expenditures on final goods and services produced by the agricultural sector as the sum of the value of the marginal contributions of each input used in producing the agricultural good. That is, the expenditure on final agricultural goods is the sum of the value of labor $(n_1)$, capital $(k_1)$, an environmental input $(Z_1)$, effective farmland $(T_1)$ and the stock of groundwater $(W_1)$ that is used to produce the agricultural good. The inputs used to produce the agricultural good are valued in terms of the marginal contribution of the agricultural good to the utility of society $(\partial U/\partial q)$. The second line in the net welfare equation represents expenditures on total goods and services produced in the non-agricultural sector. Expenditure on these goods is a function of the value of labor $(n_2)$, capital $(k_2)$ water quality $(Y)$ and land $(L_2)$ used to produce non-agricultural goods, valued in terms of the marginal contribution of these goods to the utility of society $(\partial U/\partial x_2)$. The third line in the net welfare equation represents expenditures on intermediate inputs used to produce the agricultural and non-agricultural goods and services. Intermediate expenditures are excluded from NNP to avoid double counting.

Deleterious environmental effects from agricultural production increase the cost of production and require devoting additional productive resources to improve damaged water quality. These additional intermediate inputs in the production of non-agricultural output are reflected in lower current measured output in final consumer goods. The long-term effects on the production of final consumption goods caused by environmental damages from agricultural production are not included in conventionally measured NNP.

The fourth line in the net welfare equation represents the marginal value $(\partial U/\partial Y)$ of the stock of clean water $(Y)$ to consumers. This value is also not captured in conventionally measured NNP. The final line in the net welfare equation reflects the addition of the value of net investment in both reproducible capital $(\dot{k}_i)$ and natural capital: effective farmland $(\dot{T})$, water quality $(\dot{Y})$, and groundwater quantity $(\dot{W})$. Current period production is valued in terms of its marginal contribution to the utility of society today. Net investments in both reproducible and natural capital are valued by their marginal contributions to the utility of society today and their marginal contribution to the utility of society in the future.[8]

The last two lines in the net welfare equation represent our adjustment to NNP. We suggest that the conventional measure of NNP be corrected to reflect environmental impacts of agricultural production on the stock of clean water as well as the future environmental impacts of agricultural production on the stocks of effective farmland $(T)$, water quality $(Y)$ and groundwater quantity $(W)$.

## Effective Farmland and Soil Productivity

The link between agricultural production practices, erosion and farmland's ability to produce output has been studied extensively (Crosson, 1986). In 1989, as part of the Second Resources Conservation Act (RCA) Appraisal, the U.S.

Department of Agriculture (USDA, 1989) estimated a 3 percent loss in productivity over the next 100 years if farming/management practices remained as they were in 1982 (Table 5.3). Similarly, Alt et al. (1989) found that the net present value of both the crop yield losses and the additional fertilizer and lime expenses associated with agricultural production totaled $28 billion. Both studies employ a crop production model, Erosion Productivity Impact Calculator (EPIC), which links production practices, erosion rates and productivity to provide estimates of physical depreciation rates of land.[9] Linking physical depreciation rates with crop prices can provide an estimate of economic losses attributable to soil erosion over time. However, a productivity loss of 3 percent over 100 years will not change NNP significantly.

While our theoretical model for adjusting NNP for the impact of erosion on loss of soil productivity is straightforward, it is more difficult to assess a more comprehensive view of land quality over time (National Academy of Sciences, 1993). For example, the RCA report also concluded that less than 50 percent of all agricultural land was 'adequately' protected. Adequately protected soil was defined as soil within acceptable limits with respect to soil erosion and other factors limiting sustained use. Soil scientists have developed 'soil loss tolerance values' or '$T$-values' which vary by type of soil. A general rule of thumb is that erosion rates of less than 5 tons per acre per year ($T$) do not result in damage to crop yields. Although results from the RCA seem to indicate that soil erosion's effect on productivity is economically unimportant, the report also indicates that about 40 percent of cropland was eroding at rates greater than $T$.

*Table 5.3   Productivity loss on cropland associated with soil erosion, 1982*

| Region | Sheet and rill erosion (Percent loss) | Wind erosion (Percent loss) |
|---|---|---|
| Northeast | 7.1 | – |
| Appalachia | 4.7 | – |
| Southeast | 1.3 | – |
| Lake States | 0.9 | 0.7 |
| Corn Belt | 3.5 | – |
| Delta | 1.6 | – |
| Northern Plains | 0.6 | 0.3 |
| Southern Plains | 0.2 | 2.1 |
| Mountain | 0.4 | 1.4 |
| Pacific | 2.3 | 0.2 |
| Total | 1.8 | 0.5 |

*Note:*   – = less than 0.01 percent.
*Source:* USDA (1989).

**Water Quality**

More important than the productivity impacts of agricultural production on effective farmland are the impacts of erosion on water quality and therefore on recreation, commercial fishing, navigation, water storage, drinking supplies, industrial supplies and irrigation. Ribaudo (1989) estimated the average annual off-site erosion costs for the United States at $1.78 per ton ($1986). Even if productivity effects are negligible, soil erosion associated with an acre of land causes, on average, $9 in off-site damages.

Because data are limited on wind erosion, our estimates focus on the off-site effects associated with sheet and rill erosion. We link sheet and rill erosion and the adsorption of nutrients to soil particles to estimate the effects of agricultural production on siltation, stream sedimentation and water pollution. Table 5.4 presents estimates of sheet and rill erosion for cropland and pastureland for 1982, 1987 and 1992 from the National Resources Inventory (USDA, 1994a).

It is possible for agents to mitigate the effects of pollution through defensive expenditures of capital, labor and other intermediate inputs. For example, increased siltation diminishes the usefulness of a reservoir for producing electricity. Dredging can offset the effects of siltation. The attempt to offset the effects of soil erosion may result in additional costs (expenditures) in electricity generation. In this case, part of the costs of agricultural production is shifted to electricity generation. Similar arguments can be made for other industries. Economy-wide NNP, therefore, should not be increased or decreased to reflect the transfer of costs from one industry to another because aggregate NNP is

*Table 5.4   Gross annual sheet and rill erosion, cropland and total (million tons)*

| Region | 1982 | | 1987 | | 1992 | |
|---|---|---|---|---|---|---|
| | Cropland | Total | Cropland | Total | Cropland | Total |
| Northeast | 63 | 68 | 62 | 67 | 52 | 57 |
| Appalachia | 166 | 209 | 152 | 197 | 108 | 154 |
| Southeast | 52 | 56 | 41 | 44 | 32 | 36 |
| Lake states | 124 | 128 | 118 | 122 | 99 | 102 |
| Corn Belt | 606 | 651 | 501 | 537 | 394 | 428 |
| Delta | 116 | 128 | 99 | 444 | 79 | 91 |
| Northern Plains | 256 | 336 | 224 | 320 | 189 | 268 |
| Southern Plains | 115 | 264 | 109 | 251 | 101 | 230 |
| Mountain | 91 | 301 | 84 | 285 | 66 | 277 |
| Pacific | 737 | 167 | 676 | 152 | 48 | 131 |
| Total | 1,661 | 2,307 | 1,474 | 2,085 | 1,168 | 1,773 |

*Note:*   Total includes both cropland and pasture.
*Source:*   USDA (1994a).

correct. There is, however, a misallocation of income among sectors. Conventionally measured farm income is higher if the costs of repairing the reservoir are included as an intermediate expense of the affected industries rather than as an intermediate expense of agricultural production.

Soil erosion also affects consumer utility. An increase in sedimentation in a reservoir can reduce recreational activities. Because many recreational activities are unpriced and therefore are not included in conventionally measured NNP, the diminished value of the resource does not directly affect the income accounts although decreases in expenditures on complementary goods will appear. In the inter-industry example there was a misallocation of income but economy-wide NNP was accurate. In the second case, conventionally measured NNP fails to fully reflect the loss of welfare due to the loss of the recreational resource. Therefore, the off-site damages to consumers caused by agricultural production should be counted as an overall decline in NNP.

Similarly, the non-commercial loss of fish and waterfowl populations associated with increased sedimentation is not fully represented in NNP. In addition to the impacts on recreation, there may be an 'existence' value component for the health of these riparian ecosystems. Such a value is also excluded from the national accounts as currently measured.

We do not measure the stock of water quality ($Y$) or the marginal utility of water quality ($\partial U/\partial Y$). Because no comprehensive measure exists, we use Ribaudo's (1989) estimate of the off-site damages to water quality from soil erosion. The off-site damages in dollars per ton of soil erosion (converted to $1982) are listed in Table 5.5. The estimates reflect the off-site effects of soil erosion on freshwater and marine recreation, water storage, navigation, flooding, roadside ditches, irrigation ditches, freshwater and marine

*Table 5.5   Off-site damages associated with soil erosion, 1982 ($/ton)*

| Region | Industry | Consumer | Total |
|---|---|---|---|
| Northeast | 3.74 | 2.66 | 6.40 |
| Appalachia | 0.96 | 0.32 | 1.29 |
| Southeast | 1.74 | 0.00 | 1.74 |
| Lake states | 2.45 | 0.95 | 3.40 |
| Corn Belt | 0.49 | 0.55 | 1.04 |
| Delta | 1.97 | 0.25 | 2.22 |
| Northern Plains | 0.53 | 0.09 | 0.61 |
| Southern Plains | 1.22 | 0.61 | 1.83 |
| Mountain | 0.85 | 0.17 | 1.02 |
| Pacific | 1.39 | 0.77 | 2.16 |
| Total | 1.05 | 0.49 | 1.52 |

*Source*:  Ribaudo (1989).

commercial fishing, municipal water treatment, municipal and industrial uses, and steam power cooling. We reorganize the damages into those affecting industry (water storage, navigation, flooding, roadside ditches, irrigation ditches, freshwater and marine commercial fishing, municipal water treatment, municipal and industrial uses, and steam power cooling) and those directly affecting consumers (freshwater and marine recreation). The industry and consumer damages per ton of soil erosion are highest in the Northeast.

The value of total damages presented in Tables 5.6 and 5.7 is calculated by applying Ribaudo's per ton estimates to the total level of sheet and rill erosion for

*Table 5.6   Estimated inter-industry annual soil erosion damages*

| Region | 1982 | | 1987 | | 1992 | |
|---|---|---|---|---|---|---|
| | $/ton | Million $ | $/ton | Million $ | $/ton | Million $ |
| Northeast | 3.74 | 255.0 | 4.47 | 298.3 | 5.41 | 305.5 |
| Appalachia | 0.96 | 200.7 | 1.15 | 225.7 | 1.39 | 214.6 |
| Southeast | 1.74 | 98.0 | 2.08 | 91.5 | 2.52 | 89.8 |
| Lake states | 2.45 | 312.0 | 2.92 | 355.5 | 3.54 | 360.5 |
| Corn Belt | 0.49 | 319.8 | 0.59 | 314.8 | 0.71 | 303.4 |
| Delta | 1.97 | 252.9 | 2.36 | 261.6 | 2.85 | 259.8 |
| Northern Plains | 0.53 | 176.3 | 0.63 | 200.6 | 0.76 | 203.3 |
| Southern Plains | 1.22 | 322.2 | 1.46 | 365.7 | 1.76 | 405.8 |
| Mountain | 0.85 | 255.3 | 1.01 | 288.7 | 1.23 | 339.2 |
| Pacific | 1.39 | 231.9 | 1.66 | 251.3 | 2.01 | 262.5 |
| Total | 1.05 | 2,424.0 | 1.27 | 2,653.7 | 1.55 | 2,744.4 |

*Source*:   Ribaudo (1989) and authors' calculations.

*Table 5.7   Estimated annual consumer soil erosion damages*

| Region | 1982 | | 1987 | | 1992 | |
|---|---|---|---|---|---|---|
| | $/ton | Million $ | $/ton | Million $ | $/ton | Million $ |
| Northeast | 2.66 | 181.0 | 3.17 | 211.8 | 3.84 | 216.9 |
| Appalachia | 0.32 | 67.4 | 0.39 | 75.8 | 0.47 | 72.0 |
| Southeast | 0.00 | 0.0 | 0.00 | 0.0 | 0.00 | 0.0 |
| Lake states | 0.95 | 121.2 | 1.13 | 138.1 | 1.37 | 140.1 |
| Corn Belt | 0.55 | 359.5 | 0.66 | 353.9 | 0.80 | 341.1 |
| Delta | 0.25 | 32.0 | 0.30 | 33.1 | 0.36 | 32.9 |
| Northern Plains | 0.09 | 28.7 | 0.10 | 32.6 | 0.12 | 33.1 |
| Southern Plains | 0.61 | 162.4 | 0.73 | 184.3 | 0.89 | 204.4 |
| Mountain | 0.17 | 51.9 | 0.21 | 58.7 | 0.25 | 68.9 |
| Pacific | 0.77 | 128.3 | 0.92 | 139.0 | 1.11 | 145.2 |
| Total | 0.49 | 1,132.3 | 0.59 | 1,227.3 | 0.71 | 1,254.7 |

*Source:*   Ribaudo (1989) and authors' calculations.

cropland and pasture by region.[10] Total damages are $4 billion for 1992, with $2.7 billion associated with industry affects. Interestingly, Table 5.6 shows that while the dollar-per-ton effects are highest in the Northeast, the total industrial damages are greatest in the Southern Plains.

The effects of sheet and rill erosion on consumers totaled $1.1 billion in 1982, $1.2 billion in 1987 and $1.3 billion in 1992. In addition to reducing farm income, these adjustments reflect a decline in NNP and overall welfare. The effects on other industries were about twice as large as the consumer impacts. Estimated industry effects are $2.4 billion in 1982, $2.7 billion in 1987 and $2.7 billion in 1992. While these adjustments lower agricultural income, they do not reflect a decline in NNP and overall welfare. They are treated as a transfer from one production sector of the economy to another.

## Groundwater Quantity

Our final adjustment to the national and agricultural sector accounts is an adjustment for the value of the change in the stock of groundwater over time. In the long run, an equilibrium is generally reached in terms of recharges (precipitation, imports from other regions) and discharges (natural evapotranspiration, exports to other regions, consumptive use and natural outflow) from any groundwater system. However, in five water resource regions, the rate of discharge has consistently been greater than the rate of recharge and has led to a continued decline in the stock of groundwater (U.S. Department of the Interior, 1984). Those five regions are: the Missouri Basin (Montana, Wyoming, North Dakota, South Dakota, Nebraska, and parts of Colorado and Kansas), the Arkansas-White-Red (southern Kansas, Oklahoma, north Texas and western Arkansas), the Texas-Gulf (most of Texas), the Lower Colorado (Arizona), and California. While it is difficult to assess agriculture's contribution to the overall change in groundwater stocks in those regions, the sector accounted for 79 to 88 percent of total groundwater withdrawals in the United States (Table 5.8).

*Table 5.8    Groundwater withdrawals by water resource region (billion gallons per day)*

| Region | 1980 Agriculture | 1980 Total | 1985 Agriculture | 1985 Total | 1990 Agriculture | 1990 Total |
|---|---|---|---|---|---|---|
| Missouri Basin | 11.3 | 12.0 | 8.4 | 9.5 | 7.4 | 8.5 |
| Arkansas-Red-White | 8.5 | 9.4 | 7.0 | 7.7 | 6.8 | 7.4 |
| Texas-Gulf | 4.0 | 5.1 | 3.7 | 5.1 | 4.0 | 5.5 |
| Lower Colorado | 3.9 | 4.5 | 2.6 | 3.3 | 2.3 | 3.1 |
| California | 18.0 | 21.0 | 10.3 | 14.8 | 10.8 | 14.4 |
| Total | 45.7 | 52.0 | 32.0 | 40.4 | 31.3 | 38.9 |

*Source:* Solley et al. (1983, 1993).

Because the most recent estimate of the change in the stock of groundwater for the United States is for 1980 (U.S. Department of the Interior, 1984) and because the data are not specified by sector of use, we adopt the following four-step procedure. First, we employ the 1980 water resource budgets and use agriculture's share of total groundwater withdrawals (Solley, et al., 1983, 1993) to allocate the change in the stock of groundwater for each of the five water resource regions exhibiting declines in the stock of groundwater in 1980. For example, in 1980 agriculture accounted for about 86 percent of groundwater withdrawals in the California water resource region (Table 5.8). Therefore, we assume that agriculture accounted for 86 percent (1.2 billion gallons per day (BGD)) of the total decline in the stock of groundwater in the California water resource region (1.4 BGD) for 1980 (Table 5.9).

Second, because water use data are collected every five years, we use the change in total groundwater withdrawals to update the total change in the stock of groundwater for each of the water resource regions. For example, from 1980 to 1985, the total (both agricultural and non-agricultural) withdrawals of groundwater for the California region fell by about 30 percent from 21.0 to 14.8 BGD. Therefore, we assume that the rate of groundwater depletion in the region fell by about 30 percent, from 1.4 BGD to 1.0 BGD.

Third, we again use agriculture's share of total groundwater withdrawals to allocate the change in the stock of groundwater. Continuing with our California example, in addition to the decline in overall groundwater withdrawals, the share of withdrawals attributed to agriculture fell from 86 percent to about 70 percent. Therefore, the rate at which agriculture contributed to the decline in the overall stock of groundwater in the California water resource region fell from 1.2 BGD in 1980 to 0.7 BGD in 1985 (Table 5.9).

Table 5.9    *Effects of agriculture on groundwater storage*

| Region | 1982 | | 1987 | | 1992 | |
|---|---|---|---|---|---|---|
| | BGD | Million $ | BGD | Million $ | BGD | Million $ |
| Missouri Basin | 2.1 | 73 | 1.5 | 65 | 1.4 | 70 |
| Arkansas-Red-White | 3.2 | 49 | 2.7 | 48 | 2.6 | 57 |
| Texas-Gulf | 2.4 | 109 | 2.2 | 120 | 2.4 | 159 |
| Lower Colorado | 1.8 | 87 | 1.2 | 69 | 1.1 | 73 |
| California | 1.2 | 51 | 0.7 | 35 | 0.7 | 44 |
| Total | 10.8 | 369 | 8.3 | 337 | 8.2 | 403 |

*Note:* BGD = billion gallons per day.

*Source:*
1980 data from U.S. Department of the Interior (1984). Data for 1982, 1987 and 1992 from authors' calculation. 1980, 1985 and 1990 groundwater withdrawals are used to reflect 1982, 1987 and 1992 rates of groundwater depletion.

This process leads to some interesting comparisons over time. The change in overall groundwater withdrawals coupled with changes in agricultural uses indicates that by 1990, agriculture's contribution to overall decline in the stock of groundwater had declined since 1980 and remained stable since 1985. Regionally, however, there are some differences. For the Lower Colorado and California water resource regions, both total groundwater withdrawals and the share of groundwater withdrawals attributed to agriculture fell significantly. In both regions, the share of groundwater withdrawals attributed to agriculture fell from close to 90 percent in 1980 to about 75 percent by 1990. Much of this decline in groundwater withdrawals can be attributed to the decline in irrigated acres in the Pacific coast over that period.[11] However, for the Missouri Basin, Arkansas-Red-White and Texas-Gulf, agriculture's share of total withdrawals of groundwater has remained fairly constant since 1980.

Finally, we need to associate values with the estimated changes in the rate of groundwater depletion. As a proxy for the shadow value of groundwater we use the returns to irrigation estimated by Aillery (1995). The returns to irrigation include returns to water, fixed capital, and management above variable water costs and net of returns to dryland alternatives. Ideally, one would want to separate the returns to water from returns to management and fixed capital. However, by netting out variable water costs and returns to dryland alternatives, Aillery's estimates provide a reasonable proxy of the value added to agriculture from an additional unit of the stock of groundwater. For 1992, the values range from $0.14 to $0.19 per 1,000 gallons in the Missouri Basin, Texas Gulf, Lower Colorado and California to $0.06 per 1,000 gallons in the Arkansas-Red-White. The adjustment to farm income present in Table 5.9 combines the value of groundwater with the rate of groundwater depletion associated with agriculture. Total nominal damages range from $337 million in 1987 to $403 million in 1992.

**Impacts on Income**

Agriculture affects production in other sectors of the economy and consumer utility through its use of environmental and natural resource assets. Production in other sectors of the economy is affected because changes in environmental assets affect the productivity of other inputs and therefore the cost of producing non-agricultural goods and services. Consumer utility is affected directly through changes in consumption and indirectly through changes in option or existence value.

The approach here is to extend the existing flow-of-output accounts to value environmental goods and services. Double counting is avoided by recognizing that the inter-industry externalities caused by agricultural production are captured in the existing accounting framework as intermediate expenses in non-agricultural production. Accounting for intermediate external effects is needed only to compute sectoral income. If, however, an accurate measure of national income alone is sought, then intermediate external effects can be ignored. The production externality is an intermediate good whose value is imbedded in the bundle of final goods and services. Agriculture's contribution to the decline in surface-water quality caused a transfer of accounting income from the agricultural sector to the non-agricultural sector of the economy in 1982 of $2.4 billion, in 1987 of $2.7 billion and in 1992 of $2.7 billion. These adjustments reduce agricultural income and increase income in other sectors of the economy but do not reduce economy-wide NNP. Including intermediate goods in the income accounts is double counting. Similarly, economic rents generated by a non-market externality are captured in payments to factors of production in the flow-of-income approach. This is not the case, however, when consumer utility is affected directly through changes in consumption and indirectly through changes in option or existence value.

Our estimates suggest that only minor adjustments to NNP are made necessary by the effects of agricultural production on the environment and natural resource base. This result follows partly from agriculture's small share (less than 2 percent) of GDP. Even large changes in net farm income have only modest effects on NNP. Adjustments to total farm income and economy-wide NNP for 1982, 1987 and 1992 are displayed in Table 5.10. In each year, total farm income is reduced by about $4 billion when adjustments are made for agriculture's contribution to the decline in surface-water quality and stock of groundwater. Overall, agriculture's contribution to economy-wide NNP falls by $1.50 billion in 1982, $1.56 billion in 1987 and $1.66 billion in 1992 when adjustments are made for agriculture's contribution to the decline in surface-water quality and stock of groundwater. About 85 percent of the adjustment is caused by agriculture's contribution to the decline in surface-water quality.

The relative effects on net farm product are significantly greater. Adjustments to net farm product range from 6 to 8 percent. The relative share of environmental adjustments to conventional net farm product, however, decreased from 1987 to 1992. Measured agricultural environmental costs per dollar of farm income are declining. This suggests that estimated environmental costs flowing from agriculture are not growing as fast as farm income. One possible explanation is that policies and programs for controlling soil erosion were effective during this period. In particular, highly erodible acreage enrolled in the Conservation Reserve Program increased from 13.7 to 35.4 million acres from 1987 to 1992. Removing nearly 22 million acres of highly erodible land from production contributed to a nearly 21 percent decrease in estimated soil erosion on cropland during this period, even though planted acreage for grains increased by 6 percent. Conservation compliance requirements promulgated under the 1985 farm legislation have provided additional incentives for reducing erosion.

The estimates are consistent with Smith's (1992) work on environmental costing. Smith aggregates the effects of off-site soil erosion, wetland conversion and groundwater contamination, and estimates environmental costs relative to the

*Table 5.10    Summary of national income and product accounts, 1982, 1987 and 1992*

| Income components | 1982 | 1987 $ billions | 1992 |
|---|---|---|---|
| *Traditional farm income:* | 54.0 | 54.3 | 66.8 |
| Water quality: | | | |
| Industry transfer | -2.4 | -2.7 | -2.7 |
| Consumer effects | -1.1 | -1.2 | -1.3 |
| Water quantity | -0.4 | -0.3 | -0.4 |
| Green farm income | 50.1 | 50.1 | 62.4 |
| *Traditional non-farm income:* | 2,468.5 | 3,638.0 | 4,769.8 |
| Water quality: | | | |
| Industry transfer | 2.4 | 2.7 | 2.7 |
| Consumer effects | | | |
| Water quantity | | | |
| Green non-farm income | 2,470.9 | 3,640.7 | 4,772.5 |
| *Traditional national income:* | 2,522.5 | 3,692.3 | 4,836.6 |
| Water quality: | | | |
| Industry transfer | 0.0 | 0.0 | 0.0 |
| Consumer effects | -1.1 | -1.2 | -1.3 |
| Water quantity | -0.4 | -0.3 | -0.4 |
| Green national income | 2,521.0 | 3,690.8 | 4,834.9 |

value of crops produced in 1984. His estimates range from 0.08 to 7.5 percent in the Mountain region to 3.5 to 40 percent in the Northeast. Corn Belt estimates range from 6 to 7 percent.[12]

Our estimated adjustments represent average costs of environmental damages and resource use. Marginal costs are likely to be higher. It is possible that the distortionary effect of commodity programs is alone sufficient to lead to marginal decreases in social welfare. Accounting for natural resource deterioration and environmental injury, in such a case, would lead to further reductions in social welfare. In addition, our national estimates may be masking significant regional or local problems. Estimated costs of erosion, in terms of lost productivity, for example, is not a significant national problem, but may be a significant regional or state problem. Faeth (1993) shows negative net economic value per acre after accounting for soil depreciation and off-site costs for Pennsylvania's best corn–soybean rotation over five years. The work demonstrates that there may be significant regional variation in resource depreciation and off-site costs of agricultural production.

Regional issue

# 6   SUMMARY

Growing interest in the environment has raised questions about the adequacy of
current measures of national income, particularly when these measures are used
as social welfare indicators. The intent of this chapter is to more accurately
measure agriculture's contribution to national income. Improving the measure of
current economic activity requires incorporating non-market final goods and bads
into the existing accounts. We focus attention on treating natural capital assets
used or affected by agricultural production parallel to how reproducible capital is
treated in the national accounts. Net national income and agricultural income are
adjusted to reflect the value of changes in the stock of effective farmland, surface-
water quality and groundwater.

 We first develop a theoretically consistent framework for incorporating natural
capital and environmental goods into the existing income accounts. Next, we
apply the framework and adjust agricultural income and national income to
reflect the value of the depletion of agricultural natural capital (land and water)
and the non-market effects of agricultural production on output in other sectors of
the economy and consumers. Specifically, the effects of soil erosion on
agricultural productivity and income, the economic effects of decreased surface-
water quality and the depletion of groundwater stocks are presented as examples
of the potential scope of accounting adjustments needed in the agricultural sector.
Our estimates suggest only minor adjustments to NNP are made necessary by the
effects of agricultural production on the environment and the natural capital base.
This result follows from agriculture's small share of GDP and because the
environmental effects considered in this chapter are largely captured in the
existing accounts. Adjustments to net farm income are relatively greater and fall
in the range of 6 to 8 percent.

 Our estimates of 'green' adjustments to net farm income are consistent with a
view of U.S. agriculture where environmental problems exist and the resource
base is depreciating, but the extent of the effects is in the range that can
adequately be addressed by thoughtful policy. Our estimates suggest that
agriculture's contribution to social welfare far exceeds the environmental
damages and deterioration of the stock of natural capital resulting from the
production of food.

 Estimates of adjusted or 'green' income presented here are incomplete.
Because the objective of our analysis is to illustrate some of the adjustments
necessary to improve NNP and NFP as measures of social welfare, we restrict our
scope to consider a few key agricultural effects. Other adjustments, including
additional environmental damages and valuing environmental services, are
necessary before a credible measure of welfare can emerge. We have not, for
example, estimated the cost of farm chemical volatilization on air quality, or
valued the benefits of landscape preservation or increasing wildlife habitat. In
addition, on the cost side, we have not examined how soil quality characteristics,

other than erodibility, affect productivity or wildlife habitat. The valuation of farm program benefits warrants further exploration. Program payments are currently treated as income transfers, included in net farm income but excluded from gross farm income. An alternative approach views the government purchasing environmental benefits such as scenic value or wildlife habitat.

## APPENDICES

### Appendix A: Theoretical Model

The model includes three production sectors (agriculture, non-agriculture and household production), three roles for land, and equations of motion for the 'effective' productivity of farmland, surface-water quality and the stock of groundwater. Land, surface-water quality and the stock of groundwater are treated as natural capital.

### Definitions
Output of the agricultural sector ($q$) is given by the production function:

$$q = q(n_1, k_1, Z_1, T_1, eW_1) \tag{A.1}$$

where: $n_1$:  agricultural labor,
$k_1$:  agricultural capital,
$Z_1$:  environmental input,
$T_1$:  'effective' stock of land used in agricultural production,
$e$:   groundwater extraction rate, and
$W_1$:  stock of groundwater.

Output of the non-agricultural sector ($x$) is given by the production function:

$$x = x(n_2, k_2, Y, L_2) \tag{A.2}$$

where:  $x$:   non-agricultural good,
$n_2$:  non-agricultural labor,
$k_2$:  non-agricultural capital,
$Y$:   water quality effect on non-agricultural production ($\partial x/(\partial Y > 0$), and
$L_2$:  land used in non-agricultural production.

Household or non-market production ($h$) is given by:

$$h = h(n_6, x_6, k_6) \qquad (A.3)$$

where:  $n_6$:  household labor,
        $x_6$:  intermediate inputs used in household production, and
        $k_6$:  household capital.

The household production function includes activities beyond those related to the environment. The equation of motion for the effective productivity of farmland is:

$$\dot{T_1} = \gamma(\frac{n_3}{L_1}, \frac{x_3}{L_1}, \frac{k_3}{L_1})L_1 - dL_1 \qquad (A.4)$$

where land can be managed (improved) by adding labor, intermediate inputs (fertilizer) and capital according to a management function:

$$\gamma = \gamma(\frac{n_3}{L_1}, \frac{x_3}{L_1}, \frac{k_3}{L_1}) \qquad (A.5)$$

where:  $L_1$:  land used in agriculture,
        $\gamma$:  is a rate of appreciation,
        $n_3$:  labor used in managing land,
        $x_3$:  intermediate inputs used in managing land,
        $k_3$:  capital used in managing land, and
        $d$:  soil erosion rate.

The management function $\gamma(\cdot)$ is assumed linearly homogeneous in its arguments $(n_3/L_1, x_3/L_1, k_3/L_1)$ and in $n_3$, $x_3$ and $k_3$.
     The equation of motion for water quality is:

$$\dot{Y} = [a - D(Z_1) + \eta(n_4, x_4, k_4)]Y \qquad (A.6)$$

where the impact of agricultural production on water quality is represented by:

$$D = D(Z_1) \qquad (A.7)$$

Water quality can be managed by adding labor, intermediate inputs and capital:

$$\eta = \eta(n_4, x_4, k_4) \qquad (A.8)$$

where: $n_4$: labor used in managing water quality,
  $x_4$: intermediate inputs used in water quality,
  $k_4$: capital used in managing water quality, and
  $a$: natural repair of water quality.

The damage function $D(Z_l)$ and the repair function $\eta(\cdot)$ are also assumed linearly homogeneous in their respective arguments. Our equation of motion for the stock of groundwater is:

$$\dot{W}_1 = \left[\psi - e(n_5, x_5, k_5)\right]W_1 \qquad (A.9)$$

where the extraction of groundwater for use in agriculture is represented by:

$$e = e(n_5, x_5, k_5) \qquad (A.10)$$

where: $n_5$: labor used in extracting groundwater,
  $x_5$: intermediate inputs used in extracting groundwater,
  $k_5$: capital used in extracting groundwater, and
  $\psi$: the rate groundwater is replenished.

Each natural capital asset is regenerative or renewable but could be exhausted from over-use. The net rate of regeneration, as captured by the equations of motion, is a function of the intensity of use, the effectiveness of management to offset the intensity of use of an asset, the level of the stock of the resource itself, and the natural rate of regeneration.

## The model

Social welfare ($U$) is defined as a function of final goods and services ($q$, $x_2$), household production ($h$), an index of water quality ($Y$), land in its natural state ($L_0$), land used in agriculture ($L_1$), and leisure ($n_7$). The social planner's goal is to maximize:

$$Max \int_0^\infty e^{-rt} U(q, x_2, h, Y, L_0, L_1, n_7) dt \qquad (A.11)$$

where: $q$: agricultural output (final good),
  $x_2$: non-agricultural (final) goods and services,
  $h$: household production,
  $Y$: index of water quality, ($\partial U / \partial Y > 0$),
  $L_0$: unused land (natural state),

$L_1$ :  land used in agriculture,

$n_7$ :  leisure, and

$r$:    social discount rate

subject to the equations of motion for the stock of effective land, surface-water quality and the stock of groundwater:

$$\dot{T}_1 = \gamma(\frac{n_3}{L_1}, \frac{x_3}{L_1}, \frac{k_3}{L_1})L_1 - dL_1 \tag{A.12}$$

$$\dot{Y} = \left[a - D(Z_1) + \eta(n_4, x_4, k_4)\right]Y \tag{A.13}$$

$$\dot{W}_1 = \left[\psi - e(n_5, x_5, k_5)\right]W_1 \tag{A.14}$$

In addition, there are equations of motion for each type of reproducible capital:

$$\dot{k}_i = I_i - \delta_i k_i \quad \text{for } i = 1,\ldots,6 \tag{A.15}$$

where $I_i$ represents gross investment and the '$i$' subscript represents depreciation rates for each type of reproducible capital.

A materials balance equation and constraints for labor and land complete the model:

$$x(n_2, k_2, Y, L_2) = x_2 + x_3 + x_4 + x_5 + x_6$$
$$+ I_1 + I_2 + I_3 + I_4 + I_5 + I_6 \tag{A.16}$$

$$N = \sum_{i=1}^{7} n_i \tag{A.17}$$

$$L = \sum_{i=0}^{2} L_i \tag{A.18}$$

The materials balance equation accounts for the output of the non-agricultural sector, $x$, in the economy. For example, some non-agricultural output goes to final non-agricultural consumption goods and services $x_2$. Non-agricultural output is also used as investment goods $I_i$; inputs that go into managing the stock of effective farmland $x_3$, water quality $x_4$, and the stock of groundwater $x_5$; and as inputs in the household production function $x_6$.

Recasting the materials balance equation in terms of final non-agricultural consumption goods and services $x_2$ results in:

---

---

$$x_2 = x(n_2, k_2, Y, L_2) - x_3 - x_4 - x_5 - x_6$$
$$-I_1 - I_2 - I_3 - I_4 - I_5 - I_6 \tag{A.19}$$

Equation (A.19) can then be directly substituted into the social planner's objective function (equation A.11).

The current value Hamiltonian in flow-of-output terms is:

$$H \equiv U\{q(n_1, k_1, Z_1, T_1, eW_1),$$

$$x(n_2, k_2, Y, L_2) - x_3 - x_4 - x_5 - x_6 - I_1 - I_2 - I_3 - I_4 - I_5 - I_6,$$

$$h(n_6, x_6, k_6), Y, L_0, L_1, n_7\}$$

$$+ \rho_3 \left[ \gamma(\frac{n_3}{L_1}, \frac{x_3}{L_1}, \frac{k_3}{L_1}) L_1 - dL_1 \right]$$

$$+ \rho_4 [a - D(Z_1) + \eta(n_4, x_4, k_4)] Y$$

$$+ \rho_5 [\psi - e(n_5, x_5, k_5)] W_1$$

$$+ \sum_{i=1}^{6} \mu_i [I_i - \delta_i k_i]$$

$$- \omega \left[ \sum_{i=1}^{7} n_i - N \right]$$

$$- \Omega \left[ \sum_{i=0}^{2} L_i - L \right] \tag{A.20}$$

where $\rho_i$, $\mu_i$, $\omega_i$ and $\Omega_i$ are co-state variables.

## Measurement of net welfare

The Hamiltonian along the optimal trajectory is the national welfare measure in utility terms (Mäler, 1991; Hung, 1993). The linear approximation of the Hamiltonian along the optimal path is the exact correspondence to the net national welfare measure. It measures the current utility of consumption (of goods and services and environmental services) and the present value of the future utility stream from current stock changes. This follows because stock prices measure the present value of the future contribution to welfare from a marginal increase in the stocks.

Net welfare is measured as:

$$NWM = \frac{\partial U}{\partial q}\left[\frac{\partial q}{\partial n_1}n_1 + \frac{\partial q}{\partial k_1}k_1 + \frac{\partial q}{\partial Z_1}Z_1 + \frac{\partial q}{\partial T_1}T_1 + \frac{\partial q}{\partial W_1}W_1\right]$$

$$+ \frac{\partial U}{\partial x_2}\left[\frac{\partial x}{\partial n_2}n_2 + \frac{\partial x}{\partial k_2}k_2 + \frac{\partial x}{\partial Y}Y + \frac{\partial x}{\partial L_2}L_2\right]$$

$$- \frac{\partial U}{\partial x_2}\left[x_3 + x_4 + x_5 + x_6 + I_1 + I_2 + I_3 + I_4 + I_5 + I_6\right]$$

$$+ \frac{\partial U}{\partial h}\left[\frac{\partial h}{\partial n_6}n_6 + \frac{\partial h}{\partial x_6}x_6 + \frac{\partial h}{\partial k_6}k_6\right] + \frac{\partial U}{\partial L_0}L_0 + \frac{\partial U}{\partial L_1}L_1 + \frac{\partial U}{\partial Y}Y + \frac{\partial U}{\partial n_7}n_7$$

$$+ \sum_{i=1}^{6}\mu_i\left[I_i - \delta_i k_i\right]$$

$$+ \rho_3\left[\gamma(\frac{n_3}{L_1},\frac{x_3}{L_1},\frac{k_3}{L_1})L_1 - dL_1\right]$$

$$+ \rho_4\left[a - D(Z_1) + \eta(n_4, x_4, k_4)\right]Y$$

$$+ \rho_5\left[\psi - e(n_5, x_5, k_5)\right]W_1 \qquad (A.21)$$

Recognizing the relationship between net welfare and net product, equation (A.21) can be viewed as the flow-of-output or expenditure approach to income accounting. That is, GDP = consumption + gross investment and NNP = GDP – capital depreciation = consumption + net investment. The first line in equation (A.21) represents final expenditures on the agricultural good. We assume all output of the agricultural sector (food) is a final consumption good, thus abstracting from the food processing sector. The second line captures total expenditures on the non-agricultural good $x$. Some $x$ is, however, used as intermediate goods or inputs into the production of other goods. The expenditures on $x$ that do not represent final consumption are subtracted in the third line of equation (A.21). The second and third line, therefore, capture expenditures on the final consumption of the non-agricultural good.

The fourth line of equation (A.21) captures implied expenditures on the household product, natural-state land, aesthetic farm landscape, water quality and leisure. The fourth line contains most of the extensions to the traditional GDP accounts. However, some of these expenditures may already be included in the GDP accounts. For example, government expenditures to improve water quality and explicit expenditures by environmental groups to save natural-state land such as old growth forests already show up in the accounts. The fifth line of equation (A.21) captures net investment in each of the six types of physical capital, while the last three lines report net investment in the three types of natural capital. The gross investment components of these last three lines are also extensions of the GDP accounts.

The first three lines of equation (A.21) and the gross investment components of line 5 sum to the traditional measure of GDP. Adding line 4 and the gross investment components of lines 6, 7 and 8 gives the extended GDP measure. Lines 1, 2, 3 and 5 sum to the traditional NNP measure. The entire expression given by equation (A.21) represents the extended NNP measure.

Two final observations stemming from equation (A.21) are worth noting. First, concern for sustainability and properly valuing natural resource depletion leads to extending the accounts by including lines 6, 7 and 8 of equation (A.21). Second, concern with including 'non-market' goods (e.g. housework, land in its natural state, rural landscape, water quality and leisure) in the accounts leads to expanding the accounts by including line 4.

## Appendix B: The Optimality Conditions

The optimality conditions are obtained by partially differentiating the Hamiltonian (equation A.20) with respect to the control and state variables. The control variables are the seven uses of labor, the uses of the manufactured output $x$, gross investment in the six types of reproducible capital, the three uses of land and the level of water pollution, $Z_l$. For labor, the optimality conditions are:

$$\frac{\partial H}{\partial n_1} = \frac{\partial U}{\partial q}\frac{\partial q}{\partial n_1} - \omega = 0 \tag{B.1}$$

$$\frac{\partial H}{\partial n_2} = \frac{\partial U}{\partial x_2}\frac{\partial x}{\partial n_2} - \omega = 0 \tag{B.2}$$

$$\frac{\partial H}{\partial n_3} = \rho_3 \frac{\partial \gamma}{\partial n_3} - \omega = 0 \tag{B.3}$$

$$\frac{\partial H}{\partial n_4} = \rho_4 \frac{\partial \eta}{\partial n_4} Y - \omega = 0 \tag{B.4}$$

$$\frac{\partial H}{\partial n_5} = \frac{\partial U}{\partial q} \frac{\partial q}{\partial e} \frac{\partial e}{\partial n_5} W_1 - \rho_5 \frac{\partial e}{\partial n_5} W_1 - \omega = 0 \tag{B.5}$$

$$\frac{\partial H}{\partial n_6} = \frac{\partial U}{\partial h} \frac{\partial h}{\partial n_6} - \omega = 0 \tag{B.6}$$

$$\frac{\partial H}{\partial n_7} = \frac{\partial U}{\partial n_7} - \omega = 0 \tag{B.7}$$

Equations (B.1), (B.2) and (B.6) indicate that the value of the marginal product of labor is equalized across the three production sectors. This value, the shadow wage rate, is also the marginal value of leisure, equation (B.7), and the marginal value of labor in enhancing land, equation (B.3), repairing water quality, equation (B.4), and depleting groundwater stocks, equation (B.5).

The manufactured good $x$ can be directly consumed $(x_2)$, used as an intermediate input or for investment. The optimality conditions for $x$ as an intermediate input for improving land, water quality and depleting groundwater stocks are:

$$\frac{\partial H}{\partial x_3} = -\frac{\partial U}{\partial x_2} + \rho_3 \frac{\partial \gamma}{\partial x_3} = 0 \tag{B.8}$$

$$\frac{\partial H}{\partial x_4} = -\frac{\partial U}{\partial x_2} + \rho_4 \frac{\partial \eta}{\partial x_4} Y = 0 \tag{B.9}$$

$$\frac{\partial H}{\partial x_5} = \frac{\partial U}{\partial q} \frac{\partial q}{\partial e} \frac{\partial e}{\partial x_5} W_1 - \frac{\partial U}{\partial x_2} - \rho_5 \frac{\partial e}{\partial x_5} W_1 = 0 \tag{B.10}$$

These conditions show that the value of the marginal product of the manufactured good in each of its intermediate uses must equal $\partial U/\partial x_2$, the opportunity cost of direct consumption.

The optimality conditions for $x$ as investment in reproducible capital are:

$$\frac{\partial H}{\partial I_i} = -\frac{\partial U}{\partial x_2} + \mu_i = 0 \qquad (i = 1,\ldots,6) \tag{B.11}$$

As with intermediate goods, the marginal value of investment in each type of capital $(\mu_i)$ must equal the marginal value of the consumption good $x_2$ $(\partial U/\partial x_2)$.

Partially differentiating with respect to each land type determines the distribution of land across sectors:

$$\frac{\partial H}{\partial L_0} = \frac{\partial U}{\partial L_0} - \Omega = 0 \tag{B.12}$$

$$\frac{\partial H}{\partial L_1} = \frac{\partial U}{\partial L_1} + p_3 \left[ \gamma(\cdot) - \frac{\partial \gamma}{\partial A} \frac{n_3}{L_1} - \frac{\partial \gamma}{\partial B} \frac{x_3}{L_1} - \frac{\partial \gamma}{\partial C} \frac{k_3}{L_1} \right] - p_3 d - \Omega = 0 \tag{B.13}$$

where $A = n_3/L_1$, $B = x_3/L_1$, and $C = k_3/L_1$. Because $\gamma$ is assumed homogeneous of degree one in $A$, $B$ and $C$, equation (B.13) reduces to:

$$\frac{\partial H}{\partial L_1} = \frac{\partial U}{\partial L_1} - p_3 d - \Omega = 0 \tag{B.14}$$

The remaining use of land, $L_2$, is chosen so that:

$$\frac{\partial H}{\partial L_2} = \frac{\partial U}{\partial x_2} \frac{\partial x}{\partial L_2} - \Omega = 0 \tag{B.15}$$

Recall the unique character of each type of land. Land in its natural state, $L_0$, has only a direct welfare effect and no productivity effect. Land used in non-agricultural production, $L_2$, affects welfare indirectly as an input in production. Farmland, $L_1$, however, has both a productivity effect in agriculture and a direct welfare effect in utility in terms of providing rural landscape.

The shadow value $\Omega$ gives the price of land in its natural state. This price exceeds the direct marginal contribution of farmland to welfare because some farmland erodes, while pristine land and non-agricultural land are assumed not to erode. This price $\Omega$ also equals the value of the marginal product of land in the non-agricultural sector.

An additional control variable to consider is $Z_1$, the environmental input to agricultural production. The optimality condition for this variable is:

$$\frac{\partial H}{\partial Z_1} = \frac{\partial U}{\partial q}\frac{\partial q}{\partial Z_1} - p_4 \frac{\partial D}{\partial Z_1}Y = 0 \qquad (B.16)$$

Here the choice of $Z_1$ can be interpreted as the optimal use of an environmental input, water quality. Equation (B.16) indicates that the value of the marginal product of water pollution in agricultural production is equal to the marginal change in welfare from increasing water quality.

The optimality conditions associated with the state variables describe the choice of stock levels for the six types of physical capital and the three types of natural capital. For the physical capital variables, the optimality conditions are:

$$\frac{\partial U}{\partial q}\frac{\partial q}{\partial k_1} = (r + \delta_1)\mu_1 - \dot{\mu}_1 \qquad (B.17)$$

$$\frac{\partial U}{\partial x_2}\frac{\partial x}{\partial k_2} = (r + \delta_2)\mu_2 - \dot{\mu}_2 \qquad (B.18)$$

$$p_3 \frac{\partial \gamma}{\partial k_3} = (r + \delta_3)\mu_3 - \dot{\mu}_3 \qquad (B.19)$$

$$p_4 \frac{\partial \eta}{\partial k_4}Y = (r + \delta_4)\mu_4 - \dot{\mu}_4 \qquad (B.20)$$

$$\frac{\partial U}{\partial q}\frac{\partial q}{\partial e}\frac{\partial e}{\partial k_5}W_1 - p_5 \frac{\partial e}{\partial k_5}W_1 = (r + \delta_5)\mu_5 - \dot{\mu}_5 \qquad (B.21)$$

$$\frac{\partial U}{\partial h}\frac{\partial h}{\partial k_6} = (r + \delta_6)\mu_6 - \dot{\mu}_6 \qquad (B.22)$$

These conditions demonstrate that the value of the marginal product of reproducible capital in each activity (including land enhancement, water quality repair and diminishing groundwater stocks) is equal to a rental price of capital. Because the investment good is treated as the undifferentiated intermediate good, $\mu_1 = \mu_2 = \mu_3 = \mu_4 = \mu_5 = \mu_6$. However, the rental prices may differ because of different economic depreciation rates.

The final optimality conditions involve our natural capital stocks: effective farmland, water quality, and groundwater stocks. These conditions are:

$$\frac{\partial U}{\partial q}\frac{\partial q}{\partial T_1} = r\rho_3 - \dot{\rho}_3 \qquad (B.23)$$

$$\frac{\partial U}{\partial Y} + \frac{\partial U}{\partial x_2}\frac{\partial x}{\partial Y} = (r\rho_4 - \dot{\rho}_4) - \rho_4[a - D(Z_1) + \eta(n_4, k_4, x_4)] \qquad (B.24)$$

$$\frac{\partial U}{\partial q}\frac{\partial q}{\partial W_1}e = (r\rho_5 - \dot{\rho}_5) - \rho_5[\psi - e(n_5, k_5, x_5)] \qquad (B.25)$$

Equation (B.23) has a straightforward interpretation as rental price of effective farmland. Unlike the conditions for physical capital stocks, equation (B.23) does not have a depreciation rate. Soil erosion, which is similar to a physical depreciation rate, is already captured in equation (B.23). The optimality condition for the stock of water quality is also a rental rate similar to those for physical capital. However, given the form of equation (B.24), this rental rate is adjusted for water quality appreciation rather than depreciation.

Finally, it is interesting to compare the shadow values for reproducible capital to natural capital. For example, a unit of reproducible capital that is used in the agricultural sector has a value:

$$\mu_1 = \frac{\dfrac{\partial U}{\partial q}\dfrac{\partial q}{\partial k_1}}{(r + \delta_1)} + \frac{\dot{\mu}_1}{(r + \delta_1)} \qquad (B.26)$$

or

$$\mu_1(t) = \int_t^\infty e^{-(r+\delta_1)(s-t)} \frac{\partial U}{\partial q}\frac{\partial q}{\partial k_1}(s)ds \qquad (B.27)$$

In other words, the value of a unit of reproducible capital in time $t$ is equal to the discounted value of the future services it will provide in terms of agricultural output. An increase in the discount rate ($r$) or the rate of depreciation ($\delta_1$) will reduce the value of capital.

Our shadow value of natural capital has similar characteristics. For example, a unit of water quality has a shadow value:

$$\rho_4 = \frac{\dfrac{\partial U}{\partial Y} + \dfrac{\partial U}{\partial x_2}\dfrac{\partial x}{\partial Y}}{[a - D(Z_1) + \eta(n_4, k_4, x_4)]} + \frac{\dot{\rho}_4}{[a - D(Z_1) + \eta(n_4, k_4, x_4)]} \qquad (B.28)$$

or

$$\rho_4(t) = \int_t^\infty e^{-[(r-a+D(Z_1)-\eta(n_4,k_4,x_4)](s-t)} \frac{\partial U}{\partial Y} + \frac{\partial U}{\partial x_2}\frac{\partial x}{\partial Y}(s)ds \qquad (B.29)$$

For natural capital, an increase in the natural rate of regeneration or human efforts to improve the water quality reduces the discount rate and increases the shadow value. Unlike reproducible capital, the shadow value captures the discounted value of water quality to both consumers $(\partial U/\partial Y)$ and producers of the manufactured good $[(\partial U/\partial x_2)(\partial x/\partial Y)]$.

## NOTES

1. Our definition of non-marketed goods includes environmental amenities and disamenities.
2. Smith (1992) suggests his work should be characterized as environmental costing rather than environmental accounting.
3. This interpretation requires a re-normalization of the current value Hamiltonian.
4. Possible increases in the value of natural or environmental capital are not excluded.
5. However, the current NIPA system attributes household and government investment to current consumption.
6. See United Nations (1992) and Bartelmus et al. (1991).
7. The net rate of regeneration defines the equation of motion for each asset.
8. The conditions for optimality are presented in Appendix B.
9. EPIC is a physical-process model that simulates interaction of the soil–climate–plant management processes in agricultural production. EPIC was developed by USDA/ARS scientists and has been used extensively in the RCA and elsewhere (e.g. Faeth, 1993).
10. Ribaudo's 1982 estimates are inflated to 1987 and 1992 by the change in the GDP implicit price deflator.
11. Irrigated acres in the Pacific coast fell from 12 million to 10.5 million from 1978 to 1992 (USDA, 1994b).
12. Smith suggests the work on Viscusi and Magat (1991) on energy implies that the environmental costs of agriculture are comparable to those estimated from several energy sources. Both the Smith and Viscusi and Magat work differ from Nestor and Pasurka's estimates of total value-added for environmental protection of 0.3 percent.

## REFERENCES

Ahmad, Y., El Serafy, S. and Lutz, E. (eds) (1989), *Environmental Accounting for Sustainable Development,* Washington, DC: World Bank.

Aillery, M.P. (1995), 'Federal Commodity Programs and Returns to Irrigation in the West', ERS staff paper 9502, U.S. Department of Agriculture, Economic Research Service.

Alt, K., Osborn, C.T. and Colacicco, D. (1989), 'Soil Erosion: What Effect on Agricultural Productivity?', Agricultural Information Bulletin No. 556, U.S. Department of Agriculture, Economic Research Service.

Arrow, K. and Kurz, M. (1970), *Public Investment, the Rate of Return and Optimal Fiscal Policy,* Baltimore, MD: Johns Hopkins University Press.

Bartelmus, P., Stahmer, C. and Van Tongeren, J. (1991), 'Integrating Environmental and Economic Accounting: Framework for a SNA Satellite System', *Review of Income and Wealth,* 37, pp. 111–147.

Crosson, P. (1986), 'Soil Erosion and Policy Issues', in Phipps, T., Crosson, P. and Price, K. (eds), *Agriculture and the Environment,* Washington, DC: Resources for the Future, pp. 35–72.

Faeth, P. (1993), 'Evaluating Agricultural Policy and the Sustainability of Production Systems: An Economic Framework', *Journal of Soil and Water Conservation,* 48, pp. 94–99.

Harrison, A. (1989), 'Environmental Issues and the SNA', *Review of Income and Wealth,* 35, pp. 377–388.

Hartwick, J. (1990), 'Natural Resources, National Accounting and Economic Depreciation', *Journal of Public Economics,* 43, pp. 291–304.

Hung, N.M. (1993), 'Natural Resource, National Accounting, and Economic Depreciation: Stock Effects', *Journal of Public Economics,* 51, pp. 379–389.

Mäler, K.-G. (1991), 'National Accounts and Environmental Resources', *Environmental and Resource Economics,* 1, pp. 1–15.

National Academy of Sciences, National Research Council (1993), *Soil and Water Quality: An Agenda for Agriculture,* Washington, DC: National Academy Press.

Nestor, D.V. and Pasurka, C.A. (1994), 'Environment-Economic Accounting and Indicators of the Importance of Environmental Protection Activities', paper presented at the 1993 Annual Meeting of the Southern Economic Association, March.

Nordhaus, W.D. and Tobin, J. (1972), 'Is Economic Growth Obsolete?', in *Economic Growth,* 5th Anniversary Colloquium, V, New York: National Bureau of Economic Research.

Prince, R. and Gordon, P. (1994), 'Greening the National Accounts', CBO Papers, Congressional Budget Office, March.

Repetto, R. (1992a), 'Accounting for Environmental Assets', *Scientific American,* 266, pp. 94–100.

Repetto, R. (1992b), 'Earth in the Balance Sheet: Incorporating Natural Resources into National Income Accounts', *Environment,* 34, pp. 13–20, 43–45.

Ribaudo, M. (1986), 'Reducing Soil Erosion: Offsite Benefits', Agricultural Economics Report No. 561, U.S. Department of Agriculture, Economic Research Service.

Ribaudo, M. (1989), 'Water Quality Benefits from the Conservation Reserve Program', Agricultural Economics Report No. 606, U.S. Department of Agriculture, Economic Research Service.

Rutledge, G. and Leonard, M.L. (1993), 'Pollution Abatement and Control Expenditure, 1987–91', *Survey of Current Business,* U.S. Department of Commerce, Bureau of Economic Analysis, Vol. 73, No. 5, pp. 55–62, May.

Samuelson, P.A. (1961), 'The Evaluation of Social Income: Capital Formation and Wealth', in Lutz, P. and Hague, D. (eds), *The Theory of Capital,* Proceedings of an IEA Conference, New York: St. Martin's Press.

Schafer, D. and Stahmer, C. (1989), 'Input–Output Model for the Analysis of Environmental Protection Activities', *Economic Systems Research,* 1, pp. 203–228.

Smith, V.K. (1992), 'Environmental Costing for Agriculture: Will It Be Standard Fare in the Farm Bill of 2000?', *American Journal of Agricultural Economics*, **74**, pp. 1076–1088.

Solley, W.B., Chase, E.B. and Mann, W.B., IV (1983), 'Estimated Use of Water in the United States in 1980', U.S. Geological Survey Circular 1001.

Solley, W.B., Pierce, R.R. and Perlman, H.A. (1993), 'Estimated Use of Water in the United States in 1990', U.S. Department of Interior Circular 1081.

Solow, R. (1986), 'On the Intertemporal Allocation of Resources', *Scandinavian Journal of Economics*, **88**, pp. 141–156.

Solow, R. (1992), 'An Almost Practical Step Towards Sustainability', An Invited Lecture on the Fortieth Anniversary of Resources for the Future. Mimeo.

United Nations (1993), 'Integrated Environmental and Economic Accounting', Interim Version, Studies in Methods, Series F., No. 61. Handbook on National Accounting. Department for Economic and Social Information Policy Analysis, United Nations: New York.

U.S. Department of Agriculture (1989), 'The Second RCA Appraisal: Soil, Water, and Related Resources on Nonfederal Land in the United States, Analysis of Conditions and Trends', June.

U.S. Department of Agriculture (1994a), Soil Conservation Service, 'Summary Report 1992 National Resources Inventory', July.

U.S. Department of Agriculture (1994b), Economic Research Service, 'Agricultural Resource and Environmental Indicators', Agricultural Handbook No. 705, December.

U.S. Department of Commerce (1993), Bureau of Economic Analysis, 'Survey of Current Business', August.

U.S. Department of Commerce (1994), Bureau of Economic Analysis, 'Accounting for Mineral Resources: Issues and BEA's Initial Estimates', April.

U.S. Department of the Interior (1984), U.S. Geological Survey, 'National Water Summary 1983 – Hydrological Events and Issues', Water Supply Paper 2250, p. 26.

Viscusi, W.K. and Magat, W.A. (1991), 'Interim Draft Report On Efficient Energy Pricing', Washington, DC: USEPA, Report to U.S. Environmental Protection Agency.

Weitzman, M. (1976), 'On the Significance of Net National Product in a Dynamic Economy', *Quarterly Journal of Economics*, **90**, pp. 156–162.

# 6 Vulnerability of Crops to Climate Change: A Practical Method of Indexing

## David Schimmelpfennig and Gary Yohe

## 1 INTRODUCTION

Consideration of how to respond to climate change frequently turns upon the evaluation of the undesirable consequences of some possible effect of that change. For coastal property, for example, sea level rise might inundate homes or cause salt water to intrude on sources of fresh water. In the agricultural sectors, hotter climates might cause crop yields to fall, with or without prudent adaptation. If we think of the consequences of climate change as the result of crossing a physically determined threshold, then it can be instructive to consider the probability of reaching that threshold under various states of the world. Initially ignoring the potential for adaptation can allow the research to focus on crops and growing regions where adaptation might be the most helpful.

We begin with the notion that the probability of crossing a threshold can be a workable metric of vulnerability. The idea of action thresholds was proposed by participants in a landmark international conference held in Villach, Austria (SCOPE, 1985) and it has been emphasized again in the highly visible Intergovernmental Panel on Climate Change (IPCC) assessment reports (IPCC, 1996). This chapter will add to that discussion and to our knowledge about thresholds by developing a uniformly applicable index to characterize probabilistically, the crossing of one or more thresholds. The vulnerability index accounts for uncertainty in our understanding of how the climate might be changing *and* uncertainty in our understanding of the consequences of climate change. A complementary index of sustainability is simply one minus the vulnerability index.

The choice of a threshold level is crucial for policy applicability. In the past, attempts to identify and avoid thresholds have led to the development of several rules of thumb that have been useful in policy settings. Roumasset (1976) discusses three safety-first rules of thumb. The 'safety principle' minimizes the probability of crossing the threshold, and the 'strict safety-first principle' maximizes an objective, like farm profits, subject to the constraint that the threshold should not be crossed. The third general category of threshold avoidance strategies is the 'safety-fixed principle' that attempts to hold the probability of crossing the threshold constant while maximizing the lowest level that farm profits can fall to.

In choosing the level of the threshold in the chapter we considered that, if the threshold were too low, it would be reached under circumstances that might be considered innocuous. If the threshold is too high it will be reached after the majority of the damage has been done. The threshold that we consider is a 10 percent reduction below trend in the yields of six major cereal crops. This is probably too high in some circumstances and too low in others. As will be shown, U.S. corn historically shows more natural variation to changes in weather patterns than some of the other crops considered and, for that reason, it might be appropriate to consider a higher threshold for U.S. corn.

In the final analysis, though, it is likely to be the individual farm affected by climate change that matters. For socio-economic reasons, important thresholds might be different for different farms in different regions even growing the same crop. Adaptation to climate change would proceed at different rates at different farms, so the effects of climate change should be offset at different rates (Morrisette and Rosenberg, 1992). Systems, in general, can and will adapt to change; and that adaptation can be encouraged and supported by policy. That is the point of recent studies conducted by the IPCC (1990, 1992, 1996), the U.S. National Academy of Science (1992), the Office of Technology Assessment (1993), Lewandrowski and Brazee (1993) and Schimmelpfennig (1996).

Adaptation will take place, but it is a mistake to think of adaptation as occurring simultaneously with perceived changes in the environment. Some of the lags in the adoption of agricultural adaptation measures are quite long even on the time scale of global warming, as the summary of related research in Table 6.1 shows. These time lags reflect the fact that many adaptation measures require investments in capital that are expensive and lock a farmer into the use of the new technology, at least until the investment pays for itself. In fact, the new technology is probably replacing another technology that is itself on an amortization schedule, further slowing down the adoption of new technologies as the farmer waits for the old technology to wear out. Several other factors contribute to time lags in adaptation. Time is required to carry out test plot experiments in the development of new seed varieties. Time is required to educate farmers about new practices. More commonly in developing countries, the lack of adequate infrastructure, an extension service and even cleared land can slow adoption of new agricultural technologies. Our vulnerability index could be used to help farmers evaluate the need for new technologies by indicating the vulnerability of their current crop absent adaptation. It would be fairly straightforward, with the help of extension agents with the appropriate computer software, for a farmer to develop the limited data required to generate the index for an individual farm. The index is not a policy tool in the

*Table 6.1   Speed of adoption for some major agricultural adaptation measures*

| Adaptation | Adjustment time (yrs) | Reference |
|---|---|---|
| Variety adoption | 3–14 | Dalrymple, 1986; Griliches, 1957; Plucknett et al., 1987; CIMMYT, 1991. |
| Dams and irrigation | 50–100 | James and Lee, 1971; Howe, 1971. |
| Variety development | 8–15 | Plucknett et al., 1987; Knudson, 1988. |
| Tillage systems | 10–12 | Hill et al., 1994; Dickey et al., 1987; Schertz, 1988. |
| New crop adoption: soybeans | 15–30 | FAO, Agrostat – various years. |
| Opening new lands | 3–10 | Medvedev, 1987; Plusquellec, 1990. |
| Irrigation equipment | 20–25 | Turner and Anderson, 1980. |
| Transportation system | 3–5 | World Bank, 1994. |
| Fertilizer adoption | 10 | Pieri, 1992; Thompson & Wan; 1992. |

*Source:*   Adapted from Reilly (1995).

sense that it tells decision makers what to do. It does indicate directions where the in-depth analysis necessary for policy decisions can be fruitfully applied.

## 2   RELATED RESEARCH ON POSSIBLE RESPONSES TO CLIMATE CHANGE

Any thought of trying to mitigate against the speed or magnitude of global change must weigh the cost of mitigation against the potential harm, net of any adaptation which might be forthcoming, but including the cost of that adaptation. That is the point of integrated assessments, that attempt to integrate these factors together for global warming (Manne and Richels, 1992; Nordhaus, 1991, 1992, 1994; Yohe, 1993, 1994).

Research into the relative costs of various mitigation strategies has made great strides over the past few years (Gaskins and Weyant, 1993), but evaluation of the relative vulnerability, given potential adaptation, has lagged behind. Individual sectors have been studied, but there does not yet exist a consistent, organizational method with which to compare vulnerabilities across the extended time dimension of most global change phenomena.

A weakness of studies of the effects of climate change on agriculture is that they have focused on mean effects when higher order moments are also important (Schimmelpfennig, 1996). Agriculture depends on the specific realization of climate variables like temperature and precipitation that make up our weather. The random draw from the climate distribution that gives us our weather can come from the tails of the distribution. The vulnerability index we develop is a simple metric that summarizes all of the information by evaluating a series of points spread throughout the relevant distributions.

The details of this procedure are given in the Appendix, but the underlying idea can be illustrated graphically. To see how, consider some subset of real numbers $A_0$ defined to reflect variability in the current climate of some region expressed in terms of precipitation (denoted $X$) and temperature ($Y$). The set $A_0$ can be bounded, for the sake of simplicity but without loss of generality, by thinking of it as a confidence region of some predetermined level ($\varepsilon \cdot 100$ percent) for the current climate. Meanwhile, define a second set, $B_{n0}$, to reflect the viable region for some natural or engineered system ($N$), also expessed in terms of variability in precipitation and temperature. The notion here is that system $N$ would be viable if $X$ and $Y$ were to occur within region $B_{n0}$, but that it would suffer severely if $X$ and $Y$ were to occur elsewhere.[1] The intersection of $A_0$ and $B_{n0}$ represents a region of sustainability that can be expected to occur for system $N$ with likelihood $\varepsilon \cdot 100$ percent. Probabilistically weighting these areas according to the techniques described in the Appendix places the value of the (area of) the intersection between zero and one and defines a 'sustainability index' that also lies between zero and one. The closer to one it is, the more secure is the existence of the system; the closer to zero, of course, the more likely it is that the system will expire. Defining a minimum value for this sustainability index is thus the functional equivalent of establishing a practical threshold of extinction.

Some systems may be close to that threshold, while others may not. Figures 6.1 and 6.2 show the difference. The left-hand side of Figure 6.1 shows a system with a relatively large portion of set $A_0$ covered by its $B_{n0}$ region. If the density function were uniform, then $S_0(N)$ would appear to exceed 0.5 because the area of the intersection $A_0 \cap B_{n0}$ is greater than half the size of the climate set $A_0$. If the density function were to concentrate relatively more likelihood near the means of precipitation and temperature, of course, then $S_0(N)$ would be correspondingly higher.

Figures 6.2, 6.3 and 6.4 show, by way of contrast, systems whose regions of sustainability indices are small. In Figure 6.2, the index is small because the $B_{n0}$ region is small and centered away from the means of temperature of precipitation $A_0$. In Figure 6.3, the $B_{n0}$ straddles the means of $A_0$ well enough, but its orientation does not match the natural correlation of $A_0$. Uncorrelated variability finally swamps $B_{n0}$ in Figure 6.4, where $A_0$ is enormous relative to $B_{n0}$. Finding any of these systems surviving their environments would be evidence that they have a low threshold of extinction. Some may be robust, but their low sustainability

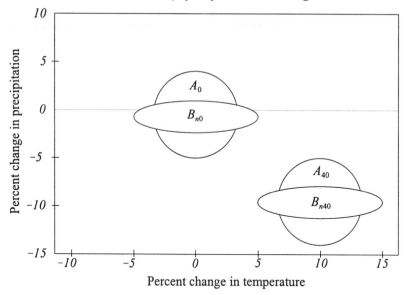

*Figure 6.1   Sustainability indices represented by intersection of
climate ($A_0$, $A_{40}$) and viability ($B_{n0}$, $B_{n40}$)*

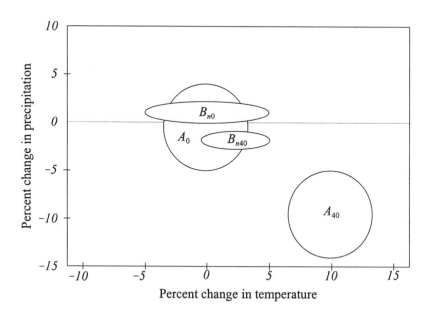

*Figure 6.2   Smaller sustainability indices than represented in Figure 6.1*

indices could indicate that their existence was, at best, very tenuous – marginal systems that might be threatened by even small climate change in the wrong direction.

Figures 6.1 and 6.2 also show what might happen as the climate changes. Suppose that 40 years of climate change produced, for example, a new distribution of temperature and precipitation, denoted $f_{40}(X, Y)$. If only the means were to change, then set $A_{40}$ would apply. If variability were to change, as well, then the shape of $A_{40}$ would have changed, of course. The point here is simply that changing climate can be easily reflected by a migration of the associated confidence region.

Figure 6.1 shows what might happen if system $N$ were to adapt perfectly as the climate changed. Notice that its region of sustainability has simply moved in synch with the climate so that the critical intersection, now between sets $A_{40}$ and $B_{n40}$, is the same size. If the shift in climate were simply higher moment preserving shifts to a drier and warmer climate, though, neither the index of sustainability nor the index of vulnerability would change. Figure 6.5 shows a time trajectory for this fortunate case.

Figure 6.2 illustrates what might lie ahead as the climate changes for the less fortunate marginal system whose ability to adapt might be overwhelmed by the warmer and drier climate. The new climate region, $A_{40}$, does not intersect the new region of sustainability, $B_{n40}$, at all. The system quite simply must have perished well before the new climate was established. Figure 6.6 shows a time trajectory for this type of climate change extinction. It assumes that the climate changes over the course of 40 years but that the threshold of extinction is crossed after only 15 years. At that point, regions $A_t$ and $B_{nt}$ intersect with such low frequency that system collapse occurs precipitously.[2] Notice, too, that a similar trajectory would emerge from Figure 6.1 if the system had not adapted; region $A_{40}$ does not intersect region $B_{n0}$.

Trajectories like the ones drawn in Figures 6.5 and 6.6 could be employed to calibrate adaptation options for aggressive, moderate and recalcitrant decision makers and political activists. Assuming a certain trajectory of climate change, a number of systems could be cataloged according to (1) the time they might cross their extinction thresholds absent adaptation and (2) the effectiveness of a range of adaptive responses. Comparisons of each might generate a robust list of 'vulnerability criteria' that could be applied beyond the set of specific examples studied. The timing scale on the horizontal axis could, of course, be stretched or contracted according to the speed with which people foresee climate changing. Timing sensitivity and sensitivity to various climate change scenarios could thereby be explored as well. This could allow decision makers to respond to threats on various systems on more than philosophical grounds.

The method outlined here is, above all else, designed to be practical. It recognizes the need for assessing vulnerability across a wide range of systems in support of planning processes that must assign priorities in allocating scarce resources to both the research and development of adaptive strategies and their

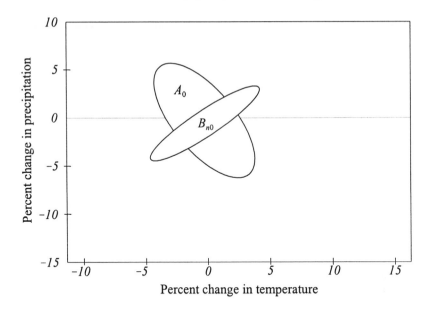

*Figure 6.3   Mismatched climate ($A_0$) and viability ($B_{n0}$)*

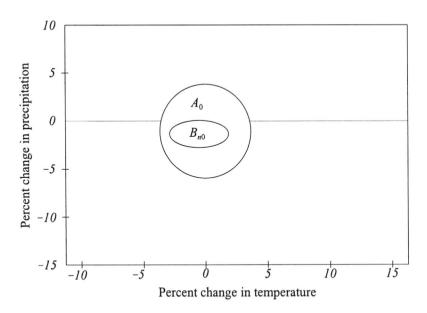

*Figure 6.4   Climate ($A_0$) swamps viability ($B_{n0}$)*

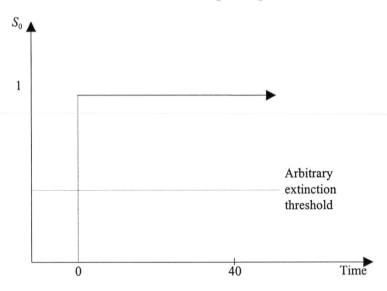

*Figure 6.5   Sustainability index (S$_0$) above extinction level*

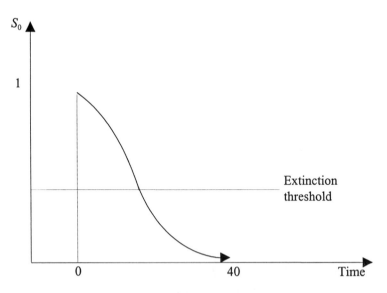

*Figure 6.6   Extinction occurs after index (S$_0$) falls below threshold*

implementation. It also recognizes that these judgements must be made in the context of large uncertainties and enormous time horizons. At the same time, though, it recognizes that the full range of quality data and theoretical tools that would be required to undertake complete and comprehensive analyses of vulnerable systems will not always be available. Indeed, the method is designed to apply simple and straightforward techniques to limited data to canvass a wide range of potentially vulnerable systems. This first step can help identify those systems where the collection of more complete data sets and the development of more comprehensive analytical tools will pay the largest dividends. The method developed here is, in short, deliberately 'low brow' and simplistic. It will not yield precise insights upon which policy and planning decisions can be made. It will, instead, support gross comparisons across disparate systems, like the major world agricultural crops, so that the long-term process of targeting various systems for detailed study will make as few errors of omission and commission as possible.

The next section gives a brief description of a simple statistical approach that can, with limited data, support the broad method outlined in the Appendix and applies the technique to selected crops throughout the world. Sections 3 and 4 turn to the issue of characterizing the future climate and the uncertainty with which we view it for these examples, allowing a means of tracking the index into the future. Section 5 concludes by drawing lessons from the illustrative applications. The notion that is developed is that there is more to tracking how and why vulnerability indices might change over time than simply positing a correlation with a plausible scenario for global mean temperature.

## 3  REPRESENTING CLIMATE VARIABILITY WITH DISCRETE DISTRIBUTIONS

The method outlined in the Appendix and to be implemented in this section requires several bits of information. First of all, useful representations of climate variability must be produced. In the notation of the Appendix, these are the $A_i$ subsets. To that end, consider a collection of ordered pairs that reflect climate: deviations in temperature and precipitation around their mean, for example, which reflect the current climate. Represent the temperature and precipitation data by $X$ and $Y$. Represent deviations around their means by $x$ and $y$. The idea will be to identify a second, systematically chosen set of ordered pairs that can all be assigned the same probability but which nonetheless reflect the distribution of experience captured in the original data. A simple linear regression of $y$ on $x$,

$$y_i = \alpha + \beta x_i + u_i, \tag{6.1}$$

will be used to summarize the climate. Let

$$y = \alpha + \beta x \tag{6.2}$$

represent the estimated equation; the estimated intercept $\alpha$ must, of course, be constrained in the estimation process to equal zero.[3]

The procedure suggested here will work from the regression results to offer a discrete portrait of the resulting statistical summary of climate. It begins by producing a discrete representation of the underlying distribution for $x$ – the independent variable for equation (6.1). Let $\{x_i\}$ support that representation with each $x_i \in \{x_i\}$ assigned probability $p_i$ so that $\Sigma p_i = 1$, the mean $\Sigma p_i x_i = 0$, and the variance of $x$ from the original sample is preserved. Elements in $\{x_i\}$ should be chosen so that $p_i = p$.

The next step produces similar representations of corresponding conditional distributions for $y$ for each of the $x_i \in \{x_i\}$. Let $\{y_j(x_i)\}$ support these representations with each $y_j(x_i) \in \{y_j(x_i)\}$ to be assigned some probability $p_j$. The key is to choose the $y_j(x_i) \in \{y_j(x_i)\}$ so that it is possible to assign the same probability $p_j = p$ with $\Sigma p_j = 1$, the mean $\Sigma p_j y_j(x_i) = \beta x_i$, and the variance of the prediction error surrounding equation (6.1) given $x_i$ preserved. The distribution of prediction error $y_i - \beta x_i$ can be characterized by

$$\{y - \beta x_i\} / s_u \{1 + [1/n] + [(x_i - \mu_x)^2 / \Sigma (x_j - \mu_x)^2]\}^{1/2} \sim t_{n-2}, \tag{6.3}$$

where $s_u^2 = \{\Sigma [y_j - \beta x_j]^2\} / (n-2)$ is an unbiased estimate of the variance of the error term in equation (6.1) (Johnson, 1984).

The collection of ordered pairs $\{(x_i, y_j(x_i))\}$, all being assigned equal probability $p_{ij} = p^2$, can finally be proposed as a reasonable representation of the original climate data expressed in a way that can easily accommodate the calculation of a vulnerability index number – they are a workable representation of the necessary $A_0$ subset from the Appendix. Superimposing a climate response surface on a grid mapping of the pairs $\{(x_i, y_j(x_i))\}$ and counting the number of points that are not covered is then a practical and simple way to begin implementing the method of section 2. If $m$ points are not covered, more specifically, the initial vulnerability index is simply $mp^2$.

### A 25-Point Illustration

A joint distribution for $(x, y)$ can be summarized by 25 equally probable ordered pairs if each of the conditional distributions rooted on five equally probable values of $x_i$ are represented by five equally (conditionally) probable values of $y_j(x_i)$.

Table 6.2 records the specifics of this case. The mean of the $x$ values combines with the mean plus and minus $(.5)^{1/2}$ and $(2)^{1/2}$ times the estimated standard deviation of the $x$ values to form the underlying discrete values for the $\{x_i\}$. Each can be given a probability of 0.2; as a set, they represent the 8th, 24th, 50th, 76th and 92nd percentiles of the original climate distribution for $x$.

*Table 6.2   Specifics of a 25-point representation*

| Point value | Percentile |
|---|---|
| $x_i$: | |
| $\mu_x$ | 50 |
| $\mu_x \pm \sigma(0.5)^{1/2} = \mu_x \pm 0.71\sigma$ | 24 and 76 |
| $\mu_x \pm \sigma(2.0)^{1/2} = \mu_x \pm 1.41\sigma$ | 8 and 92 |
| | |
| $y_j(x_i)$: | |
| $\beta x_i$ | 50 |
| $\beta x_i \pm \{s_u[1 + (1/n) + (x_i - \mu_x)]^2 / \Sigma (x_j - \mu_x)^2 \} t_{n-2}\,(.24)$ | 24 and 76 |
| $\beta x_i \pm \{s_u[1 + (1/n) + (x_i - \mu_x)]^2 / \Sigma (x_j - \mu_x)^2 \} t_{n-2}\,(.08)$ | 8 and 92 |

Each of these $x_i$ values can then be assigned a set of five conditional $y_j$ values using the $t$-distribution for the percentiles identified above and the regression results from equation (6.2). The central value should be $\beta x_i$, of course. The four outside values are determined by $\beta x_i$ plus or minus the denominator of the right-hand side of equation (6.3) multiplied by $t_{n-2}(.08)$ and $t_{n-2}(.24)$. Each conditional distribution assigns a probability of 0.2 to each $y_j(x_i)$, so each of the resulting 25 ordered pairs should be assigned probabilities of 0.04.

**An 81-Point Illustration**

Tables 6.3 and 6.4 repeat the process for 81 points, with nine $x_i$ values and nine contingent $y_j(x_i)$ values for each $x_i$. Each ordered pair should therefore be assigned a probability of $(1/81)$. Two alternatives are offered. The first moves along the range of $x$ values uniformly and produces an equally uniform spread for the contingent $y$ values. The other is based on a geometric spread which moves the third, fourth and fifth outside values away from the mean by factors of 2, 4 and 8 times the deviation of the second value from the mean. The alternatives may produce slightly different vulnerability indices in practice. When that is a problem, a finer grid of, say, 121 points might be more appropriate. Because the purpose is to provide gross representations of vulnerability to focus research and planning exercises, it is probably sufficient to average the two indices.

*Table 6.3　Specifics of an 81-point representation – uniform spread*

| Point value | Percentile |
|---|---|
| $x_i$: | |
| $\mu_x$ | 50 |
| $\mu_x = \mu_x \pm 0.39\sigma$ | 35 and 65 |
| $\mu_x = \mu_x \pm 0.78\sigma$ | 22 and 78 |
| $\mu_x = \mu_x \pm 1.17\sigma$ | 12 and 88 |
| $\mu_x = \mu_x \pm 1.56\sigma$ | 6 and 94 |
| $y_j(x_i)$: | |
| $\beta x_i$ | 50 |
| $\beta x_i \pm \{s_u[1 + (1/n) + (x_i - \mu_x)]^2 / \Sigma (x_j - \mu_x)^2\}t_{n-2}(.35)$ | 35 and 65 |
| $\beta x_i \pm \{s_u[1 + (1/n) + (x_i - \mu_x)]^2 / \Sigma (x_j - \mu_x)^2\}t_{n-2}(.22)$ | 22 and 78 |
| $\beta x_i \pm \{s_u[1 + (1/n) + (x_i - \mu_x)]^2 / \Sigma (x_j - \mu_x)^2\}t_{n-2}(.12)$ | 12 and 88 |
| $\beta x_i \pm \{s_u[1 + (1/n) + (x_i - \mu_x)]^2 / \Sigma (x_j - \mu_x)^2\}t_{n-2}(.06)$ | 6 and 94 |

*Table 6.4　Specifics of an 81-point representation – geometric spread*

| Point value | Percentile |
|---|---|
| $x_i$: | |
| $\mu_x$ | 50 |
| $\mu_x = \mu_x \pm 0.23\sigma$ | 42 and 58 |
| $\mu_x = \mu_x \pm 0.46\sigma$ | 33 and 67 |
| $\mu_x = \mu_x \pm 0.93\sigma$ | 18 and 82 |
| $\mu_x = \mu_x \pm 1.85\sigma$ | 3 and 97 |
| $y_j(x_i)$: | |
| $\beta x_i$ | 50 |
| $\beta x_i \pm \{s_u[1 + (1/n) + (x_i - \mu_x)]^2 / \Sigma (x_j - \mu_x)^2\}t_{n-2} (.42)$ | 42 and 58 |
| $\beta x_i \pm \{s_u[1 + (1/n) + (x_i - \mu_x)]^2 / \Sigma (x_j - \mu_x)^2\}t_{n-2} (.33)$ | 33 and 67 |
| $\beta x_i \pm \{s_u[1 + (1/n) + (x_i - \mu_x)]^2 / \Sigma (x_j - \mu_x)^2\}t_{n-2} (.18)$ | 18 and 82 |
| $\beta x_i \pm \{s_u[1 + (1/n) + (x_i - \mu_x)]^2 / \Sigma (x_j - \mu_x)^2\}t_{n-2} (.03)$ | 3 and 97 |

## An Application – the U.S. Corn Belt

July is the critical month for determining the effect of precipitation and temperature on corn yields in the United States. It is the month that corn tassels form and
is referred to as the heading month (Lawrence, 1986, Table V-I). Figure 6.7
displays precipitation and temperature data for the Corn Belt 'weighted by harvested cropland' as reported by the U.S. Department of Agriculture (USDA)

(Teigen and Singer, 1992). The sloped line is the corresponding estimate of equation (6.3). Table 6.5 records the results of applying the 81-point procedure outlined above to these data; notice that both the uniform and geometric spreads are reported.

Yield contours for corn in the United States are, meanwhile, available from the Research Directorate of the U.S. Department of Defense (DOD) (Lawrence, 1986). Figure 6.8 displays a 90 percent yield contour. Surveys of experts conducted by DOD determined that anticipated yields for corn in the U.S. are higher than 90 percent of the base-period expected yield for combinations of (1) deviations in the percentage change in precipitation around their mean and (2) deviations in temperature around its mean, on the inside of the contour. Superimposing this contour on the discrete representations of current climate recorded in Table 6.5 produces initial vulnerability indices (for 1990): 0.46 for the geometric spread and 0.23 for the uniform spread. A 0.345 average conforms to a sustainability index of 0.655.

This procedure is repeated below for the major crop-growing regions in the world. Historical data for temperature and precipitation in the crop-growing

*Table 6.5  Discrete representations of current climate*

| Percentage change in precipitation | Temperature change | | | | | | | | |
|---|---|---|---|---|---|---|---|---|---|
| Uniform spread: | | | | | | | | | |
| 45.2 | 1.18 | 0.73 | 0.14 | −0.19 | −0.63 | −1.07 | −1.41 | −1.99 | −2.44 |
| 33.9 | 1.29 | 0.85 | 0.28 | −0.04 | −0.47 | −0.90 | −1.23 | −1.80 | −2.24 |
| 22.6 | 1.42 | 0.99 | 0.43 | 0.11 | −0.32 | −0.74 | −1.06 | −1.62 | −2.05 |
| 11.3 | 1.56 | 1.13 | 0.58 | 0.26 | −0.16 | −0.57 | −0.89 | −1.45 | −1.88 |
| 0.0 | 1.71 | 1.29 | 0.73 | 0.41 | 0.00 | −0.41 | −0.73 | −1.29 | −1.71 |
| −11.3 | 1.87 | 1.44 | 0.89 | 0.57 | 0.16 | −0.26 | −0.58 | −1.13 | −1.56 |
| −22.6 | 2.05 | 1.62 | 1.06 | 0.74 | 0.31 | −0.11 | −0.43 | −0.99 | −1.42 |
| −33.9 | 2.24 | 1.80 | 1.23 | 0.90 | 0.47 | 0.04 | −0.28 | −0.86 | −1.30 |
| −45.2 | 2.44 | 1.99 | 1.41 | 1.07 | 0.63 | 0.19 | −0.15 | −0.73 | −1.18 |
| Geometric spread: | | | | | | | | | |
| 53.7 | 1.49 | 0.33 | −0.25 | −0.51 | −0.74 | −0.98 | −1.24 | −1.83 | −2.99 |
| 27.0 | 1.74 | 0.64 | 0.09 | −0.15 | −0.38 | −0.60 | −0.84 | −1.40 | −2.49 |
| 13.3 | 1.90 | 0.82 | 0.27 | 0.04 | −0.19 | −0.41 | −0.65 | −1.19 | −2.27 |
| 6.7 | 1.98 | 0.91 | 0.37 | 0.13 | −0.09 | −0.32 | −0.55 | −1.09 | −2.17 |
| 0.0 | 2.07 | 1.00 | 0.46 | 0.22 | 0.00 | −0.22 | −0.46 | −1.00 | −2.07 |
| −6.7 | 2.17 | 1.09 | 0.55 | 0.32 | 0.09 | −0.13 | −0.37 | −0.91 | −1.98 |
| −13.3 | 2.27 | 1.19 | 0.65 | 0.41 | 0.19 | −0.04 | −0.27 | −0.82 | −1.90 |
| −27.0 | 2.49 | 1.39 | 0.84 | 0.60 | 0.38 | 0.15 | −0.09 | −0.65 | −1.74 |
| −53.7 | 2.98 | 1.83 | 1.24 | 0.99 | 0.75 | 0.51 | 0.25 | −0.33 | −1.50 |

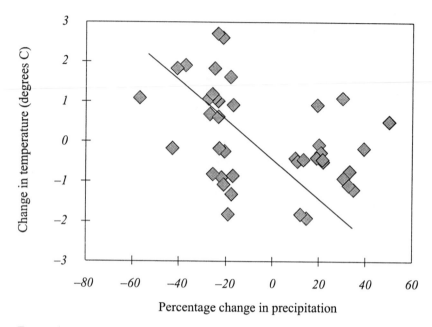

*Figure 6.7   Actual climate for U.S. Corn Belt*

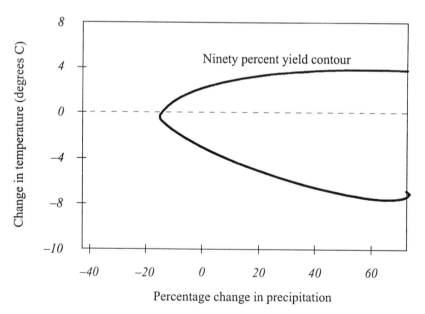

*Figure 6.8   Actual viability for U.S. corn*

regions of the United States are available in several formats from USDA. Descriptions of the world growing regions are also available in Strommen (1994). This USDA publication with specific detail about crop locations allows us to select weather data from over 6,000 weather stations that give the longest temperature and precipitation records in the appropriate region for an individual crop. Precipitation records are often longer than temperature records, and for several cases, our data are continuous from the 1800s. The world weather data are available on CD-ROM (Vose et al., 1992).

U.S. corn yields are sensitive to the variability of the historical temperature record from 1950 to 1990 in the Corn Belt. This explains why U.S. corn yields have followed long-term boom and bust cycles. The overall trend in yield has been positive, but the long-term trajectory has tended to mask variability. Yield fell by 2.02 metric tonnes/hectare (MT/ha) or 28 percent between 1982 and 1983, 2.21 MT/ha or 29 percent between 1987 and 1988, and 1.93 MT/ha or 23 percent between 1992 and 1993 (Hazell, 1984; Webb and Gudmunds, 1992). This variability in corn production in the Midwest is captured by the method proposed here as a measure of vulnerability. A low sustainability index or a high vulnerability index indicates a greater susceptibility to the extreme weather events in the tails of the weather distribution.

# 4 IMPOSING FUTURE CLIMATE CHANGE ACROSS THE GLOBE

Projecting vulnerability indices into the future requires that trajectories of temperature change and precipitation patterns be specified; and it would be most useful if these specifications could accommodate variability in both the natural environment and the international policy arena. There are undoubtedly huge uncertainties associated with both estimates of future climate and policy responses, so we diversify our approach to characterizing the future. First we project vulnerability indices into the future based on regional results from Global Circulation Models (GCMs).

As part of the IPCC Working Group II's effort to make the assessments of different authors on different aspects of the climate change problem comparable, Greco et al. (1994) produced regional results from several GCMs and made them available to the Second Assessment Report lead authors. We use their unpublished transient, coupled ocean-atmosphere GCM results from the Geophysical Fluid Dynamics Laboratory (GFDL) for 2050 and 2100 in each of the appropriate crop-growing regions. The method is the same as before. The only difference is that the temperature and precipitation distributions like the ones in Table 6.5 for the Corn Belt are no longer centered at zero change in temperature and zero percentage change in precipitation on the yield contour graph; they are, instead, shifted by the predicted change in temperature and precipitation from the GCM. The distribution is shifted twice, once for the predicted change in 2050 and again for 2100, and sustainability indices are recalculated each time. Sustainability indices for major world food crops are reported for 1990, 2050 and 2100 in Table 6.6.

Most of the sustainability indices reported in Table 6.6 do not deteriorate significantly under the future climate predicted by the GFDL GCM. Indeed, some even improve. This is because the GFDL model generally predicts increases in precipitation that offset the effects on crop yields of predicted increases in temperature. So the effect of climate change on yield is not pronounced even in the absence of any adaptation.

*Table 6.6*    *Future sustainability indices for major world food crops, based on GFDL climate scenario*

|                       | 1990 | 2050 | 2100 |
|-----------------------|------|------|------|
| Russia winter wheat   | 0.87 | 0.87 | 0.94 |
| Canada spring wheat   | 0.85 | 0.84 | 0.89 |
| Australia winter wheat| 0.83 | 0.83 | 0.83 |
| Russia spring wheat   | 0.79 | 0.77 | 0.88 |
| Argentina corn        | 0.79 | 0.82 | 0.85 |
| U.S. winter wheat     | 0.75 | 0.78 | 0.75 |
| Brazil soybeans       | 0.73 | 0.90 | 0.95 |
| Argentina winter wheat| 0.71 | 0.65 | 0.69 |
| China rice            | 0.68 | 0.74 | 0.70 |
| U.S. soybeans         | 0.68 | 0.64 | 0.81 |
| U.S. spring wheat     | 0.68 | 0.85 | 0.84 |
| China winter wheat    | 0.67 | 0.72 | 0.89 |
| U.S. corn             | 0.66 | 0.64 | 0.79 |
| India winter wheat    | 0.65 | 0.63 | 0.56 |
| India rice            | 0.41 | 0.17 | 0.43 |

*Note*: The GFDL model generally predicts increases in both temperature and precipitation.

Adaptation needs to be considered especially (but not exclusively) if the anticipated increase in precipitation does not materialize. The index suggested here can accommodate some of the more obvious possibilities. Crop migration may, for example, be one way that agriculture might adapt to future climate change. Crops might then continue to be grown in climates with temperature patterns that closely match their current environments. Preliminary insight into the potential success of this sort of planned migration can be supported by the indexing method suggested here. It is enough to replace the home region's future climate distribution with the future distribution from another region to produce a sustainability index *cum* migration.

Could future corn production, for example, migrate profitably under future climate regimes into regions where spring wheat is presently being grown?

Computing a sustainability index *cum* migration for this move suggests that this is, indeed, an idea worth considering. Moving corn production to a northern spring wheat-growing region shows that its sustainability index would rise from .66 to .72 under the present climate. More importantly, the index would rise from .64 to .85 in 2050 and from .79 to .84 in 2100. Even with favorable changes in precipitation patterns, the sustainability ranking of U.S. corn would, in the *ceteris paribus* context of Table 6.6, climb from thirteenth to eighth in 1990, from thirteenth to second in 2050 and from tenth to seventh in 2100.[4] More detailed analysis of opportunity cost, conducted within the full spectrum of alternative adaptive strategies, would be required to conclude that corn should be expected to be grown in the northern United States as the climate changes. These preliminary results do, at least, suggest that such analysis should include corn in the set of alternatives for the northern United States. Indeed, systematic application of the indexing method might fill in a sizeable portion of that set.

Turning finally to explore how changes in abatement policy might influence vulnerability, consider the time trajectories of global mean temperature that emerge from integrated assessment models – models that can accommodate wide ranges of mitigating policy intervention. Objection will certainly be raised that temperature change in the middle of the United States need not match the global mean, and that criticism is fair. It should be expected, however, that temperature change in the Midwest should at least be *correlated* with change in the global mean. It should therefore be a simple matter to adjust the regional temperature trajectory once that correlation is deduced and thereby maintain an important link to the effect of mitigating policies. One question remains, though: is calibrating that correlation enough?

Table 6.7 records three different global mean temperature trajectories that emerge from the baseline runs of some recent integrated assessment modeling conducted by Yohe (1991, 1994) – a modeling exercise that weds the probabilistic aggregate production structure of Nordhaus and Yohe (1983) with the integrating structure of Nordhaus' DICE framework (Nordhaus, 1992, 1994).[5] The second column reflects the unregulated trajectory. The third reflects the temperature trajectory that emerges when carbon emissions are optimally regulated (subject to informational constraints on decision makers over time). The fourth reflects the temperature trajectory that emerges when carbon emissions are sub-optimally restricted to a cumulative total equal to 20 percent of the unregulated total through the year 2100.[6]

Tables 6.8 and 6.9 record sustainability indices, averaged across the uniform and geometric spreads, for the 90 percent Corn Belt yield contour that correspond to the unrestricted and the 20 percent emissions reduction temperature trajectories under two sets of assumptions. The second temperature trajectory is omitted because the underlying 3.6 percent reduction in cumulative emissions through the year 2100 make so little difference relative to the unrestricted case. In the first, only the mean temperature changes along the indicated global mean trajectory

*Global Environmental Change and Agriculture*

*Table 6.7   Global mean temperature trajectories based on Yohe (1991, 1994)*

| Year | No regulation | Optimal regulation | 20 percent emission reduction |
|------|------|------|------|
| 1975 | 0.44 | 0.44 | 0.44 |
| 1990 | 0.93 | 0.93 | 0.93 |
| 2000 | 1.21 | 1.21 | 1.20 |
| 2010 | 1.47 | 1.47 | 1.45 |
| 2020 | 1.72 | 1.71 | 1.67 |
| 2030 | 1.97 | 1.95 | 1.89 |
| 2040 | 2.21 | 2.18 | 2.09 |
| 2050 | 2.43 | 2.39 | 2.29 |
| 2060 | 2.65 | 2.60 | 2.46 |
| 2070 | 2.85 | 2.80 | 2.62 |
| 2080 | 3.03 | 2.97 | 2.76 |
| 2090 | 3.20 | 3.13 | 2.88 |
| 2100 | 3.34 | 3.28 | 2.97 |

*Table 6.8   Sustainability indices for U.S. corn along the unrestricted emissions trajectory*

| Year | Temperature change only | Temperature change with precipitation reduction |
|------|------|------|
| 1975 | 0.66 | 0.66 |
| 1990 | 0.63 | 0.54 |
| 2000 | 0.61 | 0.50 |
| 2010 | 0.58 | 0.46 |
| 2020 | 0.56 | 0.41 |
| 2030 | 0.53 | 0.35 |
| 2040 | 0.51 | 0.31 |
| 2050 | 0.48 | 0.26 |
| 2060 | 0.43 | 0.24 |
| 2070 | 0.42 | 0.20 |
| 2080 | 0.38 | 0.18 |
| 2090 | 0.35 | 0.17 |
| 2100 | 0.32 | 0.14 |

*Note:*   Results are based on climate change scenarios from Yohe (1991, 1994).

while the annual variability in temperature and precipitation that is reflected in Table 6.5 is preserved. In the second, the variability of Table 6.5 is still preserved, but precipitation falls steadily as the mean temperature rises so that, by 2050, average precipitation will have fallen by 20 percent.

Several points become clear from even brief consideration of Tables 6.8 and 6.9. The sustainability index falls discernibly in all cases, but the fall is more dramatic when changes in temperature are accompanied by reductions in rainfall.

*Table 6.9  Sustainability indices for U.S. corn along a 20 percent emission reduction trajectory*

| Year | Temperature change only | Temperature change with precipitation reduction |
|------|------|------|
| 1975 | 0.66 | 0.66 |
| 1990 | 0.63 | 0.54 |
| 2000 | 0.61 | 0.50 |
| 2010 | 0.58 | 0.46 |
| 2020 | 0.56 | 0.39 |
| 2030 | 0.54 | 0.37 |
| 2040 | 0.52 | 0.33 |
| 2050 | 0.49 | 0.29 |
| 2060 | 0.47 | 0.26 |
| 2070 | 0.44 | 0.24 |
| 2080 | 0.43 | 0.21 |
| 2090 | 0.40 | 0.19 |
| 2100 | 0.39 | 0.18 |

*Note:*  Results are based on climate change scenarios from Yohe (1991, 1994).

This is not a surprise. Perhaps more surprising is the recognition that moving to a 20 percent emissions reduction trajectory has so little effect even when agriculture appears to be so vulnerable. If a 50 percent reduction in the sustainability index were determined to be a measure of the critical level for the commercial viability of growing corn, for example, then a 20 percent reduction in cumulative emissions would buy only an extra ten years of viability along the temperature and precipitation trajectory. This small effect is surely rooted in the fact that the yield contours reflect absolutely no adaptation to climate change in the way farmers grow corn. In terms of the planning function that this indexing method is designed to inform, then, Tables 6.8 and 6.9 surely highlight adaptation in corn farming as a likely target for productive and worthwhile consideration.

## 5   CONCLUDING REMARKS

Beyond the creation of a simplistic and practical indexing method designed explicitly to help planners distinguish across a wide range of systems that might be vulnerable to climate change, this chapter offers two insights that can be drawn from its agriculturally based illustrations. First, the full range of possible adaptive strategies should be surveyed even if the climate change news does not turn out to be so bad. Change will, in such cases, be more of a purveyor of opportunity than carrier of trouble. But the economic cost of missing an opportunity to improve can be every bit as large as the cost incurred by failing to respond to a problem. Good news does not, therefore, diminish the potential value of a practical method for assessing vulnerability to change.

It is true that an index of vulnerability of farm profits, rather than the index of crop yield vulnerability presented here, would provide more information in support of policy decisions. Unfortunately it is not possible to sign the effect of changes in yield vulnerability on farm profits. An example makes it clear why this is so. Let farm profits ($\pi$) be the difference between revenue and cost. Revenue is made up of output price ($p$), acres planted ($A$) and yield per acre ($y$). Cost is a function of $A$, which is independent of the yield vulnerability index. This assumption is only true if the prices of inputs like fertilizer, seed and irrigation water are not affected by climate change. The derivative of farm profits with respect to the index is:

$$\frac{d\pi}{d\ index} = \frac{dp}{d\ index}\ Ay + pA\ \frac{dy}{d\ index}. \tag{6.4}$$

We would like to be able to sign the first term. This requires that the signs on the other two derivative terms be the same. The derivative of output with respect to the index is negative because the higher the yield vulnerability index the lower the output. The derivative of the price with respect to the index can be positive or negative.

If an individual farm supplied the entire market for an agricultural crop, the higher the level of output the lower the price would be with normal downward sloping demand. Some studies have assumed this is the case (Kaiser et al., 1992). It is plausible, however, that climate change will not affect all world agriculture the same, and that there may be regional differences in the effects on one commodity. This is why we developed a different vulnerability index for each crop in each region. If output rises in one region and falls in another, international trade effects and differences in the market power of different countries will determine the net effect of a change in the vulnerability index on the world price of a commodity. What is driving the change in the index is a change in climate and this change may not affect the indices equally around the world, so the effect on world price is indeterminate and it is not possible to sign the left-hand side of equation (6.4). Even if the index were affected by climate change in the same way throughout the world, and a decrease in yield were accompanied by an unequivocal increase in world price, the effect on farm profits would still be indeterminate. There might also be scale effects where profits rise for small decreases in yield (the price effect dominates) but fall for large decreases in yield (the output effect dominates). Abstracting from farm programs and other institutions that affect farm profits, price and yield are going in opposite directions and profits could go up or down. It is therefore inadvisable to draw any conclusion about changes in farm profits from changes in the yield index.

Secondly, and perhaps most importantly, comparing the sustainability trajectories recorded in Tables 6.8 and 6.9 with the corn sustainability estimates offered for 2050 and 2100 in Table 6.6 clearly shows that tracking temperature change is not enough to completely describe the future effects of global climate change. Precipitation clearly matters, not only in distinguishing the role to be played by adaptation, but also in defining size and even the direction of the effect. This observation is not a new insight by any means. Yet, most of the integrated assessment exercises being conducted by researchers around the world use only temperature to link emissions of greenhouse gases and their associated atmospheric concentrations with the economic cost of the physical and biological impacts of global climate change. This is a practice whose validity must continue to be questioned until it is shown that future regional temperature patterns can be sufficiently correlated both with the trajectories of other critical variables *and* with the global mean, to assert that a unidimensional impact index like global mean temperature captures enough of the variance to be useful.

## APPENDIX

This section outlines steps to create an index of vulnerability of economic or natural systems within the current environment and vulnerability to change in that environment. Let $A_0$ reflect variability in the current climate of some region expressed in terms of $X$ and $Y$. Let $A_0$ be a confidence region of some predetermined level ($\varepsilon \cdot 100$ percent) for the current climate. Define a second set, $B_{n0}$, to reflect the viable region for some natural or engineered system ($N$), also expressed in terms of variability in precipitation and temperature. As noted in the text, system $N$ would be viable if $X$ and $Y$ were to occur within region $B_{n0}$, but would suffer severely if $X$ and $Y$ were to occur elsewhere. The intersection of $A_0$ and $B_{n0}$ represents a region of sustainability which can be expected to occur for system $N$ with likelihood $\varepsilon \cdot 100$ percent.

Let $f_0(X, Y)$ be the probability density function which defines set $A_0$ so that:

$$\int_A f_0(X, Y)dX\,dY = \varepsilon, \tag{A.1}$$

$$\int_A X f_0(X, Y)dX\,dY = 0, \tag{A.2}$$

$$\int_A Y f_0(X, Y) dX \, dY = 0, \tag{A.3}$$

where $\varepsilon$ is very small. The index of sustainability for system $N$ in the current climate, $S_0(n)$, can now be suggested:

$$S_0(N) \equiv \{\textstyle\int\int_{A_0 \cap B_{n0}} f_0(X, Y) dX \, dY\} / \{\textstyle\int\int_{A_0} f_0(X, Y) dX \, dY\} \tag{A.4}$$

$$= \{\textstyle\int\int_{A_0 \cap B_{n0}} f_0(X, Y) dX dY\} / \varepsilon \tag{A.5}$$

A corresponding index of vulnerability,

$$V_0(N) \equiv [1 - S_0(N)], \tag{A.6}$$

may prove to be more instructive. For each system a minimum value for the sustainability index might be established to indicate a threshold of extinction. Finding a value below this threshold would cause the index of vulnerability to climb to one over the near term while the index of sustainability would fall to zero.

## NOTES

1.  Issues of exposure to environmental stress are germane, here. The sustainability of a system might suffer after a single episode beyond the boundaries of $B_{n0}$ or it may require repeated and/or successive episodes. The discussion presented in this approach will assume the former case. Requirements for prolonged exposure to stress could probably be handled by adjusting the definition $A_0$ to reflect likelihood of multiple episodes. This is, of course, a theoretical question which must be overcome in the process of creating a detailed structure for this method.
2.  This defines both threshold and dynamics of collapse. The literature has little if anything to present in terms of a consistent method for indexing vulnerability. The early contributions to what will undoubtedly grow to be a substantial literature on biodiversity have begun to appear in print (Weitzman, 1992; Solow et al., 1993).
3.  Recall that $y$ and $x$ both represent deviations around the means of the original data, $Y$ and $X$.
4.  It is perhaps most interesting to note that the index for corn in North Dakota ranks higher than winter wheat in 2050 and falls just short in 2100.
5.  These runs are based upon a Cobb–Douglas aggregate production function in labor, capital, fossil fuel and non-fossil fuel with a wide range of random variables and parameters assigned their median values. Future applications will create Monte Carlo simulation results over all of those sources of uncertainty in the context of aggregate production which accommodates, at least in year to year approximation, non-unitary elasticities of substitution between fossil and non-fossil fuels *and* between energy and labor and capital. See Yohe (1984) for the approximation procedure.

6. This restriction is accomplished by a two-part carbon tax. The first part reflects the perceived marginal damage of emissions; the second adds a scarcity rent which grows at the underlying rate of interest.

# REFERENCES

CIMMYT (1991), *Annual Report: Improving the Productivity of Maize and Wheat in Developing Countries: An Assessment of Impact*. Mexico City: Centro Internacional de Mejoramiento de Maiz y Trigo.

Dalrymple, D.G. (1986), *Development and Spread of High-Yielding Rice Varieties in Developing Countries*, 7th ed., Washington, DC: U.S. Agency for International Development.

Dickey, E.C., Jasa, P.J., Dolesh, B.J., Brown, L.A. and Rockwell, S.K. (1987), 'Conservation Tillage: Perceived and Actual Use', *Journal of Soil and Water Conservation,* 42, pp. 431–434.

Food and Agriculture Organization, *Agrostat*, 1961–1990, Rome.

Gaskins, D. and Weyant, J. (1993), *Global Climate Change: Energy Sector Impacts and Greenhouse Gas Control Strategies*. Report of EMF-12, Energy Modeling Forum, Stanford University.

Greco, S., Moss, R., Viner, D. and Jenne, R. (1994), 'Climate Scenarios and Socioeconomic Projections for IPCC WGII Assessment', Intergovernmental Panel on Climate Change: Working Group II, WMO/UNEP for WGII lead authors, March.

Griliches, Z. (1957), 'Hybrid Corn: An Exploration in the Economics of Technological Change', *Econometrica*, 25, pp. 501–522.

Hazell, P.B.R. (1984), 'Sources of Increased Instability in Indian and U.S. Cereal Production', *American Journal of Agricultural Economics*, 66, pp. 302–311.

Hill, P.R., Griffith, D.R., Steinhardt, G.C. and Parsons, S.D. (1994), 'The Evolution and History of No-Till Farming in the Midwest', T-by-2000 Erosion Reduction/Water Quality Program, West Lafayette, IN: Purdue University.

Howe, C. (1971), *Benefit Cost Analysis for Water System Planning: Water Resources Monograph 2*. Washington, DC: American Geophysical Union.

Intergovernmental Panel on Climate Change (IPCC) (1990), *Climate Change – Final Report of Working Group I*, New York: Cambridge University Press.

Intergovernmental Panel on Climate Change (IPPC) (1992), *Climate Change – Scientific Assessment Update*, New York: Cambridge University Press.

Intergovernmental Panel on Climate Change (IPCC) (1996), *Climate Change, 1995: Impacts, Adaptations and Mitigation of the Climate Change,* Cambridge: Cambridge University Press.

James, L.D. and Lee, R.R. (1971), *Economics of Water Resource Planning,* New York: McGraw-Hill.

Johnson, J. (1984), *Econometric Methods* 3rd ed., New York: McGraw-Hill Book Co.

Kaiser, H.M., Riha, S.J., Rossiter, D.G. and Wilks, D.S. (1992), 'Agronomic and Economic Impacts of Gradual Global Warming: A Preliminary Analysis of Midwestern Crop Farming', in Reilly, J.M. and Anderson, M. (eds), *Economic Issues in Global Climate Change: Agriculture, Forestry, and Natural Resources*, Boulder, CO: Westview Press, pp. 91–116.

Knudson, M. (1988), 'The Research and Development of Competing Biological Innovations: The Case of Semi- and Hybrid Wheats', unpublished Ph.D. dissertation, University of Minnesota.

Lawrence, R.D. (president)(1986), *Crop Yields and Climate Change to the Year 2000, Volume II: Climate Model and Technical Appendixes*, Washington, DC: Research Directorate of the National Defense University.

Lewandrowski, J.K. and Brazee, R.J. (1993), 'Farm Programs and Climate Change', *Climatic Change*, **23**, pp. 1–20.

Manne, A. and Richels, R. (1992), *Buying Greenhouse Insurance – the Economic Costs of Carbon Dioxide Emissions Limits*, Cambridge, MA: MIT Press.

Medvedev, Z.A. (1987), *Soviet Agriculture*, New York: W.W. Norton & Company.

Morrisette, P.M. and Rosenberg, N.J. (1992), 'Climate Variability and Development', in Darmstadter, J. (ed.), *Global Development and the Environment: Perspectives on Sustainability*, Washington, DC: Resources for the Future, pp. 73-82.

Nordhaus, W. (1991), 'To Slow or Not to Slow: The Economics of the Greenhouse Effect', *Economic Journal*, **101**, pp. 920–937.

Nordhaus, W. (1992), 'An Optimal Transition Path for Controlling Greenhouse Gases', *Science*, **258**, 1315–1319.

Nordhaus, W. (1994), *Managing the Global Commons: The Economics of Climate Change*, Cambridge, MA: MIT Press.

Nordhaus, W. and Yohe, G. (1983), 'Future Carbon Dioxide Emissions from Fossil Fuels', in *Changing Climate*, Washington, DC: National Academy Press, pp. 87–152.

Office of Technology Assessment (1993), *Systems at Risk*, Washington, DC: U.S. Government Printing Office.

Pieri, C. (1992), *Fertility of Soils: The Future for Farmers in the West African Savannah*, Berlin: Springer Verlag.

Plucknett, D.L., Smith, N.J.H., Williams, J.T. and Anishetty, N.M. (1987), *Gene Banks and the World's Food,* Princeton: Princeton University Press.

Plusquellec, H. (1990), 'The Gezira Irrigation Scheme in Sudan: Objectives, Design, and Performance', World Bank Technical Paper, no. 120. Washington, DC: World Bank.

Reilly, J. (1995), 'Climate Change and Global Agriculture: Recent Findings and Issues', *American Journal of Agricultural Economics (Proceedings)*, **77**, pp. 727–733.

Roumasset, J. (1976), *Rice and Risk: Decision Making Among Low-Income Farmers*, Amsterdam: North Holland Press.

Schertz, D.L. (1988), 'Conservation Tillage: An Analysis of Acreage Projections in the United States', *Journal of Soil and Water Conservation,* **43**, pp. 256–258.

Schimmelpfennig, D.E. (1996), 'Uncertainty in Economic Models: Climate Change Impacts Agriculture', *Climatic Change*, **33**, pp. 213–234.

Scientific Committee on Problems of the Environment (SCOPE) (1985), *Climate Impact Assessment*, Sussex, England: John Wiley and Sons Limited.

Solow, A., Polasky, S. and Broadus, J. (1993), 'On the Measurement of Biological Diversity', *Journal of Environmental Economics and Management*, **24**, pp. 60–68.

Strommen, N.D. (chief) (1994 revised), *Major World Crop Areas and Climatic Profiles*, United States Department of Agriculture, World Agricultural Outlook Board, Agriculture Handbook Number 664.

Teigen, L.D. and Singer, F. (1992), *Weather in U.S. Agriculture*, United States Department of Agriculture, Economic Research Service, Statistical Bulletin Number 834.

Thompson, T.P. and Wan, X. (1992), 'The Socioeconomic Dimensions of Agricultural Production in Albania: A National Survey', # PN-ABQ-691, Washington, DC: International Fertilizer Development Center, U.S.A.I.D.

Turner, H.A. and Anderson, C.L. (1980), *Planning for an Irrigation System,* Athens, GA: American Association for Vocational Instructional Materials.

United States National Academy of Science (1992), *Policy Implications of Greenhouse Warming*, Washington, DC: National Academy of Science Press.

Vose, R.S., Schmoyer, R.L., Steurer, P.M., Peterson, T.C., Heim, R., Karl, T.R. and Eischeid, J.K. (1992), *The Global Historical Climatology Network: Long-Term Monthly Temperature, Precipitation, Sea Level Pressure, and Station Pressure Data*, Oak Ridge, Tennessee: Oak Ridge National Laboratory.

Webb, A. and Gudmunds, K. (1992), *Production, Supply and Distribution View '92: Users Manual and Database*, United States Department of Agriculture, Economic Research Service.

Weitzman, M. (1992) 'On Diversity', *Quarterly Journal of Economics*, **107**, pp. 363–403.

World Bank (1994), personal communication with Mr Antte Talvitie, Central Technical Department, Transportation Division.

Yohe, G. (1984), 'Constant Elasticity of Substitution Production Functions with Three or More Inputs', *Economics Letters*, **15**, pp. 29–34.

Yohe, G. (1991), 'Selecting "Interesting" Scenarios with which to Analyze Policy Response to Potential Climate Change', *Climate Research*, **1**, pp. 169–177.

Yohe, G. (1993), 'Sorting Out Facts and Uncertainties in Economic Response to the Physical Effects of Global Climate Change', in Darmstadter, J. and Toman, M. (eds), *Assessing Surprises and Nonlinearities in Greenhouse Warming*, Washington, DC: Resources for the Future, pp. 109–132.

Yohe, G. (1994), 'Integrated Assessment Using an Aggregate Model with Energy – The Abatement of Carbon Emissions', mimeo, Middletown, CT: Wesleyan University.

# PART III

# Climate Change: Adaptation and Mitigation

# 7 Assessing Research on the Impacts of Climate Change on Agriculture

**Harry M. Kaiser**

## 1 INTRODUCTION

The temperature of the earth may rise in the future due to increased emissions of greenhouse gases. These gases, which include carbon dioxide ($CO_2$), methane ($CH_4$), nitrous oxides ($N_2O$), water vapor, tropospheric ozone ($O_3$) and chlorofluorocarbons (CFCs), affect the earth's global energy balance by partially absorbing outgoing infrared radiation. Increases in atmospheric concentrations of greenhouse gases enhance the heat trapping ability of the atmosphere, and thereby result in global warming. Experiments with current climate models now predict a range of increase from 1.5 to 4.5 °C in the earth's surface temperature over the next 100 years due to increasing greenhouse gas emissions (Intergovernmental Panel on Climate Change (IPCC), 1992). Any change in temperature will likely be accompanied by new precipitation patterns. Unfortunately, there is less agreement among scientists on how precipitation will change, as illustrated in Table 7.1. In general, changes in climatic variables become more difficult to predict as the area of interest becomes smaller.

These anticipated changes in temperature and precipitation will impact agricultural productivity, land use, farm profitability, food supply and availability, trade, prices, regional comparative advantage and water availability among other things. The ultimate impact of climate change on agriculture will depend upon the magnitude of change in climatic variables and the accompanying indirect environmental effects as well as how well society is able to adapt to these changes.

A growing body of literature has emerged examining various aspects of potential economic effects of climate change on agriculture. This chapter assesses these studies and offers recommendations for future research. The chapter begins with a review of previous studies. This is followed by a discussion of a proposed

*Table 7.1   Climate model predictions of changes in global temperature and precipitation due to $CO_2$ doubling*

| Climate model | Change in surface air temperature (°C) | Change in precipitation (%) |
|---|---|---|
| Princeton University Geophysical Fluid Dynamics Laboratory (GFDL) | 4.0 | 8.7 |
| Goddard Institute of Space Studies (GISS) | 4.2 | 11.0 |
| National Center for Atmospheric Research (NCAR) | 3.5 | 7.1 |
| Oregon State University (OSU) | 2.8 | 7.8 |
| United Kingdom Meteorological Office (UKMO) | 5.2 | 15.8 |

*Source*:   Karl et al. (adapted from Rosenzweig, 1989).

research agenda for future studies in this area. This chapter draws from, as well as builds on, some of the ideas set forth in several previous analyses.[1]

## 2   REVIEW OF PAST STUDIES

**Agronomic Impacts**

Changes in temperature and precipitation will not be uniformly distributed over the earth. Consequently, some regions may experience losses in agricultural productivity, while others may become more productive due to a changing climate. Unfortunately, the studies that have been conducted are subject to a high degree of uncertainty due to the relatively large degree of inaccuracy and inconsistency among climate models, as well as in crop simulation models. Consider the yield impacts among countries summarized in Table 7.2, which are findings from Rosenzweig et al. (1993). Even using the same crop yield simulation models, it is clear that the magnitude, as well as relative distribution of yield effects across countries, varies with each climate model. Thus, the following summary of results should be interpreted with this uncertainty in mind.

As reported by Tobey et al. (1992), scientific studies suggest that most countries in the northern latitudes may experience increased precipitation in addition to higher temperatures.[2] This predicted increase in precipitation is expected to enhance crop yields in the northern regions of Canada, Europe and the former Soviet Union (IPCC, 1990; Kettunen et al., 1988; Rosenzweig et al., 1993). The anticipated yield increases in the northern latitudes are due to several factors including a longer growing season and a reduction in frost kill (Rosenzweig et al., 1993). Southern middle latitude countries such as regions of

*Table 7.2    Changes in wheat yields among countries due to a $CO_2$ doubling with and without the $CO_2$ fertilizer effect*

| | Percentage change in simulated yields | | | | | |
|---|---|---|---|---|---|---|
| | Without $CO_2$ fertilizer effect | | | With $CO_2$ fertilizer effect | | |
| Country | GISS | GFDL | UKMO | GISS | GFDL | UKMO |
| Australia | -18 | -16 | -14 | 8 | 11 | 9 |
| Brazil | -51 | -38 | -53 | -33 | 17 | -34 |
| Canada | -12 | -10 | -38 | 27 | 27 | -7 |
| China | -5 | -12 | -17 | 16 | 8 | 0 |
| Egypt | -36 | -28 | -54 | -31 | -26 | -51 |
| France | -12 | -28 | -23 | 4 | -15 | -9 |
| India | -32 | -38 | -56 | 3 | -9 | -33 |
| Japan | -18 | -21 | -40 | -1 | -5 | -27 |
| Pakistan | -57 | -29 | -73 | -19 | 31 | -55 |
| Uruguay | -41 | -48 | -50 | -23 | -31 | -35 |
| Former USSR: | | | | | | |
|    winter wheat | -3 | -17 | -22 | 29 | 9 | 0 |
|    spring wheat | -12 | -25 | -48 | 21 | 3 | -25 |
| United States | -21 | -23 | -33 | -2 | -2 | -14 |
| World | -16 | -22 | -33 | 11 | 4 | -13 |

*Source:* Rosenzweig et al. (1993).

Latin America, Northern Africa and central India may also experience enhanced crop yields since the increase in precipitation anticipated is projected to more than offset the negative effects of warmer temperatures (IPCC, 1990; Pittock, 1989; Pittock and Nix, 1986; Walker et al., 1989).

Climate change may decrease agricultural productivity in many northern middle latitude countries such as the United States, Western Europe and most of Canada's agricultural regions (IPCC, 1990; Santer, 1985; Smit, 1989; U.S. EPA, 1990; Williams et al., 1988). Crop yields may be reduced due to several factors. Vernalization, or the requirement of a period of low winter temperature to initiate plant development, may be inhibited. A combination of increased evapotranspiration rates, losses in soil moisture and (in some cases) decreases in precipitation may result in less available water for the plant. In addition, increased temperatures may shorten the growing period for the crop by accelerating plant development, particularly during the grain filling stage, which decreases crop yields. Lower agricultural productivity may not occur for all countries in the northern middle latitude. China and Japan may benefit from, or be less severely impacted by, climate change since their agriculture is located primarily in coastal regions and, as a result, will probably not experience the interior continental drying predicted by some climate models (Tobey et al., 1992).

**World Economic Impacts**

Three recent studies have examined the potential economic effects of global climate change at the world level. In the first study, Rosenzweig et al. (1993) linked the results of climate models, crop yield simulation models and a computable general equilibrium world trade model to simulate potential economic effects of climate change. The authors simulated a variety of scenarios with different climate change, $CO_2$ fertilization and adaptation assumptions. The authors used three climate change scenarios based on the results of doubled-$CO_2$ experiments conducted with three climate models: (1) Goddard Institute of Space Studies (GISS) model, (2) Geophysical Fluid Dynamics Laboratory (GFDL) model, and (3) United Kingdom Meteorological Office (UKMO) model. The change in average global surface temperature and percentage change in precipitation predicted from these three models are: +4.2 °C and +11 percent for the GISS model, +4.0 °C and +8 percent for the GFDL model, and +5.2 °C and +15 percent for the UKMO model.

The findings of this study were sensitive to assumptions regarding $CO_2$ fertilization and potential adaptation.[3] In the no $CO_2$ fertilization and no adaptation scenario, climate change reduced world grain production by 20 percent under the worst climate change scenario. On the other hand, global production was predicted to decrease by 5 percent with $CO_2$ fertilization and modest levels of adaptation (e.g. shifts in planting dates and changes in crop cultivars). The authors found that the reductions in worldwide production could be largely offset if more major adaptation strategies, such as irrigation, could be implemented. However, they argued that disparities in grain production between developing and developed countries would nevertheless increase. It was found that developed countries may actually experience increased production, while production in many developing countries was generally predicted to decrease. Adaptation strategies do little to reduce these disparate effects since developed countries have more resources to utilize in adaptation strategies than do developing countries. The economic model used by Rosenzweig et al. (1993) predicted that commodity prices could rise substantially. The combination of decreased production by developing countries and increased prices due to climate change would increase the number of people at risk of hunger according to their study. This result held even at high levels of assumed adaptation strategies with $CO_2$ fertilization.

In the second study, Reilly et al. (1993) used a partial equilibrium world trade model called SWOPSIM (Static World Policy Simulation) along with the crop yield results of Rosenzweig et al. (1993) to determine the economic impacts of climate change based on the SWOPSIM model. Unlike Rosenzweig et al.'s economic model, SWOPSIM can summarize the economic impacts of climate change into changes in country welfare, as well as changes in prices and production. The results of Reilly et al. (1993) are similar to Rosenzweig et al. (1993), which implies that the two economic models generate relatively robust results based on the same crop yield impact. A similar conclusion was reached by Kokoski and Smith (1987), who demonstrated that partial equilibrium welfare measures could provide a reasonable approximation of welfare changes estimated from computable general equilibrium models for large exogenous changes in developed countries.

Reilly et al. (1993) found sizable global welfare losses in the case of no adaptation and no $CO_2$ fertilization, ranging from $115.5 billion (in 1989 U.S. dollars) to $248.1 billion, depending on climate change scenario. Inclusion of $CO_2$ fertilization, however, lowered these losses substantially with welfare losses ranging from $0.1 billion to $61.2 billion. When modest adaptation responses were factored in as well, these losses either became gains or were further mitigated, depending on climate change scenario. A main conclusion of this study was that the change in a country's economic welfare due to climate change depends, in large part, on whether the country is an exporter or importer of agricultural commodities, and on the direction of domestic crop yield effects. Countries with substantial agricultural exports may gain from climate change if world prices rise as a result. Exporting countries that experience yield losses may actually have improved welfare if the increase in welfare due to increased export revenue more than offsets domestic losses in welfare due to higher prices.

Reilly et al. (1993) also found that developing countries are generally worse off than developed countries due to climate change. For example, under no adaptation and no $CO_2$ fertilization, developing countries, in the aggregate, experience losses in economic welfare ranging from $89.6 to $173.1 billion, depending on climate scenario, which compares with losses of $13.4 to $17.6 billion for OECD (Organization for Economic Cooperation and Development) countries. With $CO_2$ fertilization and moderate adaptation, developing countries experience losses in economic welfare ranging from $1.2 to $26.3 billion, depending on climate change scenario, while developed countries have changes in welfare ranging from a $8.2 billion increase to a $11.4 billion decrease. The worst case scenario of no adaptation and no $CO_2$ fertilization would cause serious problems for developing countries in terms of malnutrition and starvation. However, the authors believe that the worst case scenario should be considered as the extreme bounds on potential negative impacts.

In the third, and most recent study, Darwin et al. (1995) (and Chapter 9 of this volume) used monthly mean temperature and precipitation levels from four global general circulation models (GCMs) to examine impacts on regional and world agriculture. The four GCMs were the GISS, GFDL, UKMO and Oregon State University (OSU) models. These scenarios were used to adjust growing seasons and water supplies in eight global regions with six alternative land classes. The impact of climate change was incorporated by modifying the production possibilities associated with regional land and water resources. A computable general equilibrium model of the world economy was used in conjunction to examine climate change impacts on production, consumption, prices, trade and income. Adaptation was modeled by allowing for reallocation of resources to their most productive uses following the change in climate. However, the authors did not include the direct effects of $CO_2$ fertilization on enhancing crop yields.

There were three general findings of the Darwin et al. (1995) study regarding global agriculture. First, even with extensive on-farm adaptation, the authors found that global climate change would likely reduce productivity of existing agricultural land worldwide. However, the losses in agricultural productivity could be more than offset by expanding production into new areas, particularly the higher latitudes. The net effect would be an increase in global food supply. Second, there would be regional gainers and losers due to climate change. For example, production of wheat, other grains, non-grains, livestock and forestry products were found to increase in Canada, but decrease in Southeast Asia under the climate change scenarios. In general, this study found positive economic impacts in higher latitude countries, negative impacts in tropical areas and mixed results in mid-latitude regions. Third, farmers will respond to climate change by using such adaptation strategies as using new inputs and outputs more suitable to the new climate, and by expanding production into new areas. The authors found that world cropland increased from 7 to almost 15 percent, while world forest land decreased by 1.5 to almost 5 percent across climate change scenarios. However, similar to Rosenzweig et al. (1993) and Reilly et al. (1993), the authors found that it may be difficult for some regions to achieve all of these adjustments due to climate change impacts on productivity and constraints on land expansion.

## U.S. Agriculture and Climate Change

A number of studies have looked at the potential effects of climate change on U.S. agriculture. In one of the first studies, Adams et al. (1990) analyzed the potential effects of a change in climate on regional comparative advantage in U.S. agriculture. The authors used two climate change scenarios based on the results of doubled-$CO_2$ experiments conducted with the GISS and GFDL models. The GISS model predicted that a doubled $CO_2$-induced climate change would cause an increase in average U.S. temperature of 4.6 °C and an 8 percent increase in precipitation, while the more extreme GFDL model predicted a temperature increase of 5.0 °C and a decrease in precipitation of 0.8 percent for the United States. As in the study by Rosenzweig et al. (1993), Adams et al. (1990) generated separate yield impacts due to climate change with and without $CO_2$ fertilization. Not surprisingly, the crop yield results were substantially different between the two climate scenarios, as well as between the $CO_2$ scenarios. The negative impacts of climate change on crop yields under the two climate change situations were substantially mitigated and, in some cases, yields actually increased under the $CO_2$ fertilization scenario. Regions in the northern United States were generally less severely affected, while regions in the south suffered the largest yield losses.

Using the yield results with a sector level mathematical programming model of the United States, Adams et al. (1990) simulated the impact of the two climate change scenarios on prices, regional and national production, consumption, consumer and producer surplus, and other market variables. The economic results also varied tremendously in magnitude and even direction among the various scenarios. For example, when no $CO_2$ fertilization of yields was assumed, the less severe climate scenario resulted in a 10 percent decrease in U.S. crop production and an 18 percent increase in prices; while the more severe climate change scenario resulted in a 39 percent decrease in production and a 109 percent increase in prices. In both cases, society is worse off in terms of economic welfare (consumer plus producer surplus changes of -$6.5 billion and -$35.9 billion for the two climate change scenarios). On the other hand, when $CO_2$ fertilization was assumed, the predicted changes from both climate models were less severe. The less severe climate change scenario actually resulted in a 10 percent increase in crop production and an 18 percent decrease in prices, while the more severe climate change scenario resulted in a 19 percent decrease in production and a 28 percent increase in crop prices. The change in economic welfare associated with the two climate change scenarios assuming $CO_2$ fertilization was +$9.9 and -$10.5 billion, respectively.

In a more recent study, Kaiser et al. (1994) examined the potential agronomic and economic impacts of several climate change scenarios on grain farming in the United States. The analysis was based on a protocol that links climatic, agronomic and economic models to form an integrated model. Three climate scenarios were investigated for their relative impacts on crop yields, cropping patterns and farm-level profitability: (1) a baseline, no climate change scenario, (2) a mildly warmer and wetter climate change scenario and (3) a more severe hotter and drier climate change scenario. The climate scenarios were simulated for representative farms in the states of Iowa, Illinois, Nebraska, Minnesota, Ohio, Georgia and North Carolina. Unlike previous studies, climate change was modeled as a gradual, transient phenomenon and was simulated over the period 1990–2079 using a stochastic weather generator. The variability, as well as the averages of temperature and precipitation, was assumed to be affected by climate change.

The agronomic results indicated that the mild climate scenario had little impact on crop yields and that farmers could adapt to increasing temperatures and precipitation by selecting later maturing varieties. Corn and soybean yields fell at all sites in the more severe climate scenario. Similar to the findings in Adams et al. (1990), northern states were less severely affected by both climate change scenarios (soybean and sorghum yields). Crop prices were fairly sensitive to the rate and form of the assumed climate change. Under the milder climate change scenario, inflation-adjusted corn prices increased and sorghum and wheat prices decreased. Soybean prices increased, but at a lower rate than in the no climate change case. In the more severe climate change scenario, sorghum prices, as well as soybean and corn prices, had the largest increase over time. Farm profits were lower under climate change than in the no climate change case. However, there was little difference in farm profits between the mild and the severe climate change scenarios.

Easterling et al. (1993) examined potential impacts of climate change on agriculture in Missouri, Iowa, Nebraska and Kansas (MINK). Rather than using a general circulation model, this study constructed an 'analog' climate from historical data for the 1930s, which was one of the warmest decades on record for the United States. This warmer and drier climate was superimposed onto two technological and economic scenarios, one reflecting current conditions (1984–87) and the other representing technical and economic conditions predicted for the year 2030. The impact of this climate on crop yields was captured using the EPIC model, and the direct effects of $CO_2$ fertilization based on laboratory experiments were incorporated. Under the worst case scenario, where there is no $CO_2$ fertilization and no farm-level adjustments to the new climate, production of corn, sorghum and soybeans decreased, while dryland wheat production remained the same and irrigated wheat production increased for both the current and 2030 scenarios. About 80 percent of the negative effects from the analog climate were eliminated assuming farm-level adjustments with current technologies and $CO_2$ fertilization. For the 2030 scenario, there was actually a small increase in overall production given $CO_2$ fertilization and farm-level adjustments, based on anticipated technologies for 2030. Animal agriculture was virtually unaffected by the analog climate, except for feed prices.

**Agricultural Adaptation to Climate Change**

Agriculture can adapt to a changing climate in several ways, including changes in technology, in agricultural land areas and in use of irrigation. Several studies have examined how effective such actions might be in mitigating negative climate change effects. Kaiser et al. (1993) considered some relatively minor farm-level adaptations to climate change, including switching cultivars (plant varieties) for a particular crop, altering crop mix and making adjustments in the scheduling of field operations. The findings indicated that farmers in cooler locations such as Minnesota could successfully adapt to, and in fact benefit from, climate warming in some instances. However, producers in warmer locations such as Nebraska were worse off, even when using adaptation strategies, under the more severe climate change scenario. An interesting result of this study was the comparison of crop yields when adaptive farm management strategies over time were included (adaptation case) and when it was assumed that farmers could not adapt by changing cultivars, crop selection, and timing of planting and harvesting (no adaptation case). Under the no adaptation case, simulated crop yields for all climate warming scenarios were drastically lower than those in the adaptation case. For instance, the difference in corn yields between the adaptation and no adaptation cases for even the mild climate change scenario reached 40 bushels per acre (about one-third of average 1980 yields) by the year 2060.

In the Easterling et al. (1993) study of the MINK region, a variety of adaptation scenarios were examined. This study found that crop yields and production would decrease from 15–20 percent under the occurrence of a hot and dry climate (based on 1930s weather patterns) assuming farmers could not make management adjustments and there was no $CO_2$ fertilizer effect. However, the assumption of farm-level adaptation to this climate eliminated over 50 percent of the production losses. Hence, it appears that agricultural adaptation will greatly reduce the predicted negative effects of climate change and, in some cases, will lead to positive economic effects for agriculture in some locations.

Rosenzweig et al. (1993) also simulated yield effects under two adaptation levels. Adaptation strategies in Level 1 included one month shifts in crop planting, additional watering of crops already under irrigation and switches in plant cultivars in response to the new climate. The more optimistic Level 2 adaptation strategies included shifts in crop-planting dates by more than one month, increased fertilization and installation of irrigation systems. While some adaptation will take place, farmers, particularly in developing countries, will not be able to use all of these strategies (e.g. install irrigation, increase fertilizer amounts). Under Level 1 adaptation, the negative effects of climate change on crop yields were somewhat mitigated in developed countries, but still tended to be negative in the developing countries. In the case of Level 2 adaptation, the negative effects of climate change on yield were almost all mitigated for two of the three climate change scenarios, but not for the most severe scenario. For the most severe climate change scenario, neither adaptation scenario could fully overcome the negative yield effects due to climate change, even under the $CO_2$ fertilization scenario.

## Summary: What Have We Learned?

It is difficult to form generalizations from these, as well as other economic analyses of agricultural impacts from climate change. This is due to differences in climate change scenarios, crop yield models, spatial coverage, economic models and various assumptions made among studies. Nevertheless, there are six observations that most would probably agree with.

First, climate change will have distributional impacts, with developing countries generally worse off than developed countries. Poorer countries have less resources to invest in adaptation strategies, and their agricultural research bases are inadequate to deal with a change in climate. Also, developing countries have substantially lower per capita income than developed countries, and are therefore much more at risk of starvation and malnutrition, particularly if climate change leads to major increases in commodity prices. Finally, evidence suggests that the harshest impacts of climate change on agricultural productivity will occur in tropical regions, where many developing countries are situated.

Second, the impact of climate change (under a doubling of atmospheric $CO_2$) on economic welfare in developed countries may generally be rather small compared with national income. Developed countries, which tend to have substantial agricultural research capacities, will likely be able to adapt quite successfully to climate change. Under most analyses that predict higher commodity prices due to climate change, losses in consumer surplus in developed countries are typically offset by gains in producer surplus. Thus, total welfare losses are relatively small compared with national income.

Third, many studies have concluded that the economic effects of climate change will be very different than the physical effects (e.g. Adams et al., 1990; Kaiser et al., 1993; Reilly et al., 1993; Rosenzweig et al., 1993).[4] Generally speaking, the economic impacts will not be as severe as the yield impacts due to market adjustments. One of the main conclusions of a report by Tobey et al. (1992) is that climate change-induced welfare effects on individual countries will not only depend upon changes in domestic yields, but also on changes in world prices, and the country's relative strength as an exporter and importer. With even large negative yield effects, the inter-regional adjustments in the world market may cushion the impacts on economic welfare.

Fourth, climate change will be evolutionary and gradual, as opposed to instantaneous. In this context, there will be change in other important factors as well (population, income, barriers to trade, institutions, political regimes) which may have equally, if not more, important impacts on agricultural markets than the change in climate.

Fifth, farmers and agricultural institutions will not stand by and do nothing if climate change has negative impacts on agriculture. Farmers will adapt to climate change by changing what they grow and how they grow it. Likewise, climate change will also induce institutional change, from changes in agricultural policy to new water markets for allocating water between agricultural and non-agricultural uses.

Sixth, the agronomic and economic effects of climate change depend critically on the magnitude of the $CO_2$ fertilizer effect. An example of how this assumption affects the outcome is Rosenzweig et al. (1993). This study considered several scenarios where $CO_2$ fertilization was assumed not to accompany climate change, and reported a world average decrease in yields for wheat, rice, maize and soybeans. However, when $CO_2$ fertilization was assumed in this study, world average crop yields did not decline as much, or in several cases, actually increased under the climate change scenarios.[5] Other studies (e.g. Easterling et al., 1993; Adams et al., 1990) have similar findings. The general result is that crop yields decrease under climate warming when there is no $CO_2$ fertilization, but these decreases in crop yields can be largely offset by assuming a positive $CO_2$ fertilization effect.

# 3    DIRECTIONS FOR FUTURE RESEARCH

While previous studies on the potential impacts of climate change on agriculture have provided valuable insight to policy makers, much uncertainty remains and there is a need for a lot more research on this topic before any consensus is reached. In this section, I offer several suggestions for research areas that I believe are among the most important for future endeavors.

**A Universal Base Scenario**

One priority for future research is the development of a universal base scenario for economic, demographic, technical and political change, as well as climate change, to be used to compare study results. All future economic studies could include the universal base scenario, among other scenarios, so that one could make consistent comparisons of the results of each study. While not everyone would agree with the base scenario projections of climate, political, technical and economic change, it would nevertheless be useful for each study to include it to serve as a benchmark for comparisons with other studies. Currently, it is next to impossible to make adequate comparisons across studies because each one has addressed non-comparable scenarios. This makes it difficult to form generalizations of results for policy purposes.

The construction of the universal base scenario needs to be quite detailed in terms of the climate, economic, demographic, technical and political change parameters. With respect to climate change, for instance, a time path for changes in temperature, precipitation and solar radiation for a designated time period would need to be constructed on some regional basis. Assumptions would be necessary for regional economic and population trajectories under the base scenario. The base scenario would need projections of technological change for agriculture, such as new plant varieties, new management techniques and other technical factors. Also, this scenario would need to include adaptation strategies available to agriculture (e.g. irrigation possibilities, availability of inputs) on a regional basis over time. Finally, a specification of the political environment for both domestic agricultural policy, world trade liberalization and other institutional change is necessary.

How should this universal base scenario be constructed? The IPCC has already developed a base scenario for 2020 and 2050 for climate variables, population and some economic variables, which is an excellent start. Probably the easiest way to build on this would be to have a workshop inviting people that have conducted economic research on agriculture and climate change. The U.S. Department of Agriculture would be a logical organizer of this workshop. Workshop participants could then identify and work out additional parameters for the universal base scenario, which would be published and made available to future researchers.

## Improved Understanding of the $CO_2$ 'Fertilizer Effect'

The predicted impact of climate change on crop yields is highly sensitive to the assumptions about $CO_2$ fertilization. However, not everyone agrees that a large $CO_2$ fertilizer effect will accompany climate change. Wolfe and Erickson (1993) contend that many studies overstate the benefits of $CO_2$ fertilization. They argue that the magnitude of the $CO_2$ fertilizer effect used in many studies is based on short-term laboratory experiments which have ideal environmental conditions with unlimited water and nutrients, optimal temperatures, and no weeds, diseases or insects present. Extrapolating the results of laboratory experiments to actual conditions in the field, therefore, will likely overstate the benefits from $CO_2$ fertilization. This is especially the case in developing countries where irrigation, fertilizers, herbicides and pesticides are either not available or are generally so expensive that most farmers cannot afford to use them. Furthermore, Wolfe and Erickson (1993) argue that current crop models do not consider the interactions between $CO_2$ and other environmental factors. As an example, they point out that there may be no benefit, or even a negative effect, from increased atmospheric $CO_2$ at low temperatures (less than 15 °C). In addition, there is evidence that growth stimulation from high $CO_2$ is a short-term phenomenon that does not continue with prolonged exposure.

Further, most of the increase in $CO_2$ emissions will come from increased fossil fuel consumption, which will also cause increased air pollution. There are three air pollutants associated with fossil fuel that will have a negative impact on crop yields: ozone, sulfur oxide and nitrogen dioxide. Of these three, ozone has the largest negative effect on reducing crop yields; one study estimated yield losses at a seven-hour day average ozone concentration of 0.09 parts per million to be 12.5 percent for corn, 30.7 percent for soybeans and 27.4 percent for wheat (Heck et al., 1984). Wolfe and Erickson (1993) argue that if one includes the $CO_2$ fertilizer effect to study yield impacts of climate change, then one should include the negative effects of these three air pollutants as well.

Since there is debate over the magnitude of this potentially beneficial effect, it is recommended that research on $CO_2$ fertilization be one of the top priorities for future work on agricultural impacts of climate change. Additional research on the impact of ozone and other pollutants on crop yields is also warranted. Until these uncertainties are resolved, impact analyses should continue to be conducted with and without $CO_2$ fertilization included in the crop simulation models so the full range of possibilities are presented.

## Improved Climate Models

One major observation from previous studies is that there are tremendous discrepancies in predictions among climate models. There is disagreement on the magnitude and even the sign of predicted changes in precipitation due to climate change. Furthermore, the discrepancy among model results becomes larger as the region being studied gets smaller. This is due primarily to the relatively coarse spatial resolutions specified in these models. GCMs divide the globe into grids that have spatial dimensions typically about 4° latitude by 5° longitude (Rosenzweig, 1989). This is quite a sizable area and one that does not capture smaller scale climate factors.

One of the most important research needs is to improve the climate models in order to achieve a higher degree of accuracy and consistency. There is ongoing research that will hopefully produce more accurate climate models in the future. Some of this research includes improving the representation of land surfaces and clouds in existing models. Another area involves adding a dynamically interactive component, which has a very important influence on climate. These and other areas of research by atmospheric scientists should improve the overall accuracy of GCMs.

Predictions of GCMs have been used mainly to examine changes in mean values of climatic variables due to climate change. However, there is also scientific evidence to suggest that changes in climatic variability may also occur (Rind et al., 1989). Changes in climatic variability such as frequency of drought will likely have as much impact on agricultural productivity as changes in mean values. Also, because some crops are more drought resistant (e.g. sorghum) than others (e.g. corn), failure to capture the potential increased frequency of drought may result in erroneous predictions in regional cropping patterns. Consequently, another important research area is generation and analysis of climatic variability due to climate change.

## Role of Irrigation

One factor that will be an extremely important determinant of climate change impacts is the demand and supply of irrigation. Few studies have considered irrigation in the impact analysis, and those that have incorporated irrigation have made simplifying assumptions. For example, the Adams et al. (1990) study considered irrigation, but it was assumed that there were no limits on water supply. They found that yield impacts due to climate change were much less severe for irrigated crops than for non-irrigated crops. This study also found that the costs of irrigation would increase and irrigated acreage in the United States would increase substantially by 5 million (GISS climate change scenario) to 18 million (GFDL climate change scenario) acres, with most of the increase occurring in the Northwest and Northern Plains. This predicted expansion has major implications for natural resource and land use.

The impact of climate change on irrigated crops is fairly easy to incorporate into crop simulation models given assumptions about water supply availability. For example, under unlimited water availability, crop yield simulation models can be modified so that the plant always has as much water as is needed and consequently there is no water stress. The difficult part, however, is modeling how water supply (and demand) will be impacted under climate change. Because irrigation is one of the more important strategies for adapting to climate warming, it is important that future economic impact studies incorporate irrigation. It is also important that better model linkages be developed between changes in temperature and precipitation, and the availability and cost of irrigation.

### Moving Beyond Analyses of Doubled $CO_2$ Concentrations

Almost every impact study has examined climate change due to a doubling of $CO_2$ emissions from pre-Industrial Revolution levels. There is nothing magical about this level of $CO_2$ and climate change will, of course, not stop once this point is reached in greenhouse gas emissions. Consequently, we need to do some longer-term analyses with climate, crop and economic models of the impacts of higher greenhouse gas emission levels than the conventional doubling analyses. This is important because the degree of climate change may be quite different when looking at alternative greenhouse gas concentration levels. Moreover, if the relationship between greenhouse gas atmospheric concentrations and climate change is not linear, then analyses of only doubled $CO_2$ concentrations may be misleading.

### Need for More Dynamic Economic Analyses

Many of the market level studies completed thus far have used a comparative static approach. However, climate change will occur gradually and a static framework fails to capture important factors which might run counter to the results predicted by static models. In reality, farmers will have to adapt to an evolving change in climate not a sudden, abrupt change in climate. Consequently changes in agricultural technology that are induced by an evolving climate will lessen the negative impacts of climate change. It is important that technological change be incorporated dynamically in the economic models because changes in technology will also be evolutionary, not abrupt. The rate of farmer adoption of new technologies should also be made explicit. As was previously argued, other factors such as changes in population, income and institutions will also have important market-wide effects and should be captured within the economic model in a dynamic framework. These factors will be especially important in the context of analyzing climate change impacts on food availability relative to world demand.

### Role of Institutional Adaptation

There is a need to examine the role of government intervention in agricultural markets in the context of climate change. This issue is discussed in detail by Lewandrowski and Brazee (1993). The authors contend that agricultural programs can discourage such farm management adaptation strategies as altering crop mix (e.g. support prices of crops not well suited to the new changed climate, or provide disaster payments when crop fails, or prohibiting imports through import quotas), and investing in water conservation techniques (e.g. subsidize irrigation water). Because U.S. farm programs alter expected returns, as well as the risk associated with production decisions, the behavior of the farmer is also affected by these programs. Thus, while programs can hinder farmer adaptation, these programs could be modified to encourage adaptation to climate change. In addition, Lewandrowski and Brazee argue that government policies affecting irrigation will become even more important if the changing climate results in less rain for crop production. Unless programs become more flexible, the economic and budgetary costs will likely become greater as climate change occurs. A detailed policy analysis of various options including current programs, deregulation and other alternatives as they relate to climate change and social welfare is needed.

### Linking Macro and Microeconomic Models

Most of the economic studies conducted thus far have either been highly aggregated (e.g. global, national or regional), or detailed farm-level analyses. The more global studies have been useful in determining climate change impacts on supply, demand and prices. The farm-level studies have been valuable in examining the impact of climate change on farm-level organization. The information from both types of studies are important to policy makers.

An important priority for future research will be to link the more aggregated, macro models with the farm-level, micro models to study climate change impacts in a comprehensive way. Such comprehensive studies, while undoubtedly major undertakings, should shed valuable insight on climate change impacts on agricultural prices, supply, demand, farm profits, resource shadow prices and farm management strategies. Linking macro with microeconomic models will also bring more consistency in results, which is not present in the more piece-meal approaches that do not link models.

# 4  SUMMARY

A growing body of literature has emerged on various aspects of potential economic effects of climate change on agriculture. The purpose of this chapter was to assess these studies and offer recommendations for future research directions. While previous studies have shed a lot of light on the impacts climate change may have on agricultural markets, there is still a lot of uncertainty, primarily due to inaccuracies in climate change predictions.

While there is tremendous uncertainty regarding the implications of climate change, this does not justify ignoring its potential impacts on agriculture and social welfare. Economic analyses play a critical role, particularly in the policy debate over climate change. The results of future research efforts in the physical, biological and economic disciplines should contribute greatly to our understanding of this extremely important topic.

## NOTES

1.  The interested reader is referred to the following studies for additional insight: Antle (1992), Downing (1996), IPCC (1996), Kaiser (1991), Mendelsohn and Reilly (1993), Mount (1992), Schimmelpfennig et al. (1996), and Sonka and Lamb (1987).
2.  The summary of potential impacts of climate change on agricultural productivity is based on the summary provided by Tobey et al. (1992). The reader is also referred to Table 7.2.
3.  $CO_2$ fertilization, or the $CO_2$ fertilizer effect as it is sometimes called, refers to an enhancement in crop yields due to elevated atmospheric $CO_2$, which increases rates of net photosynthesis and reduces stomatal openings, resulting in increased water use efficiency by the plant.
4.  See also Chapters 8 and 9 of this volume.
5.  For example, simulated yield changes for wheat without $CO_2$ effects ranged from -16 to -33 percent; with $CO_2$ fertilization included, the range became +11 to -13 percent. Similarly, rice yield changes of -24 to -25 percent changed to -2 to -5 percent; maize yield changes of -20 to -31 percent changed to -15 percent to -24 percent; while soybean yield changes of -19 to -57 percent shifted to +16 to -33 percent.

## REFERENCES

Adams, R.M., Rosenzweig, C., Peart, R.M., Ritchie, J.T., McCarl, B.A., Glyer, J.D., Curry, R.B., Jones, J.W., Boote, K.J. and Allen, L.H., Jr (1990), 'Global Climate Change and U.S. Agriculture', *Nature*, **345**, pp. 219–224.

Antle, J.M. (1992), 'Setting Priorities for Global-Change Research in Agriculture', in Reilly, J. and Anderson, M. (eds), *The Economics of Global Climate Change:*

*Implications for Agriculture, Forestry, and Natural Resources*, Boulder, CO: Westview Press, pp. 232–238.

Darwin, R., Tsigas, M., Lewandrowski, J. and Raneses, A. (1995), *World Agriculture and Climate Change: Economic Adaptations*, Agricultural Economics Report No. 703, Washington, DC: Economic Research Service, U.S. Department of Agriculture.

Downing, T.E. (ed.) (1996), *Climate Change and World Food Security*, Heidelberg: Springer.

Easterling, W.E., III, Crosson, P.R., Rosenberg, N.J., McKenney, M.S., Katz, L.A. and Lemon., K.M. (1993), 'Agricultural Impacts of and Response to Climate Change in the Missouri–Iowa–Nebraska–Kansas (MINK) Region', *Climatic Change*, 24, pp. 23–61.

Heck, W.W., Cure, J.D., Rawlings, J.O., Zaragoza, L.J., Heagle, A.S., Heggestad, H.E., Kohut, R.J., Kressk, L.W. and Temple, P.J. (1984), 'Assessing Impacts of Ozone on Agricultural Crops: II. Crop Yield Functions and Alternative Exposure Statistics', *Journal of Air Pollution Control Association*, 34, pp. 810–817.

Intergovernmental Panel on Climate Change (IPCC) (1990), *Climate Change: The IPCC Impact Assessment*, Canberra, Australia: Australian Government Publishing Service.

Intergovernmental Panel on Climate Change (IPCC) (1992), *Climate Change 1992: The Supplementary Report to the IPCC Scientific Assessment*, Cambridge: Cambridge University Press.

Intergovernmental Panel on Climate Change (IPCC) (1996), *Climate Change, 1995: Impacts, Adaptations and Mitigation of the Climate Change*, Cambridge: Cambridge University Press.

Kaiser, H.M. (1991), 'Climate Change and Agriculture', *Northeastern Journal of Agricultural and Resource Economics*, 20, pp. 151–163.

Kaiser, H.M., Riha, S.J., Wilks, D.S. and Sampath, R. (1993), 'Adaptation to Global Climate Change at the Farm-Level', in Kaiser, H.M. and Drennen, T.E. (eds), *Agricultural Dimensions of Global Climate Change*, Del Ray Beach, Florida: St. Lucie Press, pp. 136–152.

Kaiser, H.M., Riha, S.J., Wilks, D.S. and Sampath, R. (1995), *Potential Implications of Climate Change for Farm-Level Adaptation*, ERS Staff Paper Number AGES 9522, Washington, DC: Economic Research Service, U.S. Department of Agriculture.

Karl, T.R., Diaz, H. and Barnett, T. (1990), *Climate Variations of the Past Century and the Greenhouse Effect* (a report based on the First Climate Trends Workshop), Rockville, MD: National Climate Program Office/NOAA.

Kettunen, L., Mukula, J., Pohjonen, V., Rantanen, O. and Varjo, U. (1988), 'The Effects of Climatic Variations on Agriculture in Finland', in Parry, M., Carter, T. and Konijn, N. (eds), *The Impact of Climatic Variations on Agriculture, Vol. 1: Assessments in Cool Temperate, and Cold Regions*, Dordrecht, The Netherlands: Kluwer Academic Publishers, pp. 513–614.

Kokoski, M.F. and Smith, V.K. (1987), 'A General Equilibrium Analysis of Partial Equilibrium Welfare Measures: The Case of Climate Change', *American Economic Review*, 77, pp. 331–341.

Lewandrowski, J.K. and Brazee, R.J. (1993), 'Farm Programs and Climate Change', *Climatic Change*, 23, pp. 1–20.

Mendelsohn, R. and Reilly, J. (1993), 'A Research Agenda to Study Global Climate Change Impacts on Agriculture', unpublished paper, March 1993.

Mount, T. (1992), 'Global Climate Change: Effects on Agriculture', in Reilly, J. and Anderson, M. (eds), *The Economics of Global Climate Change: Implications for Agriculture, Forestry, and Natural Resources*, Boulder, CO: Westview Press, pp. 395–401.

Pittock, A. (1989), 'The Greenhouse Effect, Regional Climate Change, and Australian Agriculture', paper presented at the Fifth Agronomy Conference of the Australian Society of Agronomy, Perth, Australia.

Pittock, A. and Nix, N. (1986), 'The Effects of Changing Climate on Australian Biomass Production: A Preliminary Study', *Climatic Change*, **8**, pp. 243–255.

Reilly, J., Hohmann, N., and Kane, S. (1993), 'Climate Change and Agriculture: Global and Regional Effects using an Economic Model of International Trade', MIT-CEEPR 93-012WP, Center for Energy and Environmental Policy Research, Massachusetts Institute of Technology.

Rind, D., Golberg, R. and Ruedy, R. (1989), 'Change in Climate Variability in the 21st Century', *Climatic Change*, **14**, pp. 5–37.

Rosenzweig, C. (1989), 'Global Climate Change: Predictions and Observations', *American Journal of Agricultural Economics*, **71**, pp. 1265–1271.

Rosenzweig, C., Parry, M., Frohberg, K. and Fisher, G. (1993), 'Climate Change and World Food Supply', Environmental Change Unit, University of Oxford.

Santer, B. (1985), 'The Use of General Circulation Models in Climate Impact Analyses: A Preliminary Study of the Impacts of a $CO_2$ Induced Climate Change on West European Agriculture', *Climatic Change*, **7**, pp. 71–93.

Schimmelpfennig, D., Lewandrowski, J., Reilly, J., Tsigas, M. and Parry, I. (1996), *Agricultural Adaptation to Change: Issues of Longrun Sustainability*, Agricultural Economic Report No. 740, Washington, DC: Economic Research Service, U.S. Department of Agriculture.

Smit, B. (1989), 'Climate Warming and Canada's Comparative Position in Agriculture', *Climatic Change Digest*, **87**, pp. 1–9.

Sonka, S.T. and Lamb, P.J. (1987), 'On Climate Change and Economic Analysis', *Climatic Change*, **11**, pp. 291–311.

Tobey, J., Reilley, J. and Kane, S. (1992), 'Economic Implications of Global Climate Change for World Agriculture', *Journal of Agricultural and Resource Economics*, **17**, pp. 195–204.

U.S. Environmental Protection Agency (1990), *The Potential Effects of Global Climate Change on the United States, Vol. 1: Regional Studies*, Report to Congress. Washington, DC.

Walker, B., Young, M., Parslow, J., Crocks, K., Fleming, P., Margules, C. and Landsberg, J. (1989), *Global Climate Change and Australia: Effects on Renewable Natural Resources*, CSIRO Division of Wildlife and Ecology, Canberra, Australia.

Williams, G., Fautley, R., Jones, D., Stewart, R. and Wheaton, E. (1988), 'Estimating Effects of Climatic Change on Agriculture in Saskatchewan, Canada', in Parry, M., Carter, T. and Konijn, N. (eds), *The Impact of Climatic Variations on Agriculture, Vol. 1: Assessments in Cool Temperate, and Cold Regions*, Dordrecht, The Netherlands: Kluwer Academic Publishers, pp. 221–379.

Wolfe, D.W. and Erickson, J.D. (1993), 'Carbon Dioxide Effect on Plants: Uncertainties and Implications for Modeling Crop Response to Climate Change', in Kaiser, H.M. and Drennen, T.E. (eds), *Agricultural Dimensions of Global Climate Change*, Del Ray Beach, FL: St. Lucie Press, pp. 153–178.

# 8  Climate Change and Agriculture: Effects on Developing Countries

## Paul Winters, Rinku Murgai, Alain de Janvry, Elisabeth Sadoulet and George Frisvold

## 1  INTRODUCTION

Climate change has received increased attention in recent years, with considerable debate over the degree to which developed countries, or the world as a whole, should take steps to mitigate global warming. An answer to this central question requires information about both the costs of alternative mitigation strategies (e.g. carbon taxes, tradable quotas) and the costs of allowing global warming to occur. Most economic analyses have focused on measuring either the gross costs of mitigation (*mitigation studies*) or the gross costs of climate change (*impact studies*).[1] Others have attempted more comprehensive cost–benefit analyses (Nordhaus, 1991; Cline, 1992).

Most impact studies have concentrated on the implications of climate change for agriculture, the sector most sensitive to climate change. The first generation of such studies focused primarily on the impacts of climate change on the agricultural sectors of grain-exporting developed countries, Japan and the former Soviet Union (Sonka, 1991). Analysis broadened to consider consequences of climate change on the world's capacity to meet future food demands (Rosenzweig and Parry, 1993; Reilly et al., 1993). In general, these studies suggest that climate change would have very modest economy-wide impacts on developed countries, the effects on grain-exporting countries (particularly in higher latitudes) could be positive and that the world's overall capacity to produce food will not be severely threatened.

Agricultural impact studies, however, suggested very different implications for developing countries. Global climate change is expected to lead to more significant agricultural productivity losses in the tropics, where a majority of these countries lie. Moreover, by the year 2050 when climate change impacts might be felt, these countries will be home to two-thirds of the world's population. The differential impact of climate change on developing countries is noted by a number of writers (Cline, 1992; Schelling, 1992; Nordhaus, 1991). Nordhaus writes:

> [S]mall and poor countries, particularly ones with low population mobility in narrowly restricted climatic zones, may be severely affected. Much more work on the potential impact of climate change on developing countries needs to be done. (Nordhaus, p. 993)

This chapter is concerned with the disparate repercussions of climate change on developing economies in Asia, Africa and Latin America. We focus on low income, net food-importing economies since we are interested in examining impacts on those countries most vulnerable to environmental and world market changes. Such economies deserve particular attention considering the rising trend in net food importation in developing countries (UN/FAO, 1993). We are also interested in climate change impacts on the level of cereal import demand which has implications for grain-exporting developed countries.

Many economic consequences of climate change will be felt via two types of agricultural change. First, agricultural sectors of individual countries will be affected by changes in domestic yields (domestic productive capacity). Second, because of the global nature of climate change, world prices of traded agricultural commodities will also be subject to change. These agricultural effects determine the economy-wide impacts of climate change on macroeconomic indicators, sectoral resource allocation and income distribution.

To examine these economy-wide impacts, we construct archetype multisector and multi-class computable general equilibrium (CGE) models for groups of countries with similar structural features. It would be very costly to construct complete models for individual countries and summarize climate change impacts and policy implications by structural group. De Melo and Robinson (1982) have pioneered the alternative approach of constructing country averages (archetypes) and deriving impacts and policy implications for the corresponding country group.[2] For this chapter, we have constructed three archetype economies for cereal-importing countries in Latin America, Sub-Saharan Africa and Asia.

The chapter is divided into six sections. In section 2, we discuss the methods used to predict the effects of climate change on a subset of developing economies. It focuses on the characterization of the archetype economies, determination of the effects of climate change on agricultural sectors and the use of CGE models to determine the economy-wide impact of agricultural shocks due to climate change.

Sections 3–5 discuss the results of our simulations. Section 3 focuses on the consequences of climate change on macroeconomic variables such as income per capita and the exchange rate. Section 4 discusses sectoral responses to climate change, which include not only the agricultural sectors, but also the non-agricultural sectors such as industry and services. In section 5, the effects on household groups in terms of income distribution and demand are discussed. Policy implications and conclusions are drawn in section 6.

In our simulation results, climate change has a negative effect on each archetype economy, but African, Asian and Latin American countries are affected differently. The disparities hinge on the relationship of each economy to the international market, the substitution possibilities within the economy, the relative importance of agriculture and the composition of production of the agricultural sector. Economies that are more able to substitute imported foods for domestic foods will be less affected by climate change, particularly if world food prices do not rise significantly. Economies with a greater supply responsiveness, with a smaller agricultural sector, and with a crop portfolio less affected by climate change scenarios will suffer less than primarily agrarian, closed economies. The most important channel of impacts on the economy will be via lower food yields because food crops constitute the bulk of agricultural production in developing countries and because food is a significant share of consumption.

## 2 METHODS

Our aim is to determine the impact of climate change on developing economies, in particular cereal-importing countries. We have therefore constructed three archetype economies to represent cereal importers in Africa, Asia and Latin America. These archetypes contain features that are characteristic of each set of countries. The experiments we conduct to analyze the effects of climate change are on these archetype economies.

Although climate change may have a number of potential impacts on economies, one of the most important, particularly for developing economies, is the impact it will have on agriculture. Two direct effects on agriculture are expected. First, there will be an effect on overall crop yields which will depend not only on the predictions of the climate model, but also on the composition of agriculture in the country – that is, the importance of certain crops in total production and how they are affected by climate change. Second, since climate change is a global phenomenon, there will be an effect on global output and therefore on world prices. As with yields, the transmission of world price shocks into an individual economy will depend on the relative importance of different crops in the export and import portfolios of the country.

In order to determine the impacts of shocks to agriculture on developing economies, we use CGE models with a multi-market agricultural sector. The multi-market agricultural sector allows for direct substitution possibilities in production within the agricultural sector. Such reallocations of resources across crops and livestock would occur if climate change had disparate impacts on agricultural commodities. The CGE models trace economy-wide effects of agricultural shocks by highlighting sectoral and institutional linkages between the agricultural sector and the economy as a whole. The archetype economies for Africa, Asia and Latin America, the agricultural shocks to yield and prices caused by climate change, and the CGE models for each archetype are discussed below.

**Archetype Economies**

The archetype models developed for Africa, Asia and Latin America are based on social accounting matrices (SAMs) which have been designed to represent the distinctive aspects of the specific regions being analyzed (Sadoulet et al., 1992). The archetypal SAMs depict the features of low income, food-importing countries in each region. They replicate the average levels of the macroaggregates for the countries grouped in each archetype. Linkage effects and household income structures for the African archetype are taken from a SAM for the Kenyan economy, for the Asian archetype from a Sri Lankan SAM, and for the Latin American archetype principally from an Ecuadorian SAM. Each basic matrix is modified to emphasize various 'average' structural characteristics from other countries. The following countries are represented in each archetype:

> *Africa*: Benin, Burkina Faso, Central African Republic, Ethiopia, Ghana, Guinea, Kenya, Lesotho, Liberia, Madagascar, Mali, Mauritania, Mozambique, Rwanda, Senegal, Sierra Leone, Somalia, Sudan, Tanzania, Togo and Zaire.

> *Asia*: Bangladesh, Indonesia, Pakistan, Papua New Guinea, Philippines and Sri Lanka.

> *Latin America*: Brazil, Chile, Colombia, Costa Rica, Dominican Republic, Ecuador, El Salvador, Guatemala, Honduras, Jamaica, Mexico, Nicaragua, Panama and Peru.

Climatologists have developed global circulation models to estimate the climatic effects of a doubling of carbon-dioxide-equivalent greenhouse gases above pre-industrial concentrations (Houghton et al., 1992). These effects are expected to be felt around the year 2050. Parry (1990) argues that under a business-as-usual scenario the date at which a doubling of carbon-dioxide-equivalent above pre-industrial levels is reached is about 2025 and under a low scenario this will occur in about 2070. In Rosenzweig and Iglesias (1993) the agricultural shocks from a carbon-dioxide-equivalent doubling are assumed to occur in 2060. In the MINK study (Crosson, 1993) the shocks occur in 2030. We have used 2050 as an intermediate position.

Because climate change impacts may not be felt until well into the next century, our simulations must be based on what the archetype economies will be like at that future date. Agricultural impact studies frequently assume climate change occurs in the current economy. This seems inappropriate in our context because the effects of climate change depend on an economy's structure, which changes over time.[3]

Three steps were taken to develop SAMs for the year 2050 (see Appendix A for details). First, archetype SAMs were determined for the present. Second, future growth rates, in GDP per capita, from the present until 2050 were determined for each archetype based on projections by the Intergovernmental Panel on Climate Change (1990) and past growth rates of the represented economies (World Bank Tables, 1994). Third, given the growth rates, for each region a new SAM was constructed, which included not only the increase in the size of the economy, that is, a higher GDP per capita, but also predicted changes in the structural characteristics of the economy following the 'normal patterns of growth' established by Chenery and Taylor (1968). These normal patterns predict that as GDP per capita increases, there is expected to be a decrease in the relative size of the agricultural sector, an urbanization of the labor force, a decrease in the share of food consumption in total consumption and an increase in international trade. While Asia and Latin America are expected to experience future growth in GDP per capita, African population growth will outweigh its GDP growth, leaving little change in the economy in terms of income per capita or structure. As a country becomes more developed it is likely to be less vulnerable to climate change (Nordhaus, 1991). Therefore, while Asia and Latin America become less vulnerable, Africa does not.

The future archetype SAMs for Africa, Asia and Latin America are shown in Tables 8.1, 8.2 and 8.3 (details of the structure of the SAMs are discussed in Appendix A). Per capita incomes in 2050 for Africa, Asia and Latin America are $243, $901 and $3,047 (in 1985 dollars). In Africa and Asia there are three agricultural sectors (agricultural exports, food crops and other agriculture) and five non-agricultural sectors (agricultural processing, energy, industry, construction and services, and administration). Food crops include cereals while other agriculture is primarily animal products. In Latin America, there are two agricultural sectors (agricultural exports and other agriculture – which includes cereals) and five non-agricultural sectors (oil and minerals, energy, industry, construction and services, and administration). The agricultural sectors account for a high share of GDP in Africa. These sectors generate over 38 percent of total income in Africa while for Asia and Latin America the corresponding figures are 18 percent and 7.6 percent. Industry and services are most important in Latin America, making up 39.9 percent and 52.5 percent of GDP per capita compared to 36.3 percent and 45.7 percent for Asia and only 20.8 percent and 41.1 percent for Africa. Considering the relative size of the agricultural sectors, it would appear that the negative effects of climate change would be felt most in Africa and least in Latin America. However, we shall see later that the size

*Table 8.1    SAM for the archetype poor African economy (1985 U.S. dollars per capita)*

|  | Agricultural exports | Food | Other agriculture | Agricultural processing |
|---|---|---|---|---|
|  | [1] | [2] | [3] | [4] |
| **Activities:** |  |  |  |  |
| 1 Agricultural exports | 1.7 |  |  | 0.7 |
| 2 Food crops |  | 2.4 | 3.1 | 15.0 |
| 3 Other agriculture |  |  |  |  |
| 4 Agricultural processing |  |  | 1.3 | 3.2 |
| 5 Energy | 0.3 | 0.3 |  | 1.3 |
| 6 Industry | 2.3 | 3.3 |  | 6.0 |
| 7 Construction services |  |  |  | 5.3 |
| 8 Administration |  |  |  |  |
| **Labor:** |  |  |  |  |
| 9 Unskilled | 4.4 | 3.8 |  | 3.4 |
| 10 Skilled | 1.1 |  |  | 5.6 |
| 11 Public employees |  |  |  |  |
| **Households:** |  |  |  |  |
| 12 Urban poor |  |  |  |  |
| 13 Urban rich |  |  |  |  |
| 14 Small farmers |  | 8.4 | 8.3 |  |
| 15 Medium farmers | 8.8 | 16.3 | 18.1 |  |
| 16 Large farmers | 10.3 | 10.2 |  |  |
| **Firms:** |  |  |  |  |
| 17 Agricultural processing |  |  |  | 5.7 |
| 18 Industry/energy |  |  |  |  |
| 19 Construction services |  |  |  |  |
| 20 Government subsidies |  |  |  |  |
| 21 Taxes – transfers |  |  |  | 6.6 |
| 22 Import tariffs |  |  |  | 0.7 |
| 23 Export taxes | 2.9 |  |  |  |
| 24 Trade margins | 2.4 | 3.2 | 2.0 | 5.8 |
| 25 Private capital |  |  |  |  |
| 26 Public capital |  |  |  |  |
| 27 Rest of world |  | 7.7 |  | 2.1 |
| Total | 34.3 | 55.5 | 32.9 | 61.4 |

| Energy | Industry | Construction services | Administration | Unskilled labor | Skilled labor | Public labor |
|---|---|---|---|---|---|---|
| [5] | [6] | [7] | [8] | [9] | [10] | [11] |
|  | 1.2 |  |  |  |  |  |
| 0.3 | 2.7 | 5.7 | 2.2 |  |  |  |
|  | 3.1 | 3.8 | 0.6 |  |  |  |
| 1.9 | 10.3 | 17.7 | 0.8 |  |  |  |
| 1.0 | 7.9 | 14.2 | 4.3 |  |  |  |
| 0.5 | 3.5 | 21.1 |  |  |  |  |
| 0.8 | 6.4 | 27.3 |  |  |  |  |
|  |  |  | 30.6 |  |  |  |
|  |  |  |  | 9.6 | 13.0 | 16.1 |
|  |  |  |  |  | 3.8 | 14.5 |
|  |  |  |  | 7.0 | 1.8 |  |
|  |  |  |  | 12.0 | 7.2 |  |
|  |  |  |  | 8.0 | 15.5 |  |
| 1.1 | 8.6 |  |  |  |  |  |
|  |  | 18.0 |  |  |  |  |
| 0.8 | 7.4 | 2.8 |  |  |  |  |
| 1.0 | 8.5 |  |  |  |  |  |
| 1.8 | 15.6 | 1.4 |  |  |  |  |
| 3.1 | 36.9 | 10.6 |  |  |  |  |
| 12.5 | 112.1 | 122.6 | 38.6 | 36.6 | 41.2 | 30.6 |

*Table 8.1   (continued)*

|  | Households | | | | | Firms |
|---|---|---|---|---|---|---|
|  | Urban poor [12] | Urban rich [13] | Small farms [14] | Medium farms [15] | Large farms [16] | Agricultural processing [17] |
| Activities: | | | | | | |
| 1 Agricultural exports | | | | | | |
| 2 Food crops | 1.9 | 0.7 | 8.8 | 17.9 | 5.7 | |
| 3 Other agriculture | 4.6 | 0.9 | 5.3 | 11.9 | 5.4 | |
| 4 Agricultural processing | 14.6 | 4.3 | 4.7 | 11.2 | 7.2 | |
| 5 Energy | 0.7 | 0.6 | 0.2 | 0.8 | 0.8 | |
| 6 Industry | 9.4 | 8.6 | 3.4 | 11.8 | 10.9 | |
| 7 Construction services | 17.3 | 10.7 | 2.0 | 5.2 | 7.9 | |
| 8 Administration | | | | | | |
| Labor: | | | | | | |
| 9 Unskilled | | | | | | |
| 10 Skilled | | | | | | |
| 11 Public employees | | | | | | |
| Households: | | | | | | |
| 12 Urban poor | | | | | | 2.3 |
| 13 Urban rich | | | | | | 2.0 |
| 14 Small farmers | | | | | | |
| 15 Medium farmers | | | | | | |
| 16 Large farmers | | | | | | |
| Firms: | | | | | | |
| 17 Agricultural processing | | | | | | |
| 18 Industry/energy | | | | | | |
| 19 Construction services | | | | | | |
| 20 Government subsidies | | | | | | |
| 21 Taxes – transfers | | 2.2 | | | 1.8 | 0.5 |
| 22 Import tariffs | | | | | | |
| 23 Export taxes | | | | | | |
| 24 Trade margins | | | | | | |
| 25 Private capital | 2.6 | 7.0 | 1.5 | 4.2 | 6.6 | 0.9 |
| 26 Public capital | | | | | | |
| 27 Rest of world | | | | | | |
| Total | 51.2 | 35.0 | 25.9 | 63.0 | 46.4 | 5.7 |

| Firms | | Government | Trade margins | Private capital | Public capital | Rest of world | Total |
|---|---|---|---|---|---|---|---|
| Industry/ energy [18] | Construction services [19] | [20–23] | [24] | [25] | [26] | [27] | |
| | | | | | | 30.7 | 34.3 |
| | | | | | | | 55.5 |
| | | | | 4.8 | | | 32.9 |
| | | | | | | 4.1 | 61.4 |
| | | | | | | | 12.5 |
| | | | | 12.8 | 3.1 | 9.7 | 112.1 |
| | | | 32.2 | 7.7 | 6.7 | | 122.6 |
| | | 38.6 | | | | | 38.6 |
| | | | | | | | 36.6 |
| | | | | | | | 41.2 |
| | | | | | | | 30.6 |
| | 7.4 | 1.3 | | | | 1.5 | 51.2 |
| 7.9 | 6.2 | 0.4 | | | | 0.3 | 35.0 |
| | | | | | | 0.4 | 25.9 |
| | | | | | | 0.6 | 63.0 |
| | | 1.2 | | | | 1.3 | 46.4 |
| | | | | | | | 5.7 |
| | | | | | | 1.0 | 10.8 |
| | | | | | | 1.0 | 19.1 |
| −1.3 | 1.5 | | | | | 15.7 | 38.2 |
| | | | | | | | 10.3 |
| | | | | | | | 2.9 |
| | | | | | | | 32.2 |
| 2.9 | 4.1 | −4.6 | | | | | 25.3 |
| | | 9.8 | | | | | 9.8 |
| 1.3 | | 4.8 | | | | | 66.4 |
| 10.8 | 19.1 | 51.4 | 32.2 | 25.3 | 9.8 | 66.4 | |

*Table 8.2  SAM for a future archetype poor Asian economy (1985 U.S. dollars per capita)*

| | Agricultural exports | Cereals | Other agriculture | Agricultural processing |
|---|---|---|---|---|
| | [1] | [2] | [3] | [4] |
| **Activities:** | | | | |
| 1 Agricultural exports | | | | 0.5 |
| 2 Cereals | | 2.6 | | 6.4 |
| 3 Other agriculture | | | 3.1 | 2.3 |
| 4 Agricultural processing | | | 2.9 | 1.1 |
| 5 Energy | 0.9 | 0.9 | 1.3 | 2.0 |
| 6 Industry | 8.1 | 8.8 | 4.8 | 5.1 |
| 7 Construction services | 3.0 | | | 4.2 |
| 8 Administration | | | | |
| **Labor:** | | | | |
| 9 Urban | | | 5.8 | 16.8 |
| 10 Rural | 16.4 | 30.6 | 18.4 | 14.7 |
| 11 Public employees | | | | |
| **Households:** | | | | |
| 12 Urban poor | | | | |
| 13 Urban rich | | | | |
| 14 Rural landless | | | 7.2 | |
| 15 Medium farmers | | 6.7 | 29.3 | |
| 16 Large farmers | 15.0 | 10.8 | 15.3 | |
| **Firms:** | | | | |
| 17 Agricultural processing | | | | 36.9 |
| 18 Industry/energy | | | | |
| 19 Construction services | | | | |
| 20 Government subsidies | | – 13.9 | | |
| 21 Taxes – transfers | | | | 9.7 |
| 22 Import tariffs | | | | 1.3 |
| 23 Export taxes | 6.7 | | | |
| 24 Trade margins | 9.4 | 5.3 | 10.7 | 12.5 |
| 25 Private capital | | | | |
| 26 Public capital | | | | |
| 27 Rest of world | | 5.0 | 5.5 | 4.2 |
| Total | 59.5 | 56.8 | 104.3 | 117.7 |

| Energy | Industry | Construction services | Admini- stration | Urban labor | Rural labor | Public labor |
|--------|----------|----------------------|------------------|-------------|-------------|--------------|
| [5] | [6] | [7] | [8] | [9] | [10] | [11] |
|  | 12.0 | 2.4 | 0.8 |  |  |  |
|  | 13.1 | 2.0 | 1.1 |  |  |  |
|  | 29.9 | 24.6 | 1.6 |  |  |  |
| 15.2 | 31.8 | 34.4 | 4.4 |  |  |  |
| 5.8 | 11.7 | 13.4 | 9.4 |  |  |  |
| 9.7 | 42.6 | 57.9 |  |  |  |  |
| 9.1 | 41.9 | 53.3 |  |  |  |  |
|  |  |  | 68.7 |  |  |  |
|  |  |  |  | 132.8 |  | 14.8 |
|  |  |  |  |  |  | 25.8 |
|  |  |  |  |  | 76.4 | 3.1 |
|  |  |  |  |  | 92.0 | 9.2 |
|  |  |  |  |  | 16.0 | 15.8 |
| 15.3 | 91.3 |  |  |  |  |  |
|  |  | 215.0 |  |  |  |  |
| 4.2 | 35.0 | 16.4 |  |  |  |  |
| 7.8 | 23.5 |  |  |  |  |  |
| 7.8 | 78.9 | 28.4 |  |  |  |  |
| 5.2 | 162.8 | 54.2 |  |  |  |  |
| 80.1 | 574.5 | 502.0 | 86.0 | 132.8 | 184.4 | 68.7 |

*Table 8.2    (continued)*

|  | Urban poor | Urban rich | Households Landless | Households Medium farms | Households Large farms | Firms Agricultural processing |
|---|---|---|---|---|---|---|
|  | [12] | [13] | [14] | [15] | [16] | [17] |
| **Activities:** |  |  |  |  |  |  |
| 1 Agricultural exports | 3.7 | 1.1 | 5.6 | 6.0 | 1.4 |  |
| 2 Cereals | 9.3 | 2.8 | 14.4 | 18.5 | 2.8 |  |
| 3 Other agriculture | 20.8 | 9.7 | 21.7 | 24.7 | 6.8 |  |
| 4 Agricultural processing | 20.8 | 7.2 | 17.4 | 22.5 | 7.2 |  |
| 5 Energy | 5.2 | 4.7 | 1.9 | 4.5 | 2.6 |  |
| 6 Industry | 61.4 | 55.6 | 43.3 | 69.5 | 27.5 |  |
| 7 Construction services | 48.6 | 35.8 | 28.6 | 54.2 | 16.7 |  |
| 8 Administration |  |  |  |  |  |  |
| **Labor:** |  |  |  |  |  |  |
| 9 Urban |  |  |  |  |  |  |
| 10 Rural |  |  |  |  |  |  |
| 11 Public employees |  |  |  |  |  |  |
| **Households:** |  |  |  |  |  |  |
| 12 Urban poor |  |  |  |  |  | 9.4 |
| 13 Urban rich |  |  |  |  |  |  |
| 14 Rural landless |  |  |  |  |  | 5.8 |
| 15 Medium farmers |  |  |  |  |  | 10.0 |
| 16 Large farmers |  |  |  |  |  |  |
| **Firms:** |  |  |  |  |  |  |
| 17 Agricultural processing |  |  |  |  |  |  |
| 18 Industry/energy |  |  |  |  |  |  |
| 19 Construction services |  |  |  |  |  |  |
| 20 Government subsidies |  |  |  |  |  |  |
| 21 Taxes – transfers | 7.8 | 13.0 |  | 6.7 | 6.1 | 1.4 |
| 22 Import tariffs |  |  |  |  |  |  |
| 23 Export taxes |  |  |  |  |  |  |
| 24 Trade margins |  |  |  |  |  |  |
| 25 Private capital | 9.0 | 14.2 | 3.8 | 25.3 | 12.2 | 10.3 |
| 26 Public capital |  |  |  |  |  |  |
| 27 Rest of world |  | 6.1 |  |  |  |  |
| Total | 186.6 | 150.2 | 136.7 | 231.9 | 83.3 | 36.9 |

| Firms | | Government | Trade margins | Private capital | Public capital | Rest of world | Total |
|---|---|---|---|---|---|---|---|
| Industry/ energy | Construction services | | | | | | |
| [18] | [19] | [20–23] | [24] | [25] | [26] | [27] | |
| | | | | | | 41.2 | 59.5 |
| | | | | | | | 56.8 |
| | | | | | | | 104.3 |
| | | | | | | 22.4 | 117.7 |
| | | | | | | | 80.1 |
| | | | | 84.8 | 15.1 | 104.7 | 574.5 |
| | | | 153.0 | 72.0 | 45.6 | | 502.0 |
| | | 86.0 | | | | | 86.0 |
| | | | | | | | 132.8 |
| | | | | | | | 184.4 |
| | | | | | | | 68.7 |
| | 16.9 | 6.3 | | | | 6.4 | 186.6 |
| 41.3 | 57.5 | 3.3 | | | | 22.3 | 150.2 |
| | 30.8 | 4.5 | | | | 8.9 | 136.7 |
| 10.3 | 50.4 | 5.9 | | | | 18.1 | 231.9 |
| | | 5.1 | | | | 5.3 | 83.3 |
| | | | | | | | 36.9 |
| | | | | | | | 106.6 |
| | | | | | | | 215.0 |
| | | 13.9 | | | | | |
| 5.3 | 9.5 | | | | | 25.3 | 140.4 |
| | | | | | | | 32.6 |
| | | | | | | | 6.7 |
| | | | | | | | 153.0 |
| 42.4 | 49.9 | - 10.3 | | | | | 156.8 |
| | | 60.7 | | | | | 60.7 |
| 7.3 | | 4.3 | | | | | 254.6 |
| 106.6 | 215.0 | 179.7 | 153.0 | 156.8 | 60.7 | 254.6 | |

*Table 8.3    SAM for the archetype Latin American economy (1985 U.S. dollars per capita)*

| | | Agricultural exports | Other agriculture | Oil/ minerals | Other energy |
|---|---|---|---|---|---|
| | | [1] | [2] | [3] | [4] |
| | Activities: | | | | |
| 1 | Agricultural exports | | | | |
| 2 | Other agriculture | | 2.7 | | |
| 3 | Oil/minerals | 1.5 | | | |
| 4 | Other energy | | | | |
| 5 | Industry | 12.5 | 20.5 | 24.1 | 25.3 |
| 6 | Trade/services | 3.9 | 2.7 | 15.3 | 9.0 |
| 7 | Government services | | | | |
| 8 | Skilled labor | 3.5 | 6.7 | 9.0 | 5.3 |
| 9 | Unskilled labor | 16.6 | 79.6 | 3.5 | 13.9 |
| | Households: | | | | |
| 10 | Urban poor | 24.9 | 5.2 | | |
| 11 | Urban rich | 5.2 | 4.4 | | |
| 12 | Small farms | 8.5 | 6.9 | | |
| 13 | Medium farms | 6.2 | 10.8 | | |
| 14 | Large farms | 9.2 | 16.3 | | |
| | Firms: | | | | |
| 15 | Agricultural exports | 7.1 | | | |
| 16 | Other agriculture | | 14.1 | | |
| 17 | Oil/minerals | | | 173.6 | |
| 18 | Industry/energy | | | | 23.2 |
| 19 | Trade/services | | | | |
| 20 | Income tax | | | | |
| 21 | Indirect tax | 3.5 | 3.1 | 24.2 | 16.6 |
| 22 | Import tariff | | -3.9 | | |
| 23 | Government | | | | |
| 24 | Trade margins | 42.1 | 53.1 | 12.9 | |
| 25 | Private capital | | | | |
| 26 | Public capital | | | | |
| 27 | Rest of world | | 32.1 | | |
| | Total | 144.7 | 254.3 | 262.6 | 93.3 |

| Industry | Trade/ services | Government services | Skilled labor | Unskilled labor | Households | | | |
| --- | --- | --- | --- | --- | --- | --- | --- | --- |
| | | | | | Urban poor | Urban rich | Small farms | Medium farms |
| [5] | [6] | [7] | [8] | [9] | [10] | [11] | [12] | [13] |
| 18.7 | | | | | 7.7 | 5.0 | 1.5 | 0.5 |
| 144.4 | 1.0 | 1.6 | | | 44.1 | 28.1 | 18.1 | 5.6 |
| 15.6 | 37.2 | 2.2 | | | 7.7 | 5.2 | 1.4 | 0.4 |
| 34.1 | 9.6 | 4.6 | | | 18.9 | 16.8 | 4.4 | 2.3 |
| 508.9 | 443.4 | 72.4 | | | 482.8 | 410.7 | 130.9 | 39.0 |
| 196.0 | 394.7 | 30.7 | | | 274.9 | 269.2 | 56.5 | 15.6 |
| 116.5 | 325.5 | 140.4 | | | | | | |
| 208.9 | 594.1 | 38.8 | | | | | | |
| 148.8 | 188.3 | | 99.6 | 489.9 | | | | |
| 90.0 | 112.6 | | 482.4 | 239.4 | | | | |
| 24.4 | 24.8 | | 11.3 | 154.1 | | | | |
| 8.1 | 7.5 | | 4.0 | 38.2 | | | | |
| 6.5 | 14.0 | | 9.6 | 33.8 | | | | |
| 202.1 | | | | | | | | |
| | 123.4 | | | | | | | |
| | | | | | 35.2 | 98.0 | | 0.8 |
| 141.8 | 25.7 | | | | | | | |
| 57.3 | | | | | | | | |
| 507.2 | | | | | | | | |
| | | | | | 131.3 | 168.1 | 22.2 | 12.8 |
| 379.9 | | | | | 6.4 | 31.6 | | 0.4 |
| 2809.2 | 2301.8 | 290.7 | 606.9 | 955.4 | 1009.0 | 1032.7 | 235.0 | 77.4 |

*Table 8.3*    *(continued)*

| | Households | Firms | | | |
|---|---|---|---|---|---|
| | Large farms | Agricultural exports | Other agriculture | Oil/ minerals | Industry/ energy |
| | [14] | [15] | [16] | [17] | [18] |
| **Activities:** | | | | | |
| 1 Agricultural exports | 0.6 | | | | |
| 2 Other agriculture | 5.2 | | | | |
| 3 Oil/minerals | 0.4 | | | | |
| 4 Other energy | 2.6 | | | | |
| 5 Industry | 38.8 | | | | |
| 6 Trade/services | 18.9 | | | | |
| 7 Government services | | | | | |
| | | | | | |
| 8 Skilled labor | | | | | |
| 9 Unskilled labor | | | | | |
| | | | | | |
| **Households:** | | | | | |
| 10 Urban poor | | | | | 5.9 |
| 11 Urban rich | | | | | 12.0 |
| 12 Small farms | | | | | |
| 13 Medium farms | | | | | |
| 14 Large farms | | | | | |
| | | | | | |
| **Firms:** | | | | | |
| 15 Agricultural exports | | | | | |
| 16 Other agriculture | | | | | |
| 17 Oil/minerals | | | | | |
| 18 Industry/energy | | | | | |
| 19 Trade/services | | 4.4 | 9.0 | 27.3 | 100.6 |
| | | | | | |
| 20 Income tax | 2.0 | 0.4 | 0.4 | | 15.3 |
| 21 Indirect tax | | | | | |
| 22 Import tariff | | | | | |
| 23 Government | | | | 116.7 | |
| | | | | | |
| 24 Trade margins | | | | | |
| | | | | | |
| 25 Private capital | 20.8 | 1.9 | 3.7 | 29.6 | 58.8 |
| 26 Public capital | | | | | |
| | | | | | |
| 27 Rest of world | 3.7 | 0.4 | 1.0 | | 32.7 |
| Total | 93.0 | 7.1 | 14.1 | 173.6 | 225.3 |

| Trade/services | Government | Trade margins | Private capital | Public capital | Rest of world | Total |
|---|---|---|---|---|---|---|
| [19] | [20–23] | [24] | [25] | [26] | [27] | |
| | | | | | 110.7 | 144.7 |
| | | | 3.5 | | | 254.3 |
| | | | | | 191.0 | 262.6 |
| | | | | | | 93.3 |
| | | | 407.6 | 34.8 | 157.5 | 2809.2 |
| | | 615.3 | 203.8 | 178.6 | 16.7 | 2301.8 |
| | 290.7 | | | | | 290.7 |
| | | | | | | 606.9 |
| | | | | | | 955.4 |
| 13.3 | 33.1 | | | | | 1009.0 |
| 31.0 | 55.7 | | | | | 1032.7 |
| 0.8 | 4.2 | | | | | 235.0 |
| 1.4 | 1.2 | | | | | 77.4 |
| 1.7 | 1.9 | | | | | 93.0 |
| | | | | | | 7.1 |
| | | | | | | 14.1 |
| | | | | | | 173.6 |
| | | | | | | 225.3 |
| 67.2 | | | | | | 331.9 |
| 39.0 | | | | | 23.9 | 215.0 |
| | | | | | | 214.9 |
| | | | | | | 53.4 |
| | 483.3 | | | | | 600.0 |
| | | | | | | 615.3 |
| 169.0 | -69.8 | | | | 66.5 | 614.9 |
| | 213.4 | | | | | 213.4 |
| 8.5 | 69.6 | | | | | 566.3 |
| 331.9 | 1083.3 | 615.3 | 614.9 | 213.4 | 566.3 | |

of the agricultural sectors in an economy is not necessarily the dominant factor influencing climate change impacts.

## Agricultural Shocks

Climate change can affect crop yields in a number of ways: through changes in temperature, precipitation, soil moisture and soil fertility, through changes in the length of the growing season and through an increased probability of extreme climatic conditions (Parry, 1990). Three of the most widely used global climate models (GCMs), which have been developed to simulate the effects of $CO_2$ equivalent doubling, are the Goddard Institute of Space Studies GCM (GISS), the Geophysical Fluid Dynamics Laboratory GCM (GFDL) and the United Kingdom Meteorological Office GCM (UKMO). Of these three GCMs, the UKMO model makes the most negative predictions about the effects of global warming.

With climatic predictions from the GCMs, Rosenzweig and Parry (1993) have used crop modeling techniques to estimate the impact of climate change on average crop yields.[4] For each GCM, Rosenzweig and Parry have created a crop yield database with information on a variety of crops for different countries and regions of the world. Since the effects of climate change on agriculture may vary depending on the response by the sector, Rosenzweig and Parry distinguish three levels of adaptation: none, level one and level two. Level one adaptation includes all farm-level adaptations including some changes in planting date (less than one month), fertilization and application of irrigation. Level two adaptation includes region-wide changes such as investment in infrastructure. Rosenzweig and Parry also distinguish between no $CO_2$ effects and positive $CO_2$ effects. Positive $CO_2$ effects relate to the potential positive benefit to plant growth of increased $CO_2$ in the atmosphere.[5] The data used here are for what Rosenzweig and Parry refer to as the yield effects given level one adaptation and positive $CO_2$ effects.[6]

A number of steps had to be taken to make the Rosenzweig and Parry data applicable to our archetypes. Yield data developed by Rosenzweig and Parry are for a variety of specific crops, such as rice and coffee, and for a number of specific countries and regions, such as Brazil and Central America. Since our archetypes represent a chosen cluster of countries, and cereal and agricultural exports include a number of crops, the yield data had to be aggregated in such a way as to make the crop yield shock applicable to the archetype economy.

The first step in this process is to make the crop-specific data represent production patterns in our archetype. For example, we needed to determine the yield shock to maize for the Latin America archetype. To do this, individual country yield shocks to maize were aggregated using weights equal to the proportion of individual country maize production to total Latin American maize production. This was done for each crop. Details of this aggregation are presented in Appendix B and Table 8.4 provides the results. The results show the predicted individual crop yield effects for the three GCMs and each archetype economy. The yield effects differ not only over the specified GCM, but also significantly by archetype.

*Table 8.4   Yield shocks by climate change scenario by crop (in percentages)*

|  | GISS | | | GFDL | | | UKMO | | |
|---|---|---|---|---|---|---|---|---|---|
|  | Africa | Latin America | Asia | Africa | Latin America | Asia | Africa | Latin America | Asia |
| Food crops: | | | | | | | | | |
| Maize | -23.0 | -19.9 | -33.8 | -25.0 | -18.1 | -24.0 | -29.0 | -25.8 | -20.3 |
| Rice | 0.0 | -15.5 | -12.2 | 0.0 | -8.7 | -2.6 | 0.0 | -25.5 | -11.7 |
| Wheat | -15.0 | -28.7 | -18.5 | -20.0 | -23.9 | -7.5 | -20.0 | -33.9 | -53.8 |
| Coarse grains | -25.0 | -21.4 | -34.1 | -28.0 | -19.1 | -23.6 | -30.0 | -26.9 | -22.1 |
| Soybeans | 8.0 | 11.6 | -8.9 | 10.0 | 10.3 | -0.9 | -2.0 | -7.8 | 9.8 |
| Cash crops: | | | | | | | | | |
| Cotton | -3.0 | -11.6 | -16.8 | -5.0 | -3.1 | 10.8 | -10.0 | -19.1 | -32.5 |
| Tobacco | 0.0 | -10.9 | -10.5 | -1.0 | -2.5 | 0.4 | -8.0 | -19.1 | -6.5 |
| Sugar | -12.0 | -17.4 | -17.8 | -12.0 | -10.0 | -2.3 | -18.0 | -25.6 | -19.0 |
| Oilseeds | -1.0 | -10.1 | -7.8 | -4.0 | -2.2 | 9.1 | -7.0 | -20.2 | -21.3 |
| Coffee | -5.0 | -6.0 | -9.0 | -7.0 | -0.8 | -1.0 | -5.0 | -16.6 | -7.0 |
| Cocoa | 7.0 | 0.0 | 0.0 | 2.0 | 1.0 | 1.0 | -2.0 | -3.0 | -4.0 |
| Tea | -5.0 | -5.7 | -9.0 | -7.0 | -3.7 | -1.0 | -15.0 | -16.7 | -7.0 |
| Bananas | -3.0 | -7.3 | -8.6 | -9.0 | -3.1 | 4.0 | -10.0 | -17.4 | -7.8 |

*Note:*
Climate change scenarios are based on the models of the Goddard Institute for Space Studies (GISS), the General Fluid Dynamics Model (GFDL) and the United Kingdom Meteorological Office (UKMO).

The SAMs contain three agricultural sectors for Asia and Africa, agricultural exports, cereals and livestock, and two for Latin America, agricultural exports and other agriculture (which includes cereals). From the data in Table 8.4, two yield shocks need to be isolated for each archetype and GCM – one for agricultural exports and one for cereals. This is done by weighting the individual crop yield shocks by the relative level of production in the archetype countries. For example, under the GISS, rice in Africa receives a zero shock. Rice, however, is not widely produced in Africa. Therefore, its weight is small and this shock has little effect in the final calculation of the shock to cereal production in Africa. On the other hand, rice in Asia, under GISS, receives a shock of -12.2 percent. Since rice is the most important cereal produced in Asia, its weight is large and this value has a large influence on the final cereal yield shock. In short, it isn't merely the size of yield shock to a crop that is important; the composition of production is equally important.[7] The total food and cash crop shocks for each of the archetypes and GCMs are presented in Table 8.5. Negative yield shocks are systematically larger on food crops than on cash crops. The shocks to both food and cash crops vary a great deal from one archetype to another by virtue of the differing relative importance of various

*Table 8.5   Total yield shocks (percent change)*

| Archetype: | GISS | | GFDL | | UKMO | |
|---|---|---|---|---|---|---|
| | Food | Cash | Food | Cash | Food | Cash |
| Africa | -17.4 | -3.5 | -19.6 | -6.2 | -21.5 | -9.8 |
| Asia | -14.5 | -11.6 | -4.8 | 1.9 | -15.0 | -13.4 |
| Latin America | -13.2 | -10.7 | -10.8 | -4.7 | -22.7 | -19.8 |

crops in domestic production. Shocks are also disparate from one GCM to another, with Asia faring worst according to GISS, Africa according to GFDL and Latin America according to UKMO.

Not only will climate change affect agriculture through country-specific yield changes, but also through changes in world prices. Individual crop price changes to maize, rice, coffee, bananas and so on depend on global changes in production and are important because our archetype economies import food and export cash crops at prevailing world prices.[8] World price changes for each crop are drawn primarily from a study by Reilly et al. (1993) that uses the same Rosenzweig and Parry data used in this study (see Appendix B for details on crop price shock determination). Table 8.6 provides data on price effects for each individual crop. Notice that both negative and positive price shocks are possible. This occurs because global warming may increase total world yields and therefore decrease prices. This could happen if warmer temperatures allowed production of certain crops where previously impossible, particularly in northern countries such as Canada and Russia (Reilly et al., 1993; Chapter 9, this volume). Price shocks tend to be larger for food crops than for cash crops (Table 8.7).

*Table 8.6   World price shocks by crop (percent change)*

| Crop | GISS | GFDL | UKMO |
|---|---|---|---|
| Food crops: | | | |
| Corn | 1.3 | 19.6 | 44.2 |
| Rice | 24.2 | 22.8 | 78.1 |
| Wheat | -21.8 | 2.2 | 49.7 |
| Other coarse grains | -6.7 | 12.8 | 42.4 |
| Soybeans | -20.3 | -7.2 | 28.3 |
| Cash crops: | | | |
| Seed cotton | -22.2 | -14.2 | 26.6 |
| Tobacco | -42.0 | -32.9 | -5.4 |
| Sugar | 14.5 | 20.1 | 78.2 |
| Oilseeds | -22.8 | -12.0 | 23.5 |
| Coffee | 16.7 | 6.8 | 33.8 |
| Cocoa | -12.0 | -4.9 | 8.2 |
| Tea | 24.7 | 5.4 | 24.8 |
| Bananas | 16.1 | 2.0 | 28.4 |

To make the price effects correspond to the archetypes, it is necessary to isolate a general price shock for an aggregate cereal crop and an aggregate cash crop. We proceed by dividing the crops into cereal and cash crops and weighting each crop by its relative value as a net import (see Appendix B for details). Table 8.7 provides the results of this aggregation and gives the price shocks to agricultural exports and cereals for each archetype and each GCM. Several combinations of beneficial and deleterious price shocks prevail – negative shocks to both cash and food crops, a negative shock to food and a positive shock to the cash crops (and vice versa), or two positive shocks. The UKMO consistently predicts positive price effects, essentially arising from the dire consequences of global warming which lead to lower world crop production and consequently, higher world prices. There is considerable variation in price shocks across archetypes, establishing that the effects of climate change will be governed by the relative importance of different crops in exports and imports of each region.

*Table 8.7   World price shocks (percent change)*

| Archetype: | GISS | | GFDL | | UKMO | |
|---|---|---|---|---|---|---|
| | Food | Cash | Food | Cash | Food | Cash |
| Africa | -8.8 | -2.3 | 8.5 | -1.2 | 56.0 | 23.9 |
| Asia | -17.1 | 15.4 | 4.1 | 5.1 | 48.4 | 32.8 |
| Latin America | -8.1 | 10.4 | 8.9 | 2.8 | 46.1 | 31.2 |

All our experiments are based on the price and yield shocks discussed above. The preceding estimations, needless to add, are imperfect. When examining the results that emerge from the simulations, one must keep in mind the various levels of analysis from the GCMs to the determination of price effects, each with their own uncertainties and generalities.

Yet, given the limited information currently available, our general intent is not to generate precise forecasts of the impacts of global warming. Rather, it is to corroborate that climate change will affect different continents and social classes within continents unequally. Our results demonstrate this unambiguously. More importantly, we wish to provide insights into economic forces determining how and why these differential impacts are felt.

## CGE Models

In order to determine the effects of crop yields and price shocks on the archetype economies, a CGE model with a multimarket agricultural sector specification was constructed for each archetype. The models used in this chapter are neoclassical. Agents respond to relative prices as a result of profit maximizing and utility maximizing behavior in determining levels of production and consumption. Markets reconcile endogenous supply and demand decisions with adjustments in relative prices. General equilibrium modeling, which emphasizes linkages between sectors on the demand and supply sides, permits us to trace the effects of agricultural shocks on the socio-economic structure, prices, sectoral structure and macroeconomic makeup of the economy.

The multi-market representation specifies a joint production function for the three agricultural sectors to allow for interaction among sectors on both the product and factor sides. In our model, it includes complementarities and substitutions among agricultural exports, cereals and other agriculture, along with reallocations across sectors of different types of labor (skilled/unskilled or urban/rural). In general, the supply elasticities which encapsulate the joint production function, particularly the own-price elasticities, are lower for Africa than for both Asia and Latin America. Underlying these values is the observation that African agriculture is not as responsive as the other two regions to external changes. The rigidity in African agriculture arises from a variety of institutional factors such as access to credit and the efficiency of marketing channels. All own-price elasticities are positive and all the product cross-price elasticities are negative (indicating that cash crops, food crops and other agriculture are substitutes in production). These cross-price elasticities within the agricultural sector will determine the extent to which economy-wide effects arising from shocks to the cash and food crop sectors can be mitigated by substitutions towards other agricultural products. The response of rural or unskilled labor to changes in the prices of the agricultural goods is greater than the response of urban or skilled labor.

Non-agricultural sectors are represented by a multi-level constant elasticity of substitution (CES) production function for the primary factors and fixed coefficients for the intermediate inputs. The closure rules focus attention on the particular variables that are needed to bring about overall macro-balance. Wage rates for urban labor in Asia, for skilled labor in Africa and Latin America, and for public employees are institutionally determined (which corresponds to the assumption of surplus labor). Unskilled/rural wage rates are, in contrast, flexible. The foreign exchange market is cleared by an endogenous determination of the real exchange rate, with foreign borrowing fixed at the initial level. Total government expenditures are fixed in order to isolate impacts of climate change shocks on the economy in the absence of policy interventions. Investment adjusts to the level of savings in the economy. All commodity markets follow the neoclassical market-clearing price system.

Macroeconomic responses of the archetypes to world price shocks and adverse yield shocks depend substantially on the ability of the economies to offset some of the burden of domestic adjustment by participating in international markets. As Reilly and Hohmann (1993) have argued, trade adjustments may play an important role as a mitigating factor against global warming. Yet the degree to which this occurs is dependent on an individual country's integration into the world market. This degree of integration is captured by the elasticities of substitution between domestic and foreign goods both on the consumption and the production sides. In particular, an increase in the international price of cereals will have relatively small effects on the producer price of food crops if imports are a poor substitute for domestic production, if the share of imports is small or if the elasticity of food supply is large. The consumer price will increase, with the rise in price being greater with lower substitutability in consumption, with lower demand elasticity and with a greater share of imports in total supply.

To distinguish between countries where domestic food crop production is competitive with the cereals they import from those where it is not, we use an index of competitiveness defined as the share of wheat, rice and maize in total domestic food crop production, with a threshold of 25 percent. For the Asian archetype a high degree of substitutability is assumed to characterize the observed high degree of competitiveness between imports and domestic food crops. Hence, we have chosen a value of 30 for the elasticity of substitution between imported and domestic food crops in Asia. Correspondingly, Africa has a low degree of substitutability with an elasticity of 0.3, while Latin America is an intermediate case with an elasticity of 1.2.

# 3   MACROECONOMIC RESPONSES TO CLIMATE CHANGE

The yield and price shocks from climate change have deleterious effects on per capita income levels for all the economies, under all climate change scenarios. This may be seen by the reduction in GDP per capita by 1.6 percent in Asia and 2.5 percent in Latin America (for the GISS simulations). Africa suffers the most, with a 6.5 percent decline in income levels (see Table 8.8). Negative yield shock effects are attenuated to some degree when the world price of the composite agricultural import to an archetype falls (all archetypes are net importers of food) or the world price for agricultural exports rises, or both.

Three main factors account for why Africa responds particularly poorly to climate change. First, with negligible structural change and per capita GDP growth expected until 2050, the archetypal African economy will remain mainly agrarian. Any shocks to the agricultural sector will reverberate in the rest of the economy disproportionately relative to the other archetypes. Second, unlike Asia and Latin America, world prices of African exports are predicted to fall under both the GISS and the GFDL climate change scenarios. According to Reilly et al. (1993) and our own estimations (Appendix B), under the GISS scenario, the world prices of cocoa, tobacco and oilseeds will fall between 12 percent and 43 percent. Tobacco and cocoa constitute over 50 percent of cash crop exports for the 'average' African economy, and thus cash crops on the

*Table 8.8    Macroeconomic and trade responses to climate change shocks (percent change)*

| Change in | GISS | | GFDL | | UKMO | |
|---|---|---|---|---|---|---|
| | Yield and price shocks | Yield shocks only | Yield and price shocks | Yield shocks only | Yield and price shocks | Yield shocks only |
| Africa: | | | | | | |
| GDP per capita | -6.5 | -6.5 | -7.8 | -7.8 | -9.5 | -9.1 |
| Absorption | -6.1 | -6.2 | -7.7 | -7.4 | -7.9 | -8.6 |
| Real exchange rate | -5.3 | -5.4 | -2.7 | -5.0 | -11.0 | -3.7 |
| Value of industrial imports | -6.7 | -6.5 | -8.6 | -8.1 | -6.3 | -9.8 |
| Value of agricultural exports | -8.3 | -8.0 | -10.0 | -10.7 | -13.2 | -13.9 |
| Value of cereal imports | -1.9 | -4.1 | -8.7 | -5.4 | -13.1 | -6.9 |
| Asia: | | | | | | |
| GDP per capita | -1.6 | -2.2 | -0.2 | -0.2 | -3.1 | -2.4 |
| Absorption | -0.5 | -2.0 | 0.0 | -0.2 | -1.6 | -2.2 |
| Real exchange rate | 3.5 | 4.3 | -1.1 | 0.3 | -5.1 | 4.8 |
| Value of industrial imports | -1.7 | -3.4 | 0.4 | -0.3 | 0.2 | -3.7 |
| Value of agricultural exports | -5.6 | -13.5 | 3.9 | 2.4 | -10.4 | -15.6 |
| Value of cereal imports | 242.4 | 95.3 | 25.9 | 38.0 | -39.9 | 96.6 |
| Latin America: | | | | | | |
| GDP per capita | -2.5 | -2.8 | -2.1 | -1.9 | -6.4 | -5.5 |
| Absorption | -2.1 | -2.9 | -2.1 | -2.0 | -6.1 | -5.6 |
| Real exchange rate | 1.0 | 3.5 | 1.8 | 1.9 | 3.5 | 6.5 |
| Value of industrial imports | -2.7 | -5.0 | -2.9 | -3.2 | -5.8 | -9.4 |
| Value of agricultural exports | -12.6 | -16.2 | -8.9 | -9.3 | -23.7 | -29.4 |
| Value of cereal imports | 28.2 | 14.6 | 5.1 | 12.0 | 2.6 | 29.4 |

whole suffer a negative price shock. Finally, consumption of domestic and imported food is characterized by a very low elasticity of substitution in Africa. This food self-sufficiency orientation prevents the economy from taking advantage of lower world food prices by shifting consumption towards imported food.[9] Unfavorable yield shocks to food production must necessarily be attenuated by sectoral shifts in production away from cash crops, livestock and other sectors, towards the food sector.

Interestingly, Asia suffers a relatively smaller decrease in GDP per capita relative to Latin America in response to the climate change shocks under all the climate change scenarios. This is true even in the GISS scenario where yield shocks to Asia are largest. A comparison of the sectoral structure of the two archetypes indicates that agricultural production remains important in Asia (21 percent of GDP per capita) while in Latin America the industrial and services sectors account for more than 83 percent of production. This is a point worth emphasizing. The conventional arguments among critics of policy efforts to slow global warming rely on the expected tendencies for developing economies to be less dependent on agriculture, and hence less vulnerable to climate change (Schelling, 1992). Our analysis suggests that the degree of dependence of an economy on agriculture is important, but an equally relevant consideration is the ability of an economy to adapt or respond to agricultural yield shocks by integrating into the international market.[10]

Asian integration into the world market, as highlighted by its ability to substitute easily between domestic and imported cereal, leads to a lower effect of climate change. Absorption (equal to domestic consumption) is everywhere less affected by the price and yield shocks than GDP.[11] This difference is more pronounced in Asia than in Africa and in Latin America. Domestic food price changes in Asia mirror changes in world prices because of the high substitutability in consumption of imported and domestic food. When world prices fall, as is predicted under the GISS scenario, domestic prices of food also fall. This, accompanied with an increase in food imports, keeps absorption levels high, despite the adverse yield shocks. In contrast, the African economy, with low substitutability, is forced to decrease absorption. Effects in Latin America lie in between those of Africa and Asia.

An appreciation of the real exchange rate reduces further the degree of openness of the African economy. For the GISS case, there is a 5 percent appreciation of the currency in response to a complex of changes but primarily due to a large decline in demand for imports. (The balance of trade is fixed at the base level observed in the initial SAM, and the exchange rate adjusts to equilibrate pressures in demand or supply on the foreign currency market.) The food sector yield shock of −17 percent cannot be compensated by an increase in food imports. In response, the domestic price of food rises. The domestic food price increase induces substitution towards food production. Import demand for food and industry declines, since real incomes of all households decrease, leading to a lower demand for foreign currency. The supply of foreign currency falls as cash crop production decreases, both because productivity falls and in order to allow a shift towards food production. The depreciating effect from lower supply of foreign currency is overwhelmed by the significant decrease in industrial imports, which are much larger in value terms than agricultural exports, causing a net appreciation. Similar reasoning may be applied to explain the change in the real exchange rate under the GFDL and UKMO cases.

In contrast to Africa, both Asia and Latin America respond to the climate change shocks by increasing demand for cereal imports, along with reductions in agricultural exports. Balance of trade equilibrium is achieved by currency depreciation, by 3.5 percent in Asia and 1 percent in Latin America. In the GISS case, both archetypes face adverse yield shocks to food, but favorable price shocks. Since imported food serves as an adequate substitute for domestic food, imports of the now cheaper cereals replace domestic food in consumption and demand for foreign currency rises. For reasons discussed later, nominal and real incomes of all households fall, leading to lower demand for industrial imports. However, the lower demand for foreign currency (from the decrease in industrial imports) is outweighed by the combination of enhanced demand (for food imports) and reduced supply (lower agricultural exports due to the cash crop yield shock). Thus, in net, the currency depreciates.[12]

Our conclusions are fairly robust across the three simulations. In Africa, GDP per capita and absorption decrease under all scenarios. Cereal imports fall by more as the climate change predictions become more pessimistic. Agricultural exports and industrial imports both decrease in value terms and the real exchange rate depreciates. Similarly, Asian GDP per capita, absorption, agricultural exports and industrial imports fall under the GISS and UKMO cases (the GFDL results are different due to the particular combination of favorable shocks to cash crops). Cereal imports rise in all cases. Results in Latin America are generally intermediate between those obtained for the Asian and African archetypes, with cereal imports also rising.

Disparities in the direction of change of variables across scenarios can be explained by looking at the combination of price shocks applied. For instance, in the UKMO case, cereal imports in Asia decrease by 40 percent. The decrease is readily explained by the predicted 48 percent increase in the world price of food under this relatively pessimistic scenario. Once again, the built-in flexibility in consumption in the Asian archetype causes the shock to be borne largely by cereal imports. For the same scenario, imports in Africa decrease only by 13 percent while there is a negligible change in Latin America. In the GFDL scenario, there is a negligible drop in income per capita in Asia while absorption does not change. Focusing on the combination of yield and price shocks elucidates why this may be the case. Yields of cash crops increase by 2 percent (Rosenzweig and Parry predict positive yield shocks to cotton, oilseeds and banana) accompanied with a 5 percent rise in world prices of Asian cash crop exports. The world price of food rises only by 4 percent, and the yield shock is also fairly low relative to other scenarios.

Finally, while aggregate welfare effects may be small (largely due to the high degree of flexibility built into the model), the impact of climate change on the sectoral structure of resource allocation, production and income distribution will be more significant.

# 4   SECTORAL EFFECTS OF CLIMATE CHANGE

Discussions of global warming often emphasize the size of impacts to cereals and other crops or the economy-wide effects of climate change, focusing on the overall loss in GDP. These studies do not consider linkages and transmission mechanisms to the various sectors of the economy. The use of CGE models allows us to examine how shocks to agriculture not only affect the agricultural sectors themselves, but also how these shocks are transmitted through the economy to the non-agricultural sectors. Transmission is a function of the backward and forward linkages in the economy and the flexibility in the reallocation of resources between sectors that occurs as relative prices change.

Agriculture is linked to the rest of the economy in a myriad of ways such as through substitution possibilities between sectors, household income and consumption, industrial inputs in agriculture, and the use of agricultural outputs in food processing. Although the yield and price shocks directly influence only the cereal and agricultural export sectors, all sectors will be affected indirectly through these linkages. These effects will vary across the archetypes depending on the relative size of the different sectors, the substitution possibilities between factors and outputs within the agricultural sectors, and the relationship between agriculture and other sectors.

The agricultural sector is relatively large in Africa, where it comprises 38.1 percent of GDP per capita as opposed to 18 percent and 7.6 percent for Asia and Latin America. Cereal is the predominant agricultural commodity in Africa, representing 45 percent of total agriculture. In Asia, other agriculture (primarily livestock) accounts for over 47 percent of total agriculture. The agricultural export sector is largest in Latin America, comprising 36 percent of all agricultural production, as opposed to 27 and 28 percent for Africa and Asia. However, agricultural exports are particularly important in Africa, where they make up 69 percent of foreign exchange earnings. Imports represent 14 percent and 13 percent of domestic cereal supply in Africa and Latin America, but only 9 percent in Asia. In examining the effects of climate change it is important to note these differences in the archetype economies. Not only will the yield and price shocks differ for each archetype, but the importance of the shocks to the economy will be related to the relative importance of that sector in GDP and in the foreign sector.

The sectoral response within agriculture from the climate change experiments are enumerated in Table 8.9. One can make six general observations from these results. First, total food production is lower in all archetypes and with all GCMs, but it does not decrease by as much as the yield shock. Second, food prices increase (except in Asia in the GISS case). Third, the quantity of agricultural exports decreases (except in Asia in the GFDL case) more than the agricultural exports yield shock, particularly when there is a lower shock to agricultural exports than to cereals. Fourth, the price of agricultural exports increases in Asia and Latin America, but not in Africa. Fifth, in Africa and Asia, both the price and production of other agriculture tends to fall. Finally, the agricultural terms of trade increase in all cases, although little in Asia, moderately in Africa and strongly in Latin America.

Comparison of Tables 8.5 and 8.9 shows that the yield shocks cause food production in the economy to decline, but this decline is less than the yield shocks themselves. For example, under GISS the yield shock to food in Africa is −17.4 percent (Table 8.5) while the decrease in food production is only 12.4

percent (Table 8.9). The decline in yields leads to a decline in food production, causing the price of food to rise. This price rise is particularly pronounced in Africa and in Latin America because the elasticity of substitution between imported and domestic cereals is relatively low. As the price of cereals rises, farmers will devote more of their land and labor to cereal production, thereby mitigating the negative effect on production of the food crop yield decline. In Asia, the price effect is much lower since domestic food supply reductions are easily replaced by imports. In fact, under the GISS, the 17 percent decline in the world price (Table 8.7) leads to a decline in the domestic food price. This contributes to food production falling by more than the yield shock.

Table 8.9 also shows that the shock to cereal yields tends to have the dominant effect on the economy, producing a more significant effect compared to the price shocks or the agricultural exports sector yield shock. The importance

*Table 8.9  Sectoral responses to climate change shocks (percent change)*

|  | GISS | | GFDL | | UKMO | |
|---|---|---|---|---|---|---|
|  | Yield and price shocks | Yield shocks only | Yield and price shocks | Yield shocks only | Yield and price shocks | Yield shocks only |
| **Africa:** | | | | | | |
| Total agricultural production | −9.0 | −8.9 | −10.7 | −10.8 | −12.6 | −12.7 |
| Production of agricultural exports | −8.2 | −7.9 | −9.9 | −10.5 | −13.1 | −1.5 |
| Production of food | −12.4 | −12.4 | −14.4 | −14.3 | −15.7 | −15.9 |
| Production of other agriculture | −4.9 | −5.0 | −6.3 | −6.1 | −7.8 | −7.3 |
| Agricultural terms of trade | 9.1 | 9.6 | 9.7 | 11.0 | 19.4 | 12.0 |
| Price of agricultural exports | −6.0 | −5.1 | −4.0 | −4.8 | 1.3 | −3.5 |
| Price of food | 28.0 | 28.3 | 30.6 | 32.2 | 41.4 | 34.8 |
| Price of other agriculture | −13.0 | −13.0 | −16.7 | −15.7 | −16.4 | −18.5 |
| Price of industry | −6.0 | −6.5 | −6.6 | −7.2 | −12.8 | −7.6 |
| Price of services | −5.3 | −5.5 | −6.0 | −6.4 | −9.9 | −7.0 |
| **Asia:** | | | | | | |
| Total agricultural production | −5.8 | −6.5 | −0.3 | −0.6 | −6.4 | −7.1 |
| Production of agricultural exports | −3.8 | −9.1 | 2.7 | 1.6 | −7.1 | −10.5 |
| Production of food | −19.3 | −13.2 | −3.9 | −4.3 | −8.2 | −13.6 |
| Production of other agriculture | 0.1 | −1.2 | −0.5 | −0.2 | −5.0 | −1.4 |
| Agricultural terms of trade | 0.4 | 4.1 | 1.7 | 0.1 | 21.7 | 4.6 |
| Price of agricultural exports | 19.7 | 7.7 | 2.4 | −0.4 | 25.4 | 8.9 |
| Price of food | −11.1 | 6.2 | 3.4 | 1.4 | 34.1 | 6.6 |
| Price of other agriculture | −1.9 | −0.2 | 0.1 | 0.0 | 0.6 | −0.2 |
| Price of industry | 0.5 | 0.1 | −0.7 | −0.1 | −5.2 | 0.1 |
| Price of services | 0.0 | −1.8 | −0.3 | −0.2 | −4.7 | −2.0 |
| **Latin America:** | | | | | | |
| Total agricultural production | −8.9 | −9.1 | −5.7 | −6.1 | −14.5 | −16.5 |
| Production of agricultural exports | −10.8 | −13.6 | −7.7 | −7.9 | −20.6 | −24.3 |
| Production of food | −7.8 | −6.4 | −4.5 | −5.0 | −10.8 | −11.8 |
| Agricultural terms of trade | 20.2 | 18.8 | 15.9 | 13.4 | 59.8 | 39.9 |
| Price of agricultural exports | 13.7 | 7.2 | 5.8 | 3.7 | 36.8 | 15.5 |
| Price of food | 21.3 | 22.0 | 19.3 | 16.8 | 62.8 | 45.6 |
| Price of industry | −5.5 | −0.3 | −0.3 | −0.2 | −1.1 | −0.6 |
| Price of services | −1.5 | −1.7 | −1.3 | −1.2 | −4.4 | −3.5 |

of yield shocks is most apparent in Africa and Latin America, where adding the price shocks to the yield shocks has little impact on either production or prices. Additionally, when examining each shock in isolation, the cereal yield shock in all cases has the most profound impact. This is because the food sector is larger than the cash crops sector in all countries, and food is important as a consumer and producer good while cash crops tend to be produced solely for external markets. Again, in Asia, the situation is somewhat different because of greater sensitivity to world prices. The effect of the cereal yields shock has the dominant impact on production but not prices. This is particularly evident in GISS and UKMO scenarios with large changes in world food prices (-17 percent under GISS and +48.4 percent under UKMO).

The substitution of inputs towards cereal production must lead to a decline in production elsewhere. This may occur in both the agricultural export and other agriculture sectors and the degree to which it occurs depends on the responsiveness of agriculture as specified by the elasticities in the multi-market. High own- and cross-price elasticities in the multi-market model would suggest a responsive agricultural sector. If agriculture is able to respond effectively to yield shocks by substituting between inputs and between agricultural outputs, then climate change will have less of an aggregate effect. Low own-price elasticities for agriculture in Africa reflect the low responsiveness of African farmers to changes in the market, while relatively high elasticities for Latin America show that farmers are responsive. If labor and land are reallocated from agricultural export and other agriculture toward cereal production, the production of these two commodities will decrease. In many cases, this causes a decrease in the production of agricultural exports that is even greater than the negative yield shock. In Latin America, under GFDL, the yield shock to agricultural exports is -4.7 percent while the decrease in production due to global warming is -7.7 percent. In all cases in Africa, the overall reduction in agricultural export production is greater than the agricultural export shock. There is also a reduction in other agriculture. In Asia, the price effect on cereals is not as strong, so there is less substitution towards cereals and less of an effect on the other agriculture commodities.

Whether substitution towards cereals, in Africa and Asia, is primarily from other agriculture or agricultural exports may depend on the world price shock to agricultural exports. Under the UKMO, in Asia the price shock to agricultural exports is 32.9 percent. In response, farmers substitute towards agricultural export production. So while the shock to agricultural export yields is -13.4 percent, the decrease in production of agricultural exports is only 7.1 percent. The production of other agriculture decreases by 5 percent, suggesting substitution from other agriculture to both food and agricultural export production. So, while there is substitution towards cereal production, the source of the factors of production reallocated to cereals varies depending on relative prices.

It is possible for both price and production of an agricultural commodity to decrease, even for a nontradable good such as other agriculture in Africa (Table 8.9). This occurs because the large rise in the price of food decreases the real income of consumers. This decline in real income reduces demand for all other commodities. In other agriculture in Africa, price falls because this demand side effect dominates the effects of the supply contraction.

While in our model climate change has no direct effect on the non-agricultural sector, there are a number of indirect effects including a demand effect and a substitution effect. The demand effect, as discussed above, is a result of decreased demand due to the lower real incomes of consumers. The cereal yield shocks lead to lower production which increases the price of food substantially, thus lowering real income. With higher expenditures on food, other expenditures must decrease. This lowers demand for all non-agricultural sectors and will also generally reduce the price these sectors receive. This is evident in the lower prices for industry and services for all scenarios except for one (Asia under GISS).

The substitution effect is related to the agricultural terms of trade. In all our simulations, the change in food price, along with the reduction of non-agricultural commodity prices, leads to an increase in the agricultural terms of trade.[13] Firms will then shift production from the non-agricultural sectors to the agricultural sectors, leading to a lower supply of non-agricultural goods.

## 5    INCOME DISTRIBUTION EFFECTS OF CLIMATE CHANGE

Although aggregate deleterious welfare effects (especially when measured in terms of absorption) are not very large, global warming induced-climate change should still be of concern to developing countries. This is because climate change has an uneven impact on incomes of various household classes. In general, households that sell food and cash crops will benefit from warming when the domestic prices of these commodities increase by more than the fall in yield. However, 'producer-consumer' peasant households suffer a loss in real income since they also consume food crops. Linkage effects emanating from the shocks to the food and cash crop sectors also lead to changes in the domestic prices of other sectors such as livestock and industry, and factor prices. The overall social impact will depend on the distribution among household classes of net buyers and net sellers of food and cash crops, and the proportion of income derived from wage payments and agricultural profits. Table 8.10 presents the percentage changes in real incomes of rural and urban households for each archetype under the three climate change scenarios.

In Africa, all household groups lose as a result of global warming. Small and medium farmers experience a loss in real income of between 9 and 13 percent while larger farmers and urban households have approximately half that loss. Incomes of rural households decrease despite the increase in food prices due to the lower prices of livestock and cash crops, and the lower wages for unskilled labor. In addition, small farmers are net buyers of food and they are hurt by rising food prices. Medium farmers are hurt more since a larger percentage of their nominal income is derived from wages and livestock. Income losses for urban households (from lower unskilled labor wages and payments from firms) are counteracted to a large degree by the fall in prices of agricultural processing, industry and services which account for the bulk of their expenditures. The income distribution impacts are similar across the three GCMs. In sum, global warming has negative real income effects on all classes and regressive income distribution effects with richer income groups in both the rural and urban areas suffering relatively less than other classes as the climate change effects get worse (i.e. moving from GISS to UKMO scenarios).

*Table 8.10    Income distribution responses to climate change shock (percent change in real income)*

|  | GISS | | GFDL | | UKMO | |
|---|---|---|---|---|---|---|
|  | Yield and price shocks | Yield shocks only | Yield and price shocks | Yield shocks only | Yield and price shocks | Yield shocks only |
| Africa: | | | | | | |
| Small farmer | -8.7 | -9.2 | -12.1 | -11.1 | -13.4 | -13.0 |
| Medium farmer | -10.1 | -10.2 | -13.0 | -12.2 | -13.1 | -14.2 |
| Large farmer | -4.7 | -4.4 | -5.9 | -5.5 | -3.2 | -6.7 |
| Urban poor | -4.9 | -5.0 | -6.2 | -5.9 | -6.7 | -6.8 |
| Urban rich | -4.0 | -3.9 | -5.3 | -4.8 | -3.6 | -5.8 |
| Asia: | | | | | | |
| Small farmer | 0.5 | -2.2 | -0.4 | -0.2 | -6.0 | -2.4 |
| Medium farmer | -2.1 | -2.6 | -0.2 | -0.3 | -3.1 | -2.8 |
| Large farmer | -2.4 | -3.0 | 2.5 | -0.5 | 19.6 | -3.2 |
| Urban poor | 0.1 | -1.8 | -0.3 | -0.1 | -4.4 | -1.9 |
| Urban rich | -0.1 | -1.3 | -0.1 | -0.1 | -2.6 | -1.5 |
| Latin America: | | | | | | |
| Small farmer | -2.2 | -3.4 | -2.4 | -2.3 | -6.2 | -6.7 |
| Medium farmer | 1.3 | 0.4 | 1.6 | 0.7 | 7.1 | 1.0 |
| Large farmer | 2.6 | 1.8 | 3.1 | 1.8 | 12.2 | 3.8 |
| Urban poor | -2.7 | -3.8 | -2.9 | -2.7 | -8.3 | -7.6 |
| Urban rich | -2.4 | -3.2 | -2.4 | -2.2 | -7.4 | -6.4 |

In contrast to Africa, income distribution changes in Asia are progressive under the GISS scenario. Small farmers and the urban poor gain in real income. The other three household groups suffer income losses, with the large farmers experiencing the most adverse impacts (2.4 percent real income loss). The size of marketed surplus of food is very unequal in Asia. The small farmer group buys most of its food, and medium farmers 74 percent of their food, while larger farmers have a net surplus of food. Thus, when the world price of food falls and is transmitted to the domestic market due to the high degree of substitutability in consumption of domestic and imported food, small farmers gain in real income terms. In the event of severe warming (UKMO predictions), the world price of food rises by 48 percent and domestic prices also rise. Real income effects are regressive. Small farmers and the urban poor take the brunt of income losses whereas larger farmers have a 20 percent real income appreciation.

The Latin American social structure is intermediate between those of Asia and Africa. Small farmers buy 72 percent of their food while both medium and large farmers are net sellers. World price shocks of food, when transmitted to the domestic market in conjunction with yield shocks, result in higher food prices under all three scenarios of warming. Consequently, net sellers of food (medium and large farmers) benefit from higher real incomes. All three rural household groups are also net sellers of the agricultural export crops, whose price rises in response to climate change impacts. The income effect is thus regressive among rural households. In the urban sector, rising food prices depress real incomes, with the urban poor losing more as they have a higher budget share for food.

To summarize, the effects of climate change on income distributions are generally regressive, with the disparity of impacts rising as global warming becomes more severe. All social classes in Africa will be hurt by climate change, which is essentially a productivity shock since world prices are not transmitted to the domestic market. In Asia and Latin America, certain groups may experience real income gains if they allocate a large proportion of their budget to food consumption and the price of food falls (as in the GISS case in Asia), or if they are net sellers of commodities whose prices rise in the domestic market. Net buyers of food will, however, lose if the price of food rises. The impacts are particularly bad for small farmers and the urban poor.

## 6   POLICY IMPLICATIONS

Our results, based on continental archetype CGEs for food importing less developed countries in Africa, Asia and Latin America, predict that global warming will have a negative income effect in all countries under all GCM scenarios. These aggregate effects are relatively small. Per capita GDP in 2050 is estimated to be 0.2 to 9.5 percent lower than it would otherwise be as a result of global warming. The models are, however, constructed not so much to predict the overall magnitude of the income effects of global warming, as to analyze the contrasted impacts of global warming across continents, sectors of economic activity and social groups by sector and income level. These contrasts are indicative of where the impact of global warming will be differentially felt and suggestive of policy interventions to countervail undesirable effects.

The negative GDP per capita effect indicates that global warming will impoverish all less developed countries analyzed compared to a no global warming alternative. However, the magnitude of this impoverishment is much larger in Africa than in Latin America, and larger in Latin America than in Asia. With Africa already the poorest continent, this implies that global warming will contribute to further widening intercontinental income gaps. From a policy standpoint, compensatory interventions will be the most urgently needed in Africa. The reason why Africa is more sensitive to the negative effects of global warming is the large share of agriculture in its economy, low substitution between domestic food consumption and imports, specialization in the production of cash crops whose prices will rise less on the world market and rigid supply response.

Total agricultural production will fall throughout all countries and under all GCM scenarios. There are, however, contrasted patterns across continents that result in large part from the differential impact of the shocks on the real exchange rate and on the domestic prices of food and export crops. In Africa, the real exchange rate appreciates and it is the only continent where the domestic price of export crops falls (GISS and GFDL). In Asia and Latin America, the real exchange rate depreciates and the domestic price of export crops rises. For Africa, this indicates that the cash crops sectors will not fare well and that stress should be placed on import substitution in food production as food prices rise. Policy implications are thus to increase the notoriously low elasticity of supply response through programs of technological change, extension, greater access to credit, sharper definition of property rights and reduction of transactions costs.

For Asia and Latin America, the policy implication is to increase the availability of foreign exchange to meet the cost of rising food imports. Within the agricultural sector this may be accomplished by increasing the production of cash crops in order to take advantage of rising producer prices.[14] With such a measure, access to international markets will play an important role in obtaining food crops and selling cash crops. This will require developed countries to maintain trade policies favorable to cash crop exports.

Cereal imports will fall in Africa but rise in Asia and Latin America. Since Latin America accounts for 54 percent and Asia 27 percent of total cereal imports by countries considered in the three archetype groups, import demand for food will clearly rise, to the benefit of grain exporting countries such as the United States. We should recall, however, that global warming induces global impoverishment in the less developed countries. As a consequence, while cereal import demand rises, the demand for industrial imports shrinks and by more than the expansion of cereal imports. The fall is largest in Africa, where the absolute level of imports is small, and in Latin America where it is large.

Thus, while global warming may be beneficial to U.S. farm export interests, it is globally detrimental to the U.S. economy in terms of aggregate demand for exports and for manufactured goods in particular. This suggests that broad-based compensatory development programs need to be put into place to maintain the level of economic activity of these countries and the dynamic of their demand for U.S. manufactured products.

In only one scenario (GFDL in Asia) does the price of food fall. In this case, poor rural net buyers and the urban poor gain. However, in all other continents and GCM scenarios, the price of food rises, and sometimes quite sharply, especially in Africa which finds little relief in imports due to low substitution in consumption between domestic production and imports. In terms of welfare, it is consequently in Africa that the real income effects are systematically negative across all classes and sharply regressive both within the rural and the urban sectors. In Latin America and Asia (GFDL, UKMO), the rural and urban poor are also hurt by rising food prices and the impact is regressive. These observations suggest the need to be watchful of the welfare effects on the poor of potentially sharp increases in food prices. Required are either development programs to correspondingly raise the income level of the rural and urban poor, or compensatory food aid to shelter them from rising food prices.

While aggregate incomes will systematically fall, not all social groups will lose. Changes in agricultural prices within a country will affect income groups differentially depending on whether they are net buyers or sellers of the commodity. Rising prices for food crops (GFDL and UKMO) and cash crops (all GCMs) benefit large farmers in Asia and medium and large farmers in Latin America. This suggests the possibility of some taxation of gainers, particularly in Latin America, to compensate losers. However, because the urban economies in Latin America are large, these tax revenues, obtained for instance through a progressive land tax, would still be far insufficient to compensate all the losers. Compensatory development interventions to stimulate incomes and shift the economy further away from agriculture would still be needed.

We conclude by recalling that these intercontinental, intersectoral and intersocial group scenarios are as tentative as the geographical and commodity-specific information derived from the GCMs. The results presented here are consequently highly tentative. They are, however, useful in suggesting problems that are likely to emerge as a consequence of global warming. Among those, we stress again the global trade shrinkage that will hurt U.S. export interests even if farm interests benefit, the differentially negative impact that will plague Africa, a continent already in distress, and the sharply regressive distribution of the costs of global warming that will hurt the rural and urban poor. It is important to start acknowledging these effects and putting into place compensatory interventions.

# APPENDICES

## Appendix A    Developing the SAMs

The three archetype SAMs were initially developed to reflect the region-specific aggregate structural characteristics in 1985, for low income, food importing countries by Sadoulet et al. (1992). Information on input–output coefficients, distribution of value-added to factor incomes, transfers and consumption shares were drawn primarily from an Ecuadorian SAM for Latin America, from a Kenyan SAM for Africa, and from a Sri Lankan SAM for Asia. These initial values were then adjusted to include information from other countries and reflect an average per capita income for Africa of $243, for Asia $339 and for Latin America $1,587.[15]

Each of the 1985 SAMs was then modified to characterize the expected size and sectoral structure of the archetypal economies in the year 2050. We determined growth rates for each of the economies and used this information to predict GDP per capita levels (size) in the future. In order to adjust the structural characteristics of the archetypes in response to higher income levels, we used information from cross-sectional analysis of *inter alia* the trends in the composition of activities, household expenditures, labor income, exports and imports with increase in GDP per capita (Chenery and Syrquin, 1975).

### Estimation of GDP per capita in 2050

The Intergovernmental Panel for Climate Change (IPCC) projects income per capita growth for less developed countries of 1.6 percent for the present until 2000, 1.3 percent for 2001 to 2025 and 1.5 percent for 2026 to 2050 (Cline, 1992). These projections are for all developing countries, including many countries not represented in our archetypes, and do not reflect differential growth rates for the archetypes we have constructed. It is expected that the growth rates in Africa, Asia and Latin America will not be the same. In order to determine appropriate growth rates for each archetype we need to compare the archetype economy growth rates – that is, the growth rates of the countries it represents – with the growth that has occurred in all developing countries. Once a relationship between these is established, the IPCC projections can be used as a base to determine the growth rates of the archetypes.

We used data on GDP per capita growth for less developed countries for 1961 to 1990 (World Bank tables). Using this World Bank data for all developing economies, with weighting by economy size, it was determined that the average GDP per capita growth for all developing economies over the period from 1961 to 1990 was 2.7 percent. With the data from the countries represented in each archetype the growth in per capita GDP, between 1961 and 1990, was found to be -0.05 for the African archetype, 2.9 percent for the Asian archetype and 1.9 percent for the Latin American archetype. The Asian countries did better than average, the Latin American slightly worse and the

African countries did not improve in GDP per capita. While Africa did experience growth in GDP over this period, it was outweighed by population growth. Using the relationship between the growth of all developing countries and the calculated growth for each archetype, along with the IPCC projections, growth rates for each archetype were determined. Table 8.A.1 provides the results for this calculation.

*Table 8.A.1   Growth rates and GDP per capita*

| Archetype | 1986–2000 | 2001–2025 | 2025–2050 | GDP/capita in 1985 ($1985) | GDP/capita in 2050 ($1985) |
|---|---|---|---|---|---|
| | | (percent annual growth) | | | |
| Africa | −0.03 | −0.03 | −0.03 | 243 | 243 |
| Asia | 1.68 | 1.36 | 1.57 | 339 | 901 |
| Latin America | 1.12 | 0.92 | 1.05 | 1,587 | 3,047 |

Since Africa is found to have negligible growth per capita over this period, its GDP per capita is expected to remain at $243 in 2050. The Asian archetype is expected to grow from a GDP per capita of $339 to $901, and the Latin American archetype expects GDP per capita to grow from $1,587 to $3,047 (all monetary values are in 1985 dollars).

### Determining the structure of future economies

In our methodology simply increasing the size of the economy in GDP/capita terms has no effect on the outcome of the experiments.[16] What matters is how the structure of the economy is altered. Chenery and Syrquin (1975) develop 'normal patterns of growth' that provide insight into the relationship between GDP per capita and the structural characteristics of an economy. Their analysis characterizes the general trends expected as countries grow. Using this information, and our initial 1985 SAMs, we can approximate the structure of the archetype economies for 2050. Some of Chenery and Syrquin's general trends may be summarized as follows (these may be viewed as occurring with growth in per capita GDP):

1. Primary production will decrease while industry, service and utility production will increase.
2. Consumption share of food will decrease and consumption share of non-food will increase.
3. Savings and investment as a percentage of per capita expenditures will increase.
4. Population will shift from the rural to urban areas. This means more labor and households will be living in urban areas than previously, thereby increasing relative urban income.

5.  More labor will be allocated to industry and services at the expense of primary production with the greater increase occurring in the service sector.
6.  Both imports and exports as a percentage of GDP will increase and the makeup of exports will shift from primary to industrial products.
7.  The percentage of income spent by households and firms on taxes will increase.

With these factors considered, the SAMs of Asia and Latin America were altered to include the GDP per capita changes and structural effects. These SAMs are presented in Tables 8.2 and 8.3 while the African SAM is presented in Table 8.1. Table 8.A.2 highlights some of the structural changes that were incorporated in the Asian and Latin American SAMs by comparing the 1985 SAMs with the 2050 SAMs.

### SAMs of the country archetypes in 2050

Per capita income levels in 1985 dollars for Africa, Asia and Latin America were computed to be $243, $901 and $3,047 (Table 8.A.1). In Africa, a large share of this income is generated in the agricultural sectors while agriculture is replaced by the industrial sectors in Asia. Less than 8 percent of GDP per capita is generated in the agricultural sectors in Latin America and over 50 percent of the income originates in the services sector (See Table 8.A.3).

The three economies exhibit similar degrees of openness on the export side, with exports equal to 15–19 percent of GDP. In contrast, imports as a percentage of GDP amount to 25 percent in Africa, 26 percent in Asia and 14 percent in Latin America. This leaves Latin America with a small balance of trade surplus, while the other two regions run large trade deficits. Imports comprise 14 percent and 13 percent of the domestic supply of food crops in Africa and Latin America, as opposed to only 9 percent in Asia. However, despite these high import ratios, the non-agricultural imports account for the majority of the total import bills. All the economies have a positive balance of agricultural trade. On the export side, the African countries are highly dependent on agriculture as a source of foreign earnings. Sixty-nine percent of African exports arise from the agricultural sectors. Asia and Latin America have a more diversified structure of exports with agriculture comprising only 25 percent and 23 percent of total exports respectively. These figures suggest that yield shocks in the agricultural export sector in Africa will lead to large pressures on the exchange rate relative to equal shocks in Asia and Latin America.

The social structures of the three archetypes are captured in the household accounts (Table 8.A.4). We consider five household classes: small farmers/landless, medium farmers and large farmers for the rural sector and two classes of urban households. Household income includes agricultural profits, wage income and various transfers from firms, government and remittances from abroad. Africa and Asia have predominantly rural populations with over 57 percent of total household incomes accruing to rural households. Latin

America is relatively more urban, as reflected in the 17 percent share of farmers in total household income.

In the African and Latin American archetypes, labor categories are decomposed between unskilled and skilled while in the Asian context, they are decomposed into urban and rural labor. These dichotomies suggest that non-

*Table 8.A.2   Comparison of present and future SAMs*

| | Asia | | Latin America | | Africa |
|---|---|---|---|---|---|
| | 1985 | 2050 | 1985 | 2050 | 1985 and 2050 |
| **Activities:** | Percentage of total activities | | | | |
| Agriculture | 35.9 | 21.4 | 10.4 | 6.5 | 39.2 |
| Energy/oil | 3.4 | 5.1 | 5.8 | 5.8 | 2.7 |
| Industry | 28.9 | 36.3 | 43.7 | 45.6 | 23.9 |
| Services | 26.3 | 31.7 | 35.3 | 37.4 | 26.1 |
| Administration | 5.5 | 5.5 | 4.6 | 4.7 | 8.2 |
| **Household expenditures:** | Percentage of household expenditures | | | | |
| Food | 47.0 | 28.5 | 7.6 | 4.8 | 28.5 |
| Non-food | 42.9 | 58.3 | 73.1 | 73.3 | 59.8 |
| Savings | 5.9 | 8.9 | 14.2 | 16.2 | 9.9 |
| Taxes | 3.6 | 4.3 | 5.1 | 5.5 | 1.8 |
| **Household labor income:** | Percentage of total labor income | | | | |
| Urban households | 30.2 | 42.7 | 75.7 | 83.4 | 52.5 |
| Rural households | 69.8 | 57.3 | 24.3 | 16.6 | 47.5 |
| **Labor types:[a]** | Percentage of total labor payments | | | | |
| Urban/skilled | 24.5 | 34.4 | 35.8 | 38.8 | 33.8 |
| Rural/unskilled | 58.7 | 47.8 | 64.2 | 61.2 | 38.0 |
| Public | 16.7 | 17.8 | – | – | 28.2 |
| **Labor allocation:** | Percentage of total labor payments | | | | |
| Agriculture | 43.7 | 26.6 | 11.1 | 6.8 | 16.9 |
| Industry/energy | 18.0 | 26.8 | 20.8 | 22.8 | 10.3 |
| Services | 21.5 | 28.7 | 56.5 | 58.9 | 44.6 |
| Administration | 16.6 | 17.8 | 11.6 | 11.5 | 28.2 |
| **Savings/investment:** | Percentage of GDP | | | | |
| Households | 5.3 | 7.2 | 11.3 | 13.0 | 9.0 |
| Firms | 8.0 | 11.4 | 9.5 | 10.0 | 3.3 |
| Total | 13.3 | 18.4 | 20.8 | 23.0 | 12.8 |
| **Trade:** | Percentage of GDP | | | | |
| Imports | 22.2 | 26.3 | 13.2 | 13.5 | 24.8 |
| Exports | 16.2 | 18.7 | 16.4 | 15.6 | 18.3 |
| **Exports:** | Percentage of exports | | | | |
| Agriculture | 53.6 | 37.8 | 32.0 | 24.1 | 78.2 |
| Industry | 46.4 | 62.2 | 26.8 | 34.3 | 21.8 |
| Oil | – | – | 41.1 | 41.6 | – |

*Notes:*
a. Urban/rural/public distinction for Asia and skilled/unskilled for Latin America and Africa.

*Table 8.A.3  Regional characteristics of the archetype economies*

|  | Africa | Asia | Latin America |
|---|---|---|---|
| General indicators: | | | |
| GDP/capita in 1985 (1985 $) | 243.0 | 339.0 | 1587.0 |
| GDP/capita in 2050 (1985 $) | 243.0 | 901.0 | 3047.0 |
| Structure of production (% of 2050 GDP): | | | |
| Agriculture | 38.1 | 18.0 | 7.6 |
| Industry | 20.8 | 36.3 | 39.9 |
| Services | 41.1 | 45.7 | 52.5 |
| International trade (% of 2050 GDP): | | | |
| Imports | 24.8 | 26.3 | 13.5 |
| Exports | 18.3 | 18.7 | 15.6 |
| % domestic supply of food from imports | 13.9 | 8.8 | 12.6 |
| % of total exports from agriculture | 69.0 | 24.5 | 23.3 |

agricultural activities are more decentralized in Asia, leading to labor markets which are local within the rural and within the urban areas. In contrast, non-agricultural activities in Africa are highly centralized, implying a lesser geographical separation in wages but a sharp dichotomy by skills due to the low levels of education of a large share of the population.

The African labor market is very thin and most value-added in agriculture is distributed to the households. There are practically no pure landless households, as even the small farmers receive about 65 percent of their income from direct agricultural production. In contrast, there are well-functioning labor markets in Asia and a considerable degree of landlessness. Consequently, we specify that self-employment occurs with an opportunity cost equal to the competitive wage, and income from self-employment has been aggregated with hired labor income. Therefore, the residual value-added represents only the return to fixed factors, which is 5 percent of income for the rural poor in Asia. In contrast, labor provides 58 percent of their income. Sources of income for the rural poor farmers in Latin America are similar to their counterparts in Asia. In Latin America, 70 percent of the income of the rural poor comes from labor payments with agricultural profits accounting for only 7 percent.

In all three archetypes, small farmers get a greater percentage of their income from unskilled labor payments relative to the other two rural households (see Table 8.A.4). Participation on the unskilled labor market is more pronounced in Latin America. In Asia, rural households do not participate in the urban labor market whereas in Africa and Asia, large farmer households get 33 percent and 10 percent of their incomes from skilled labor wages. Aside from fluctuations in nominal skilled/urban and unskilled/rural wages, changes in the price of agricultural exports will affect the three rural income groups disproportionately. Small and medium farmers in Asia and small farmers in Africa do not derive any income from profits originating in the export sector. In contrast, large farmer households in all three countries get over 10 percent of their incomes from profits in the cash crop sector.

*Table 8.A.4   Social characteristics of rural households of the archetype economies*

|  | Africa | Asia | Latin America |
|---|---|---|---|
| Rural household income (%): |  |  |  |
| Share of total households' income | 61.1 | 57.3 | 16.6 |
| Share of poorest group in rural income | 19.2 | 30.3 | 58.0 |
| Share of income of rural poor (%): |  |  |  |
| Share from agricultural profit | 64.5 | 5.3 | 6.6 |
| Share from labor income | 34.0 | 58.2 | 70.4 |
| Share from other sources | 1.5 | 36.6 | 23.1 |
| Share of income from agricultural exports (%): |  |  |  |
| Small farmers/landless | 0.0 | 0.0 | 3.6 |
| Medium farmers | 14.0 | 0.0 | 8.0 |
| Large farmers | 22.2 | 18.0 | 9.9 |
| Share of income from skilled/urban labor (%): |  |  |  |
| Small farmers/landless | 7.0 | 0.0 | 4.8 |
| Medium farmers | 11.4 | 0.0 | 5.2 |
| Large farmers | 33.4 | 0.0 | 10.3 |
| Share of income from unskilled/rural labor (%): |  |  |  |
| Small farmers/landless | 27.0 | 55.9 | 65.6 |
| Medium farmers | 19.1 | 39.7 | 49.4 |
| Large farmers | 17.2 | 19.2 | 36.3 |
| Self-sufficiency in cereals (other agriculture in Latin America) (%): |  |  |  |
| Small farmers/landless | 96.5 | 0.0 | 38.1 |
| Medium farmers | 91.1 | 36.2 | 192.9 |
| Large farmers | 177.8 | 385.7 | 313.5 |
| Self-sufficiency in agricultural exports (%): |  |  |  |
| Small farmers/landless | 0.0 | 0.0 | 566.7 |
| Medium farmers | 0.0 | 0.0 | 1240.0 |
| Large farmers | 0.0 | 1071.4 | 1533.3 |

### Rural households

On the consumption side, African small farmers and medium farmers are fairly self-sufficient in food (97 percent and 91 percent respectively). In Asia, by contrast, the small farmers/landless buy 100 percent of their food and medium farmers buy 74 percent, suggesting a high degree of exposure to increases in consumer prices for food. Inequality in the size of a marketed surplus across rural households is also much greater in Asia than in Africa. This suggests that the effect of an increase in the producer price of food crops will be much less regressive in Africa than in Asia. The Latin American social structure is in between that of Asia and Africa. Small farmers buy 72 percent of their food while both medium and large farmers are net sellers.

Output from the agricultural export sector is not consumed by any of the rural households in Africa while production in Asia and Latin America is divided between the domestic and export market. Poor rural income groups in Asia and Africa devote all their production resources to food crops and other agriculture (primarily livestock). Thus, in general, world price changes in the price of export crops affect only the larger farmers in Africa and in Asia. For Latin America, all three rural groups are net sellers of the export commodity.

## Appendix B    Calculating Yield And Price Shocks

### Yield shock estimation

The data on the effects of climate change on crop yields used in our analysis are from data provided by Rosenzweig and Parry. Using crop modeling techniques, Rosenzweig and Parry have simulated yield effects for a variety of crops over a number of countries and regions. They determined the effect on yields, due to a doubling of carbon-dioxide-equivalent gases, under the climate conditions predicted by three GCMs, the GISS, GFDL and UKMO.

We use the data for what they designate as the yield effects with level one adaptation and the positive benefits of $CO_2$ fertilization. Level one adaptation refers to the effect on yields when farmers adapt by, for example, altering the type of seeds they use. A no adaptation scenario is unlikely since it is expected that farmers will react appropriately to a change in the environment, particularly in the long run. Level two adaptation, where the government actively seeks to offset the effects of global warming, may also be unlikely in the developing country context considering the constraints of developing economies. Although there is some question on the extent of the positive effects from additional atmospheric $CO_2$ (Cline, 1992; Wolfe and Erickson, 1993) we have used the data including $CO_2$ effects to err on the side of underestimating the climatic effects of global warming.

Because we are examining three archetypes representing countries in Africa, Asia and Latin America, and each economy has two crop types, agricultural exports and cereals, six yield shocks must be isolated for each GCM. Our initial data are for a variety of crops and countries so a great deal of aggregating is necessary to make the data applicable to our archetypes.

To develop individual crop yield shocks (e.g. maize, rice, cocoa) for each archetype we first aggregated over the countries represented by the archetype. This was done for each GCM as follows. From the data, a shock was determined for each of the countries represented in the archetype. If data were available for the specific country then those data were used. If data were only available on a regional basis, for a given country the regional data were used. For example, the data for Honduras came from Central American data. Once individual crop yield shocks were determined for each country in the archetype, the individual crop shocks for the archetype were calculated by weighting each specific country shock by its proportion of total production. So the shock to Mexican maize was weighted by the ratio of Mexican maize to total archetype production and added to other countries' weighted yield shocks to create an overall yield shock to maize for the Latin America archetype. Production data were obtained from the

*FAO Production Yearbook.* The results of the individual crop aggregation for each of the three GCM models are shown in Table 8.4.

Five food crops and eight export crops are represented in Table 8.4. To isolate an individual shock, for both agricultural exports and food crops, we aggregated across each category, food and agricultural exports. This was done by weighting the crop yield shocks by their relative value of total production for the represented countries. So maize in Latin America was weighted by the ratio of the value of maize production to the value of total cereal production. Table 8.5 provides the results of this aggregation for each of the three GCMs. These are the yield shocks used in performing the experiments in this chapter.

**Price shock estimation**
As with the yield shocks, six price shocks must be isolated for each GCM to identify the effects of climate change. The price shocks will be for each of the three archetypes, and for the export price of the export crop and import price for the food crop. (The archetypes are designed to represent net food importers.) Reilly et al. (1993) also use data from Rosenzweig and Parry to run the SWOPSIM model to predict world price changes for various crops under the three GCM scenarios. For commodities that are represented in the SWOPSIM model we have used the price shocks generated by the model and presented in the Reilly et al. (1993) study. Unfortunately, the SWOPSIM model does not include all the commodities we have included in our analysis, specifically coffee, cocoa, tea and bananas. For those commodities, since they are not in the SWOPSIM model, we used demand elasticities to calculate price shocks. Given the demand elasticities, we used Rosenzweig and Parry's yield effects and FAO production data to determine the effect of climate change on world production. Using this percentage change in world production, along with world demand elasticities, we were able to calculate individual crop price shocks for bananas, cocoa, coffee and tea. The price shocks for each commodity, from our own calculations and the SWOPSIM model, and for each GCM model are represented in Table 8.6.

In order to determine the specific shocks for the price of the aggregate food crop and the price of the aggregate export crop, we must aggregate over the individual crops in Table 8.6 for each archetype. Each individual crop price shock was weighted by its proportional value of net exports for the archetype countries as a whole – with imports being negative exports. Data for exports and imports were obtained from the *FAO Trade Yearbook.* That is, the total value of all food imports, was determined for the archetype as a whole. Then the individual food crop price shocks were weighted by their relative value of food imports to get an aggregate food price shock. So if maize made up 20 percent of the value for food imports the price shock to maize was weighted by 0.2. The same procedure was repeated for cash crops. The aggregate price shocks for the aggregate food and export crops, for each archetype and GCM, are presented in Table 8.7.

# Appendix C   Structure of the CGE Model

## Overview of the model

The model used in this chapter is a standard neoclassical CGE in which agents respond to relative prices as a result of profit maximizing and utility maximizing behavior in determining levels of production and consumption, and markets reconcile endogenous supply and demand decisions with adjustments in relative prices.

CGE models differ primarily in the choices of closure rules which equilibrate commodity, factor and foreign exchange markets, in rules specified to reconcile the government budget constraint, and in the mechanism used to equilibrate savings and investment levels in the economy. In our model, all commodity markets follow the neoclassical market-clearing price system, in which jointly determined producer and consumer prices vary only by given tax rates. Labor markets have been specified to reflect some regional differences. Africa and Asia each have three categories of labor: public employees, and a division of the remaining workers by residence (urban, rural) in Asia, and by skill in Africa. The two nonpublic categories of labor are imperfect substitutes. We assume that urban labor in Asia and skilled labor in Africa are in surplus and are thus hired at an exogenous real wage. Wages for rural labor in Asia and unskilled labor in Africa are, in contrast, flexible. Public employees receive an exogenous, fixed real wage. In Latin America, labor markets are relatively more integrated, with a categorization of workers by skill only.

The foreign exchange market equilibrates via adjustments of the real exchange rate. With foreign borrowing fixed, and an additional constraint of fixed balance of payments, the balance of trade is pre-specified at a constant level. Pressures to change export or import quantities (and hence, demand and supply of foreign currency) are therefore equilibrated by adjustments in the real exchange rate.

Government earnings comprise revenues raised from indirect taxes, trade taxes and net foreign borrowing. Public outlays consist of non-targeted food subsidies, current expenditures on the services provided by the public sector, investment and some small transfers to households and firms. Government transfers, current expenditures and investment expenditures are fixed. Government deficit is covered by borrowing on the domestic credit market.

Private investment is savings driven. Savings are generated by exogenous constant rates for households and by residual savings from firms. Private savings are equal to net savings available after government borrowing is covered.

The relationship between the rest of the world and the domestic economy is determined, for each sector, by the substitutability between imported and domestic goods on the consumption side and by the substitutability in production for the domestic market and for the international market. Allocations between the domestic and international markets for demand and supply occur in response to the relative prices of foreign goods, themselves defined by international prices, the exchange rate and government policies (taxes, subsidies and tariffs).

The model is homogeneous of degree one in all prices and nominal values. Our numeraire is the global producer price index at its initial level. All nominal values are measured in real terms relative to this price. Fixed wages in this context should be interpreted in terms of production cost. Real incomes are computed with social group-specific consumer price indices which, unlike the global producer price index, include the prices of imported goods, taxes and subsidies. The model solves for a one-period equilibrium and results should be interpreted in comparative static terms.

Our model is different from a standard CGE in the production specification for the agricultural sectors. A joint production function is specified for the agricultural export, cereals and other agriculture sectors following the profit function approach used in multi-market modeling. This approach characterizes the nature of agricultural production at the farm level, in which combinations of crops produced and factors employed are jointly chosen as part of a single income strategy and where a variety of common fixed factors affect the levels of all activities. Non-agricultural sectors, in contrast, are represented by traditional multi-level CES production functions for primary factors and by fixed coefficient functions for intermediate inputs.

**Equations of the model**
The equations of the model and a list of variables are reported in Table 8.C.1. Our model allows for imperfect substitution in consumption and production between domestic and foreign goods. Import and export prices (equations (A.1) and (A.3)) are equal to the world prices $PWM_i$ and $PWE_i$ converted into domestic prices at the exchange rate $ER$ and adjusted for import taxes $tm_i$, export taxes $te_i$ and indirect taxes $td_i$ on domestic sales. A constant trade margin coefficient $mg_i$ is also added to each transaction (hence, included in the price) and the corresponding services will be added (see below) to the demand for the trade sector. Goods $D_i$ sold on the domestic market are combined with imports $M_i$ in a CES aggregation function resulting in the total supply $Q_i$ on the domestic market. The consumer price of this composite good for each sector is thus a CES function of the consumer price of $D_i$ and the import price $PM_i$ (equation (A.2)). Since domestically produced goods $X_i$ are allocated between exports $E_i$ and domestically sold goods $D_i$ within a CET aggregation, the producer price $PX_i$ is a CET function of the export price $PE_i$ and the producer price of goods sold on the domestic market $PD_i$ (equation (A.4)). Equations (A.5) to (A.7) compute the value-added price $PN_i$ received by the producer, the aggregate consumer price index (*CPI*) and an aggregate producer price index (*PINDEX*).

For the non-agricultural sectors, sectoral gross output $X^s_i$ is a CES function of the given capital stock $K_i$ and labor (equation (A.8)). Demand for intermediate use of good $j$ in the production of sector $i$, $N_j$, is determined by a Leontief technology (equation (A.9)). Labor is divided in $L$ imperfect substitute categories corresponding to skill or residence and aggregated in the production function with a Cobb–Douglas (CD) function. Sectoral labor demand by category $L^d_{li}$ is derived from profit maximization by the firms and depends on the net price of output and the vector of wages $w$ (equation (A.10)). For the agricultural sectors, a system of output supply for the three commodities and labor demand for the two categories is derived from the maximization of a generalized Leontief profit function (equations (A.11) and (A.12)). Labor allocation between the three crops is based on proportional adjustment of the initial labor/output ratios (equation (A.13)). For all sectors, total factor productivity is a function of sectoral private investment and total public investment (equation (A.14)).

Labor supply by category $L^s_l$ is assumed to be given in the current period (equation (A.15)). The labor market can be closed in two ways: in the neoclassical closure (equation (A.17)) the wage rate is flexible and adjusts to clear the market. In the Keynesian closure, the wage is exogenous and there is a labor surplus (equations (A.17′) and (A.18)). Labor surplus is determined by endogenously generated total labor demand (equation (A.16)).

Each sector's capital income $KINC_i$ is given by value-added net of labor payments (equation (A.19)). A firm's net income $Y_i$ is equal to its net capital income plus government transfers (equation (A.20)). Their disposable income $YD_i$ is income net of taxes and payments to the rest of the world (equation (A.21)). Household $h$ receives income (equation (A.22)) from labor of each category $l$ (in proportion $\alpha_{hl}$ to its ownership share in the category), distributed profit from each sector $i$ (in proportion $\alpha_{hi}$ to its ownership in the sector), transfers from different firms and government transfers. Their disposable income $YD_h$ is income net of taxes and transfers abroad (equation (A.23)). Government revenue consists of direct taxes on firms' profits and households' income, import tariffs and export taxes, indirect taxes on domestic sales and foreign transfers (equation (A.24)).

The government budget constraint (equation (A.27)) states that revenues less expenditures on consumption and investment, subsidies, transfers to firms, household and rest of the world is equal to the budget deficit. The budgetary rule maintains investment (equation (A.26)) and consumption expenditures fixed while the deficit adjusts in response to changing revenues. Sectoral allocations of government commodity demand are given by fixed coefficients (equation (A.25)).

Households' consumption demand for goods is a function of their disposable income, savings and the vector of consumer prices. A linear expenditure system (LES) is specified to derive household demands subject to a budget constraint (equation (A.28)). Savings behavior is given by a fixed savings rate, with savings proportional to disposable income (equation (A.37)).

Demand for goods for investment purposes is derived from private sectoral and public investment demands through the matrix of coefficients $g_{ij}$ and $g_{ig}$ that specifies the composition of investment goods in each sector. Total demand for investment is $Z_i$ (equation (A.29)).

*Table 8.C.1   Equations of the general equilibrium models*

### Price system

$$PM_i = \overline{PWM}_i ER(1 + tm_i + td_i + mg_i) \tag{A.1}$$

$$P_i(1 + sub_i) = CES(PD_i(1 + td_i + mg_i)PM_i) \tag{A.2}$$

$$PE_i(1 + te_i + mg_i) = \overline{PWE}_i ER \tag{A.3}$$

$$PX_i = CET(PD_i, PE_i) \tag{A.4}$$

$$PN_i = PX_i - \sum_j a_{ji} P_j \tag{A.5}$$

$$CPI = \sum_i v_i P_i \tag{A.6}$$

$$PINDEX = \sum_i \mu_i PX_i \tag{A.7}$$

### Production

$$X_i^s = a_i CES\left(\overline{K}_i, CD\left(L_{li}^d\right)\right), i \in NAg \tag{A.8}$$

$$N_{ji} = a_{ji} X_i^s, \; i \in NAg \tag{A.9}$$

$$L_{li}^d = l_{li}(PN_i, w), \; i \in NAg \tag{A.10}$$

$$X_i^s = a_i GLT\left(PX_j, / PX_i, w_l / PX_i, \overline{K}_A\right), i, j \in Ag \tag{A.11}$$

$$L_{LA}^d = GLT\left(PX_j / w_l, w_k, \overline{K}_A\right) \tag{A.12}$$

$$L_{li}^d = L_{LA}^d X_i^s \lambda_i / \left(\sum_j \lambda_j X_j^s\right), i, j \in Ag \tag{A.13}$$

$$a_i = a_{io} I_g^{\varepsilon g_i} I_i^{\varepsilon p_i} \tag{A.14}$$

### Labor market

$$L_l^s = \overline{L}_l^s \tag{A.15}$$

$$L_l = \sum_i L_{li}^d \tag{A.16}$$

$$L_i = L_l^s \; \text{full employment} \tag{A.17}$$

$$or \quad w_l = \overline{w}_l \; \text{fixed wage} \tag{A.17'}$$

$$U_l = L_l^s - L_l \tag{A.18}$$

*Institutions income*

$$KINC_i = PN_i X_i^s - \sum_l w_l L_{li}^d \tag{A.19}$$

$$Y_i = \alpha_{ii} KINC_i + PINDEX\, T_{ig} \tag{A.20}$$

$$YD_i = (1 - t_i)Y_i - ER\, T_{wi} \tag{A.21}$$

$$Y_h = \sum_l \alpha_{hl} w_l L_l + \sum_i \alpha_{hi} KINC_i + \sum_i \theta_{hi} YD_i + PINDEX\, T_{hg} \tag{A.22}$$

$$YD_h = (1 - t_h)Y_h - ER\, T_{wh} \tag{A.23}$$

$$Y_g = \sum_i t_i Y_i + \sum_h t_h Y_h + \sum_i tm_i\, ER\, \overline{PWM}_i M_i + \sum_i te_i\, PE_i E_i$$
$$+ \sum_i td_i \left( PD_i D_i^d + \overline{PW}_i ERM_i \right) + ER\overline{FF} \tag{A.24}$$

*Government budget*

$$C_{gi} = gcons_i k_g CG_o \tag{A.25}$$

$$I_g = k_g GI_o \tag{A.26}$$

$$Y_g - \sum_i P_i C_{gi} - \sum_i P_i \gamma_{ig} I_g - \sum_i sub_i P_i Q_i$$
$$- PINDEX \left( \sum_h T_{hg} + \sum_i T_{ig} \right) - ER\, T_{wg} = \overline{S}_g \tag{A.27}$$

*Product demand*

$$C_{hi} = LES\big((1 - s_h)YD_h, P\big)$$

*subject to the household budget constraint:* $\tag{A.28}$

$$\sum_i P_i C_{hi} \equiv (1 - S_h)YD_h$$

$$Z_i = \sum_j \gamma_{ij} I_j + \gamma_{ig} I_g \tag{A.29}$$

*Table 8.C.1 (continued)*

$$Q_i = \sum_h C_{hi} + C_{gi} + Z_i + \sum_j N_{ij} \tag{A.30}$$

$$Q_i = CES\left(D_i^d, M_i\right) \tag{A.31}$$

$$\frac{M_i}{D_i^d} = CES^*\left[\frac{PM_i}{PD_i\left(1 + td_i + mg_i\right)}\right] \tag{A.32}$$

$$X_i^s = CET\left(D_i^s, E_i\right) \tag{A.33}$$

$$\frac{E_i}{D_i^s} = CET^*\left(\frac{PE_i}{PD_i}\right) \tag{A.34}$$

$$MG = \sum_i mg_i\left(\overline{PWM_i}\ ER\ M_i + PE_i E_i + PD_i D_i^d\right) \tag{A.35}$$

$$D_i^s = D_i^d \qquad\qquad i \neq trade\ sector$$

$$D_i^s = D_i^d + \frac{MG}{P_i} \qquad i = trade\ sector \tag{A.36}$$

### Savings and investment

$$S_h = s_h YD_h \tag{A.37}$$

$$S_i = \left(1 - \sum_h \theta_{hi}\right) YD_i \tag{A.38}$$

$$I_i = kinv_i\,INV \tag{A.39}$$

$$\sum_{ij} P_j \gamma_{ji} I_i = \sum_h S_h + \sum_i S_i + \overline{S}_g \tag{A.40}$$

### Foreign exchange market

$$\sum_i \overline{PWE}_i E_i - \sum_i \overline{PWM}_i M_i - \sum_h T_{wh} - T_{wg} - \sum_i T_{wi} = \overline{FF} \tag{A.41}$$

*Table 8.C.2   Variable definitions for the general equilibrium models*

|  |  |
|---|---|
| | *Endogenous variables* |
| $PM_i$ | Import price in domestic currency |
| $P_i$ | Price of composite good |
| $PD_i$ | Price of domestically produced good for domestic market |
| $PE_i$ | Export price in domestic currency |
| $PX_i, PN_i$ | Average producer price; net producer price |
| $CPI$ | Aggregate consumer price index |
| $a_i$ | Total factor productivity |
| $X_i^s$ | Domestic production |
| $N_{ji}$ | Use of input $j$ in sector $i$ |
| $L_{li}^d$ | Demand of labor of category $l$ in sector $i$ |
| $L_{lA}^d$ | Demand of labor of category $l$ in the agricultural sectors |
| $L_l^s; w_l$ | Supply of labor of category $l$; wage of labor of category $l$ |
| $L_l; U_l$ | Employment/unemployment of labor category $l$ |
| $KINC_i$ | Capital income in sector $i$ |
| $Y_i; YD_i$ | Income and disposable income of firm $i$ |
| $Y_h, YD_h$ | Income and disposable income of household $h$ |
| $Y_g$ | Government revenues |
| $I_g; Inv$ | Public investment; private investment |
| $k_g$ | Adjustment scalar in government budget |
| $C_{gi}; C_{hi}$ | Government consumption; private consumption |
| $Z_i$ | Demand for good $i$ for investment |
| $Q_i$ | Domestic demand for composite good |
| $M_i; E_i$ | Imports; exports |
| $D_i^d; D_i^s$ | Domestic demand for/supply of domestically produced good |
| $MG$ | Trade margin revenues |
| $S_h, S_i$ | Savings of household $h$, of firm $i$ |
| $I_i$ | Investment in sector $i$ |
| $ER$ | Exchange rate |
| | |
| | *Policy variables* |
| $sub_i$ | Subsidy on good $i$ ($\neq 0$ for food only) |
| $T_{hg}$ | Transfer from government to household |
| | |
| | *Exogenous variables and coefficients* |
| $\overline{K}_A$ | Fixed factors in agricultural sectors |
| $\overline{K}_i$ | Capital stock in sector $i$ |

*Table 8.C.2 (continued)*

| | |
|---|---|
| $PWM_i, PWE_i$ | World price of imported and exported good $i$ |
| $\overline{FF}$ | Foreign borrowing |
| $\overline{S}_g$ | Government savings (deficit if negative) |
| $T_{ig}$ | Transfer from government to firm $i$ |
| $T_{wi}, T_{wh}, T_{wg}$ | Transfer from firm $i$, household $h$ and government to rest of world |
| $te_i$, $tm_i$ | Export and import tax rates on good $i$ |
| $mg_i$ | Trade margin on good $i$ |
| $td_i$ | Indirect tax rate on good $i$ |
| $t_i$, $t_h$ | Tax rate on income of firm $i$, household $h$ |
| $a_{ij}$ | Input–output coefficient |
| $\gamma_{ig}, \gamma_{ij}$ | Share of good $i$ in government and sector $j$ investment |
| $v_i, \mu_i$ | Weights in price indices |
| $\alpha_{hl}, \alpha_{hi}; \alpha_{ii}$ | Ownership share of household $h$ in labor $l$, capital of sector $i$; share of firm $i$ in capital of sector $i$ |
| $gcons_i$ | Share of good $i$ in government consumption |
| $CG_o, CI_o$ | Initial values of government consumption and investment |
| $kinv_i$ | Share of sector $i$ in private investment |

*Functions*

| | |
|---|---|
| CES | Constant elasticity of substitution function |
| CET | Constant elasticity of transformation function |
| CES* | Derived relation from cost minimization in a CES |
| CET* | Derived relation from revenue maximization in a CET |
| CD; GLT | Cobb–Douglas function; generalized Leontief function |

*Indices and sets*

| | |
|---|---|
| $i, j$ | Index for activities/commodities, $i, j \in J$ |
| $l, h$ | Index for labor categories, $l \in L$ and households, $h \in H$ |
| $Ag$ | Set of agricultural activities, $Ag \subset J$ |
| $NAg$ | Set of non-agricultural activities, $NAg \subset J$ |

*Numeraire*

| | |
|---|---|
| $PINDEX$ | Aggregate producer price |

Total demand for goods $Q_i$ (equation (A.30)) is shared between imports and domestically produced goods depending on the price of the imported good relative to the domestic good (equations (A.31) and (A.32)). The supply of goods $X_i^s$ is allocated for sale on the export and domestic markets depending on the relative prices (equations (A.33) and (A.34)). Equation (A.35) defines the revenues from the trade margin, which are considered to be a source of demand for the trade sector output. Equilibrium between demand and supply in the goods market is imposed in equation (A.36).

Total private savings consists of household savings (equation (A.37)) and firm savings (equation (A.38)). Private investment is determined by the amount of funds available from savings, after the necessary funds for financing government borrowing have been subtracted, and investment is allocated among sectors in fixed proportions (equations (A.39) and (A.40)).

Equilibrium on the foreign exchange market is achieved by changes in the real exchange rate, such that the (fixed) balance of trade less transfers abroad made by households, government and firms, is equal to capital inflow (equation (A.41)).

### Calibration of the model

*Initial quantities and prices, and share parameters*    Measurement units for labor categories are chosen such that all wages are initially equal to unity. Similarly, measurement units for the domestic commodities $D_i$, imports $M_i$ and exports $E_i$ are chosen such that consumer prices $P_i$ and $PM_i$, the world price $PWE_i$ and the exchange rate $ER$ equal one in the base year.

With these normalization rules, all initial quantities and other prices can be computed, rendering the parameters that are directly computed from these values a matter of simple algebra. Indirect tax rates $td_i$, tariff rates $tm_i$, exports tax rates $te_i$ and trade margins $mg_i$ are jointly determined with the quantities transacted, from the tax collection, trade margins and nominal transaction flows recorded in the original SAMs. Other initial quantities such as labor–output ratios in the agricultural sectors, distributional shares of labor income, capital income and firms' income, sectoral distribution of government consumption and investment, and various transfers simply reflect the values observed in the base data. Input–output coefficients $(a_{ij})$ are computed from observed payments to the sectors. Weights $m_i$ and $n_i$ used in the price indices are the sectoral shares in total domestic production and household consumption, respectively. The distribution of private investment by sector is assumed to be constant. Thus, relative changes in sectoral private investment are all equal to the relative change of aggregate private investment.

*Parameters of the generalized Leontief profit function in agriculture*    Output supplies for the three agricultural products and factor demands for the two labor categories are derived from profit maximization of a generalized Leontief profit function. In calibrating the model, two difficulties are encountered. None of the consistent systems of output supply and factor demands (i.e. those which obey symmetry and homogeneity constraints to be compatible with an underlying profit function) exhibit constant elasticities over all values of production and factor use. The second problem is that whatever set of elasticities we can draw from the literature will usually not be a consistent set. Calibration of the model thus consists of finding parameters that give a consistent set of elasticities for the initial production structure represented in the SAM and that simultaneously reproduces as closely as possible a first guess on elasticities.

First guesses for supply and demand elasticities were mostly derived from the catalog of elasticities developed by Sullivan et al. (1989) for different regions of the world. These elasticities were then forced to satisfy the additivity and symmetry constraints of a full system by using an algorithm to minimize the distance to the base values while maintaining unchanged the base values for the direct price elasticities (in simpler terms, only cross-price elasticities were adjusted). The consistent set of elasticities are of the same order of magnitudes as our initial guesses, and are reported in Table 8.C.3.

For Asia, the product elasticities were computed from the figures suggested for Other South Asia, Indonesia, the Philippines and Other East Asia in Sullivan et al. (1989). Since direct price elasticities across these regions were fairly similar, averages were used. Livestock elasticities are reported only for the Philippines and Other East Asia. In both cases, the cross-price elasticity with

*Table 8.C.3   Elasticities of output supply and factor demand for the agricultural sector*

|  | Agricultural exports | Food crops | Other agriculture | Unskilled labor | Skilled labor |
|---|---|---|---|---|---|
| **African archetype:** |  |  |  |  |  |
| Agricultural exports | 0.30 | −0.16 | −0.10 | −0.03 | 0.00 |
| Food crops | −0.10 | 0.20 | −0.07 | −0.03 | 0.00 |
| Other agriculture | −0.10 | −0.10 | 0.20 | 0.00 | 0.00 |
| Unskilled labor | 0.12 | 0.14 | 0.01 | −0.30 | 0.02 |
| Skilled labor | 0.01 | 0.05 | 0.00 | 0.15 | −0.20 |
| **Asian archetype:** | Agricultural exports | Food crops | Other agriculture | Rural labor | Urban labor |
| Agricultural exports | 0.45 | −0.11 | −0.09 | −0.27 | 0.00 |
| Food crops | −0.08 | 0.35 | −0.22 | −0.06 | 0.00 |
| Other agriculture | −0.05 | −0.15 | 0.40 | −0.19 | −0.01 |
| Rural labor | 0.17 | 0.05 | 0.26 | −0.50 | 0.01 |
| Urban labor | 0.02 | 0.02 | 0.19 | 0.17 | −0.40 |
| **Latin American archetype:** | Agricultural exports | Food crops | Other agriculture | Rural labor | Urban labor |
| Agricultural exports | 0.50 | −0.35 | − | −0.14 | −0.01 |
| Food crops | −0.20 | 0.45 | − | −0.24 | −0.01 |
| Rural labor | 0.15 | 0.42 | − | −0.60 | 0.03 |
| Urban labor | 0.09 | 0.15 | − | 0.26 | −0.50 |

respect to cereals is approximately $-1$, while cross-price elasticities with respect to cash crops are not provided. The latter were assumed to be small. Cross-price elasticities of cash crops with respect to cereals prices are also reported for the Philippines and Other East Asia. These are $-0.15$ and $-0.1$.

Elasticities of rural labor with respect to crop prices were those estimated for India by Quizon and Binswanger (1986). The demand for urban labor is sufficiently small that the parameters have no significant effect on the model results. Having no information, we use a slightly lower direct elasticity and assume that most of the indirect effects would come from its substitutability with the rural labor force.

For Africa, the available information is sparse. There are some elasticities in Sullivan et al. (1989) for Nigeria and Other Sub-Saharan Africa. However, neither livestock nor any of the root crops that constitute a large share of food production are reported. Direct price responses for cereals and cash crops are of the same order of magnitude as the Asian average. Thus, we choose the same elasticities with respect to the cash crop prices, and we assume lower values of direct price elasticities for food crops, livestock and labor, drawing from the common understanding that markets are less developed in this continent. Correspondingly, cross-price elasticities have to be lowered relative to Asia.

*Other elasticities (see Sadoulet et al., (1992) for details)*    Tables 8.C.4 and 8.C.5 list the parameters that are needed beyond the data collected in the SAM for the archetypes. For the consumption elasticities for the Latin American archetype, we use the econometric estimates obtained by Kouwenaar (1988). Production elasticities were also econometrically estimated by Kouwenaar. However, their values are by all measures extremely low, much below the range of elasticities usually used in CGE models, reflecting a very rigid economy. We thus decided to pursue the analysis with a more neutral assumption of medium-to-low elasticities between 0.7 and 0.95.

Tables 8.C.4 and 8.C.5 also show the parameters for the African and Asian models. The demand system is an LES, for which the parameters are derived from the observed shares of consumption (in the SAM) and from estimated income elasticities by income class. For the four aggregation functions (CES for labor categories in the non-agricultural sectors, for capital and labor in the non-agricultural supply functions, for imports and domestic commodities in consumption, and a CET aggregation of exports and domestic sales in domestic production), the share parameters are derived from the observed initial values once the elasticities of substitution have been determined. The elasticities are derived as follows.

First, on the supply side, all non-agricultural production functions are CES in capital and labor, with a medium value of substitutability between these factors equal to 0.8. Labor is a CES aggregate of the two labor categories with a low value of substitutability equal to 0.2.

Second, for the aggregation elasticities between imports and domestic products in consumption, a relatively low value of substitutability (elasticity of 0.5)

*Table 8.C.4    Elasticities and parameters used in the models*

| | Urban households | | Rural households (farm size) | | |
|---|---|---|---|---|---|
| | Poor | Rich | Small | Medium | Large |
| **Latin America:** | | | | | |
| **Income elasticities** | | | | | |
| Agricultural exports | 0.88 | 0.83 | 0.88 | 0.87 | 0.84 |
| Other agriculture | 0.77 | 0.73 | 0.88 | 0.87 | 0.84 |
| Oil | 0.78 | 0.74 | 0.97 | 0.95 | 0.98 |
| Industrial goods | 0.92 | 0.92 | 0.98 | 0.99 | 0.99 |
| Services | 1.22 | 1.18 | 1.12 | 1.10 | 1.10 |
| Frisch parameter | −4.00 | −2.00 | −4.00 | −3.00 | −2.00 |
| **Asia and Africa:** | | | | | |
| **Income elasticities** | | | | | |
| Food crops | 1.27 | 0.56 | 1.13 | 1.13 | 0.65 |
| Other agriculture | 1.21 | 0.98 | 1.04 | 1.04 | 0.89 |
| Agricultural processing | 1.08 | 0.97 | 1.01 | 1.01 | 0.99 |
| Industrial goods | 0.76 | 1.11 | 0.79 | 0.79 | 1.13 |
| Services | 0.78 | 1.15 | 0.96 | 0.96 | 1.21 |
| Frisch parameter | −4.00 | −2.00 | −4.00 | −3.00 | −2.00 |

*Table 8.C.5    Sectoral elasticities and parameters used in the models*

| | Substitution elasticity in import CES | Substitution elasticity in export CET | Capital–labor substitution elasticity in production CES | Labor aggregation parameter |
|---|---|---|---|---|
| **Latin America:** | – | | | |
| Agricultural exports | 0.6 | 0.8 | – | 0.2 |
| Food crops | 1.2 | – | – | 0.2 |
| Food processing | 0.8 | 0.9 | – | 0.2 |
| Oil/energy | 0.9 | 0.9 | 0.8 | 0.2 |
| Industry | 0.9 | 0.9 | 0.8 | 0.2 |
| Services | 0.6 | 0.95 | 0.8 | 0.2 |
| Government services | – | – | 0.8 | 0.2 |
| **Asia and Africa:** | | | | |
| Agricultural exports | – | 1.2 | – | 0.2 |
| Food crops | 30 (0.3) | – | – | 0.2 |
| Other agriculture | 3 (0.5) | 0.5 | – | 0.2 |
| Food processing | 0.5 | 0.5 | 0.8 | 0.2 |
| Oil/energy | 0.5 | 0.8 | 0.8 | 0.2 |
| Industry | 0.5 | 0.8 | 0.8 | 0.2 |
| Services | 0.5 | 0.5 | 0.8 | 0.2 |
| Government services | – | – | 0.8 | 0.2 |

*Note:*
Agricultural sectors do not employ CES production function specification. Elasticities for Africa in parentheses when different from Asia.

has been assumed for the non-agricultural products. This reflects an assumption of product differentiation between the domestically produced commodities and the imports of these large aggregates. For the other agriculture sector (predominantly livestock), high substitutability (elasticity of 3) is assumed in Asia. However, with the observed very low share of imports in domestic consumption for Asia, the transmission of an external price increase to domestic price is not very high. For the African archetype, foreign price changes are irrelevant since there are no imports. The elasticity of substitution between imported and domestic food crops, which is key to our analysis, has been calibrated as follows: For the Asian archetype, an almost infinite substitutability (an elasticity of substitution of 30) is chosen to characterize the observed high degree of competitiveness; for the African archetype for which domestically produced food crops are different from the imported cereals, the calibration is based on the relation between these elasticities and the cross-price elasticity of demand for these domestic commodities with respect to the price of imported cereals. Based on Sullivan et al. (1989), these cross-price elasticities are all equal to zero for the Sub-Saharan African countries, indicating that the elasticity of substitution is equal to the direct price elasticity of consumption for the aggregated food crop good. Although these direct price elasticities vary across households, they are close to 0.5 for the larger poor consumer classes. Thus, the elasticity of substitution was set to 0.5 for this archetype. Sensitivity analysis (not reported here) shows that the results are not qualitatively sensitive to the specific choices of these values.

Third, on the export side, levels of elasticities of transformation depend on the homogeneity of the aggregated sectors. But, as we observed on the consumption side, these elasticities are bound to be of medium values. Therefore, a medium-high elasticity of transformation (1.2) is used for the agricultural export sector, a medium-low value (0.8) for the industrial sector, and a lower value (0.5) for the food processing sector, which is dominated by mills that produce for the domestic market.

## NOTES

1. A number of mitigation studies are cited in Dornbusch and Poterba (1993) and OECD (1991). Sonka (1991) provides a good survey of early impact studies. More recent studies of climate change and food security appear and are referenced in recent special issues of *Food Policy* (vol. 19, no. 2, April 1994) and *Global Environmental Change* (vol. 4, no. 1, March 1994).
2. The archetype approach has also been used by Loo and Tower (1990) and by Sadoulet and de Janvry (1992) to analyze impacts of trade liberalization.
3. The 19 impact studies summarized in Table 1 of Sonka (1991) all assume that climate change affects the current economy as do more recent studies (Reilly et al., 1993; Darwin et al. this volume (Chapter 9); Mendelsohn et al., 1994).
4. See Mendelsohn et al. (1994) for a critique of the crop modeling or production function approach.
5. Wolfe and Erickson (1993) note that estimated positive effects of $CO_2$ fertilization are derived from experimental plot studies. In actual field conditions optimum circumstances for

full $CO_2$ benefits are seldom maintained. In developing countries in particular the irrigation and fertilizer requirements needed to achieve $CO_2$ fertilization benefits may not be met. Also see Cline (1992), pp. 89–92 and Kaiser this volume (Chapter 7) for a discussion of the issue.
6. We thank Dr Cynthia Rosenzweig of the Goddard Institute of Space Studies and Professor Martin Parry of Oxford University for providing data for use in this study.
7. Table 8.4 shows that, under GISS, individual food yield shocks in Asia are always worse than individual food shocks in Africa. Yet, the overall shock to food in Africa is worse than Asia. This is a result of the weighting of the different shocks. In Asia, rice, which has a relatively low shock, is weighted heavily, while in Africa coarse grains, which receives a worse shock than Asian rice, is weighted heavily.
8. We assume the archetypes are 'small' in the world markets. Domestic changes in supply and demand of goods will not have an effect on world prices.
9. This corresponds to Reilly et al. (1993) who state, 'Subsistence agricultural systems are most at risk because they cannot avail themselves of the risk pooling value of markets.'
10. Integration into the world food market is at the expense of food security motivations for food self-sufficiency. To the extent that countries will impose self-sufficiency orientation on themselves, aggregate welfare in GDP terms will decrease. Food production could be maintained at high levels at the expense of production in other sectors such as industry.
11. Absorption equals national income plus imports minus exports.
12. Appreciation in Asia under the UKMO and GFDL is explained by the price shock effects. Notice the depreciation which results when only the yield shock is applied. Food imports rise. When the adverse price shocks are included in the simulations, imports decrease. The currency appreciates to equilibrate the excess supply of foreign currency which results from this demand deficiency.
13. The agricultural terms of trade ratio is defined as the ratio of the price of agricultural commodities over the price of non-agricultural commodities.
14. The degree to which an increased emphasis on cash crop production makes sense for Latin America and Asia *as a whole* will depend on the impact of aggregate regional production shifts on world prices of export commodities. While individual countries may face horizontal demand curves, whole regions may well face highly inelastic demand for cash crop exports.
15. The average incomes per capita for the archetypes are weighted averages of the income per capita of the countries represented in the archetype.
16. In CGE models it is the relative magnitudes of variables that matter. Simply multiplying the SAM by a scalar will not alter the results since the relative structure of the economy will not change.

# REFERENCES

Adams, R., Rosenzweig, C., Peart, R., Ritchie, J., McCarl, B., Glyer, J., Curry, R., Jones, J., Boote, K. and Allen, L., Jr (1990), 'Global Climate Change and U.S. Agriculture', *Nature*, **345**, pp. 219–222.
Chenery, H. and Syrquin, M. (1975), *Patterns of Development, 1950–1970*, London: Oxford University Press (for the World Bank).
Chenery, H. and Taylor, L. (1968), 'Development Patterns: Among Countries and Over Time', *Review of Economics and Statistics*, **50**, pp. 391–416.
Chourcri, N. (1982), *Energy and Development in Latin America*, Lexington: Lexington Books.
Cline, W.R. (1992), *The Economics of Global Warming*, Washington, DC: Institute for International Economics.
Crosson, P. (1993), 'Impact of Climate Change on the Agriculture and Economy of Missouri, Iowa, Nebraska and Kansas (MINK) Region', in Kaiser, H. and Drennen, T. (eds), *Agricultural Dimensions of Global Climate Change*, Delray Beach, FL: St. Lucie Press.

de Janvry, A., Sadoulet, E. and Fargeix, A. (1991), *Adjustment and Equity in Ecuador*, Paris: Organization for Economic Cooperation and Development.

de Melo, J. and Robinson, S. (1982), 'Trade Adjustment Policies and Income Distribution in Three Archetype Developing Countries', *Journal of Development Economics*, **10**, pp. 67–92.

Desai, A. (1990a), *Energy in Africa*, New Delhi: Wiley Eastern Limited.

Desai, A. (1990b), *Energy in Latin America*, New Delhi: Wiley Eastern Limited.

Dornbusch, R. and Poterba, J. (1993), *Global Warming: Economic Policy Responses*, Cambridge: MIT Press.

Hoeller, P., Dean, A. and Nicolaisen, J. (1991), 'Macroeconomic Implications of Reducing Greenhouse Emissions: A Survey of Empirical Studies', *OECD Economic Studies No. 16*, pp. 45–79.

Houghton, J., Callander, B. and Varney, S. (eds), *Climate Change 1992, Supplementary Report to the IPCC Scientific Assessment*, Cambridge: Cambridge University Press.

Huang, K. (1991), 'U.S. Demand for Food: A Complete System of Quantity Effects on Prices', *Technical Bulletin No. 1795*, USDA-ERS.

Intergovernmental Panel on Climate Change (1990), *Scientific Assessment of Climate Change*, New York: World Meteorological Association and U.N. Environment Programme.

James, W.E. (1989), *The Energy Economy Link: New Strategies for the Asia-Pacific Region*, New York: Praeger Publishers.

Kaiser, H. and Drennen, T. (1993), *Agricultural Dimensions of Global Climate Change*, Delray Beach, FL: St. Lucie Press.

Kane, S., Reilly, J. and Tobey, J. (1991), *Climate Change: Economic Implications for World Agriculture*, AER-647, USDA-ERS, October 1991.

Kokoski, M. and Smith, V.K. (1987), 'A General Equilibrium Analysis of Partial-Equilibrium Welfare Measures: The Case of Climate Change', *American Economic Review*, **77**, pp. 331–341.

Kouwenaar, A. (1988), 'A Basic Needs Policy Model: A General Equilibrium Analysis with a Special Reference to Ecuador', *Contributions to Economic Analysis Series, No. 175*, Amsterdam: North-Holland.

Loo, T. and Tower, E. (1990), 'Agricultural Liberalization, Welfare, Revenue and Nutrition in Developing Countries', in Golden, I. and Knudsen, O. (eds), *Agricultural Trade Liberalization: Implications for Developing Countries*, Paris: Organization of Economic Development and Cooperation and The World Bank.

Mendelsohn, R., Nordhaus, W. and Shaw, D. (1994), 'The Impact of Global Warming on Agriculture: A Ricardian Analysis', *American Economic Review*, **84**, September, pp. 753–771.

Nordhaus, W. (1991), 'To Slow or Not to Slow: The Economics of the Greenhouse Effect', *Economic Journal*, **101**, pp. 920–937.

O'Keefe, P., Raskin, P. and Bernow, S. (1984), *Energy and Development in Kenya: Opportunities and Constraints*, Stockholm: The Beijer Institute and The Scandinavian Institute of African Studies.

Organization for Economic Cooperation and Development (OECD) (1991), *The Economics of Climate Change: Proceedings of an OECD/IEA Conference*, Paris: OECD.

Parry, M. (1990), *Climate Change and World Agriculture*, London: Earthscan Publications Limited.

Quizon, J. and Binswanger, H. (1986), 'Modeling the Impact of Agricultural Growth and Government Policy on Income Distribution in India', *World Bank Economic Review*, **1**, pp. 103–148.

Reilly, J. and Anderson, M. (1992), *Economic Issues in Global Climate Change.* Boulder, CO: Westview Press Inc.

Reilly, J. and Hohmann, N. (1993), 'Climate Change and Agriculture: The Role of International Trade', *American Economic Review, AEA Papers and Proceedings*, **83**, pp. 306–312.

Reilly, J., Hohmann, N. and Kane, S. (1993), *Climate Change and Agriculture: Global and Regional Effects Using an Economic Model of International Trade*, MIT-CEEPR 93-012WP, MIT Center for Energy and Environmental Policy Research.

Rosenzweig, C. and Iglesias, A. (eds) (1993), *Implications of Climate Change for International Agriculture: Crop Modeling Study*, Washington, DC: Environmental Protection Agency.

Rosenzweig, C. and Parry, M. (1993), 'Potential Impacts of Climate Change on World Food Supply: A Summary of a Recent International Study', in Kaiser, H. and Drennen, T. (eds), *Agricultural Dimensions of Global Climate Change*, Delray Beach, FL: St. Lucie Press.

Rosenzweig, C. and Parry, M. with Fisher, G. and Frohberg, K. (1992), 'Climate Change and World Food Supply: A Preliminary Report', manuscript, May 1992.

Sadoulet, E. and de Janvry, A. (1992), 'Agricultural Trade Liberalization and the Low Income Countries: A General Equilibrium Multimarket Approach', *American Journal of Agricultural Economics*, **74**, pp. 268–280.

Sadoulet, E., Subramanian, S. and de Janvry, A. (1992), 'Adjusting to a Food Price Increase in the Context of Stabilization Policies: An Analysis Using Archetype Financial CGEs for Developing Countries', Working Paper, Department of Agricultural and Resource Economics, University of California at Berkeley, April.

Schelling, T. (1992), 'Some Economics of Global Warming', *American Economic Review*, **82**, pp. 1–14.

Sonka, S. (1991), 'Methodological Guidelines for Assessing the Socio-economic Impacts of Climate Change on Agriculture', in OECD (eds), *Climate Change: Evaluating the Socio-economic Impacts*, Paris: OECD.

Sullivan, J., Wainio, J. and Roningen, V. (1989), *A Database for Trade Liberalization Studies*, Washington, DC: USDA-ERS-Agricultural and Trade Analysis Division.

Tobey, J., Reilly, J. and Kane, S. (1992), 'Economic Implications of Global Climate Change for World Agriculture', *Journal of Agricultural and Resource Economics*, **17**, pp. 195–204.

United Nations, Food and Agriculture Organization (UN–FAO) (1993), *Agriculture: Toward 2010*, Rome: FAO.

Wolfe, D. and Erickson, J. (1993), 'Carbon Dioxide Effects on Plants: Uncertainties and Implications for Modeling Crop Response to Climate Change', in Kaiser, H. and Drennen, T. (eds), *Agricultural Dimensions of Global Climate Change*, Delray Beach, FL: St. Lucie Press.

# 9 Climate Change, World Agriculture and Land Use

## Roy Darwin, Marinos Tsigas, Jan Lewandrowski and Anton Raneses

## 1 INTRODUCTION

Many studies project that the earth's climate will warm by 1.5 to 5.0 °C during the next century. A substantial portion of this warming may occur even if global efforts are taken to reduce emissions of heat-trapping gases. Better estimates of the impacts of climate change on economic and ecological systems are important for determining how aggressive such emissions control activities should be and how best to adapt to unavoidable climate changes.

The agricultural consequences of climate change are two-fold. First, climate change may affect crop and livestock productivity. Second, ensuing economic responses may alter the regional distribution and intensity of farming. This means that, for some regions, (1) the long-term productivity and competitiveness of agriculture may be at risk, (2) farm communities could be disrupted, and (3) environmental conflicts over land and water resources may become increasingly contentious.

A substantial amount of research has now been conducted on the potential impacts of climate change on agricultural productivity (Leemans and Solomon, 1993; Parry, 1990; Parry et al., 1988; Rosenzweig and Iglesias, 1994). A few studies have used climate-induced changes in crop yields to estimate potential global economic impacts (Kane et al., 1991; Reilly et al., 1993; Rosenzweig and Parry, 1994; Rosenzweig et al., 1993). These global studies, however, have generally failed to consider that climate change would affect the availability of agriculturally suitable land, that economic factors drive farm-level adaptations, and that farmers must compete with other economic agents for land and water resources.

This research effort is unique in that it directly links detailed climate projections with land and water resource endowments that are, in turn, integrated within a global economic model. This enables us to simulate how climate change might affect water supplies and the availability of agriculturally suitable land, and to analyze how these impacts might affect total world production of goods and services.

This effort is also unique in modeling the extent to which farmers respond to climate change. Farmer adoption of alternative production systems or expansion (or abandonment) of agricultural lands, is completely simulated within the economic model. This reflects the fact that farmers are likely to consider the economic viability of their responses to climate-induced changes in yield. It avoids the arbitrariness that attends projections of farmer responses that do not explicitly consider economic variables.

Finally, this effort is unique in that impacts on major resource-using sectors (crops, livestock and forestry) are estimated simultaneously. Crop, livestock and forestry sectors often compete for land resources. Failure to jointly consider these sectors' demands for land may implicitly lead to the same land being used over several times so that the impacts of climate change in these sectors would be underestimated. Treating these demands explicitly and simultaneously avoids such problems and enables us to provide quantitative estimates of land use changes. The combination of these unique features enables us to generate comprehensive and economically consistent projections of how climate change might alter the location and intensity of farming.

## 2   PROCEDURES

The methodology employed in this research assumes that (1) changes in climate will directly affect land and water resources and (2) changes in land and water resources will affect economic activity. The economic insight embodied in this approach is that climate change would affect production possibilities associated with land and water resources throughout the world and the resultant shifts in regional production possibilities would alter current patterns of world agricultural output and trade.[1] By explicitly incorporating land and water resources, our framework enables us to simulate climate change's impacts on the availability of land suitable for agriculture and allows economic factors to determine the nature and extent of adaptive responses to climate change by farmers. We also can estimate changes in land use.

**Modeling Framework**

Figure 9.1 presents an overview of our modeling framework. The framework is embedded in the Future Agricultural Resources Model (FARM). FARM is composed of a geographic information system (GIS) and a computable general equilibrium (CGE) economic model. The GIS links climate with production

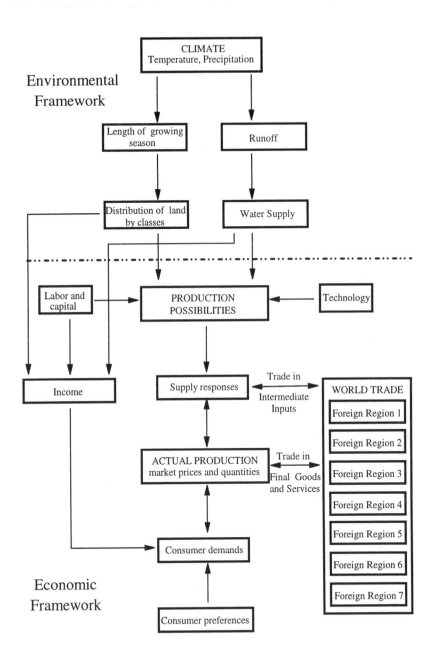

*Figure 9.1    FARM modeling framework*

possibilities in eight regions. The CGE model determines how changes in production possibilities affect production, trade and consumption of 13 commodities.

### Environmental framework

The 'Environmental Framework' portion of Figure 9.1 shows how regional climates are linked with production possibilities in FARM. Climate, which is defined in terms of mean monthly temperature and precipitation, affects production possibilities by determining a region's length of growing season and its water runoff. Length of growing season is defined as the longest continuous period of time in a year that soil temperature and moisture conditions support plant growth. Growing season length is the primary constraint to crop choice and crop productivity within a region. Water runoff is that portion of annual precipitation that is not evapotranspirated back to the atmosphere. Runoff limits a region's water supply, thereby constraining its ability to irrigate crops, generate hydropower and provide drinking water.

Growing season lengths are provided in FARM's GIS. The GIS can be thought of as a grid overlaid on a map of the world. Grid cells have a spatial resolution of 0.5° latitude and longitude (360 rows by 720 columns) and contain information from various global databases on climate and current land use and cover. Two data sets on growing season lengths are derived from current climatic conditions.[2] One data set is computed from monthly temperature and precipitation data (Leemans and Cramer, 1991) using Newhall's (1980) method. The other data set is derived from monthly temperature data only and is used to determine length of growing seasons on irrigated lands. For any GIS grid cell, growing season length can range from 0 to 365 days. To obtain a broader picture of the distribution of growing conditions around the world, we divide the world's land into six classes (Table 9.1). A region's distribution of land classes is a major determinant of its agricultural and silvicultural possibilities. Current distributions of land classes are presented in Table 9.2.

Land classes 1 and 2 (LC 1 and 2) have growing seasons of 100 days or less. LC 1 occurs where cold temperatures limit growing seasons – mainly polar and alpine areas. High latitude regions (e.g. Canada and the former Soviet Union) contain 79.3 percent of the world's stock of LC 1. LC 2 occurs where growing seasons are limited by low precipitation levels – mostly deserts and semi-desert shrublands and grasslands. Africa, Latin America and Western Asia hold 56.1 percent of the world's stock of LC 2. Crop production on LC 1 and rain-fed LC 2 is marginal and restricted to areas where growing seasons approach 100 days. LC 1 and 2 (without irrigation) are limited to one crop per year. LC 2 may be an important crop-producing land class where irrigation extends growing seasons. Almost half of the world's land is either LC 1 or 2. This means that, without irrigation, 50 percent of the world's land is, at best, marginal for crop production due to cold temperatures, limited precipitation, or both.

*Table 9.1    Land class boundaries in the FARM*

| Land class | Length of growing season (days) | Days with soil temperatures above 5 °C | Principal crops and cropping patterns | Sample regions |
|---|---|---|---|---|
| 1 | 0 to 100 | 125 or less | Sparse forage for rough grazing | US: northern Alaska World: Greenland |
| 2 | 0 to 100 | more than 125 | Millets, pulses, spare forage for rough grazing | US: Mojave Desert World: Sahara Desert |
| 3 | 101 to 165 | | Short season grains, forage: one crop per year | US: Palouse, western Nebraska World: southern Manitoba |
| 4 | 166 to 250 | | Maize: some double cropping possible | US: Corn Belt World: northern European Union |
| 5 | 251 to 300 | | Cotton, rice: double cropping common | US: Tennessee World: Zambia, non-penisular Thailand |
| 6 | 301 to 365 | | Rubber, sugar cane: double cropping common | US: Florida and southeast coast World: Indonesia |

*Table 9.2    Current land class endowments by region (million hectares)*

| Land class | Region | | | | | | | | |
|---|---|---|---|---|---|---|---|---|---|
| | US | Canada | EU | Japan | OEA[a] | SEA[b] | ANZ[c] | ROW[d] | Total |
| 1 | 120.45 | 504.10 | 3.10 | 0.22 | 225.57 | 0.00 | 3.55 | 1413.10 | 2270.09 |
| 2 | 300.97 | 79.11 | 7.07 | 0.00 | 308.40 | 0.00 | 506.47 | 2985.81 | 4187.82 |
| 3 | 116.21 | 309.72 | 33.27 | 9.62 | 121.71 | 1.34 | 91.13 | 1014.91 | 1697.91 |
| 4 | 198.80 | 29.18 | 117.63 | 18.62 | 87.56 | 4.36 | 91.48 | 785.08 | 1332.71 |
| 5 | 68.96 | 0.00 | 45.07 | 7.64 | 69.31 | 39.80 | 29.04 | 748.14 | 1007.95 |
| 6 | 111.26 | 0.00 | 16.69 | 1.54 | 130.07 | 249.48 | 69.58 | 2003.79 | 2582.42 |
| Total | 916.66 | 922.10 | 222.82 | 37.65 | 942.61 | 294.98 | 791.24 | 8950.83 | 13078.98 |

*Notes:*
a.    Other East Asia (China, Hong Kong, Taiwan and South Korea).
b.    Southeast Asia (Thailand, Indonesia, Philippines and Malaysia).
c.    Australia and New Zealand.
d.    Rest of world.

The other land classes are more suitable for agricultural production. LC 3 has growing seasons of 101 to 165 days; principal crops are wheat, other short season grains and forage. LC 3 is limited to one crop per year. Growing seasons on LC 4 range from 166 to 250 days and are long enough to produce maize. Some double cropping occurs on LC 4. LC 5 has growing seasons of 251 to 300 days; major crops include cotton and rice. Two or more crops per year are common on LC 5. Year round growing seasons characterize LC 6, which is the primary land class for rice, tropical maize, sugar cane and rubber. Two or more crops per year are common on LC 6. LC 6 accounts for 20 percent of all land. Most (87.2 percent) LC 6 land is located in tropical areas of Africa, Asia and Latin America.

FARM's benchmark water runoff and water supplies (see Table 9.3) are derived from country-level data compiled by the World Resources Institute (WRI, 1992). Changes in a region's water supply are linked to changes in runoff by elasticities of water supply. These elasticities measure percentage changes in regional water supplies in response to 1 percent increases in runoff. Runoff elasticities are positive, implying that water supplies increase when runoff increases. Regional differences in elasticities are related to differences in hydropower capacity. Production of hydropower depends on dams, which enable a region to temporarily store water. The ability to store water allows people within a region to consume water during dry as well as rainy seasons of the year.

*Table 9.3    Water runoff, water supply and water supply elasticities with respect to runoff*

| Region | Runoff[a] | Supply[a] | Elasticity[b] |
|--------|-----------|-----------|----------------|
| US     | 2,478     | 467       | 0.469          |
| Canada | 2,901     | 42        | 0.448          |
| EU     | 818       | 254       | 0.342          |
| Japan  | 547       | 108       | 0.426          |
| OEA[c] | 2,863     | 471       | 0.412          |
| SEA[d] | 3,420     | 88        | 0.279          |
| ANZ[e] | 740       | 19        | 0.341          |
| ROW[f] | 26,940    | 1,791     | n/a[g]         |
| Total  | 40,707    | 3,240     | n/a            |

*Notes:*
a.   Source: World Resources Institute (WRI), 1990. *World Resources 1991–92: A Guide to the Global Environment.* Oxford University Press, Oxford. 'Table 22.1, Freshwater Resources and Withdrawals', pp. 330–331.
b.   Estimated from regression analysis.
c.   Other East Asia (China, Hong Kong, Taiwan and South Korea).
d.   Southeast Asia (Thailand, Indonesia, Philippines and Malaysia).
e.   Australia and New Zealand.
f.   Rest of world.
g.   Elasticities of Rest of world include those for the former USSR (0.453), Other European (0.299), Western and Southern Asia (0.324), Latin America (0.318) and Africa (0.223).

### Economic framework

The 'Economic Framework' portion of Figure 9.1 outlines how production possibilities interact with consumer preferences to determine a region's output. A region's production possibilities, that is, what it can supply, depend on its primary factor endowments (land, water, labor and capital) and existing technology. We consider regional endowments of land, labor and capital to be fixed; climate change scenarios, however, may alter regional water endowments and the distribution of land among the land classes. Although there are upper limits to what can be produced, the combination of different product mixes is infinite. What actually gets produced depends on how firms and consumers interact in commodity markets. Preferences and income drive consumer demands. Firm supplies, consumer demands and their interactions are embedded within FARM's CGE component.[3]

The CGE model contains eight regions. Each region has 11 sectors that produce 13 commodity aggregates (Table 9.4). All 13 commodities are traded internationally and are used as both intermediate inputs and as consumption goods. This enables FARM to simulate how international trade offsets reduced production potential in some regions by gains in others. Finally, households own all primary factors and derive income from their sale as well as from net tax collections. Consumption and savings exhaust regional income. The main advantage of a general equilibrium approach is that it fully accounts for all income and expenditures and, therefore, provides comprehensive measures of economic activity.

To translate factor endowments into production possibilities, regional land and water resources are appropriately distributed as inputs to the production of goods and services. Land resources are distributed by land class. The distributions capture three economic realities: (1) land is used by all sectors, (2) water is used in the crops, livestock and services sectors, and (3) different areas within a region are often associated with distinct product mixes. Within the CGE model, these assignments serve three purposes. First, major differences in the potential productivity of land are captured. Second, all sectors compete for the services of all land. Third, major water-using sectors compete for the services of water. A summary of the distribution of land and water resources to the economic sectors follows.

Owners of land within a land class provide productive services to all 11 sectors. Table 9.5 shows the distribution of land to cropland, permanent pasture, forestland and other land by region and land class for 1990. Other land, which includes urban land as well as deserts and ice fields, is used by the manufacturing and services sectors. Within a land class, quantities of land supplied to the various sectors reflect the land class's productive capabilities. For example, LCs 3, 4 and 5 make up only 31 percent of all land but 58 percent of all cropland.

Water is used for irrigation by the crops and livestock sectors and for other uses by the services sector (see Table 9.6). Table 9.6 also shows the distribution of irrigation water across land classes within each region. These distributions are based on the amount of irrigated land in a given land class and the amount of irrigation water required per hectare. Crops grown on desert-like LC 2, for example, use more irrigation water per hectare than crops grown on Midwestern LC 4. Also, agricultural land on LC 2 is more likely to be irrigated than agricultural land on other land classes. This is reflected in Table 9.6, where 66 percent of the world's irrigation water is allocated to LC 2. Another 21 percent is assigned to LCs 5 and 6, which are heavily used for production of paddy rice and sugar cane.

*Table 9.4   Regions, sectors and commodities in the FARM*

|  | World product (percent of total) |
|---|---|
| Regions[a] | 100.0 |
| United States | 22.2 |
| Australia and New Zealand | 1.6 |
| Canada | 2.7 |
| Japan | 14.8 |
| Other East Asia | 4.2 |
|    China, Hong Kong, Taiwan, South Korea | |
| Southeast Asia | 1.4 |
|    Thailand, Indonesia, Philippines, Malaysia | |
| European Union | 25.3 |
|    Belgium, Denmark, Federal Republic of Germany, France, Greece, Ireland, Italy, Luxembourg, Netherlands, Portugal, Spain United Kingdom | |
| Rest of world | 27.7 |
| Sectors (and commodities) | 88.1[b] |
| Crops[c] | 2.5 |
|    Wheat | 0.2 |
|    Other grains | 0.9 |
|    Non-grain crops | 1.4 |
| Livestock | 1.4 |
| Forestry | 0.4 |
| Coal, oil and gas | 2.0 |
| Other minerals | 1.2 |
| Fish, meat and milk | 1.8 |
| Other processed foods | 4.1 |
| Textiles, clothing and footwear | 2.6 |
| Other non-metallic manufacturers | 1.8 |
| Other manufacturers | 13.3 |
| Services | 47.0 |

*Notes:*
a.   The regions listed are for FARM's CGE model. FARM's geographic information system disaggregates Rest of World into: the former USSR, Mongolia, Other Europe, Other Asia and Oceania, Latin America and Africa.
b.   Saving (equal to investment) is 11.9 percent.
c.   The crops sector produces three crop commodities, that is, wheat, other grains and non-grains. Each of the other sectors produces one commodity.

*Table 9.5   Cropland, permanent pasture, forest land and land in other uses by region and land class (million hectares)*

| Land use and class | Region | | | | | | | | |
|---|---|---|---|---|---|---|---|---|---|
| | US | Canada | EU | Japan | OEA[a] | SEA[b] | ANZ[c] | ROW[d] | Total |
| **Cropland** | | | | | | | | | |
| 1 | 0.06 | 0.00 | 0.54 | 0.00 | 1.22 | 0.00 | 0.00 | 15.36 | 17.18 |
| 2 | 37.01 | 15.64 | 2.38 | 0.00 | 31.11 | 0.00 | 3.45 | 200.08 | 289.68 |
| 3 | 22.68 | 20.42 | 11.72 | 0.42 | 14.19 | 0.40 | 12.42 | 178.54 | 260.79 |
| 4 | 85.93 | 9.90 | 41.24 | 2.74 | 14.67 | 1.32 | 13.41 | 169.43 | 338.64 |
| 5 | 23.97 | 0.00 | 16.70 | 1.01 | 14.61 | 10.92 | 3.35 | 107.09 | 177.67 |
| 6 | 20.27 | 0.00 | 5.25 | 0.47 | 22.79 | 44.03 | 16.73 | 248.63 | 358.17 |
| Total | 189.92 | 45.96 | 77.84 | 4.64 | 98.59 | 56.68 | 49.36 | 919.14 | 1442.12 |
| **Pasture** | | | | | | | | | |
| 1 | 13.49 | 10.48 | 0.00 | 0.00 | 66.82 | 0.00 | 3.16 | 210.01 | 303.96 |
| 2 | 137.11 | 8.34 | 2.23 | 0.00 | 149.30 | 0.00 | 341.24 | 896.82 | 1535.04 |
| 3 | 18.18 | 6.64 | 9.38 | 0.11 | 45.81 | 0.36 | 29.63 | 241.59 | 351.71 |
| 4 | 39.71 | 2.73 | 29.86 | 0.39 | 31.64 | 0.91 | 27.54 | 264.79 | 397.56 |
| 5 | 13.71 | 0.00 | 10.88 | 0.13 | 32.07 | 2.41 | 10.53 | 214.53 | 284.26 |
| 6 | 19.26 | 0.00 | 2.72 | 0.02 | 74.45 | 10.16 | 19.58 | 404.35 | 530.52 |
| Total | 241.47 | 28.20 | 55.07 | 0.64 | 400.08 | 13.84 | 431.67 | 2232.10 | 3403.06 |
| **Forest** | | | | | | | | | |
| 1 | 36.07 | 136.89 | 0.59 | 0.00 | 12.73 | 0.00 | 0.08 | 658.38 | 844.75 |
| 2 | 48.76 | 21.77 | 1.45 | 0.00 | 7.71 | 0.00 | 33.78 | 115.90 | 229.37 |
| 3 | 56.20 | 184.22 | 7.40 | 8.34 | 38.85 | 0.17 | 28.96 | 436.40 | 760.54 |
| 4 | 58.48 | 15.12 | 29.14 | 11.44 | 26.63 | 0.60 | 26.97 | 204.20 | 372.57 |
| 5 | 26.77 | 0.00 | 9.50 | 4.88 | 17.24 | 14.99 | 9.36 | 340.89 | 423.63 |
| 6 | 67.62 | 0.00 | 6.33 | 0.44 | 29.86 | 142.22 | 14.17 | 1143.22 | 1403.86 |
| Total | 293.90 | 358.00 | 54.41 | 25.11 | 133.01 | 157.98 | 113.32 | 2898.99 | 4034.72 |
| **Other** | | | | | | | | | |
| 1 | 70.84 | 356.73 | 1.96 | 0.22 | 144.81 | 0.00 | 0.31 | 529.34 | 1104.20 |
| 2 | 78.08 | 33.35 | 1.01 | 0.00 | 120.28 | 0.00 | 128.00 | 1773.01 | 2133.73 |
| 3 | 19.15 | 98.43 | 4.77 | 0.75 | 22.86 | 0.40 | 20.12 | 158.38 | 324.87 |
| 4 | 14.68 | 1.43 | 17.39 | 4.05 | 14.62 | 1.53 | 23.56 | 146.66 | 223.94 |
| 5 | 4.51 | 0.00 | 7.98 | 1.62 | 5.39 | 11.48 | 5.79 | 85.62 | 122.40 |
| 6 | 4.12 | 0.00 | 2.39 | 0.62 | 2.97 | 53.08 | 19.11 | 207.59 | 289.87 |
| Total | 191.38 | 489.94 | 35.50 | 7.27 | 310.93 | 66.49 | 196.90 | 2900.61 | 4199.00 |

*Notes:*
a.   Other East Asia (China, Hong Kong, Taiwan and South Korea).
b.   Southeast Asia (Thailand, Indonesia, Philippines and Malaysia).
c.   Australia and New Zealand.
d.   Rest of world.

Each region in the CGE has three land-intensive sectors: crops, livestock and forestry. These sectors are divided in up to six subsectors, each utilizing land from only one of the six land classes. In addition, crop producers may, on a given land class, produce up to three crop aggregates – wheat, other grains and non-grains. Table 9.7 depicts the major components of these commodities by region. There are substantial regional differences. In the United States, for example, maize is a major component of 'other grains'; produce (i.e. fruits and vegetables), soybeans and sugar crops are major components of 'non-grains'; and cattle and pigs are major components of 'livestock'. Most U.S. forest products are softwood prod-

*Table 9.6   Water use by land class and region (cubic kilometers)*

| Use and land class | US | Canada | EU | Japan | OEA[a] | SEA[b] | ANZ[c] | ROW[d] | Total |
|---|---|---|---|---|---|---|---|---|---|
| Agriculture | 196 | 4 | 92 | 53 | 408 | 64 | 6 | 1396 | 2219 |
| 1 | 0 | 0 | 0 | 0 | 8 | 0 | 0 | 2 | 10 |
| 2 | 149 | 4 | 46 | 0 | 284 | 0 | 6 | 971 | 1460 |
| 3 | 14 | 0 | 19 | 0 | 7 | 0 | 0 | 96 | 136 |
| 4 | 19 | 0 | 26 | 4 | 16 | 0 | 0 | 85 | 150 |
| 5 | 4 | 0 | 0 | 29 | 36 | 23 | 0 | 182 | 273 |
| 6 | 10 | 0 | 0 | 20 | 57 | 41 | 0 | 60 | 189 |
| Other uses | 271 | 39 | 163 | 54 | 62 | 24 | 13 | 395 | 1021 |
| Grand total[e] | 467 | 42 | 254 | 108 | 471 | 88 | 19 | 1791 | 3240 |

*Notes:*
a.   Other East Asia (China, Hong Kong, Taiwan and South Korea).
b.   Southeast Asia (Thailand, Indonesia, Philippines and Malaysia).
c.   Australia and New Zealand.
d.   Rest of world.
e.   Totals may not add up due to rounding.

*Source:*
World Resources Institute (WRI), 1990. *World Resources 1991–92: A Guide to the Global Environment.* Oxford University Press, Oxford. 'Table 22.1 Freshwater Resources and Withdrawals', pp. 330–331.

*Table 9.7   Major components of agricultural and silvicultural production by region[a]*

| Region | Other grains | Non-grains | Livestock[b] | Forest product (%) Hardwood | Fuelwood |
|---|---|---|---|---|---|
| US | Maize | Produce, soybeans, sugar | Cattle, pigs | 34 | 17 |
| Canada | Barley, maize | Oils, produce, roots and tubers | Cattle, pigs | 10 | 4 |
| EU | Maize | Produce, sugar | Sheep and goats, pigs, cattle | 32 | 13 |
| Japan | Rice | Produce | Pigs, cattle | 34 | 1 |
| Other East Asia | Rice, maize | Produce, roots and tubers | Pigs, sheep and goats | 52 | 67 |
| Southeast Asia | Rice | Sugar, roots and tubers | Pigs, sheep and goats, cattle | 100 | 69 |
| Australia and New Zealand | Barley | Sugar | Sheep and goats | 42 | 9 |
| Rest of world | Rice, maize, barley | Sugar, produce | Sheep and goats, cattle | 69 | 62 |

*Notes:*
a.   Commodities that make up more than 20 percent of the total are listed from the most to least dominant.
b.   Does not include poultry.

*Source:*
United Nations. Food and Agriculture Organization (FAO), 1992. *Agrostat.* Rome, Italy.

ucts, that is, derived from coniferous trees, and only 17 percent of U.S. forest products are used for fuel. In Southeast Asia, however, 'other grains' is primarily rice, 'non-grains' is sugar cane and roots and tubers (i.e. cassava), and 'livestock' is pigs, sheep, goats and cattle. All forest products in Southeast Asia are hardwood products, that is, derived from deciduous trees, and 69 percent is used for fuel. Because of such regional differences in the composition of these and other commodities (including wheat), each region's commodities are treated as heterogeneous goods when traded.

This structure supports the capability of FARM's CGE model to simulate a number of adaptive responses to climate change by farmers. With respect to outputs, farmers adopt the crop and livestock mix best suited to their climatic and economic conditions. If changing climatic conditions alter their growing season enough to shift their land to a new land class, farmers may adopt a much different crop and livestock mix. This is like incorporating the 'analogous regions' methodology into a formal economic structure. Farmers also may adjust their mix of crops and livestock in response to climate-induced price changes. If the price of wheat were to rise, for example, farmers would tend to increase both their cropland and the amount of wheat produced per hectare relative to other crops.

Farmers also adopt the mix of primary factor inputs best suited to their climatic and economic conditions.[4] If water supplies are adversely affected and cause water prices to increase, for example, farmers may use less irrigation water and more land, labor and/or capital. This might be done within a particular land class or, alternatively, by shifting production from land classes that require relatively large amounts of irrigation water to classes of land that require less. Similarly, if climate change reduces the amount of land in an agriculturally important land class, farmers may use less of that land and more water, labor and/or capital. They may also use more land in other land classes. Thus, FARM's framework enables us to analyze how climate change might alter the distribution and intensity of farming within a region.

## Simulating Climate Change

In FARM, we simulate climate change by altering water supplies and the distribution of land across the land classes within each region. This section describes the methods used to transform temperature and precipitation changes generated by general circulation models (GCMs) into changes in land and water resources and from there into economic impacts.

### GCMs

Climate change scenarios are derived from monthly temperature and precipitation estimates generated by GCMs of the Goddard Institute for Space Studies (GISS) (Hansen et al., 1988), Geophysical Fluid Dynamics Laboratory (GFDL) (Manabe and Wetherald, 1987), United Kingdom Meteorological Office (UKMO) (Wilson and Mitchell, 1987) and Oregon State University (OSU) (Schlesinger and Zhao, 1989). The scenarios represent equilibrium climates given a doubling of atmospheric trace gases.[5] Summary statistics for the scenarios are presented in Table 9.8. The Intergovernmental Panel on Climate Change (IPCC) recently concluded that a doubling of trace gases would lead to an increase in mean global temperature of 1.5 to 5.0 °C by 2090 (IPCC, 1992). The GCM scenarios considered here are at the upper end of the IPCC's range.

*Table 9.8    Summary statistics for the GCMs used as the basis for climate change scenarios*

| Model | Year calculated | Resolution (lat. * long.) | CO$_2$ (ppm) | Change in average temperature (°C) | Change in average global precipitation (%) |
|-------|-----------------|---------------------------|--------------|-------------------------------------|---------------------------------------------|
| GISS | 1982 | 7.83° * 10.0° | 630 | 4.2 | 11.0 |
| GFDL | 1988 | 4.44° * 7.5° | 600 | 4.0 | 8.0 |
| UKMO | 1986 | 5.00° * 7.5° | 640 | 5.2 | 15.0 |
| OSU | 1985 | 4.00° * 5.0° | 652 | 2.8 | 7.8 |

*Note:*
Climate change scenarios generated by, respectively, the GCMs of the Goddard Institute for Space Studies (GISS), the Geophysical Fluid Dynamics Laboratory (GFDL), the United Kingdom Meteorological Office (UKMO) and Oregon State University (OSU).

*Sources:*
For GISS, GFDL and UKMO scenarios, Rosenzweig, C., Parry, M., Fischer, G. and Frohberg, K. (1993), 'Climate Change and World Food Supply', Environmental Change Unit, University of Oxford, Research Report No. 3. For the OSU scenario, Dr Sanjay Dixit, Department of Meteorology, Pennsylvania State University, University Park, Pennsylvania (personal communication).

**Impacts on land resources**
Revised data sets of monthly temperature and precipitation are obtained for each GCM by: (1) adding to Leemans and Cramer (1991) temperature data, differences in mean monthly temperatures obtained in GCM runs with current $(1 \times CO_2)$ and double $(2 \times CO_2)$ atmospheric $CO_2$ levels; and (2) multiplying Leemans and Cramer (1991) precipitation data by the ratio of precipitation in the $2 \times CO_2$ GCM run to precipitation in the $1 \times CO_2$ GCM run.[6]

Using the revised temperature and precipitation data, new sets of growing season lengths (one with and one without precipitation constraints) are computed for each GIS grid cell.[7] Each GIS grid cell is assigned the appropriate land class. The revised growing season length may alter the land class to which a given cell is assigned. In this way, climate change can alter regional endowments of the six land classes.

Two sets of land class changes are computed for each GCM scenario. One set contains regional net changes in land classes and is used to evaluate all potential economic impacts of global climate change, including impacts generated by changes in land use. The second set contains net changes in land classes on existing land use and cover patterns in the regions. This enables us to evaluate economic impacts of climate change while constraining total quantities of crop-land, permanent pasture and forestland in each region to their 1990 levels. This has two purposes. First, it serves as a check on situations where land uses cannot change as easily as indicated in our model. Second, it measures climate change's potential impacts on existing agricultural and silvicultural systems.

### Impacts on water supplies

Changes in regional water supplies are also estimated with the revised temperature and precipitation data. First, estimates of annual runoff under current climatic conditions are calculated using Leemans and Cramer (1991) mean monthly temperature and precipitation data. Annual runoff is the sum of monthly runoff in an area. Monthly runoff is that portion of monthly precipitation that is not evapotranspirated back to the atmosphere. Monthly evapotranspiration estimates are obtained from monthly temperature data (Thornthwaite, 1948).[8]

Second, water runoff in each region is derived for the four GCM scenarios using the appropriate revised temperature and precipitation data. Third, regional percentage changes in water runoff are calculated by comparing the GCM-based runoff estimates with runoff estimates derived from the original Leemans and Cramer (1991) temperature and precipitation data.[9] Fourth, regional percentage changes in water supplies are computed using the runoff elasticities of water supply presented in Table 9.3, that is, $\%\Delta W = \%\Delta R \cdot E$, where $\%\Delta W$ is the percentage change in a region's water supply, $\%\Delta R$ is the percentage change in a region's runoff, and $E$ is the runoff elasticity of water supply.

### Simulating climate change in FARM's CGE model

Economic impacts of the shifts in regional water supplies and the redistribution of land across land classes is computed by FARM's CGE model. The CGE model is implemented using the GEMPACK suite of model development software (Codsi and Pearson, 1988; Pearson, 1988). GEMPACK solves a system of non-linear equations via a linearized representation (Pearson, 1991). The solution algorithm does *not* have the problems associated with previous 'linearized' models (see Hertel et al., 1992).

### Limitations and Strengths

The FARM framework contains several strengths that significantly advance our ability to evaluate potential impacts of global climate change on regional and world agriculture. At the same time, a number of limitations should be made explicit.

### Land and water resources

One limitation is that land classes are defined by climatic variables and do not account for soil characteristics or other factors that affect productivity. These non-climatic factors may not accompany climate-induced shifts in length of growing season. While we assume that productivity per unit area follows the migration of growing seasons, it is more likely to decrease or increase in a given instance. This means that farmer adaptations simulated by FARM are somewhat uncertain and subject to independent verification. Assuming that per unit area productivity of natural ecosystems will automatically follow the migration of growing seasons is even more naive. Some natural ecosystems will find it difficult or impossible to migrate, even with direct human assistance.

Procedures for simulating water resources are limited in three ways. First, water storage in alpine snowpack is not taken into account. Alpine snowpack is an important source of irrigation water in the western United States, northern Africa, the Middle East, India and China. Reductions in snowpack might cause shortages of irrigation water in some of these regions during critical times of the year. Second, water is treated as though it could be utilized anywhere within a given region; hence, water is considerably more mobile in our model than in reality. Third, in the model, water is always beneficial. In fact, too much water can wash away crops, waterlog soils, delay planting or inhibit harvesting. These limitations suggest that our estimates of climate-induced changes in water supplies are probably optimistic and that negative impacts attributable to water resource changes are probably underestimated.

### Economic impacts

Four limitations of FARM's economic framework need to be made clear. First, substitution between intermediate goods or between intermediate and primary factors is not allowed. This means that increases in fertilizer cannot be used to offset climate-induced productivity losses. Second, FARM only considers the commodity value of land. The value of land *in situ* is not included. This means, for example, that values of sawlogs, pulpwood and similar forest commodities are tracked, but environmental amenities of forests are not. Third, the 'Rest of world' region includes Latin America, Africa, West Asia, much of South Asia, the former Soviet Union and countries in Europe outside the European Union. For a large portion of the world then, it is difficult to obtain precise information about how the economic impacts of climate change would be distributed.

Finally, our benchmark is the world economy as it existed in 1990. This means that: (1) some potential adaptations (i.e. new cultivars or new livestock breeds)[10] are not considered, (2) direct costs of physically converting land from one use to another (e.g. building roads, clearing trees, burning brush) are ignored, and (3) current economic distortions such as subsidies and tariffs are in place.

### Climate change scenarios

Our climate change scenarios are limited to how alternative global patterns of mean monthly temperature and precipitation affect land and freshwater resources. We do not simulate all potential impacts associated with climate change. We do not consider, for example, possible rises in sea level or increased variability in weather.

We also do not consider physiological effects of greater atmospheric concentrations of $CO_2$ or other trace gases on plant growth. Increases in atmospheric concentrations of $CO_2$ would act like a fertilizer for some plants and improve water-use efficiency for others (IPCC, 1990). Productivity gains associated with these phenomena probably would more than offset acid deposition and ozone pollution damages induced by other trace gases emitted by burning fossil fuels.

**Strengths**

The above limitations aside, FARM extends previous research by linking land and water resources directly to climate conditions and economic activity; hence human responses to climate change are economically consistent and follow from environmental impacts. FARM also integrates many advances made in earlier works. Specifically, FARM (1) utilizes GIS data similar to Leemans and Solomon (1993), (2) incorporates multi-sector impacts as in Bowes and Crosson (1991), and (3) simulates global impacts on production and trade as in Kane et al. (1991) and Rosenzweig and Parry (1994). The result is a framework that (1) includes climate effects on crops, livestock and forestry simultaneously, (2) simulates endogenous adaptive responses to climate change by farmers, (3) explicitly simulates land and water resource markets, (4) includes detailed interactions with the rest of the economy, and (5) provides global coverage of responses to climate change.

# 3   RESULTS

We begin this section by examining the impacts on land resources generated by the four GCM climate change scenarios. Then we present subsequent changes in production of agricultural and other commodities, land use patterns and overall economic activity. Special emphasis is placed on land use changes as an adaptive response to new climatic conditions. By necessity, many regional and sectoral effects are not discussed.[11]

**Impacts on Land Endowments**

Table 9.9 shows how climate change is likely to affect the distribution of land across the land classes for the world as a whole. Across scenarios, the global endowment of LC 1 (land with short growing seasons due to cold temperatures) decreases. This implies that climate change is likely to increase the amount of land suitable for agriculture and silviculture, especially in arctic and alpine areas. However, LC 6 (land with growing seasons longer than ten months, primarily in the tropics) decreases in each scenario and LC 2 (desert/dry grasslands) increases in three scenarios. This indicates that soil moisture losses are likely to reduce

*Table 9.9    Impacts of climate change on the distribution of land across land classes under different climate change scenarios*

| Scenario | Land class | | | | | |
|----------|------|------|------|------|------|------|
|          | 1 | 2 | 3 | 4 | 5 | 6 |
| GISS | −39.77 | −1.44 | 28.71 | 51.64 | 4.68 | −10.06 |
| GFDL | −47.72 | 17.22 | 28.74 | 36.98 | 18.21 | −31.05 |
| UKMO | −62.45 | 16.39 | 38.81 | 78.09 | 4.37 | 39.20 |
| OSU | −32.57 | 6.87 | 16.68 | 21.87 | 17.76 | 11.69 |

agricultural possibilities in many areas of the world. These results are consistent with Leemans and Solomon (1993).

Table 9.10 shows that 28.6 to 46.2 percent of the world's land endowment (outside Antarctica) faces changes in climatic conditions that are large enough to result in new land class assignments.[12] The scenario ranking, from lowest to highest, is OSU, GISS, GFDL and UKMO. This ranking is not perfectly correlated with either GCM temperature or precipitation changes. We use this ranking when referring to the strength of climatic shocks generated by the four GCM scenarios, that is, we consider the OSU climatic shock to be 'weaker' than the UKMO climate shock. The shock pattern generally follows the same order in each region as for the world as a whole. The major exception is Australia/New Zealand. This indicates that respective differences in the GCMs are relatively consistent.

*Table 9.10    Percentage of total land changing land class by region and climate change scenario*

| Scenario | Region | | | | | | | | |
|----------|------|--------|------|-------|------|------|------|------|-------|
|          | US | Canada | EU | Japan | OEA[a] | SEA[b] | ANZ[c] | ROW[d] | Total |
| GISS | 40.0 | 37.7 | 71.8 | 65.9 | 34.9 | 21.9 | 18.5 | 31.2 | 32.3 |
| GFDL | 47.0 | 48.7 | 84.0 | 73.9 | 34.5 | 27.1 | 25.1 | 38.6 | 39.4 |
| UKMO | 55.3 | 58.8 | 85.7 | 78.8 | 43.9 | 34.3 | 24.6 | 45.6 | 46.2 |
| OSU | 38.9 | 35.3 | 59.3 | 63.8 | 26.1 | 16.0 | 26.4 | 26.8 | 28.6 |

*Notes:*
a.   Other East Asia (China, Hong Kong, Taiwan and South Korea).
b.   Southern Asia (Thailand, Indonesia, Philippines and Malaysia).
c.   Australia and New Zealand.
d.   Rest of world.

Climate-induced impacts on agriculturally important land in various areas are presented in Table 9.11. Agriculturally important land increases in high latitude regions, but decreases in tropical regions. In mid-latitude regions, changes in agriculturally important land may be positive or negative. These results suggest that, under global climate change, agricultural possibilities are likely to increase in high latitude regions and decrease in tropical areas.

Table 9.12 summarizes climate-induced impacts on existing cropland by GCM scenario. Globally, 41.2 to 59.6 percent of existing cropland faces changes in

*Table 9.11    Percentage changes in agriculturally important land by area and climate change scenario*

| Scenario | High latitudes[a] | Tropics[b] | Other areas[c] |
|---|---|---|---|
| GISS | 58.6 | −20.5 | −0.5 |
| GFDL | 21.2 | −39.7 | 1.2 |
| UKMO | 49.3 | −52.0 | −3.6 |
| OSU | 7.8 | −18.6 | 6.8 |

*Notes:*
a.    Land with growing season length from 101 to 250 days in Canada, non-EU and the former USSR.
b.    Land with growing season length greater than 300 days in Africa, Latin America and Asia (except Japan, China and South Korea).
c.    Land with growing season length from 101 to 300 days.

*Table 9.12    Global changes in land classes on existing cropland and in the value of existing cropland and agricultural land under existing rents (percentage change)*

| Scenario | Cropland land class changes | | Value changes | |
|---|---|---|---|---|
| | Total | To shorter land classes | Cropland | Agricultural land |
| GISS | 43.8 | 21.9 | 0.7 | -0.3 |
| GFDL | 43.4 | 37.0 | -3.2 | -1.8 |
| UKMO | 59.7 | 41.3 | -5.4 | -3.5 |
| OSU | 41.2 | 25.1 | -0.5 | -0.8 |

*Note*: Agricultural land includes cropland and pasture.

climatic conditions that result in new land class assignments.[13] Under each scenario, more than half of the cropland that does change land class shifts to a class with a shorter growing season. Table 9.12 also shows that, using *current* rents, the total value of existing agricultural land declines under the land class distributions generated by the four climate change scenarios. These results imply that climate change's impacts on the existing agricultural system are likely to be negative overall.

**Impacts on Commodity Markets**

Climate-induced changes in natural resource endowments will affect the production of basic agricultural and silvicultural commodities around the world. Changes in agricultural production in turn will affect the output of various processed food commodities. We examine how the four GCM climate change scenarios affect production of these and other selected commodities when farmers are allowed to take advantage of newly available agricultural land as well as under the existing pattern of agricultural production. We also evaluate the role that on-farm adaptations might play in responding to climate change.

**Agricultural and silvicultural commodities**
Table 9.13 shows how each climate change scenario affects production of crops, livestock and forest products when land use changes are and are not allowed. When land use changes are allowed, world wheat production increases, while production of non-grains falls in all climate change scenarios. Output of other grains increases or decreases depending on the scenario. Production of livestock and forest products generally increases.

These global impacts mask more pronounced variations in regional impacts. In Canada, FARM's only unambiguously high latitude region, production of wheat, other grains, non-grains, livestock and forest products increase in all scenarios. In Southeast Asia, FARM's only unambiguously tropical region, production of these commodities generally decreases in all scenarios (exceptions are non-grains in the GISS, GFDL and UKMO scenarios). These changes in regional production of agricultural and silvicultural commodities reflect longer and warmer growing seasons at high latitudes and shorter and drier growing seasons in the tropics.

*Table 9.13*    *Percentage changes in world production of food, agricultural and forest products with and without land use restrictions*

| GCM scenario | GISS | GISS | GFDL | GFDL | UKMO | UKMO | OSU | OSU |
| --- | --- | --- | --- | --- | --- | --- | --- | --- |
| Land use changes allowed | Yes | No | Yes | No | Yes | No | Yes | No |
| Wheat | 1.9 | 0.6 | 0.5 | -1.0 | 3.3 | 1.2 | 0.8 | -0.4 |
| Other grains | 0.4 | 0.0 | 0.3 | -0.4 | 0.3 | -0.8 | -0.1 | -0.5 |
| Non-grains | -0.5 | -1.3 | -0.4 | -0.6 | -1.3 | -2.6 | -0.2 | -0.4 |
| Livestock | 0.9 | 0.6 | 0.7 | 0.3 | 0.9 | 0.4 | 0.7 | 0.7 |
| Forest products | 0.3 | 0.1 | 0.0 | -0.2 | 0.0 | -0.3 | 0.1 | 0.0 |
| Fish, meat, milk | 0.4 | 0.0 | 0.3 | -0.2 | 0.3 | -0.3 | 0.3 | 0.0 |
| Other processed foods | 0.4 | -0.1 | 0.2 | -0.4 | 0.2 | -0.6 | 0.3 | -0.1 |

Impacts on mid-latitude regions are mixed. In the United States, output of wheat increases, while output of other grains (primarily maize) decreases across all scenarios. Production of non-grains increases or decreases depending on the scenario. Livestock production decreases in all scenarios, and forestry production decreases in three scenarios. These results indicate that climate change is likely to have negative impacts on some important U.S. agricultural sectors.

**Processed food commodities**
Although climate-induced changes in production possibilities will be most pronounced for agriculture and silviculture, other sectors will be affected as well. Output of fish, meat, milk and other processed foods, for example, increases in all scenarios when land use changes are allowed (Table 9.13). This indicates that climate change's *overall* impact on world food production is likely to be beneficial.

Regional production of processed food commodities tends to follow regional production of agricultural commodities. For example, production of processed food commodities increases in all scenarios for Canada and decreases in all scenarios for Southeast Asia. In the United States, production of processed food commodities generally declines. The decreases in production of fish, meat and milk are associated with decreases in output of other grains (primarily maize) and livestock in all four scenarios. U.S. production of other processed foods decreases in three scenarios. The increase in the severity of the GISS scenario is associated with a relatively large increase in non-grain production.

## Adaptation

Our results are more positive for world food production than those reported in earlier research, even in research that includes the beneficial effects of atmospheric $CO_2$ on plant growth. This can be illustrated by focusing on cereals, that is, wheat plus other grains. After taking $CO_2$ fertilization and various adaptations into account, climate-induced impacts on world cereal production in Rosenzweig and Parry (1994) are approximately 1.0, 0.0 and –2.5 percent, respectively, for the GISS, GFDL and UKMO scenarios. As shown in the fifth column of Table 9.14, however, our research indicates that, *without* $CO_2$ fertilization, world cereal production increases by 0.9, 0.3 and 1.2 percent, respectively, for the GISS, GFDL and UKMO scenarios.[14]

These different impacts on production of cereals could be due to a number of reasons. First, our direct climate-induced impacts on world cereals supply might be less severe than the impacts underlying Rosenzweig and Parry's (1994) analysis. Second, our methodology may assign a larger role to adaptation (i.e. switching to alternative crops, adjusting primary factor inputs, and taking advantage of new climatically-suitable agricultural lands) when farmers respond to changing climate conditions. Third, other factors may be responsible. We consider all three reasons.

Table 9.14 shows how our climate change scenarios affect world *supply* and *production* of cereals under various constraints. *Changes in supply* are the additional quantities (positive or negative) that firms would be willing to sell at 1990 prices under the alternative climate. *Changes in production* are the equilibrium quantities (positive or negative) that both firms and consumers would be willing to sell and buy at equilibrium prices under the alternative climate. The former can be represented as a shift in a supply curve. The latter result from simultaneous shifts in supply and demand curves. Land use is fixed in both supply cases, that is, cropland is not allowed to increase.

Supply effects for two types of farmers, *naive* and *smart*, are evaluated. Naive farmers take no adaptive measures in response to climate change. Supply changes for naive farmers are simulated with FARM's GIS by first assuming that crops are planted where they originally occurred no matter what the new land class turned out to be. How much is harvested then depends on the average products of the crops on the new land class with one constraint – the average products cannot be greater than the average products of the original land class. These supply effects capture the direct climate-induced impacts on world cereals and are comparable

Table 9.14   Changes in United States and world supply and production of cereals under various constraints, by climate change scenario[a]

| Region/ scenario | Supply[b] | | Production | |
|---|---|---|---|---|
| | No farm-level adaptation | Farm-level adaptation[c] | Land use fixed | Land use variable[d] |
| | Percent change | | | |
| World: | | | | |
| GISS | −22.9 | −2.4 | 0.2 | 0.9 |
| GFDL | −23.2 | −4.4 | −0.6 | 0.3 |
| UKMO | −29.6 | −6.4 | −0.2 | 1.2 |
| OSU | −18.8 | −3.9 | −0.5 | 0.2 |
| | | | | |
| United States: | | | | |
| GISS | −24.4 | −8.7 | −2.0 | −3.0 |
| GFDL | −38.0 | −22.3 | −4.6 | −2.0 |
| UKMO | −38.4 | −19.4 | −3.2 | −5.0 |
| OSU | −33.3 | −20.9 | −5.6 | −5.2 |

*Notes:*

a.   Changes in supply represent the additional quantities (positive or negative) that firms would be willing to sell at 1990 prices under the alternative climate. Changes in production represent changes in equilibrium quantities (changes in quantities that firms are willing to sell and consumers are willing to buy at new market prices under the alternative climate).
b.   Land use is fixed (cropland is not allowed to increase) in both supply cases.
c.   Includes switching to alternative crops and adjusting primary factor inputs.
d.   Expansion into new agriculturally suitable lands is allowed.

to Rosenzweig and Parry's (1994) scenarios that do not include $CO_2$ fertilization and adaptation. Smart farmers, on the other hand, adapt by switching to alternative crops or adjusting primary factor inputs on existing cropland. Supply changes for smart farmers are estimated with the CGE by fixing prices of all intermediate goods (as well as land use) at their 1990 levels.

Under our naive farmer scenarios, world cereals supply decreases 22.9, 23.2 and 29.6 percent, respectively, for the GISS, GFDL and UKMO climates (Table 9.14). For naive farmer scenarios in Rosenzweig et al. (1993), world cereals supply decreases 19.9, 24.5 and 30.0 percent, respectively, for the GISS, GFDL and UKMO climates.[15] A comparison of these results indicates that direct climate-induced impacts on world cereals supply are similar in the two modeling frameworks. With smart farmers (and cropland fixed), world supplies of cereals decrease by 2.4, 4.4, 6.4 and 3.9 percent for the GISS, GFDL, UKMO and OSU scenarios. Comparing these changes with the naive farmer supply changes indicates that from 78 to 90 percent of the initial climate-induced reductions in world cereals supply might be offset by allowing farmers to select the most profitable mix of inputs and crops on existing cropland.

Farmers are assumed to be smart in both production cases. After allowing for trade and changes in demand (but still holding cropland fixed), changes in world cereals production range from −0.6 to +0.2 percent, thereby mitigating more than 97 percent of the original negative impacts. Finally, after allowing farmers to take advantage of new agriculturally suitable lands, changes in world production of cereals range from 0.2 to 1.2 percent. These results indicate that farmer adaptations are likely to offset many of the economic losses that global climate change may otherwise induce.

The relatively small impacts on cereals production are also due to how FARM's CGE component simulates consumption of final goods and services. Simply put, household consumption of food is less likely to vary than consumption of non-food items during periods of economic change. This means that climate-induced impacts may spill over into sectors only distantly related to food production.

Adaptation in specific regions may be more difficult for a number of reasons. First, initial regional impacts may be more negative. Table 9.14 shows that, under our naive farmer scenarios, initial impacts on U.S. cereals supplies are more severe than for the world as a whole. Second, farm-level adaptations may not be as effective. Selecting the most profitable mix of inputs and crops on existing cropland in the United States mitigates from 37 to 64 percent (rather than 78 to 90 percent) of initial climate-induced shocks to cereals supply. Further allowing for trade and changes in demand mitigates from 83 to 92 percent (instead of more than 97 percent) of these shocks. Finally, greater availability of potential cropland in foreign regions could have an adverse effect on domestic agricultural production. Table 9.13, for example, shows that after all the world's farmers take advantage of newly available agricultural land, U.S. production of cereals would be smaller in the GISS and UKMO scenarios than if agricultural land were fixed.

**Impacts on the existing system**
By restricting land uses and covers to their current patterns, we get an idea of how climate change might impact existing agricultural systems. Table 9.13 also shows production changes of selected commodities when land use changes are not allowed. In general, world production of these commodities is generally lower when land use movements are not allowed. This phenomenon is most striking with regard to processed foods. When land use changes are not allowed, world production in the processed foods sectors decreases in all four GCM scenarios; just the opposite of what we found when farmers were allowed to take advantage of newly available agricultural land.[16] This suggests that climate change is likely to reduce productivity on earth's *current* agricultural land.

**Impacts on aggregate economic activity**
Real gross domestic product (GDP) is used as a measure of aggregate economic activity. Changes in GDP reflect changes in the prices of all goods and services consumed by households as well as changes in primary factor income and income from other sources.[17] In this section, we evaluate climate change's potential impacts on GDP for the world as a whole and for the regions represented in FARM.

Table 9.15 shows how each climate change scenario affects GDP when cropland expansions are and are not allowed. When cropland expansions are allowed, world GDP increases or decreases depending on the scenario. The size of the impacts are relatively small, ranging from about −0.1 to +0.1 percent of 1990 world GDP, that is, losses of $24.5 billion to gains of $25.2 billion per year. The rank ordering of the impacts is inversely correlated with the strength of the climate change shocks. That is, world economic welfare appears to increase at relatively low levels of climate change and to decrease at higher levels.[18] When land use movements are restricted, world economic activity declines slightly; up to 0.35 percent (from $0.7 to $74.3 billion per year) across the four scenarios.

*Table 9.15    Percentage changes in GDP by region and climate change scenario*

| Scenario | Region | | | | | | | | |
|---|---|---|---|---|---|---|---|---|---|
| | US | Canada | EU | Japan | OEA[a] | SEA[b] | ANZ[c] | ROW[d] | Total |
| Base GDP ($U.S. trillions) | 5.5 | 0.6 | 5.9 | 3.0 | 0.7 | 0.3 | 0.4 | 4.6 | 21.0 |
| Percentage change in GDP with cropland expansion | | | | | | | | | |
| GISS | 0.1 | 1.9 | −0.9 | 0.8 | 0.4 | −0.9 | 0.1 | 0.4 | 0.0 |
| GFDL | −0.1 | 2.3 | −0.7 | 0.6 | 0.4 | −0.6 | −0.2 | 0.3 | 0.0 |
| UKMO | 0.0 | 2.8 | −1.1 | 0.3 | 0.4 | −1.3 | −0.4 | 0.3 | −0.1 |
| OSU | −0.1 | 1.9 | −0.3 | 0.7 | 0.2 | −0.2 | 0.8 | 0.3 | 0.1 |
| Percentage change in GDP without cropland expansion | | | | | | | | | |
| GISS | 0.1 | 1.7 | −1.1 | 0.6 | 0.2 | −1.6 | 0.2 | 0.2 | −0.1 |
| GFDL | −0.2 | 2.0 | −0.9 | 0.3 | 0.0 | −1.3 | −0.1 | 0.1 | −0.3 |
| UKMO | −0.0 | 2.4 | −1.3 | 0.0 | −0.2 | −2.6 | −0.2 | 0.0 | −0.4 |
| OSU | −0.1 | 1.6 | −0.5 | 0.5 | 0.0 | −0.6 | 1.0 | 0.1 | 0.0 |

*Notes:*
a.    Other East Asia (China, Hong Kong, Taiwan and South Korea).
b.    Southeast Asia (Thailand, Indonesia, Philippines and Malaysia).
c.    Australia and New Zealand.
d.    Rest of world.

The latter results indicate the importance of incorporating climate-induced impacts on the availability of potential agricultural land into global climate change analysis. The latter results also may serve as a corrective for overly optimistic land use changes, changes that may be limited by agronomic, environmental or other factors. Because of poor soil conditions, for example, some land may not be suitable for agriculture regardless of how favorable temperature and precipitation conditions become. One also might consider the difference between cropland expansion and no expansion scenarios as equivalent to the value of expanding cropland. This analysis, however, only considers commercial use values associated with land and water resources. Not included here is the value of these resources (and their associated ecosystems) *in situ*.

## Land Use

Previous results show that the ability of farmers to take advantage of newly available agricultural land will help to offset the negative impacts that global climate change is likely to induce in the world's current agricultural and food processing system. Here we examine how some of the land use changes that such activity is likely to generate might alter the distribution and intensity of farming.

### Net land use changes

Table 9.16 shows that, under climate change, more land will be devoted to agriculture. Across GCM scenarios, cropland and pasture increase by 7.1 to 14.8 percent and by 1.5 to 4.7 percent, respectively, for the world as a whole. Changes in total crop and livestock production, however, range from −0.3 to 0.0 and from 0.7 to 0.9, respectively (see Table 9.13, Land use changes allowed scenarios). This implies that crop and livestock yields will decline, on average, under climate change.

Cropland generally increases in all regions and scenarios. In percentage terms, the largest net increases of cropland occur in Canada, ranging from 49.1 to 112.3

*Table 9.16   Net percentage changes in cropland, permanent pasture, forest land and land in other uses by region and climate change scenario*

| Land use scenario | Region | | | | | | | | |
|---|---|---|---|---|---|---|---|---|---|
| | US | Canada | EU | Japan | OEA[a] | SEA[b] | ANZ[c] | ROW[d] | Total |
| Cropland: | | | | | | | | | |
| GISS | 9.7 | 63.0 | 6.8 | 17.9 | 10.1 | 19.4 | 2.8 | 10.1 | 11.7 |
| GFDL | 3.9 | 78.8 | 8.7 | 26.7 | 7.0 | 21.9 | 1.6 | 6.7 | 9.2 |
| UKMO | 4.9 | 112.3 | 9.3 | 40.7 | 12.1 | 30.8 | −5.3 | 12.7 | 14.8 |
| OSU | 1.6 | 49.1 | 4.0 | 17.6 | 7.5 | 9.5 | 22.0 | 5.3 | 7.1 |
| Pasture: | | | | | | | | | |
| GISS | −0.1 | 2.6 | −9.0 | −9.5 | 1.5 | 57.1 | −2.3 | 3.8 | 2.5 |
| GFDL | 0.7 | 15.8 | −4.0 | −13.8 | 6.5 | 48.1 | −2.0 | 4.3 | 3.7 |
| UKMO | 7.0 | 35.0 | −11.9 | −17.7 | 6.3 | 66.4 | 1.7 | 4.3 | 4.7 |
| OSU | 7.4 | 4.4 | 5.8 | −12.0 | 1.6 | 20.7 | −10.6 | 3.0 | 1.5 |
| Forest: | | | | | | | | | |
| GISS | 2.9 | 6.9 | 8.8 | −21.1 | 5.6 | −8.6 | 5.8 | −6.1 | −3.6 |
| GFDL | 2.3 | −1.9 | −0.6 | −26.4 | −6.3 | −9.5 | 5.5 | −9.6 | −7.5 |
| UKMO | 0.6 | −0.1 | 7.7 | −33.8 | 4.0 | −16.4 | −0.3 | −11.8 | −9.1 |
| OSU | −0.8 | 2.4 | −4.5 | −21.2 | 6.1 | −4.5 | 18.5 | −6.8 | −4.4 |
| Other land: | | | | | | | | | |
| GISS | −13.9 | −11.1 | −14.5 | 62.3 | −7.5 | −7.9 | 1.1 | 0.0 | −2.6 |
| GFDL | −8.4 | −6.9 | −11.9 | 75.4 | −7.8 | −6.1 | 0.7 | 4.2 | 1.1 |
| UKMO | −14.6 | −12.5 | −13.9 | 92.2 | −13.7 | −1.1 | −2.1 | 4.5 | −0.1 |
| OSU | −9.7 | −6.7 | −10.9 | 63.0 | −7.1 | −1.8 | 7.1 | 2.8 | 0.5 |

*Notes:*
a.   Other East Asia (China, Hong Kong, Taiwan and South Korea).
b.   Southeast Asia (Thailand, Indonesia, Philippines and Malaysia).
c.   Australia and New Zealand.
d.   Rest of world.

percent (22.6 to 51.7 million hectares) across scenarios. Other regions with relatively large net increases in cropland are Japan and Southeast Asia. In the United States, cropland increases by 1.6 to 9.7 percent.

Coincident with the global expansion of cropland, Table 9.16 shows that forest land decreases by 3.6 to 9.1 percent. These changes suggest that expansion of agricultural land into new areas is likely to be at the expense of existing forest. However, although this may be true in the aggregate, it might not be true for all forests. Because of their importance to biodiversity and carbon sequestration, we conducted a more detailed analysis of climate-induced impacts on tropical rain forests.

Rain forests are located primarily on LC 6 in tropical areas. Table 9.17 depicts direct climate–induced losses on LC 6 in tropical areas (from 18.4 to 51.0 percent) along with the indirect losses of forest (from 18.7 to 51.6 percent), cropland (from 18.3 to 49.3 percent) and pasture (from 20.5 to 55.7 percent) on LC 6 estimated by FARM's CGE. The decline in forest is larger (while the decline in cropland is smaller) than the decline in total LC 6 in all scenarios. These results indicate that competition from crop production could aggravate climate-induced losses of tropical rain forests.

*Table 9.17   Impact of climate change on LC 6 in tropical areas: percentage changes in total area and land use*

| Scenario | Percentage change in LC 6 acreage | | | |
|---|---|---|---|---|
| | Total | In forest | In cropland | In pasture |
| GISS | −20.1 | −20.5 | −19.6 | −22.1 |
| GFDL | −39.5 | −40.0 | −38.7 | −42.9 |
| UKMO | −51.0 | −51.6 | −49.3 | −55.7 |
| OSU | −18.4 | −18.7 | −18.3 | −20.5 |

**Land use movements**
Behind the net land use changes lie various conversions of land from one use to another.[19] Table 9.18 shows aggregate land use movements generated by the GCM climate change scenarios. Minimum estimates of global land movements range from 6.5 to 10.2 percent of total acreage. In most regions, minimum estimates of land converted from one use to another are less than 15 percent. In the European Union and Japan, however, estimated land use changes range from 10.5 to 20.4 and from 15.2 to 23.9 percent, respectively. Minimum estimates of land use changes in the United States range from 8.3 to 15.1 percent of total acreage.

In some areas, negative impacts of climate change would cause farmers to abandon existing cropland. Table 9.19 summarizes these effects. For the world as a whole, 4.2 to 10.5 percent (60.2 to 150.7 million hectares) of existing cropland would be converted to other uses. In percentage terms, cropland losses are greatest in the European Union and the United States – from 7.3 to 15.6 percent (from 5.6

*Table 9.18*   *Percentage of land changing use by region and climate change scenario*

| Scenario | US | Canada | EU | Japan | OEA[a] | SEA[b] | ANZ[c] | ROW[d] | Total |
|---|---|---|---|---|---|---|---|---|---|
| GISS | 8.3 | 8.4 | 16.6 | 15.8 | 7.7 | 7.5 | 2.4 | 5.9 | 6.4 |
| GFDL | 14.1 | 13.0 | 20.4 | 18.8 | 6.8 | 7.5 | 4.9 | 9.1 | 9.5 |
| UKMO | 15.1 | 13.9 | 19.8 | 23.9 | 9.7 | 13.2 | 7.9 | 10.8 | 11.3 |
| OSU | 11.6 | 8.1 | 10.5 | 15.2 | 6.7 | 3.5 | 8.1 | 5.4 | 6.4 |

*Notes:*
a.    Other East Asia (China, Hong Kong, Taiwan and South Korea).
b.    Southeast Asia (Thailand, Indonesia, Philippines and Malaysia).
c.    Australia and New Zealand.
d.    Rest of world.

*Table 9.19*   *New and abandoned cropland by region and climate change scenario*

| Scenario | Region | | | | | | | | |
|---|---|---|---|---|---|---|---|---|---|
|  | US | Canada | EU | Japan | OEA[a] | SEA[b] | ANZ[c] | ROW[d] | Total |
| New cropland (% of current) | | | | | | | | | |
| GISS | 18.3 | 63.0 | 21.2 | 24.2 | 10.7 | 21.3 | 10.5 | 13.0 | 15.9 |
| GFDL | 23.1 | 87.1 | 23.1 | 31.9 | 12.2 | 23.2 | 19.0 | 8.4 | 14.9 |
| UKMO | 22.3 | 115.4 | 24.9 | 46.4 | 17.5 | 33.6 | 10.7 | 22.3 | 25.2 |
| OSU | 17.0 | 54.5 | 11.2 | 22.4 | 14.3 | 10.8 | 27.6 | 11.6 | 14.4 |
| New cropland (million hectares) | | | | | | | | | |
| GISS | 34.8 | 28.9 | 16.5 | 1.1 | 10.5 | 12.1 | 5.2 | 119.9 | 229.0 |
| GFDL | 43.8 | 40.0 | 18.0 | 1.5 | 12.1 | 13.2 | 9.4 | 77.4 | 215.4 |
| UKMO | 42.4 | 53.1 | 19.4 | 2.2 | 17.2 | 19.1 | 5.3 | 205.2 | 363.8 |
| OSU | 32.2 | 25.1 | 8.7 | 1.0 | 14.1 | 6.1 | 13.6 | 106.4 | 207.4 |
| Abandoned cropland (% of current) | | | | | | | | | |
| GISS | 8.6 | 0.0 | 14.4 | 6.3 | 0.6 | 1.9 | 7.8 | 2.9 | 4.2 |
| GFDL | 19.1 | 8.3 | 14.4 | 5.3 | 5.2 | 1.3 | 17.5 | 1.7 | 5.7 |
| UKMO | 17.5 | 3.1 | 15.6 | 5.7 | 5.3 | 2.9 | 16.1 | 9.7 | 10.5 |
| OSU | 15.3 | 5.4 | 7.2 | 4.7 | 6.8 | 1.4 | 5.6 | 6.2 | 7.3 |
| Abandoned cropland (million hectares) | | | | | | | | | |
| GISS | 16.2 | 0.0 | 11.2 | 0.3 | 0.6 | 1.1 | 3.8 | 27.0 | 60.2 |
| GFDL | 36.4 | 3.8 | 11.2 | 0.2 | 5.2 | 0.8 | 8.6 | 15.8 | 82.0 |
| UKMO | 33.2 | 1.4 | 12.1 | 0.3 | 5.3 | 1.6 | 7.9 | 88.9 | 150.7 |
| OSU | 29.1 | 2.5 | 5.6 | 0.2 | 6.7 | 0.8 | 2.8 | 57.4 | 105.0 |

*Notes:*
a.    Other East Asia (China, Hong Kong, Taiwan and South Korea).
b.    Southeast Asia (Thailand, Indonesia, Philippines and Malaysia).
c.    Australia and New Zealand.
d.    Rest of world.

to 12.1 million hectares) and from 8.6 to 19.1 percent (16.2 to 36.4 million hectares), respectively. These results imply that some U.S. and EU farm communities could be severely disrupted by climate change.

Table 9.19 also shows that land newly converted to crop production is estimated to range from 14.4 to 25.2 percent (from 207.4 to 363.8 million hectares) of existing cropland. In percentage terms, the largest increases are in Canada, ranging from 54.5 to 115.4 percent (from 25.1 to 53.1 million hectares) of existing cropland. Such large increases may not be possible in Canada, however, because poor soil quality may limit cropland expansion regardless of how favorable temperature and precipitation conditions become (Ward et al., 1989). One advantage of our methodology is its ability to map the possibilities. We leave the questions of whether and exactly where farmers might add 28.9 million hectares of cropland in Canada to soil scientists and agronomists.

# 4  CONCLUSIONS

As predicted by four major GCMs, global changes in temperature and precipitation patterns during the next century are not likely to imperil food production for the world as a whole. Although world production of non-grain crops would be likely to decline, production of grain and livestock would likely increase. The net result is that world production of processed foods would be maintained slightly above current levels. These results are more positive than those suggested in previous research, even in research that includes the beneficial effects of atmospheric $CO_2$ on plant growth.

The agricultural benefits of climate change are not equally distributed. In Canada, for example, output of agricultural and processed food commodities increases, while in Southeast Asia, output of these commodities generally decreases in all scenarios. Impacts on mid-latitude regions are mixed. These production changes are correlated with changes in the world's endowment of land resources. Under climate change, warming in polar and alpine areas is likely to increase the quantity of land suitable for agricultural production. Warming in some areas, however, particularly the tropics, is likely to reduce soil moisture, thereby shortening growing seasons and decreasing agricultural possibilities.

A key reason for maintaining world food production under climate change will be the ability of farmers to respond to new climatic conditions. Even in areas where productivity is considerably reduced for existing agriculture, adopting appropriate crop and livestock mixes could substantially alleviate the initial impacts of climate change. Ways to encourage adopting appropriate crop and livestock mixes include reducing barriers to trade and implementing commodity support programs that allow farmers more flexibility in production decisions (see Lewandrowski and Brazee, 1993). Also, though not explicitly modeled in this research, expanding technical possibilities by strengthening institutions currently involved in the identification, development and transfer of agricultural technologies would increase the set of crop and livestock possibilities available to farmers. This would help farmers adjust to changes in soil or other non-climatic characteristics not considered here.

Another key reason for maintaining world food production under global climate change will be the ability of farmers to increase the amount of land under cultivation. This could be especially important in high latitude regions, where the amount of agriculturally suitable land is expected to increase under climate change. Some farm communities could be disrupted in this process, however, particularly in areas where the only economically viable adaptation is to abandon agriculture. Some land use and cover changes we simulate, however, may be hindered by agronomic, political, environmental or other constraints not accounted for in the FARM framework. Our framework's ability to link quantitative estimates of land use changes with specific geographic locations will help to flag and resolve some of these cases.

## NOTES

1. The economic principles behind our approach are demonstrated in Darwin et al. (1994) and Darwin et al. (1995).
2. Growing season lengths were provided by the World Soil Resources Office of USDA's Natural Resources Conservation Service.
3. FARM's CGE model is an aggregation and extension of the Global Trade Analysis Project (GTAP) model (Hertel, 1997). GTAP is built, in turn, upon the SALTER database of global trade developed by Australia's Industry Commission. A more complete description of FARM's economic framework and CGE model is in Darwin et al. (1995).
4. Only primary factor inputs are substitutable for one another in production. Intermediate inputs (represented by the traded commodities) are assumed to be used in fixed proportions.
5. Equilibrium scenarios presume that atmospheric concentrations of $CO_2$, temperature and precipitation have attained some stable steady state. At present, meteorologists are working to provide 'transient' climate change scenarios that show how temperature and precipitation would respond to increasing levels of atmospheric $CO_2$ through time.
6. Results from GCM simulations of current ($1 \times CO_2$) climate sometimes differ from actual climatic conditions. Comparing $2 \times CO_2$ GCM runs with $1 \times CO_2$ GCM runs minimizes the impacts of these errors while maintaining the overall integrity of the simulation results.
7. Revised growing season lengths are provided by the World Soil Resources Office of USDA's Natural Resources Conservation Service.
8. McKenney and Rosenberg (1993) suggest that Thornthwaite's method produces estimates of potential evapotranspiration that are unrealistically high at warmer locations. In Thornthwaite's method, however, potential evapotranspiration generally (1) is equal to zero when temperature is less than or equal to 0 °C; (2) increases at an increasing rate as temperatures range between 0 °C and 26.5 °C; (3) increases at a decreasing rate as temperatures range from 26.5 °C to 37.5 °C; and (4) is constant when temperature is above 37.5 °C. McKenney and Rosenberg derive their results solely from the formula used to estimate potential evapotranspiration between 0 °C and 26.5 °C. Their results, therefore, do not accurately portray Thornthwaite's method at warmer locations.
9. GIS estimates of renewable water computed with Leemans and Cramer (1991) weather data differ from those derived from WRI (1992). Comparing estimates of renewable water based on a standard weather database minimizes the impacts of these differences.

Global Environmental Change and Agriculture

10. The model embodies some technological innovation by assuming that productivity per unit area doesn't change when following a climate-induced migration of land classes, even when the migration is to poorer quality soils.
11. For more detailed results see Darwin et al. (1994, 1995).
12. Results are reported in ranges because we examine four climate change scenarios. Results for specific scenarios are shown in Table 9.10.
13. The GIS can track how much LC 4 cropland in a given region becomes LC 2, LC 3, LC 5 or LC 6 and how much remains LC 4. This is done by combining the relevant land use and cover data in Olson (1989–91) with the current and appropriate scenario-based land class data sets.
14. Rosenzweig and Parry (1994) do not report impacts on world cereals production for scenarios with their adaptation techniques but without $CO_2$ fertilization. They would undoubtedly be negative and, hence, less than ours.
15. These values are derived from changes in simulated wheat, rice and maize yields presented in Rosenzweig et al. (1993) combined with production data for 1990 in United Nations, Food and Agriculture Organization (1992).
16. Results in Table 9.13 indicate that, when land use changes are not allowed, world production of fish, meat and milk falls even though livestock numbers increase. This anomaly is due to increases in world output of small livestock (e.g. goats and sheep) and simultaneous declines in world production of large livestock (e.g. cattle). In the United States, the livestock and fish, meat and milk sectors move together.
17. FARM uses utility functions to determine household demands for goods and services. Changes in real GDP are equivalent to changes in utility. The sensitivity of these results to 50 percent increases and decreases of selected model parameters in all regions is analyzed in Darwin et al. (1995). The analysis indicates that results presented here are robust.
18. World GDP declines even though world food production increases because of spillovers into non-food sectors. For example, world production of services, which makes up 47 percent of world output, falls in the GFDL and UKMO scenarios.
19. Estimates of the quantities of land converted are derived by comparing the CGE model's land class pattern of land uses with the land class pattern of current land uses under alternative climatic conditions. The latter are generated by the GIS. If, for example, the CGE-estimated acreage for a particular land use in a given land class is less than the GIS-estimated acreage, then one can assume that the difference was converted to other uses.

# REFERENCES

Bowes, M.D. and Crosson, P.R. (1991), *Processes for Identifying Regional Influences of and Responses to Increasing Atmospheric $CO_2$ and Climate Change – the MINK Project – Report VI – Consequences of Climate Change for the MINK Economy: Impacts and Responses*, U.S. Department of Energy/RL/01830T-H12.

Codsi, G. and Pearson, K.R. (1988), 'GEMPACK: General-Purpose Software for General Equilibrium and Other Economic Modellers', *Computer Science in Economics and Management*, **1**, pp. 189–207.

Darwin, R.F., Lewandrowski, J., McDonald, B.J. and Tsigas, M. (1994), 'Global Climate Change: Analyzing Environmental Issues and Agricultural Trade within a Global Context', in Sullivan, J. (ed.), *Environmental Policies: Implications for Agricultural Trade*. (USDA, ERS, FAER No. 252), U.S. Government Printing Office, Washington, DC.

Darwin, R.F., Tsigas, M., Lewandrowski, J. and Raneses, A. (1995), *World Agriculture and Climate Change: Economic Adaptations*. (USDA, ERS, AER No. 703), U.S. Government Printing Office, Washington, DC.

Hansen, J., Fung, I., Lacis, A., Rind, D., Lebedeff, S., Ruedy, R. and Russell, G. (1988), 'Global Climate Changes as Forecasted by the Goddard Institute for Space Studies Three-Dimensional Model', *Journal of Geophysical Research*, **93**, pp. 9341–9364.

Hertel, T.W. (ed.) (1997), *Global Trade Analysis: Modeling and Implications,* Cambridge: Cambridge University Press.

Hertel, T.W., Horridge, J.M. and Pearson, K.R. (1992), 'Mending the Family Tree: A Reconciliation of the Linearization of Levels Schools of Applied General Equilibrium Modeling', *Economic Modeling,* **9**, pp. 385–407.

Intergovernmental Panel on Climate Change (IPCC) (1990), *Climate Change: The IPCC Impact Assessment,* Canberra, Australia: Australian Government Publishing Service.

Intergovernmental Panel on Climate Change (IPCC) (1992), *Climate Change 1992: The Supplementary Report to the IPCC Scientific Assessment,* Cambridge: Cambridge University Press.

Kane, S., Reilly, J. and Tobey, J. (1991), *Climate Change: Economic Implications for World Agriculture.* (USDA, ERS, AER No. 647), U.S. Government Printing Office, Washington, DC.

Leemans, R. and Cramer, W.P. (1991), *The IIASA Database for Mean Monthly Values of Temperature, Precipitation, and Cloudiness on a Global Terrestrial Grid,* Digital Raster Data on a 30 minute Geographic (lat/long) 360 × 720 grid, Laxenburg, Austria: International Institute for Applied Systems Analysis.

Leemans, R. and Solomon, A.M. (1993), 'Modeling the Potential Change in Yield and Distribution of the Earth's Crops Under a Warmed Climate', *Climate Research,* **3**, pp.79–96.

Lewandrowski, J.K. and Brazee, R.J. (1993), 'Farm Programs and Climate Change', *Climatic Change,* **23**, pp.1–20.

Manabe, S. and Wetherald, R.T. (1987), 'Large-Scale Changes in Soil Wetness Induced by an Increase in $CO_2$', *Journal of Atmospheric Science,* **44**, pp. 1211–1235.

McKenney, M.S. and Rosenberg, N.J. (1993), 'Sensitivity of Some Potential Evapotranspiration Estimation Methods to Climate Change', *Agricultural and Forest Meteorology,* **64**, pp. 81–110.

Newhall, F. (1980), 'Calculation of Soil Moisture Regimes from the Climatic Record' (Rev. 7) USDA, Soil Conservation Service, Mimeograph.

Olson, J.S. (1989-91), *World Ecosystems (WE1.3),* Digital Raster Data on Global Geographic (lat/long) 360 × 720 grid. Boulder, CO: NOAA National Geophysical Data Center.

Parry, M. (1990), *Climate Change and World Agriculture,* London: Earthscan Publications Limited.

Parry, M., Carter, T. and Konijn, N. (eds) (1988), *The Impacts of Climatic Variations on Agriculture, Vol. 1: Assessments in Cool Temperate and Cold Regions,* IIASA/UNEP, Boston: Kluwer Academic Publishers.

Pearson, K. (1988), 'Automating the Computation of Solutions of Large Economic Models', *Economic Modeling,* **5**, pp. 385–395.

Pearson, K. (1991), 'Solving Nonlinear Economic Models Accurately Via a Linear Representation', Preliminary Working Paper No. IP-55, The Impact Project, Impact Research Centre, University of Melbourne.

Reilly, J., Hohmann, N. and Kane, S. (1993), 'Climate Change and Agriculture: Global and Regional Effects Using an Economic Model of International Trade' (MIT-CEEPR 93-012WP), Massachusetts Institute of Technology, Center for Energy and Environmental Policy Research.

Rosenzweig, C. and Iglesias, A. (eds) (1994), *Implications of Climate Change for International Agriculture: Crop Modeling Study* (U.S. Environmental Protection Agency, Office of Policy, Planning, and Evaluation. EPA 230-B-94-003), Washington, DC: U.S. Government Printing Office.

Rosenzweig, C. and Parry, M. (1994), 'Potential Impact of Climate Change on World Food Supply', *Nature,* **367**, pp. 133–138.

Rosenzweig, C., Parry, M., Frohberg, K. and Fisher, G. (1993), 'Climate Change and World Food Supply' (Research Report No. 3), Environmental Change Unit, University of Oxford.

Schlesinger, M.E. and Zhao, A.C. (1989), *Seasonal Climatic Changes Induced by Doubled $CO_2$ as Simulated by the OSU Atmospheric GCM/Mixed-Layer Ocean Model.* (Climate Research Institute, Report No. 70), Corvallis, OR: Oregon State University.

Thornthwaite, C.W. (1948), 'An Approach toward a Rational Classification of Climate', *Geographical Review*, **38**, pp. 55–94.

United Nations. Food and Agriculture Organization (1992), *Agrostat,* Rome, Italy.

Ward, J.R., Hardt, R.A. and Kuhule, T.E. (1989), *Farming in the Greenhouse: What Global Warming Means for American Agriculture*, Washington, DC: National Resources Defense Council.

Washington, W.M. and Meehl, G.A. (1984), 'Seasonal Cycle Experiment on the Climate Sensitivity Due to a Doubling of $CO_2$ with an Atmospheric General Circulation Model Coupled to a Mixed-Layer Ocean Model', *Journal of Geophysical Research*, **89**, pp. 9475–9503.

Wilson, C.A. and Mitchell, J.F.B (1987), 'A Doubled $CO_2$ Climate Sensitivity Experiment with a Global Climate Model Including a Simple Ocean', *Journal of Geophysical Research*, **92**, pp. 315–343.

World Resources Institute (WRI) (1992), *World Resources 1992–93: A Guide to the Global Environment*, Oxford: Oxford University Press.

# 10  Carbon Abatement: Lessons from Second-Best Economics

## Ian W.H. Parry

## 1  INTRODUCTION

According to the traditional approach in environmental economics, it is optimal to reduce emissions of a pollutant until the incremental environmental benefits (or damages avoided) equal the incremental economic cost. This optimum can be induced by either setting a tax on emissions equal to marginal environmental damage, or by issuing the appropriate quantity of emissions permits. The welfare gain from achieving this optimum is the difference between marginal environmental benefit and marginal abatement cost, integrated over the level of abatement. So far the attempts to develop a cost/benefit analysis of carbon dioxide ($CO_2$) abatement, in response to the possibility that atmospheric accumulations of this gas will cause future global climate change, have used this basic theory.[1] The conclusion from these studies is that the currently optimal tax on the carbon content of fossil fuels (the primary source of $CO_2$ emissions) is around $5 to $20 per ton, although there is a good deal of uncertainty and controversy surrounding these estimates.

For our purposes, the key feature of these cost/benefit studies is that they assume a first-best world. That is, they focus on the $CO_2$ externality distortion in the fossil fuel market, but they do not take into account interactions between this market and other distorted markets in the economy. Even in a market-based economy like the United States, market imperfections are very pervasive, due to distortions created by taxes, regulations, imperfect competition, other externalities, and so on. Indeed there is a long tradition in the public finance literature warning that the outcomes from second-best analyses, which do capture the secondary welfare effects of policies in other distorted markets, can be very different from those implied by a first-best analysis (Lipsey and Lancaster, 1956; Harberger, 1974).

How important are these sources of pre-existing market distortions in the context of carbon abatement policies? Fortunately, many of these distortions are small in size and are in markets that are very distant from the fossil fuel market, and incorporating them into the analysis would have negligible empirical effect. For example, Oates and Strassmann (1984) found that allowing for imperfect competition in the United States economy had little empirical significance for implementing environmental policies in general, because the price distortions created by monopoly pricing are typically small. However, this is not the case for pre-existing distortions created by the tax system. Indeed, some very recent studies have shown that allowing for taxes in factor markets can crucially affect not only the magnitude, but also the sign, of the welfare impact from environmental policies.[2]

Environmental policies interact with the tax system in two important respects (Goulder, 1995a). First, to the extent that they cause the economy-wide level of employment or investment to fall, they compound the welfare cost of pre-existing taxes in these markets. Second, environmental policies can produce an efficiency gain to counteract this loss, if they raise revenues and these are used to cut the level of pre-existing distortionary taxes. Non-auctioned emissions quotas do not directly affect revenues, and do not produce this latter efficiency benefit. Indeed the net welfare loss from interactions with the tax system can be large enough to more than offset the traditional partial equilibrium gain from imposing an emissions quota, when environmental benefits are relatively modest. In contrast, because of the efficiency value of the revenues raised, an emissions tax is potentially welfare-improving, regardless of the level of environmental benefits.

The purpose of this chapter is to pull together this recent literature on environmental policy in a second-best setting, and discuss the implications for carbon abatement policies. This is a very complex topic, so we proceed in stages. The next section summarizes the results from highly simplified analytical models, which have examined the interactions between environmental policies and a pre-existing tax distortion in the labor market. In these models, the overall welfare gain from introducing a balanced-budget environmental tax is generally lower in the presence of a labor tax than when there is no labor tax. In addition, the second-best optimal emissions tax is somewhat below the first-best optimal tax, which is equal to marginal environmental damages. Probably the most important result, however, is that given existing 'best estimates' for damages from carbon emissions, it is possible that only a revenue-raising instrument – a tax or auctioned carbon quota – can increase economic efficiency. Section 3 discusses the results from numerical models, that allow for more complex features of the tax system. In general, these results support those from the analytical models. Section 4 briefly discusses some implications for carbon abatement policies in other countries. Section 5 summarizes the main conclusions of the chapter.

## 2   RESULTS FROM ANALYTICAL MODELS

Several recent analytical papers have examined how a pre-existing tax in the labor market affects the welfare impact of an environmental tax (Bovenberg and de Mooij, 1994; Bovenberg and van der Ploeg, 1994; Parry, 1995).[3] The models have a similar structure. They assume households gain utility from consumption goods, leisure and environmental quality. Labor supplied by households is the only primary input (i.e. there is no capital input), and labor supply plus leisure equals the aggregate household time endowment. Firms use labor to produce consumption goods and intermediate goods under competition and constant returns to scale. Producing one of the goods (either a consumption or intermediate good) causes a proportional amount of waste emissions, which reduce environmental quality. The government levies a tax on labor income and also taxes emissions. These revenues finance an exogenous amount of non-distortionary spending.[4] The models focus on 'revenue-neutral' or 'balanced-budget' environmental taxes; that is, extra revenues generated by increasing the environmental tax are recycled in labor tax cuts.

The labor tax drives a wedge between the gross wage paid by firms and the net wage received by households. Firms employ labor until the value of its marginal product equals the gross wage and households supply labor until the value of foregone leisure time equals the net wage. Consequently, the labor tax creates a welfare loss because the equilibrium quantity of employment is below the point where marginal social benefit equals marginal social cost.

### Welfare Impacts of a Carbon Tax

In this setting, the welfare effect of a tax on emissions from a particular commodity, such as carbon emissions from fossil fuels, can be separated into three components.[5] First, there is the *primary welfare gain* in the regulated market from reducing the quantity of emissions, for which marginal social cost exceeds marginal social benefit. This is the focus of a first-best analysis. In the context of carbon abatement, it is the present discounted value of the benefits from avoided future climate change less the current economic costs of abatement due to the induced reduction in carbon-intensive fuels.

Second is the *revenue-recycling effect*. This is the efficiency gain from using the emissions tax revenues to reduce the rate of labor tax relative to the case where these revenues are returned to households as lump sum transfers (and have no efficiency consequences). That is, the gain from reducing the wedge between the marginal social benefit and marginal social cost of labor, thereby increasing employment towards the socially efficient level.

Third is the *tax-interaction effect*, which is the welfare loss from the reduction in aggregate labor supply indirectly caused by the emissions tax. If firms are charged a tax on their emissions, this increases their marginal cost of production, and will result in a higher final product price. Indeed, given the assumptions of competition and constant returns to scale, the full amount of the tax is passed on in a higher final product price, and there is no reduction in the net price received by producers. This causes a reduction in the real wage received by households (the nominal wage divided by an index of consumer goods prices). In general, the real wage reduction reduces aggregate labor supply because the return to work effort relative to leisure falls. This produces a welfare loss in the labor market because of the wedge between the marginal social benefit and marginal social cost of labor. In addition, the reduction in employment reduces labor tax revenues and the tax-interaction effect also incorporates the resulting efficiency loss.[6]

The effect on aggregate employment from the tax-interaction effect will be slight. In particular, it will be much less than the labor released from the fossil fuel producing and consuming industries that contract in response to the emissions tax, since most of this labor will be absorbed by other (substitute) industries rather than becoming 'unemployed'.[7] However, the welfare loss from the tax-interaction effect can still be important relative to the primary welfare effect, since the welfare loss per unit of labor is 'large'. This occurs because, when we take into account federal and state income taxes, social security taxes, sales taxes and benefit withdrawal as income rises, the marginal rate of tax on labor earnings faced by the average household is substantial, around 40 percent (Browning, 1987).

The analytical models indicate (either explicitly or implicitly) that in general the tax-interaction effect dominates the revenue-recycling effect. That is, the net effect of the emissions tax is to reduce aggregate labor supply, hence producing a net welfare loss from interactions with the tax system. This means that raising additional revenue from an emissions tax involves a higher efficiency loss (ignoring environmental benefits) than raising the same amount of revenue by increasing the labor tax. There are two reasons for this.

First of all, assume that fossil fuels are used in fixed proportions to final output, that is, raising the price of fossil fuels does not induce firms to substitute labor and other inputs for fossil fuels in production. In this case, taxing fossil fuels is equivalent to taxing final output from industries that use fossil fuels. Call this output $X$, and all other consumption $Y$. Also, note that a tax on labor income received is equivalent to a uniform tax on consumption expenditure in a static model, where there is no income from capital and all labor income is spent. If the revenue-recycling effect were larger than the tax-interaction effect, then, holding total revenue constant, introducing a small tax on $X$ and reducing the consumption (labor) tax would increase welfare. But we know from the theory of optimal commodity taxation (see, for example, Sandmo (1976)) that this result could only hold if $X$ were a sufficiently weaker substitute for leisure than $Y$. If $X$ were an equal (or stronger) substitute for leisure, then this tax change would necessarily reduce welfare. This is because the base of the tax on $X$ is smaller than the base of the consumption tax $(X + Y)$. Therefore, raising a given amount of revenue requires a higher tax rate on $X$ than it would if the tax were levied on $X + Y$. In addition, it is easier for consumers to substitute away from $X$ (into $Y$ as well as leisure) in response to the tax, compared with the broader-based tax. Both of these factors raise the welfare cost of a tax on fossil fuels relative to an equal revenue-yield labor tax.

The second reason is that the fossil fuel tax distorts the mix of inputs used in production, as well as the quantity of final goods and leisure. Relaxing the assumption of fixed proportions, the fossil fuel tax will lead to some replacement of fossil fuels by labor and other inputs in the production of $X$. This opens up another channel for substituting away from the taxed commodity, thereby increasing the welfare cost of the tax. A well-known result in public finance is that, for a given revenue-yield, taxing an input used in variable proportions is more distortionary than taxing final output (Diamond and Mirrlees, 1971; Wisecarver, 1974). In contrast, since the labor tax is equivalent to a uniform consumption tax, it does not affect production efficiency (assuming labor is the only primary input).

In summary, only if final output from industries that use fossil fuels intensively were a sufficiently weaker substitute for leisure than other consumption goods, could the revenue-recycling effect outweigh the tax-interaction effect in the analytical models described above. Fossil fuel-intensive consumption goods primarily consist of transportation and electricity-intensive goods. Very little is known about the relative degree of substitution between these goods and leisure, but there is no obvious reason to suggest that it would differ substantially from that for the average consumption good. Despite the net loss from interactions with the tax system, however, the analytical models show that the emissions tax is still potentially welfare-improving (unless the $X$ sector is a very strong substitute for leisure relative to the $Y$ sector). That is, the primary welfare gain still dominates the tax-interaction effect net of the revenue-recycling effect.

### The Rise and Fall of the Double Dividend Hypothesis

These analytical studies, and the numerical work discussed below, have refuted the widely held view that there was a 'double dividend' from environmental taxes. The essential idea behind the double dividend hypothesis was that environmental taxes could simultaneously correct environmental externality distortions and provide other gains when the revenues raised were used to cut other distortionary taxes. These gains were either defined in terms of increased economic efficiency or other desirable goals, such as reduced unemployment and increased investment. The double dividend argument took several different forms, and Goulder (1995a) has distinguished the following three:

1. *Weak form*: this asserts that using emissions tax revenues to reduce other distortionary taxes will produce an efficiency gain, relative to the case when revenues are returned to taxpayers in a lump sum fashion.
2. *Intermediate form*: the overall welfare impact of a balanced-budget emissions tax is greater in the presence of pre-existing tax distortions than where there is no pre-existing tax.
3. *Strong form*: not only is there a net welfare gain because of the pre-existing tax, but this gain more than offsets the primary costs of emissions reduction within the regulated market.

The third form asserts that the gross cost of an emissions tax (i.e. without subtracting environmental benefits) is negative. In this case, introducing a balanced-budget emissions tax could produce an efficiency gain, even if environmental benefits were very small, or even zero. This is a particularly appealing notion in the context of carbon abatement, where the benefits from emissions reduction are very difficult to quantify. It implies that we can do something to reduce the threat of possible future global climate change and, even if this threat turns out to be non-existent, we will have incurred no costs and possibly even positive economic benefits. The second form asserts that, in a static setting where the pre-existing tax is on labor income, the net effect of an emissions tax is to increase efficiency in the labor market by *increasing* employment. In this connection, Repetto et al. (1992) suggested that using the revenues from a $40 carbon tax in the United States to cut other distorting taxes could produce enormous efficiency gains of around $20–30 billion each year, in addition to any efficiency gain from offsetting the carbon externality.[8] These claims caught the attention of policy makers in Western Europe, where unemployment seems to be 'stuck' at rates often in excess of 12 percent. It was thought that, by imposing a carbon, or more broad-based energy tax, 'two birds could be killed with one stone'; that is, emissions of carbon and aggregate unemployment could be reduced at the same time.

Unfortunately, as is often the case in economics, there is no such free lunch. The double dividend hypothesis was based on an analysis which 'tacked on' the revenue-recycling effect to partial equilibrium models of emissions abatement. As discussed above, a more complete analysis would take into account the tax-interaction effect, which generally negates the hypothesis in both its strong and intermediate form. Therefore, the large revenue potential from a carbon tax does *not* strengthen the case for introducing such a tax *per se*. However, the debate over the double dividend has at least made a very valuable contribution in drawing attention to the potentially large efficiency gains to be had from using emissions tax revenues to cut distortionary taxes rather than for other purposes (this is discussed further below).[9]

## Second-Best Optimal Carbon Tax

The analytical models indicate that (when output from the polluting sector is an average substitute for leisure) the marginal cost of emissions reduction in the presence of a labor tax, $MC_t$ in Figure 10.1, has a steeper slope than the primary or partial equilibrium marginal cost $MC_p$. The first-best or Pigouvian tax, $t_p$, equals marginal environmental benefit $MB$ (assumed to be constant for simplicity), and induces an emissions reduction of $R_p$. However, this tax is too high from an efficiency-maximizing perspective. The second-best optimal emissions reduction is $R_t^*$ in Figure 10.1, where $MC_t$ and $MB$ intersect. To induce this requires a tax of $t^*$. Given existing estimates of the labor tax wedge and labor supply elasticities for the United States, the second-best optimal tax is about 90 percent of the Pigouvian tax in Bovenberg and Goulder's (1996) analytical model, and 60–80 percent of the Pigouvian tax in Parry (1995).[10]

Earlier studies suggested that the discrepancy between the optimal environmental tax and the Pigouvian tax was positively related to marginal tax revenue (Lee and Misiolek, 1986; Oates, 1995). The latter declines with the level of abatement and is negative beyond the revenue-maximizing tax, or peak of the Laffer curve. Therefore, these studies suggested that if marginal environmental benefits are low (high) relative to marginal abatement costs, then the optimal emissions tax is above (below) marginal environmental

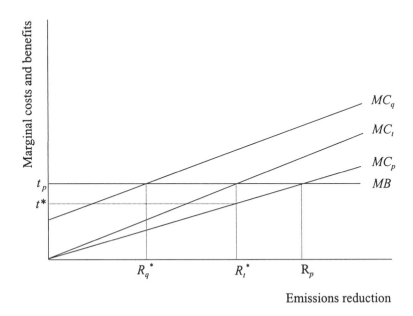

*Figure 10.1  Pre-existing taxes and the marginal cost of abatement*

benefits. Indeed Nordhaus (1993a) estimated that the optimal tax on carbon in his model increased from $5 per ton to $59 per ton, when carbon tax revenues are used to cut other taxes. Again, these studies just focused on the revenue-raising effect. However, when allowance is also made for the tax-interaction effect, the optimal emissions tax can only exceed marginal environmental benefits under fairly restrictive conditions (Parry, 1995).

## Welfare Impacts of a Carbon Quota

To date, much less attention has been paid to the welfare effects of emissions quotas (or permits) in the presence of distortionary taxes. The key difference between an emissions tax and a (non-auctioned) emissions quota in this respect is that the former directly raises revenue while the latter does not. Two recent papers (Goulder et al., 1997 and Parry, 1997) have emphasized that this distinction can imply a significant empirical difference, and even a difference in sign, between the overall welfare effects of emissions taxes and quotas.

Using a similar model structure to that described above, Goulder et al. (1997) and Parry (1997) indicate that a quota causes the same tax-interaction effect as an emissions tax. This is because the quota effectively creates a price or virtual tax on emissions (equal to the sale value of a quota) that increases marginal production costs and final product prices and thereby reduces the real wage. For a given reduction in emissions, the tax-interaction effect is the same for both the emissions tax and quota.

Parry (1997) suggested that there is no revenue-recycling effect from the quota to offset the tax-interaction effect. However, Goulder et al. (1997) point out that allocating quotas creates rents, by limiting entry into the regulated industry. These are reflected in higher firm profits which are subject to corporate income taxation, and personal income taxation when returned to households. Therefore, quotas do actually raise revenue, albeit indirectly. Still, since the effective tax rate on such rent income is around 40 percent,[11] the revenue-recycling effect from the quota is only about 40 percent of that in the emissions tax case.

This implies that, for a given level of emissions abatement, total abatement costs are higher under the quota than the tax. Indeed, in the context of $SO_2$ abatement, Goulder et al. (1997) found this discrepancy is quite striking at modest levels of abatement. For example, if the emissions reduction is below 20 percent, then the cost of the quota is more than double the cost of the tax. However, at higher levels of abatement the discrepancy is much less substantial. The addition to the revenue-recycling effect from incremental increases in the emissions tax is declining, while the incremental addition to the tax-interaction effect is approximately constant. This is because the emissions tax base declines with abatement, and the revenue loss from incremental reductions in emissions increases as the emissions tax increases. At an emissions reduction of around 50 percent, increasing the emissions tax actually starts to reduce revenue. That is, the downward-sloping part of the emissions tax Laffer curve is reached. At the limit of 100 percent emissions reduction, the overall cost of the tax and quota is the same. This is because there is no revenue raised from the tax, and hence no revenue-recycling effect.

These results have important implications for welfare. Suppose the first-best level of emissions tax or quota is introduced. If marginal environmental benefits are modest relative to the primary marginal cost of abatement, then the overall welfare impact of the quota can be negative. That is, the net loss from interactions with the tax system can be large enough to more than offset the primary welfare gain. In this case, only the emissions tax can increase welfare. However, when environmental benefits are larger, implying the first-best emissions reduction would be in the order of 50 percent or more, Goulder et al. (1997) find that the overall welfare impact of the quota is positive. Nevertheless, it can still be significantly lower than when there is no pre-existing labor tax. Returning to Figure 10.1, suppose that the first-best quantity of quotas is imposed, reducing emissions to $R_p$. This will reduce welfare if the area between $MC_q$ and $MB$ and $R_q^*$ and $R_p$, exceeds that between $MB$ and $MC_q$ from 0 to $R_q^*$. Also, note that $MC_q$ has a positive intercept. This means that if $MB$ lies below this intercept, then no level of quota can increase welfare.

No empirical studies (that I am aware of) have been done comparing the efficiency effects of carbon quotas and carbon taxes in the presence of distorting taxes. However, in a simulation from Bovenberg and Goulder's (1996) numerical model, a carbon tax where the revenues are returned as lump sum transfers (rather than used to cut other taxes) reduces welfare unless the damages per ton of carbon exceed $50. Since lump sum transfers have no efficiency consequences, this policy is equivalent to a carbon quota where none of the quota rents are received by the government. If instead, rent income is taxed at 40 percent, we can speculate that this threshold would be around $30 per ton.[12] Most of the 'best estimates' (i.e. using median parameter values from the economics and scientific literature) for carbon damages are actually *below* $30 per ton.[13] These estimates are relatively low, because most economic activity is not particularly sensitive to the modest changes in climate predicted over the next century, and because discounting over long periods of time substantially reduces the present value of economic impacts. However, under more extreme scenarios for climate change, or when the utility of future generations is not discounted, then damages per ton can rise well above this threshold.[14]

In summary, although yet to be confirmed by rigorous empirical analysis, there would appear to be a compelling case on efficiency grounds for preferring carbon taxes to carbon quotas if action is to be taken to reduce carbon emissions. Aside from more extreme scenarios for climate change, it seems possible that only the carbon tax can increase welfare using conventional cost/benefit criteria, and a quota is necessarily welfare-reducing. However, this distinction arises entirely from the revenue-raising feature of the carbon tax. If carbon quotas were auctioned rather than given away free, they could potentially generate the same revenues as a tax and hence produce the same efficiency benefits from the revenue-recycling effect.

**Some Further Issues**

Analytical studies of carbon taxes and quotas raise three further policy questions. First, should carbon tax revenues be used for purposes other than cutting taxes? Carbon tax revenues could be used for a variety of purposes other than cutting distortionary taxes. For example, they could be earmarked for further carbon-reducing policies, such as subsidies for tree growing.[15] Alternatively, they could be used to neutralize the distributional consequences of the carbon tax. Since consumption goods that are produced intensively from fossil fuels, in particular electricity and gasoline, are necessities, their share of expenditure in total consumption expenditure is greater for lower income households. Therefore a carbon tax, which drives up the price of these goods, is regressive (Poterba, 1991). This effect could be counteracted (albeit imperfectly) by, for example, using carbon tax revenues to finance an increase in the earned income tax credit or higher means-tested benefits.[16] However, the opportunity cost of using revenues for these purposes rather than to cut other taxes is the revenue-recycling effect. Only if they generated benefits to society (in terms of increased efficiency, more desirable income distribution, etc.) in excess of the dollar cost plus the revenue-recycling effect, could they be justified on cost/benefit criteria.

Second, should we tax economic 'bads' (pollution) instead of 'goods' such as employment? At first glance, the answer to this question sounds obvious: is it not better to raise a given amount of revenue from taxes that discourage pollution rather than taxes that discourage employment? However, taxes on emissions are in fact implicit taxes on labor, since they reduce the real wage received by households. Therefore, both the emissions tax and the labor tax reduce employment. Indeed, as discussed above, to raise a given amount of revenue it is more efficient to use a labor tax than an emissions tax, since it has a broader base and does not distort production efficiency. Nevertheless environmental taxes are still part of an optimal tax system, albeit at a somewhat lower level than the first-best tax.

Third, should we ever subsidize pollution? The above discussion indicated that reducing emissions by a non-auctioned quota may sometimes reduce welfare. Does this mean that a subsidy for emissions which increased production and employment can be welfare-improving? In general, the answer to this is no. There are two effects of a subsidy, as well as the primary welfare effect, when the labor market is distorted by taxes. First, the welfare cost of financing the subsidy by distortionary taxation, which is the mirror image of the revenue-recycling effect for emissions taxes. Second, the tax-interaction effect, which is now a welfare gain since the subsidy reduces the price of consumption goods, hence increasing the real wage and employment. In general there is a net loss from these two effects (Parry, 1998) in addition to the primary welfare loss.

# 3   RESULTS FROM NUMERICAL MODELS

The analytical models described above can explain the key mechanisms by which environmental policies interact with the tax system in a simple and intuitive fashion. However, their empirical usefulness is limited in a number of respects. First, although these models can be used to estimate the effects of incremental policy changes, they can only estimate the effects of 'large' policy changes if demand and the primary marginal cost of emissions reduction are taken to be linear. In general, demand curves must be non-linear in order to satisfy various adding up properties associated with the household's budget constraint (Deaton and Muellbauer, 1980), and the primary marginal cost of reducing carbon is thought to be convex (Nordhaus, 1991b). Therefore, an analytical model can only generate second order welfare approximations, which may be unreliable for 'large' reductions in emissions. Instead, solving the model by numerical simulation avoids this problem. Second, in the context of carbon abatement, numerical models are able to capture more complex features of the fossil fuel sector and tax system that are not tractable within an analytical model. This allows the sensitivity of the results from analytical models to be examined in a more general setting, with a variety of different channels for reducing carbon, and interactions with other tax distortions besides those in the labor market.

Important numerical contributions in this area include Bovenberg and Goulder (1996, 1997), which use a dynamic computable general equilibrium model of the United States economy. This model incorporates a particularly detailed treatment of how the tax system affects household consumption, saving and labor supply decisions, as well as firm investment, output and input choices.[17]

**The Implications of Taxes on Capital**

Bovenberg and Goulder (1997) address the important issue of whether incorporating capital accumulation, and the taxation of capital income, affects the results on environmental taxes discussed above. In this case, the tax-interaction effect is defined more broadly to include the welfare loss from any reduction in aggregate investment, as well as that from any reduction in

Global Environmental Change and Agriculture

aggregate labor supply, caused by an environmental tax. This more general setting with two primary factor inputs introduces the possibility of a *tax-shifting* effect. Even though the tax wedge in the capital market in the United States is around the same magnitude as that in the labor market, the former is thought to be more distorting.[18] This is because a tax on capital discourages investment, while a tax on labor discourages work effort, and investment is estimated to be relatively more sensitive to tax increases than labor supply.[19] Therefore the efficiency cost of raising an extra dollar of revenue from taxes on capital is thought to be higher than that for taxes on labor.[20] That is, capital is 'overtaxed' relative to labor. In this situation, a policy change which induced firms to substitute capital for labor at the economy-wide level would produce an efficiency gain from the tax-shifting effect and reduce the overall cost of the tax-interaction effect. This means that, even if output from the sector affected by an environmental tax is an average substitute for leisure, the net effect of the revenue-recycling and tax-interaction effects could be positive. Here the environmental tax could produce a double dividend (in the intermediate form). A revenue-neutral environmental tax is more likely to produce such a double dividend by this mechanism when: (a) the environmental tax revenues are used to cut taxes on capital rather than labor, thereby increasing the demand for capital relative to labor; and (b) when the environmental tax is levied on a relatively labor-intensive industry, so that a greater share of the tax-interaction effect is felt in the (less distorted) labor market than in the capital market.

The numerical results in Bovenberg and Goulder (1997) confirm the significance of the tax-shifting effect. They examine two taxes that have been proposed to reduce carbon emissions and other pollutants: a gasoline tax and a Btu tax. A Btu tax is a tax on all fossil fuels based on their heat content measured in British thermal units (Btus). The latter has a broader tax base and, therefore, for a given revenue yield one might expect it to have a lower efficiency cost (ignoring environmental benefits) than the gasoline tax. However, the gasoline tax causes a significant tax-shifting effect, while the Btu tax does not, and this is large enough so that the overall efficiency cost is lower under the gasoline tax.

Nevertheless, Bovenberg and Goulder (1996) find that, even when the revenues from gasoline and Btu taxes are used to reduce taxes on capital, there is still no double dividend, under a wide variety of assumptions about key parameter values. This contrasts with Jorgenson and Wilcoxen (1993), who do find a significant double dividend from environmental taxes, if the revenues are specifically targeted to reduce the most distortionary taxes in the economy. Poterba (1993, p. 55) sums up the debate as follows:

> Simply demonstrating that raising the carbon tax and reducing other onerous taxes would lead to an efficiency gain does not imply that carbon taxes should be adopted. Rather, one must compare the carbon tax policy with the set of all feasible policies that could reduce the onerous taxes and achieve a balanced budget. On reflection,

however, the revenue-recycling argument may make more sense. If there is a causal link between enacting a carbon tax and cutting particular other taxes, perhaps because of political constraints on raising existing taxes, then it *is* appropriate to consider how the funds are used in evaluating the net benefit from a carbon tax. Absent a strong basis for linking enactment of a carbon tax to other particular tax changes, a plausible assumption is that carbon taxes would be paired with a proportionate reduction in all existing revenue sources [in which case a double dividend seems unlikely].

## The Optimal Carbon Tax Revisited

Table 10.1 presents Bovenberg and Goulder's (1996) estimates for the second-best optimal carbon tax in the United States under damage scenarios varying from $25 to $100 per ton of carbon. The first row shows the optimum tax from a first-best analysis which is just equal to the damages per ton. The second row shows the second-best optimal tax from Bovenberg's analytical model, discussed in section 2, when carbon tax revenues finance reductions in taxes on labor income. This is equal to about 89 percent of the first-best tax, regardless of the level of damages per ton.

The third row shows the optimal carbon tax in the numerical model when the revenues are returned as lump sum transfers to households. It is dramatically below the first-best tax, and is zero when damages are $50 per ton or below. This reflects the role of the tax-interaction effect in shifting up the overall marginal cost of emissions reduction so that damages must be above a threshold

*Table 10.1   Differences between Pigouvian and second-best taxes*
*(all rates in dollars per ton)*

|  | Assumed marginal environmental damages (dollars/ton) | | | |
|---|---|---|---|---|
|  | 25 | 50 | 75 | 100 |
| Optimal tax from analytical models: | | | | |
| 1.  Optimal Pigouvian tax | 25 | 50 | 75 | 100 |
| 2.  Optimal tax implied by analytical model with personal income tax (PIT) replacement | 22 | 45 | 67 | 89 |
| Optimal tax from numerical models: | | | | |
| 3.  Realistic benchmark, lump sum replacement | 0 | 0 | 13 | 31 |
| 4.  Realistic benchmark, PIT replacement | 7 | 27 | 48 | 68 |
| 5.  Optimized benchmark, PIT replacement | 17 | 41 | 64 | 85 |

*Source*: Bovenberg and Goulder (1996).

level before abatement can increase welfare. In the fourth row, carbon tax revenues are used to increase efficiency by reducing the rate of personal income taxation. The optimal tax is higher in this case, about 55–65 percent of the first-best tax when damages are $50 or above, but is still significantly below that implied by the analytical model. Bovenberg and Goulder (1996) suggest that this discrepancy is due to the suboptimality of the existing tax system (which is captured in the numerical but not the analytical model). In addition, the gasoline tax is effectively a tax on carbon emissions from the transportation sector. Therefore, an optimal tax system is created in which the efficiency cost of raising an additional dollar of revenue is equalized across all taxes in the economy (and which yields the same total revenue as in the realistic tax case). This involves reducing the relative tax on capital and eliminating taxes on intermediate inputs, industry outputs and consumer goods. In this case, the second-best optimal carbon tax (fifth row) is much closer to that in the analytical model. These results indicate, therefore, that extending the analytical models of section 2 to allow for more complex features of the tax system leads to a further reduction in the second-best optimal carbon tax.

# 4    INTERNATIONAL IMPLICATIONS

This section briefly examines whether the revenue-recycling and tax-interaction effects are likely to be important in other countries, and whether a uniform carbon tax still minimizes abatement costs across countries.

**The Importance of Pre-Existing Taxes in Other Countries**

To date, empirical estimates of the revenue-recycling and tax-interaction effects have been made for the United States but not for other countries. In general, developed countries have a similar tax structure to that in the United States, with the huge bulk of revenues collected from taxes on labor and capital income or broad-based consumption taxes (which cause similar distortions to a labor tax). Therefore, the key parameters which determine the revenue-recycling and tax-interaction effects in other developed countries are essentially the same as in the United States. In the analytical models of section 2, these parameters are the ratio of emissions to gross domestic product, the primary marginal cost of percentage emissions reductions, the tax wedge between the gross and net wage, and the labor supply elasticity.

Goulder et al. (1997) illustrate that increasing the relative size of the polluting sector increases the absolute size of the revenue-recycling and tax-interaction effects, but has very little effect on their size relative to the primary welfare effect. This suggests that the proportionate increase in carbon abatement costs caused by pre-existing taxes is not significantly affected by the ratio of carbon emissions to a country's gross domestic product. The primary marginal cost of emissions reduction is determined by the ease of substituting away from carbon using other fuels, energy-saving technologies, less energy-intensive consumption goods, and so on. These substitution possibilities may vary considerably across countries. However, estimates of the marginal cost of percentage reductions in carbon emissions for the United States do not differ markedly from those for other countries (see Nordhaus, 1991b). Thus, if labor market parameters were the same, the proportionate increase in costs due to interactions with the tax system is likely to be similar in magnitude for the 'average' developed country, as in the United States.

Labor tax rates are, however, significantly higher in many other countries than in the United States, since their governments play a greater role in the provision of goods and services. The fourth column in Table 10.2 shows the effective tax wedge in the labor market for the G-7 countries, using estimates of labor income and consumption taxes in 1988 by Mendoza et al. (1994).[21] Compared with the United States, this distortion is about 75 percent higher in France, 50 percent higher in Germany and Italy, 15 percent higher in Canada and the United Kingdom, and slightly lower in Japan.[22] There is a good deal of uncertainty over the labor supply elasticity, even in the United States which has been the focus of most studies (see the discussion in CBO (1996)). This elasticity could be somewhat smaller in other countries than for the United States, given the lower labor force participation of women and the more stringent regulations on the hiring and firing of workers in Western Europe. Therefore, despite higher effective labor taxes, the revenue-recycling and tax-interaction effects are not *necessarily* more important in other countries.

A further consideration is the extent of pre-existing tax or subsidy distortions within the energy sector. Given the gasoline tax, and the reduction in tax exemptions for exploration and mining of natural resources, on balance the United States taxes energy.[23] Gasoline taxes are considerably higher in Western Europe. However, most developing countries subsidize energy. In particular, the price of electricity is typically well below long-run marginal cost, and the

*Table 10.2    International comparison of tax rates (percent)*

|  | Consumption tax rates | Labor income tax rates | Effective tax wedge |
|---|---|---|---|
| France | 21.4 | 47.2 | 56.5 |
| Germany | 14.7 | 41.2 | 48.7 |
| Italy | 14.3 | 40.9 | 48.3 |
| United Kingdom | 16.9 | 26.8 | 37.4 |
| Canada | 13.1 | 28.0 | 36.3 |
| United States | 5.2 | 28.5 | 32.0 |
| Japan | 5.3 | 26.6 | 31.1 |

*Source*: Mendoza et al. (1994) and author's calculations.

production of fuels usually receives favorable tax treatment and/or explicit subsidies (Kosmo, 1987). Shah and Larsen (1992) have estimated that total world energy subsidies exceeded $230 billion in 1990, which is equivalent to a negative carbon tax of $40 per ton! The removal of such subsidies would not only produce a primary welfare gain, but also, as discussed above, a likely gain from interactions with the tax system.

### Does a Uniform Carbon Tax Equalize Marginal Abatement Costs Across Countries?

A familiar implication of the first-best environmental policy model is that, if all emissions sources face the same tax, they will reduce emissions until the primary marginal cost is the same across all sources (and equal to the tax rate). This achieves a given aggregate emissions reduction at minimum cost. A uniform carbon tax across countries produces a parallel result. That is, the total cost of emissions reduction is minimized at the international level.

However, when there are pre-existing tax distortions, this result no longer holds. Returning again to Figure 10.1, for a given tax on emissions, the gap between $MC_p$ and $MC_t$ differs between countries because they have different labor tax rates and labor supply elasticities. Therefore the second-best optimal tax is non-uniform across countries.[24] Unfortunately, achieving agreement among countries on a set of differentiated carbon taxes could be even more difficult than achieving agreement on a single tax rate for all.

## 5    CONCLUSION

Recent studies have indicated that environmental policies can be substantially more costly when their effect on compounding pre-existing tax distortions in the economy is taken into account. However, if the policy raises revenues, and these are used to cut other distortionary taxes, then much of this additional loss can be offset. This suggests a strong efficiency case for preferring a revenue-raising instrument (an emissions tax or auctioned emissions quota) over a non-revenue-raising instrument (a non-auctioned emissions quota), should action be taken to slow atmospheric accumulations of carbon dioxide.

## NOTES

1.    Emissions of methane, nitrous oxide and chlorofluorocarbons (CFCs) may also affect future global climate. However, their potential contribution is small relative to that of $CO_2$. Moreover, methane and nitrous oxide are much more difficult to regulate than $CO_2$. CFCs are being phased out, at least in developed countries, because of their effect on depleting the ozone layer.
2.    See Bovenberg and Goulder (1996), Goulder et al. (1997) and Parry (1997).

3.  These models build on earlier contributions by Sandmo (1975) and Ng (1980).
4.  That is, either a lump sum transfer to households or a public good.
5.  The following decomposition is discussed in Parry (1995) (who used a slightly different terminology), Oates (1995) and Goulder (1995a). The models by Bovenberg and collaborators do not separate out the tax-interaction and revenue-recycling effects defined below.
6.  However, this reduction in revenue is generally small relative to the direct revenues raised by the emissions tax.
7.  This is probably why the labor market consequences of environmental policies have been ignored in the past.
8.  To put this figure in perspective, it is about seven times the efficiency gain estimated by Harberger (1954) from eliminating all product market monopolies in the United States and about 50 percent greater than the efficiency gains from eliminating a 10 percent inflation estimated by Lucas (1981) (when these figures are converted into current dollars).
9.  That is, the weak form of the double dividend is still correct.
10. One reason for this discrepancy is that Bovenberg and Goulder (1996) assume demand elasticities are constant while Parry (1995) assumes constant price coefficients and variable elasticities.
11. See for example Lucas (1990).
12. The analytical models imply that the revenue-recycling effect equals the tax-interaction effect for the first unit reduction in emissions. Therefore, a 40 percent revenue-recycling effect would produce an offsetting gain of $20.
13. These include $7/ton (Nordhaus, 1991a), $12/ton (Peck and Teisberg, 1993), $5/ton (Nordhaus, 1994) and $20/ton (Frankhauser, 1994).
14. In particular, the possibility of some discontinuity leading to dramatic climate change cannot be ruled out. For example, an induced change in North Atlantic Ocean currents could freeze Western Europe. In addition, Cline (1992) argues that the utility of future generations should not be discounted on ethical grounds. Cline (1992) also criticizes these damage estimates for neglecting some ecosystem impacts and possibly adverse effects on the distribution of world income. However, Nordhaus (1993b) gives a convincing response to these criticisms.
15. A carbon tax does *not* reward activities which remove $CO_2$ from the atmosphere such as tree growing.
16. The revenues could also be used to reduce the federal budget deficit. However, this is equivalent to reducing future taxes, and therefore produces an efficiency gain analogous to the revenue-recycling effect.
17. The model also allows for imperfect capital mobility, which limits the ability of firms to shift the burden of new carbon taxes to other sectors, and the transition dynamics as firms substitute away from fossil fuels to synthetic fuels. See Goulder (1994, 1995b), who finds that the gross efficiency cost of a fossil fuel Btu tax and a $25 per ton carbon tax are positive. That is, they reject the strong form of the double dividend hypothesis.
18. Income from capital is subject to corporate income taxation, and personal income taxation at the federal and state level.
19. Actually, since part of labor earnings are saved, a tax on future consumption (i.e. a capital tax) does discourage current work effort to some degree.
20. In Bovenberg and Goulder (1997), this efficiency cost is 0.43 per dollar of revenue for capital and 0.31 for labor.
21. With no taxes, the real wage is the nominal wage ($w$) divided by the general price level ($p$). If wages are taxed at $m$ percent, and there is a tax of $t$ percent on the value of goods, the net wage is $(1 - m)w/(1 + t)p$. Therefore, the effective tax on real labor earnings is calculated by $1 - [(1 - m)/(1 + t)]$.
22. These figures do not take account of benefit withdrawal as income rises, the other major determinant of marginal tax rates faced by the average household.
23. This does not necessarily mean that energy is taxed enough to internalize the full costs of (non-carbon) pollution externalities.
24. The same problem would arise under an internationally tradable quota scheme, since the permit price in each country is equalized to $MC_p$ rather than $MC_q$ in Figure 10.1.

# REFERENCES

Bovenberg, A.L. and Goulder, L.H. (1996), 'Optimal Environmental Taxation in the Presence of Other Taxes: General Equilibrium Analyses', *American Economic Review*, **86**, 985–1000.

Bovenberg, A.L. and Goulder, L.H. (1997), 'Costs of Environmentally-Motivated Taxes in the Presence of Other Taxes: General Equilibrium Analyses', *National Tax Journal*, **50**, 59–88.

Bovenberg, A.L. and de Mooij, R.A. (1994), 'Environmental Levies and Distortionary Taxation', *American Economic Review*, **84**, pp. 1085–1089.

Bovenberg, A.L. and van der Ploeg, F. (1994), 'Environmental Policy, Public Finance and the Labor Market in a Second Best World', *Journal of Public Economics*, **55**, pp. 349–390.

Browning, E.K. (1987), 'On the Marginal Welfare Cost of Taxation', *American Economic Review*, **77**, pp. 11–23.

CBO (1996), 'Labor Supply and Taxes', CBO Memorandum, Congressional Budget Office, Washington, DC.

Cline, W.R. (1992), *The Economics of Global Warming*, Washington, DC: Institute for International Economics.

Deaton, A. and Muellbauer, J. (1980), *Economics and Consumer Behavior*, Cambridge: Cambridge University Press.

Diamond, P. and Mirrlees, J. (1971), 'Optimal Taxation and Public Production I: Production Efficiency and II: Tax Rules', *American Economic Review*, **61**, pp. 8–27, 261–278.

Frankhauser, S. (1994), 'The Social Costs of Greenhouse Gas Emissions: An Expected Value Approach', *The Energy Journal*, **15**, pp. 157–184.

Goulder, L.H. (1994), 'Energy Taxes: Traditional Efficiency Effects and Environmental Implications', in Poterba, J.M. (ed.), *Tax Policy and the Economy*, Cambridge, MA: MIT Press, pp. 105–158.

Goulder, L.H. (1995a), 'Environmental Taxation and the "Double Dividend": A Reader's Guide', *International Tax and Public Finance*, **2**, pp. 157–184.

Goulder, L.H. (1995b), 'Effects of Carbon Taxes in an Economy with Prior Tax Distortions: An Intertemporal General Equilibrium Analysis', *Journal of Environmental Economics and Management*, **29**, pp. 271–297.

Goulder, L.H., Parry, I.W.H. and Burtraw, D. (1997), 'Revenue-Raising vs. Other Instruments for Environmental Protection: The Critical Significance of Pre-existing Tax Distortions', *RAND Journal of Economics*, **28**, .708–731.

Harberger, A.C. (1954), 'Monopoly and Resource Allocation', *American Economic Review*, **44**, pp. 77–787.

Harberger, A.C. (1974), *Taxation and Welfare*, Chicago: University of Chicago Press.

Jorgenson, D.W. and Wilcoxen, P.J. (1993), 'Reducing US Carbon Emissions: An Econometric General Equilibrium Assessment', *Resource and Energy Economics*, **15**, 7–26.

Kosmo, M. (1987), 'Money to Burn: The High Cost of Energy Subsidies', Working Paper Series, World Resources Institute, Washington, DC.

Lee, D.R and Misiolek, W.S. (1986), 'Substituting Pollution Taxation for General Taxation: Some Implications for Efficiency in Pollution Taxation', *Journal of Environmental Economics and Management*, **13**, pp. 338–347.

Lipsey, R.G. and Lancaster, K. (1956), 'The General Theory of the Second Best', *Review of Economic Studies*, **24**, pp. 11–32.

Lucas, R.E. (1981), 'Discussion of: Stanley Fischer, "Towards an Understanding of the Costs of Inflation: II"', *Carnegie–Rochester Conference Series on Public Policy,* **15**, pp. 43–52.

Lucas, R.E. (1990), 'Supply-Side Economics: An Analytical Review', *Oxford Economic Papers,* **42**, pp. 292–316.

Mendoza, E.G., Razin, A. and Tesar, L.L. (1994), 'Effective Tax Rates in Macroeconomics: Cross Country Estimates of Tax Rates on Factor Incomes and Consumption', *Journal of Monetary Economics,* **34**, pp. 297–323.

Ng, Y.K. (1980), 'Optimal Corrective Taxes or Subsidies when Revenue-Raising Imposes an Excess Burden', *American Economic Review,* **70**, 313–317.

Nordhaus, W.D. (1991a), 'To Slow or Not to Slow: The Economics of the Greenhouse Effect', *The Economic Journal,* **101**, pp. 920–937.

Nordhaus, W.D. (1991b), 'The Costs of Slowing Climate Change: A Survey', *The Energy Journal,* **12**, pp. 37–53.

Nordhaus, W.D. (1993a), 'Optimal Greenhouse Gas Reductions and Tax Policy in the "DICE" Model', *American Economic Review,* **83**, pp. 313–317.

Nordhaus, W.D. (1993b), 'Reflections on the Economics of Climate Change', *Journal of Economic Perspectives,* **7**, 11–26.

Nordhaus, W.D. (1994), *Managing the Global Commons,* Cambridge, MA: MIT Press.

Oates, W.E. (1995), 'Green Taxes: Can We Protect the Environment and Improve the Tax System at the Same Time?', *Southern Economic Journal,* **61**, pp. 914–922.

Oates, W.E. and Strassmann, D.L. (1984), 'Effluent Fees and Market Structure', *Journal of Public Economics,* **24**, pp. 29–46.

Parry, I.W.H. (1995), 'Pollution Taxes and Revenue Recycling', *Journal of Environmental Economics and Management,* **29**, S64–S77.

Parry, I.W.H. (1997), 'Environmental Taxes and Quotas in the Presence of Distortionary Taxes in Factor Markets', *Resource and Energy Economics,* **19**, pp. 203–220.

Parry, I.W.H. (1998), 'A Second-Best Analysis of Environmental Subsidies', *International Tax and Public Finance,* **5**, pp. 153–170.

Peck, S.C. and Teisberg, T.J. (1993), 'Global Warming Uncertainties and the Value of Information: An Analysis using CETA', *Resource and Energy Economics,* **15**, pp. 71–98.

Poterba, J.M. (1991), 'Tax Policy to Combat Global Warming: On Designing a Carbon Tax', in Dornbusch, R. and Poterba, J.M. (eds), *Global Warming: Economic Policy Responses,* Cambridge, MA: MIT Press, pp. 71–97.

Poterba, J.M. (1993), 'Global Warming: A Public Finance Perspective', *Journal of Economic Perspectives,* **7**, pp. 47–63.

Repetto, R., Dower, R.C., Jenkins, R. and Geoghegan, J. (1992), *Green Fees: How a Tax Shift can Work for the Environment and the Economy,* Washington, DC: World Resources Institute.

Sandmo, A. (1975), 'Optimal Taxation in the Presence of Externalities', *Swedish Journal of Economics,* **77**, pp. 86–98.

Sandmo, A. (1976), 'Optimal Taxation – An Introduction to the Literature', *Journal of Public Economics,* **6**, pp. 37–54.

Shah, A. and Larsen, B. (1992), 'Carbon Taxes, the Greenhouse Effect and Developing Countries', World Bank Policy Research Working Paper Series No. 957, World Bank, Washington, DC.

Wisecarver, D. (1974), 'The Social Costs of Input Market Distortions', *American Economic Review,* **64**, pp. 359–372.

# Index